Farah Boyuerra

Farah
Boyuerra.

Farah Boyuerra

English Revision for Leaving Certificate Higher Level

FIFTH EDITION
FOR EXAMINATIONS IN 2007, 2008 AND 2009

Anne Gormley

GILL & MACMILLAN

Gill & Macmillan Ltd
Hume Avenue
Park West
Dublin 12
with associated companies throughout the world

© Anne Gormley 2001, 2002, 2004 and 2007
978 0 7171 4140 1

Print origination in Ireland by
O'K Graphic Design, Dublin

Note: The texts, films and poems in this book are prescribed for the Higher Level Leaving Certificate examinations in June 2007, June 2008 and June 2009.

The paper used in this book is made from the wood pulp of managed forests. For every tree felled, at least one tree is planted, thereby renewing natural resources.

Contents

Acknowledgments

For permission to reproduce copyright material the publishers gratefully acknowledge the following:

HarperCollins for extracts from *Wild Swans* by Jung Chang; John Murray (Publishers) Ltd for an extract from *Wheels Within Wheels* by Dervla Murphy; Merlin Publishing for an extract from *The Reaping Race* by Liam O'Flaherty; Random House Group Ltd for an extract from *A Far-Off Place* by Laurens van der Post published by Hogarth Press, extract from *An Evil Cradling* by Brian Keenan published by Hutchinson (© Brian Keenan 1992) and an extract from *In Patagonia* by Bruce Chatwin (© Bruce Chatwin 1997) published by Jonathan Cape; Penguin Books Ltd for an extract from *How Many Miles to Babylon?* by Jennifer Johnston (Hamish Hamilton 1974; Penguin Books 1988); Faber and Faber Ltd for an extract from *Lord of the Flies* by William Golding, an extract from *Murder in the Cathedral* and for 'The Hippopotamus' by T. S. Eliot, 'Epitaph on a Tyrant' from *Collected Shorter Poems* by W. H. Auden and 'You're' from *Collected Poems* by Sylvia Plath; Curtis Brown Group Ltd, London, on behalf of The Estate of Elizabeth Bowen for extracts from 'Summer Night' from *Look at All Those Roses* (© Elizabeth Bowen 1946) and 'The Demon Lover' from *Ivy Gripped the Steps* (© Elizabeth Bowen 1941) by Elizabeth Bowen; Methuen Publishing for an extract from *How to Write a Novel* by John Braine; excerpts from *The Complete Poems 1927-1979* by Elizabeth Bishop. Copyright © 1979, 1983 by Alice Helen Methfessel. Reprinted by permission of Farrar, Straus and Giroux, LLC.

Photos: The Kobal Collection: 228 © Cecchi Gori/Tiger/Canal; 230 © Merchant Ivory/Goldcrest; 235 © Renaissance Films/BBC/Curzon Films; 237 © Paramount; 239 © Granada/Miramax; 242 © United Artists; 244 © Sam Goldwyn/Renaissance Films/BBC; 247 © M & A Film Corporation; 251 © Paramount/Gordon, Melinda Sue; 257 © WT2 Productions.

The publishers have made every effort to trace copyright holders, but if they have inadvertently overlooked any they will be pleased to make the necessary arrangements at the first opportunity.

Preface

In this revision book, guidelines are clearly set out that will enable you to revise for the Leaving Certificate course at Higher Level. The book gives a series of practical guidelines on how to tackle both Paper I and Paper II. There are notes on the different language genres, together with sample material and commentary, which will help you in dealing with questions on Paper I. There are also a number of samples of Paper I that follow the same form – that is, comprehension and composition – as the examination on Paper I.

The book also deals with Paper II. There are guidelines on how to prepare for the question on both the single study of a text and the comparative study of texts. The notes on all texts are specifically designed for Higher Level. There are also notes on Shakespeare plays, a compulsory question at Higher Level.

Guidelines are also given on answering questions on both prescribed and unseen poetry. The method of answering poetry questions in both the prescribed and the unseen section is clearly outlined. In addition, there are sample answers on both unseen poetry and some of the prescribed poetry on the course.

I hope the practical approach adopted throughout this book will enable you to prepare in an efficient and focused manner for all aspects of this course.

Anne Gormley

Revision Techniques
1

1. Make sure you are completely familiar with the syllabus and the requirements for Higher Level. Know exactly how many questions you have to answer on each paper and how much time you have for answering each one. Know what sections or questions are compulsory.

2. Prepare yourself for Paper I, which covers *comprehension* and *composition,* by reading material on topics you are interested in. Gather ideas on these topics and perhaps write them up in a notebook.

3. Study unseen passages for the comprehension section and practise writing answers to these. It can help to compare your own answers with some of the sample answers already done in this book.

4. Practise writing answers on the writing assignments in the different language genres. Make sure your expression is original and striking.

5. Identify clearly what text, whether a play or a novel, you will choose for the detailed question in Paper II, as you will need to know this more thoroughly. Practise writing essays on both the detailed study of a text and the comparative section. Give yourself the same amount of time that you will have in the examination.

6. Clearly establish which three texts you are studying for the comparative question on Paper II. Remember that you can study a film for this question. If you do choose a film, watch it several times and try to familiarise yourself with the central issues and the techniques.

7. Know your texts, whether a book or play, very well. You cannot read your texts often enough. There is no substitute for your own intimate interaction with the text. Understand what you are reading; follow what is happening. If you miss a connection in the story, you will find yourself increasingly puzzled as you read on. Ask yourself the following questions: Why are the characters behaving in this way? How is the plot constructed? Study key passages and sections in great detail. Take note of important quotations and familiarise yourself with the plot and the main features of the characters.

8. In the Shakespeare play, take note of key scenes and soliloquies. Study these in relation to the development of character and the plot.

9. Study five poets for the precribed poetry section and about five poems by each.

10. Practise writing questions on the unseen poetry section. Give yourself about 20 minutes to do this.

Examination Techniques in Paper I

2

1. The total number of marks for this paper is 200, or half the total for the examination. There are 100 marks for the comprehension and 100 marks for the composition assignment.
2. Four comprehension texts are given, each followed by two questions (question A and question B). You must answer *two* questions: question A on *any text* and question B on *any other text*. You cannot answer two questions on the same text.
3. In addition, you must answer one question on a composition or writing assignment.
4. The time limit for this paper is 2 hours and 50 minutes.
5. Spend 75 minutes on the comprehension and 75 minutes on the writing assignment.
6. Give yourself approximately 35 minutes on each comprehension question.
7. Answer the comprehension questions first, since they demand less effort at creative thinking. Both the passage and the questions are clearly laid out.

Comprehension

CHARACTERISTICS OF COMPREHENSION PASSAGES

In the comprehension passage, always look for the following:
- **Theme:** This is the subject matter of the writing. There are usually three texts which are selected under a certain theme. Take note of this theme.
- **Tone:** This is the relationship between the writer and the reader, how the writer is saying what he/she is saying.
- **Intention/purpose:** This is the reason why the writer writes the passage.

These three features are related. If a writer's intention is to condemn violence, their theme will reflect that intention. A writer may wish to tell a story, so the subject matter will be written in the form of a narrative. Another writer may wish to persuade the reader about something and therefore will use a persuasive or ironic style of writing.

TYPES OF PROSE WRITING

- Autobiographical
- Argument
- Informative
- Narrative
- Persuasive
- Descriptive

Autobiographical writing
In this kind of writing we get an insight into the mind of the writer. The use of the subjective 'I' is a feature of autobiographical writing.

Example

> In May 1953 my mother went into hospital to have her third child, who was born on 23 May – a boy called Jinming. It was the missionary hospital where she had stayed when she was pregnant with me, but the missionaries had now been expelled, as had happened all

over China. My mother had just been given a promotion to head of the Public Affairs Department for the city of Yibin, still working under Mrs Ting, who had risen to be party secretary for the city. At the time my grandmother was also in the hospital with severe asthma. And so was I, with a navel infection; my wet-nurse was staying with me in the hospital. We were being given good treatment, which was free, as we belonged to a family 'in the revolution'.

(Jung Chang, *Wild Swans*)

Comment

This is an example of autobiographical writing, in which the writer recounts some details about her life and events in her family during the Cultural Revolution in China.

Argument writing

In writing that is based on argument, the information is presented in a logical and organised manner. The method of the writer here is detached and factual.

Example

Humankind is under an obligation to preserve its physical health and well-being and to avoid anything that might endanger it. It is wrong to take alcohol in volumes that affect the rightful use of reason and one's consciousness.

Drug addiction, apart from being an offence against the individual human person, is also a destabilising factor in society as a whole. The relationship between rising crime and drug abuse is evident. For that reason, the state has a duty, in the interests of the common good, to make all forms of drug-taking illegal, not to mention trafficking in them. It would abdicate responsibility if it permissively tolerated any form of so-called 'soft' drugs.

Comment

The style of writing here is based on argument. The tone is clear and factual. The argument is based on the dangers of drug abuse. The writer establishes his argument here on a fact – the need to preserve one's physical well-being. The effects of drug addiction are clearly stated in the parallel between rising crime and drug abuse.

Informative writing

The purpose of this type of writing is to inform or to convey certain facts in a clear and terse manner.

Example

Pope John Paul has signed a decree recognising a miracle by Pope John XXIII, which will allow for his beatification. He also recognised a miracle attributed to the Dublin-born Benedictine priest Dom Columba Marmion, who died in 1923. Elected to the papacy on the death of Pope Pius XII in 1958, Pope John was already elderly. He was to become the most radical and best-loved pope of the century. The miracle is based on a vision of Pope

John by Sister Caterina Capitani at Naples in 1966. Then twenty-two, she was dying of acute peritonitis. She had received the last rites when, on 25 May 1966, she said Pope John appeared and told her he had answered her prayers. Her recovery was immediate. Still alive, she is now nursing in Sicily.

Comment

This extract is taken from a newspaper report. It is a clear example of informative writing, as it gives the reader information and facts about the beginnings of the process of beatification of Pope John XXIII.

Narrative writing

In narrative writing the writer is telling a story. There is a definite arrangement of ideas or sequence of events. Narrative prose puts an emphasis on description – describing people, actions and events in detail.

Example

One sunny frosty December morning I set out to cycle to the foot of the Knockmealdown Mountains, some eight miles north of Lismore. I took a picnic and ate it by a lively brown stream, and then thought it would be fun to climb to the top of Knockmealdown – an easy little mountain of just under 3,000 feet.

I had been up several times before, with my father and Pappa and sundry guests, and was familiar with the easiest route. But somehow the climb took longer than expected, and as I approached the top the weather began to change. The air lost its crispness and the Galtees to the north-west disappeared as clouds came rolling south over the plain of Tipperary. Before I was half way down both the clouds and the dusk had overtaken me. But I was too inexperienced to be immediately afraid. For ten or fifteen minutes it all seemed a glorious adventure and I never doubted that I would soon hear the stream and feel the road beneath my feet. Not until darkness came, and the mist turned to rain, and a wind began to moan, did panic threaten. Then I stumbled into an old turf-cutting that should not have been on my route, and burst into tears.

(Dervla Murphy, *Wheels Within Wheels*)

Comment

This is an example of narrative writing, which has a strong personal flavour and pays lively attention to small details. The writer recounts in a vivid and intimate manner an incident that affected her deeply. She uses an **anecdote** here, which is a feature of narrative writing – a single incident is told in the form of a story. This incident almost always contains a definite point. Through the incident where the writer got lost in the mountains we learn how unpredictable and dangerous the weather can be.

Persuasive writing

The purpose of persuasive writing is to sway the reader towards a certain viewpoint on the strength of feeling and emotion.

Example

In the current debate on street violence, I have to say I'm amazed at the cursory mention of alcohol. The truth is that alcohol is responsible for a substantial number of violent attacks.

I don't drink, and sometimes when I walk home at night through Temple Bar I wonder whether I've stepped into some bizarre alternative Dublin. Between the fresh vomit, the streams of urine, the shouting yobs, the general air of disorder and the occasional acts of violence, the easy availability of alcohol has to be blamed.

All my friends drink, and I don't object to people drinking. But I do object to the acceptance of an atmosphere in which drink-related civil disorder is accepted as unavoidable and the gardaí just have to contain it as best they can.

Secondly, I don't accept the age-old belief that someone who misbehaves under the influence is socially cleared of responsibility. No one is forced to drink.

So what to do? Prohibition isn't an option, politically or practically. But a tough line on public drunkenness, under-age drinking and drinking in public streets should be enforced. Heavy fines should be imposed and in particular bars that serve under-age drinkers or people obviously drunk should have their night's takings confiscated.

I'm twenty-seven years old, I'm not a reactionary, but I'm appalled at seeing the city I was born and live in deteriorate into a yobbos' paradise. Am I on my own in feeling this?

Comment

This is taken from a letter written to a daily newspaper and is an example of persuasive writing. The writer makes use of colourful analogies, such as 'some bizarre alternative Dublin' and 'a yobbos' paradise', to illustrate his points about drinking. He concludes on a rhetorical question, which is a feature of persuasive writing.

Descriptive writing

Where narrative writing tells us what people and things *do,* descriptive writing tells us what people or things *are like.* Joseph Conrad said that descriptive writing, 'by the power of the written word, makes you hear, makes you feel; before all makes you see.'

This type of writing illustrates the power of the imagination to create unusual images or to juxtapose exciting and dynamic ideas. It differs from factual or argument writing in that it links ideas through word repetition and image association rather than through logic. There is a strong emphasis on drawing descriptions of things or people.

Descriptive writing:
- gives a clear picture
- selects details with great care
- uses precise vocabulary and avoids exaggeration
- focuses on colour
- uses similes to draw comparisons
- appeals to the different senses.

Example

> As soon as the sun was down, the air was full of bats, cruising as noiselessly as cars upon asphalt; the nighthawk swept past too – the bird that sits on the road and in the eyes of which the lights of your car gleam red a moment before he flutters up vertically in front of your wheels. The little spring hares were out on the roads, moving in their own way, sitting down suddenly and jumping along to a rhythm, like miniature kangaroos. The cicadas sing an endless song in the long grass, smells run along the earth, and falling stars run over the sky, like tears over a cheek.
>
> A few miles out, in the Maasai reserve, the zebra are now changing their pasture, the flocks wander over the grey plain like lighter stripes upon it, the buffalo are out grazing on the long slopes of the hills. My young men of the farm would come by, two or three together, walking one after the other like narrow dark shadows on the lawn.
>
> (Karen Blixen, *Out of Africa*)

Comment

This is a splendid example of the use of detailed and vivid description. In this passage the writer sharply focuses on small details, which is a striking feature of good descriptive writing. For example, note the comparison between the cars and asphalt. The use of similes in writing can lend a richness and immediacy to description.

Note

Some comprehension passages will contain a mixture of styles. The intention of the writer will largely dictate what style they will use. A writer may decide to attack corruption in the political sphere, so, for example, they could use argument and an ironic tone. Another writer may wish to tell a story, so they could make use of anecdote to illustrate a point more effectively.

STRUCTURE AND FORM OF COMPREHENSION PASSAGES

A comprehension passage is made up of:
*   paragraphs
*   sentences
*   words.

The **structure** is the layout of the writing, whether it is written as one continuous piece of prose, structured in paragraphs or is simply a series of sentences.

Paragraphs

A paragraph consists of one main sentence, usually called the **topic sentence**. The rest of the paragraph consists of support for that topic sentence. In a comprehension passage, the paragraphs may be clearly outlined or the passage may simply be one independent piece of writing. When you are studying paragraphs for comprehension, examine:
*   the topic sentence – try to find where exactly in the paragraph it comes. Usually topic sentences come at the beginning or end of a paragraph

- the linking devices used by the writer to tie up the different ideas in each paragraph.

Sentences

A sentence may be defined as a group of words that makes complete sense. Sentences may be classified according to:
- their purpose
- their syntax
- their form.

Purpose

According to its mood or purpose, a sentence may be:

declarative – a statement or an assertion:

> John's wife died of cancer.
> Mary broke the vase.
> It's a lovely sunny day.

interrogative – asking a question:

> Have you seen him?
> Where's the cat?

imperative – giving a command:

> Please stop talking.
> Don't burn the toast.
> Close your books.

exclamatory – expressing surprise or shock:

> 'Oh, what a rogue and peasant slave am I!'
> My mother won the lottery!
> Imagine that!

Syntax

According to its syntax, a sentence may be:

simple – made up of one subject and one object:

> The typist made an error.

compound – just two simple sentences connected by a conjunction:

> The typist made an error and then she spilled the coffee.

complex – a simple statement followed by one or two qualifying clauses:

> Computers require a particular set of aptitudes, and if these aptitudes are missing, little can be done and misery is guaranteed to millions of people.

Form

According to form, a sentence may be:

periodic – with the main idea coming at the end:

> Spectacular though the parade was, it passed by largely unnoticed.

Surprised and excited, the scientists who witnessed the event found themselves wondering, is this how life got started?

loose – the main point coming at the beginning:

The parade was spectacular, but it passed by largely unnoticed.

We can make impersonal places, like offices and factories, bear the imprint of our personality: pin-ups on the wall behind the workbench, trendy executive toys, gold pens, silver-mounted portraits on the executive's desk (or, equally revealing, nothing at all).

balanced – having a similarity of thought and a similarity of structure. The purpose can be to create dramatic effect. Balanced sentences can also show that a writer is drawing on different aspects of the subject matter to drive home the point:

To be a woman writer long meant, may still mean, belonging to a literary movement apart from, but hardly subordinate to, the mainstream: an undercurrent, rapid and powerful.

The true gentleman is too clear-headed to be unjust; he is as simple as he is forceful, and as brief as he is decisive.

inverted – with the subject of the sentence coming in the middle or at the end:

Seeing a bullfight in Valencia, I understood why people can find it such a fascinating thing.

Now in this dawn, how or why he did not know, his brain, without help or knowledge, had made that leap and combined with impeccable logic those two simple but momentous propositions.

antithetical – creating an **antithesis**, which could be described as similar to a balanced sentence but with the balance created by opposing ideas:

The husband is a ruthless businessman, while his wife is a docile and humble woman.

The farmer is a just and loyal employer, while his employees are dishonest and unfaithful.

That girl is strong and powerful in her manner, while her brother is weak and cowardly.

The way writers construct sentences can reveal certain attitudes they may have towards the subject. A series of terse sentences can contribute to the flow of thought in a passage:

The performance came to an end with two choruses, the second more subtle in its harmonies. The choir stood still and let their voices resonate around the small German church. There was no applause. No-one moved. The conductor did not move. There was a sort of stunned silence, but it was deliberate. It lasted one minute, perhaps more. And then there was a shuffling of papers, but no coughs or whispers. The performers remained still. No-one spoke. People began to move quietly from their seats.

Simple sentences anchor a writer's thoughts securely. However, a series of too many simple sentences can cause the writing to be jerky and monotonous. Examine the following opening on the subject of success, which is made up of a series of simple sentences:

Swallowing, then inhaling deeply, I plunged forward. 'How could you, after all I have told you? What are you trying to do? What right have you to disfigure such a beautiful area?'

Beneath my steadfast gaze he slowly transformed into a tall, cruel, bellowing devil. 'Vanessa, my dear, I've won. It's all over. Construction is going ahead. All your exaggerated stabbings and jibes didn't work. Who cares about wildlife? Today the only thing that counts is money, and, along with genius, I've a lot of that.'

The sentence structure here makes the piece of writing incoherent and jerky. The following sentence structure would be more effective:

> As I plunged forward, I inhaled deeply. I began to cry out as I directed my gaze in his direction. 'How could you do this, after all I told you? What are you trying to do? Who gave you the right to devastate and disfigure the whole area, which is so beautiful?'
>
> As I looked at him he slowly changed and began to look like a tall and cruel devil-like figure. With a slow, measured voice he bellowed: 'Vanessa, my dear, it's all over. I've won. The construction is going ahead, in spite of all your jibes and criticism. In this world, the only thing that counts is money, and, as well as genius, I've got lots of that. So who cares about wildlife?'

Words

It is important to clearly understand how words are used in writing. The same word can be used to persuade, to argue or to describe something. A writer can also use words to draw pictures or images of certain things.

There are different kinds of words. *Pictorial* words draw an image or picture of something. *Concrete* words give a specific idea about something, for example, a heavy man, a round table, a tall girl, a circular motion, an oval face, a hollow cheek, a gaunt child, a green, ripe apple. *Abstract* is the opposite of concrete. It means something that is not specific or tangible, for example, goodness, loyalty, whiteness, truth.

The context of words

Examine the context of certain words. Both the *context* and the *connotations* of words can affect the writer's message or purpose. The same word or set of words can be used to provoke a totally different type of reaction in the reader, depending on its context.

(1) Bombshell from Brazil explodes onto catwalk.

(2) He dropped a bombshell in the department when he announced that he was resigning.

The first sentence is a headline taken from a magazine. The second is an informal and casual use of language, taken from a personal letter.

(1) Torrid time for retailers.

(2) Retailers will have to audit their accounts before the next budget.

(3) He works as a retailer.

The first sentence is a headline from a newspaper, written in a sensational way in order to attract attention. It is an example of an emotive statement. The second is simply a factual account of how retailers will have to organise their accounts before the next budget and it could feature in a newspaper article. The third is a simple assertion or statement that can also be spoken.

(1) Pets find their patch in star-studded glory.

(2) Pets are usually familiar with their own patch in the garden.

(3) She was mending the patch when the pets wandered over to her.

The first sentence is a headline from a newspaper. The second is taken from a book on gardening and deals with the peculiar habits of pets. The third is a statement taken from a story. Thus, we can see that the context of words can affect their meaning in a sentence.

The connotation of words

The connotation of a word is the emotive impact it may have on a reader – the associations, whether positive or negative, it conjures up in the mind. Word connotations all suggest certain attitudes to an idea. Examine the following words and consider the various connotations that spring to mind when you read them:

- cool
- upbeat
- traditional
- soap opera
- obese
- foolish
- raw.

Word connotations can be achieved in different ways: through

- syntax
- alliteration
- assonance
- cacophony
- sibilance
- repetition.

SYNTAX

Syntax can be defined as the order of words a writer uses when constructing sentences. The syntax can play a large part in the communication of certain ideas to the reader and in controlling or manipulating the reader's responses.

ALLITERATION

This is the repetition of consonant sounds, especially the initial consonants of words. Through the alliteration of certain consonants, different moods or emotions can be conveyed:

> He feared he would go mad or fall ill, yet if he once let go, the elaborate scaffolding he had so painfully erected would fall asunder.

The repetition of the *f* sound here is an example of alliteration and serves the function of underlining the emotion of fear within this man:

> I realised I had looked my last on youth and little more,
> For they are not made whole that reach the age of Christ.

The *l* sound here emphasises the sense of loss experienced by the writer.

ASSONANCE

This is the repetition of vowel sounds, which conveys a musical or sensuous impact or a sense of harmony. Look at the following lines of poetry, all of which are examples of the use of assonance, each with a different effect or a different connotation:

> only a man harrowing clods …
> with an old horse that stumbles and nods …

The repetition of the *o* sound here emphasises the sense of isolation in the lines.

> Fall, gall themselves, and gash gold-vermilion.

Repetition of the *a* and *o* sounds here depicts a sense of richness.

> … Nor does long our small
> Durance deal with that steep or deep. Here creep …

There is assonance in the repetition of the *e* sound, which emphasises a profound sense of disorientation and confusion in the writer.

CACOPHONY

Cacophony, or *dissonance*, is the opposite of assonance – it consists of the repetition of 'hard' sounds, such as *k,* to suggest a harsh or grating mood:

> Blight and famine, plague and earthquake, roaring deeps and fiery sands
> Clanging fights and flaming towns and sinking ships
> and preying hands.

The connotations underlying the use of cacophony in these lines suggest destruction and devastation.

SIBILANCE

This is the repetition of *s* and *z* sounds and its use in writing serves the function of appealing to the senses. The following lines, from two different poems, contain some striking examples of the use of sibilance:

> starlight lit my lonesomeness
> when I set out for Lyonesse …

> turning the silver out of dark grasses
> where the skylark had lain …

REPETITION

A writer can repeat the same word or set of words for purposes of emphasis. This type of emphatic repetition underlines different points more effectively for a writer:

> the beating down of the wise,
> and great Art beaten down.

> he knew he was on the point of breaking through – he knew it …

> no development has provoked more religious awe, more contentious debate, more lyrical speculation …

Word connotations can also be achieved by means of:

* irony
* simile
* metaphor.

The combined use of these different techniques can add up to what is termed the *figurative use* of language.

THE LANGUAGE OF COMPREHENSION

Style

'Style' is the ability to present a subject in a way that is best suited to achieving the writer's aim. It is important when understanding a passage to know how to 'read between the lines', to understand how language and imagery both work to create a certain tone or mood and how they all add up to a coherent style.

Note the difference between 'tone' and 'mood'. **Tone** is the relationship a writer establishes with the reader – how the writer is saying what is in the passage. **Mood** is the atmosphere of the piece of writing.

Imagery

Words can also be combined to form images or 'word pictures'. (The use of imagery will form an essential part of the 'Aesthetic Use of Language' section in Chapter 5.)

When you see imagery in comprehension pieces or writing, ask yourself the following questions:

* What does it say?
* Why is it used?
* How well does it work in the passage?
* Does it have 'sound effects' or certain connotations?

There are different kinds of imagery:

simple:

Easter Island is the loneliest inhabited place in the world. The nearest solid land the inhabitants can see is in the firmament, the moon and the planets.

original:

His instincts threw up their defences against the scandalous notion of being creative.

In some cathedrals you can see demonic winged creatures referring diplomatically to the majesties of political power. The cathedral can therefore be seen as an awesome engine of communication.

Copies of the molecule began to evolve and it began to perform new and unexpected chemical tricks.

vivid or clear:

The matador, gorgeous in green and gold, skipped with unbelievable nimbleness and daring in front of the bull, varying his blows with caresses on the soft nose and deft little side-kicks on the jaws.

exotic:

> A hedge of hibiscus bordered the airport buildings. Sunbirds glittering with green and blue iridescence played around it, darting from one scarlet blossom to another, hanging on beating wings as they probed for nectar. I noticed a chameleon motionless except for its goggling eyes, which swivelled to follow every passing insect.

startling:

> The calves sang to my horn, the foxes on the hill barked clear and cold …

> Fury had shrieked 'No lingering! Let me be fell: force I must be brief.'

> O the mind, mind has mountains cliffs of fall
> Frightful, sheer no-man fathomed.

Images can be used for different reasons in writing:

to illustrate a point:

> He is nearly as tall as a Dublin policeman, and preaching literature, he stood on the hearthrug, his feet set close together. Lifting his arms above his head (the very movement that Raphael gives to Paul when preaching at Athens)…

to provoke atmosphere:

> The edge of a colossal jungle, so dark-green as to be almost black, fringed with white surf, ran straight, like a ruled line, far, far away along a blue sea whose glitter was blurred by a creeping mist.

to provoke an emotional impact (the following lines are from an advertisement for perfume):

> Each woman should have her own subtle fragrance – one that will suit her style and that is a true expression of her personality. Each must use it as much to denote what kind of woman she is, her emotions and her aspirations, as to enhance her outward appearance.

Remember, imagery is effective when it conveys what a writer intends in a vivid and economical way. The use of imagery can also help a writer to achieve originality of expression in writing.

CHARACTERISTICS OF WELL-WRITTEN ANSWERS IN COMPREHENSION

1. Your answers must reflect a clear understanding of the content of the passage.
2. Organise your thoughts clearly. Focus on exactly what you are asked. Avoid padding or introducing irrelevant points.
3. Have a thorough grasp of the writer's intention in writing. Be able to understand whether the writing is persuasion, argument or narration.
4. Develop the ability to follow a line of argument and to evaluate the points objectively.
5. Your answers must show a basic knowledge of the constituent elements of writing – how to structure sentences and paragraphs, how to use and understand tone and imagery.
6. Use clear, correct English and lucid argument to support your statements.

7. Answers must be:
   - clear
   - logical
   - factual
   - precise
   - simple, not ambiguous or awkward.

Common errors in comprehension answers
1. Misunderstanding the content of the passage.
2. Using incorrect facts or information in answers.
3. Misunderstanding the questions. Distinguish between such terms as:
   'How does the writer reach the conclusion …?'
   'Why does the writer claim that this is the case …?'
   'Demonstrate from your own experience …'
4. Not giving reasons for answers when asked to do so.
5. Badly structured answers, where the main point is ignored and irrelevancies are introduced and developed.
6. Badly written answers, with faulty grammar, weak expression and poor punctuation.
7. Not answering the question asked, but rambling and going off the point.

Method of tackling comprehension questions
1. There are usually three different types of texts printed out in the exam. You will have to answer one question only on question A or comprehension.
2. Decide first of all what question B you are going to do. Question B is a writing exercise based on one of the passages printed out and you may find that your choices here are limited.
3. Start with your question A or the questions based on one of the passsages.
4. Generally the comprehension questions are divided into three different parts. It can help to read the passaages for each part of the question.
5. Spend approximately 35 minutes on each question.
6. Read the passage through several times in order to grasp the gist or general idea of what it is about. Try examine what the primary purpose of the passage is – is it informative, narrative or persuasive?
7. Quickly scan the layout of the passage. If the text is divided by sub-headings, many times these headings can provide you with an idea of what the passage is about and how the points are developed.
8. Sometimes it can help to write out one sentence or phrase on the main idea of the passage. This can help to focus your mind and keep to the point.
9. If the passage uses *imagery*, examine why it is used and what point is being made by it.
10. Does the writer intrude in the text and can you see why?
11. In a passage that is factual or based on argument, know how to distinguish facts from opinions. See whether there is evidence to support the points made.

12. Before beginning to write your answers, work on a rough draft – getting your points down in note form – for each question.
13. Tackle every aspect of your question. Keep control of time. Stop when your allotted time is up.
14. Use your own words as much as possible.
15. When reading back, read your answers with a purpose. Check the question and then your answer. Have you answered the question asked? Have you used examples that are relevant and useful? Is your answer clear and logical or is it repetitive and long winded?

The summary

A summary tests your ability to:
- condense material, choose the main points from a piece of writing and express them in appropriate and clear language
- organise material in a coherent and logical manner.

Method of writing a summary
1. Grasp the general gist or message of the writing.
2. Write down the main points in the form of a rough draft.
3. Rewrite the summary in the form of one main paragraph.
4. Include all dates, numbers or statistics.
5. Write your summary in the past tense.

Read the following article (from a 'healthy living' newspaper), then study the sample summary that follows.

Threat to natural health supplements
Today you can walk into any health shop and buy safe health-supporting supplements of your choice at reasonable prices – just as you have been able to do for the last twenty years or so. You can select your vitamins, your garlic or evening primrose oil or other natural remedies from the vast array that is available. You can also discuss your purchase with the sales assistant to make sure it is the right one for you.

But all this could change. In May this year the Irish Medicines Board issued a document entitled *Guide to the Definition of a Medicinal Product*. Without question, this document threatens the rights of health-conscious consumers to buy effective and safe supplements of their choice. If the proposals in this document become law, many safe and popular products could disappear from the shelves, simply because the IMB has decided to reclassify them as medicines and not food supplements. Enforcement of the proposals would require most products to have a medicinal licence, which, even if it were possible to obtain one, would cost thousands of euro and take several years of clinical trials and scientific work for each product. Of necessity, these costs would be passed on to the consumer.

The IMB claims this is an issue of safety, but reclassifying supplements would not make them safer. Products at present produced under food law have to be 100 per cent safe; medicines do not.

As you would expect, consumers are extremely unhappy with this situation and are asking why the IMB has decided to pre-empt legislation, which is expected towards the end of this year, by bringing out their own guidelines.

Sample summary

Safe health supplements of your choice can be obtained at reasonable prices from any health shop. You can select vitamins, garlic, evening primrose oil or other natural remedies that are available. This could change. In May this year the Irish Medicines Board issued a document entitled *Guide to the Definition of a Medicinal Product*. If its proposals become law, many products could be reclassified as medicines rather than food supplements. The enforcement of these proposals would require that these products have a medicinal licence. This would cost thousands of euro, which would have to be paid for by the consumer.

The IMB claims this is an issue of safety. Products now covered by food law have to be 100 per cent safe; medicines do not. Consumers are unhappy with this situation and are questioning the IMB's decision to pre-empt legislation by issuing their own guidelines.

Remember, in comprehension a good Honours pupil must be able to ask and answer the following questions:
1. What was the writer's intention in writing this passage?
2. Who is the intended audience for this passage? Are the techniques used suitable for this audience? Explain why or why not.
3. Is the writing structured clearly in paragraphs, and if so, does each paragraph fit into the scheme of the writing as a whole?
4. Is the writer appealing to our emotions or to our intellect? Why is this so?
5. Does the nature of the subject justify the use of the emotions employed? Remember that emotion must be restrained in writing if it is to achieve the desired effect.
6. If the writing is based on argument, do you find the arguments convincing? If so, why?
7. Is the style uniform or does it vary? If so, why is this? Does the style suit the subject or is it too dull or too ornate?
8. What do the style and the subject matter tell us about the writer?
9. Look at the writer's choice of words to see whether they are relevant, excessive, appropriate, precise, etc.

COMPREHENSION VOCABULARY

You should know the difference between the following words:

analyse: 'take apart' an idea or a statement in order to consider all its aspects.
compare: show the similarities or the differences between things ('compare with': make a comparison; 'compare to': suggest a similarity).
contrast: show the differences between things.
criticise: point out mistakes and weaknesses in a balanced way.

define: give the precise meaning of a concept.

discuss: explain a passage and give details, with examples.

disprove: produce arguments that show something to be false.

evaluate: discuss, but go on to judge for and against.

explain: offer a detailed and exact explanation of an idea or principle.

illustrate: give examples that demonstrate and prove a point.

justify: give the reasons for a position.

prove: give answers that demonstrate the logical position.

state: express the points briefly and clearly.

summarise/outline: give only the main points – not details.

trace: give a description in logical or chronological order of the stages of a process.

Study the meaning of the following literary terms

alliteration: repetition of the same initial consonant:

> the beating of the baton
>
> leafy with love

allusion: a reference; allusions can be:

—scientific:

> Newton's laws in physics

—literary:

> Heaney's poetry is rich in symbolism

—historical:

> the Wild Geese fled

ambiguity: the use of an expression or word that has a number of possible meanings in such a way that it is difficult to tell which meaning is intended:

> love is blind

analogy: a comparison that points out a relationship or similarity between two things

aphorism: a short, powerful maxim: a concise statement of truth:

> brevity is the soul of wit
>
> borrowing dulls the edge of husbandry

archaism: a term that is obsolete or no longer in use:

> perchance
>
> methinks
>
> thou

assonance: the rhyming of vowel sounds within words:

> thought her too proud
>
> watery hazes of the hazel

atmosphere: the feelings or emotions evoked by nature or a piece of music, art, etc.

balance: placing two parts of a sentence or words within a sentence in such a way as to be in opposition to one another:

> People who are powerful renounce coercive power but not the power that rests on persuasion.

Fools step in where angels fear to tread.

bias: a prejudice: favouring one side in an argument

cadence: the rhythmical rising and falling of language in writing or speech

caricature: the portrayal of a person in which certain characteristics are exaggerated so that the person appears ridiculous

cliché: a hackneyed expression so overused as to have lost its impact:

> slowly but surely
> up for grabs

climax: the culminating moment in a play, poem or piece of prose

colloquial: belonging to common or ordinary speech: informal language

connotations: reverberations or what is implied by a word

diction: the writer's choice of words

digression: turning aside from the main subject

ellipsis: the omission of words, usually indicated by *omission points* (…)

emotive: tending to arouse emotion or feelings

empathy: the complete association of the self with another being

epigram: a short sentence expressing a witty thought or shrewd comment

euphemism: a mild expression in place of a harsh one

figurative language: language that contains many figures of speech, such as metaphors or similes

hyperbole: exaggeration to achieve a certain effect

idiom: an expression peculiar to a certain language

image: a word picture

implication: something that is hinted at or suggested rather than stated explicitly

inference: a judgment or conclusion derived from a statement

invective: wordy abuse or denunciation

irony: an incongruous contrast between the words used and their implication

lucid: vivid or clear

lyrical: literally, like a song; figuratively, full of praise:

> he waxed lyrical about her talents

maxim: an adage: an established principle or truth expressed in a concise form:

> present fears are less than horrible imaginings
> brevity is the soul of wit

metaphor: a comparison between two things without using 'like' or 'as'

mood: the feeling or atmosphere created by a piece of writing

moral: concerned with the good or bad of human behaviour

oratorical: eloquent

paradox: a statement that is apparently contradictory but might be true in a way

parenthesis: an aside

pathos: pity, sadness or tenderness created by a writer

personification: investing inanimate things with human qualities

platitude: a trite or commonplace remark

polemics: the art of controversial discussion

precis: a summary

pun: a play on words that are similar in sound but different in meaning

quip: a sharp retort

rhetoric: persuasive and impressive speech or writing

sarcasm: bitter or wounding remarks made at the expense of another person

satire: exposing folly by means of ridicule

simile: the comparison of two things, using the words 'like' or 'as':

> as plain and as unadorned as the unclouded sky – and about as beautiful

slang: extremely informal expressions that are fashionable for a time but usually go stale very quickly

syntax: the grammatical arrangement of words in the form of sentences

tone: the voice of the writer or speaker

verbosity: wordiness: using more words than necessary, especially pompous ones:

> we would labour with all the wit of us, all the strength of us, to reach our goal [we would try with all our strength and intelligence to reach our goal]

> on a six-monthly basis [every six months]

Common vocabulary errors

Be aware of the difference in meaning between the following sets of words.

advance: progress, going forward:

> the advance of medicine, the advance of old age, the advance of time

advancement: promotion or helping forward:

> The government is working for the advancement of education

affect (a verb): This word has different meanings:

(*a*) to produce an effect on:

> The climate affected his health.

(*b*) to move or influence:

> The news affected relations with Japan.
> The film affected me deeply.

(*c*) to pretend something, to pretend to feel:

> He affected shock at the news.

effect (a noun): the result or consequence of an action:

> The effects of the nuclear fall-out were disastrous.

When used as a verb it means to cause or bring about:

> The prisoners tried to effect an escape.

agree with: to regard something with approval:

> I agree with the minister's new proposal.

agree to: to give consent:

They were forced to agree to the plans for the new building, though they did not like them.

allusion: an indirect reference:

She drew on several literary allusions in her lecture.

illusion: a false image:

He has illusions of greatness.

delusion: a false belief with no basis in fact:

He suffers from delusions ever since the accident.
She is under the delusion that she can write well.

anecdote: a short story
antidote: a medicine used to counteract the effects of a poison or disease

approve: to give consent to:

The committee has approved the budget.

approve of: to think well of, to regard with favour:

He did not approve of the plan to build an extension to the house.

artful: cunning or deceitful:

He is an artful planner when it comes to getting more money.

artless: natural, innocent:

She is a simple, artless girl.

assent/consent: both words mean 'agree to' and both take the preposition 'to'. Assent is immediate agreement; consent is agreement after some consideration

cancel: to put off altogether
postpone: to put off until later

censor: to examine books, films or plays with the intention of suppressing anything offensive
censure: to criticise strongly:

The teacher censured the pupil for cheating in the examination.

compare to: to state a resemblance between two things:

Shakespeare compared the world to a stage and men and women to actors.

compare with: to place side by side and note the resemblances, but mainly the differences:

Most working people are better off compared with how they were in the fifties.

credible: believable:

a credible story

creditable: deserving of merit:

a creditable achievement

credulous: ready to believe anything

defective: faulty:

The computer is defective.

deficient: lacking in something:

You're deficient in vitamin C.

definite: certain:

a definite offer

definitive: final, complete:

a definitive explanation

disinterested: detached, not emotionally involved, objective

uninterested: not interested, not paying attention:

A judge should be disinterested in a case, but not uninterested.

instantaneous: immediate, over in an instant:

an instantaneous reaction
death was instantaneous

simultaneous: happening at the same time:

simultaneous translation

its (a possessive adjective):

The cat is licking its paw.
The world is using up its resources.

it's: a contraction of 'it is' (a pronoun and a verb):

It's a fine day.

lose (a verb):

I lose my keys frequently.
I've lost my confidence in the government.

loose (an adjective):

The door handle is loose.

stationery (a noun):

The stationery shop is on the corner.

stationary (an adjective): at a standstill:

The car is stationary

EXERCISES ON STYLE

Examine the following sentences, then rewrite them correctly. (You can compare your answers with those on pages 290–1.)

1. Shorten and increase the vigour of the following sentences:
    (*a*) Looking at the house from the outside I would imagine there to be about twenty rooms in the house.

(b) The writer uses short to the point sentences with humour and sarcasm to keep the reader interested in the passage.

(c) Boyle full of self delusion sees himself as the man of the house.

(d) Many of these sort of teenagers result from homes where parents are unable to control them properly or the mother is at work and has no time for her children.

(e) I would be delighted if you could please write back to me and tell me if and when you are available to do it for me.

(f) What he means by this is that wherever there is a place it is made a place by people being there.

2. Criticise the following sentences under the headings repetition, punctuation and use of clichés:

(a) When he states his points of arguments he doesn't condemn himself to one side he tries to incorporate the other side too.

(b) You could find it in a magazine which rich people buy, you wouldn't find it in a newspaper because there are too many pictures.

(c) The house is enormous and is not the usual type of house, it appears to be an old house that has been restored.

(d) The environment where a person lives can tell you a lot about that person, if for instance you were in an untidy house you would presume that the owner was a laid back easy going character.

(e) The image I get from Oprah on her programme tells me what type of person she is and her way of life, and I think her home would be the best way to tell me about her.

(f) This would indicate to me that this is a family which leads a classy lifestyle by the mirror and the picture of the woman with the pearls.

3. Rewrite the following sentences by eliminating the repetition and improving the grammar:

(a) The play is filled with jealousy and betrayal one sign of this is Iago.

(b) In university students consistently analyse their actions with great scrutiny feverishly fearing that they may unwaveringly upset a fellow peer or teacher.

(c) I am writing this letter to you to let you know what type of images and photographs I want included in my photo gallery.

(d) The surplus between cost and selling price arose.

(e) Trade fairs are a commercial feature today many being in new exporting markets.

(f) I believe the writer puts across his argument very well and he also perceives human tendencies and exposes them in his argument very well.

4. Rewrite the following sentences and eliminate ambiguity:

(a) I find myself grappling to maintain my popular personage.

(b) The application of time and motion study to this section will of course result in appreciable improvement from the production standpoint.

(c) Regrettably I'm stuck steadfast in this tedious unwelcoming claustrophobic condition where no one knows the despair filled plight I must participate in every day and the lonesome state I am in.

(d) Re your order for Boxhead golf clubs of 15 ult., we beg to advise that these are out of stock.

(e) During the winter the 15:20 train (which during the summer runs on weekdays but not on Sundays) will not run on Sundays.

(f) To these people they soldier on, perhaps living on very little for many years struggling in their quest for success.

4
Composition

GENERAL NOTES ON WRITING

How to write effectively

Good, effective writing is a craft that can be acquired with hard work and a knowledge of the basics. Successful writing involves taking a number of different things into account. It means:

- knowing how to construct sentences so that they form effective and clear paragraphs
- constructing paragraphs and linking them together to achieve a coherent unity and structure
- selecting the appropriate style for your reader
- mastering the conventions of spelling and punctuation
- polishing and revising what you have written.

Every form of written communication must take into account the following elements:

- a writer
- an audience or 'receiver'
- the purpose of the communication.

Before you start writing, clearly establish:

- what the purpose of your communication is
- what your subject matter is
- the type of reader and what expectations they have.

Effective writing means that what you have written is both relevant and appropriate to the situation. For effective writing, therefore, bear in mind the following elements:

- purpose
- topic or subject
- context

* audience
* language or techniques.

Genres of writing

The prose composition should be an attempt to present a reasonable and logical interpretation of the topic you choose. The Leaving Certificate course offers you the opportunity to write in a variety of genres, including:
* the language of narration
* the language of argument
* the language of information
* the language of persuasion
* the aesthetic use of language.

As we have already seen in the section on comprehension, none of these methods are completely clear cut. In other words, a piece of informative writing will involve some amount of persuasive techniques, while writing an argument means that you must communicate information in a certain way.

The art of writing a composition can be mastered with time and effort. It is essential in writing a composition that you take into account certain things, such as pre-composition writing and the different features of the language genres, together with some basic knowledge of how sentences work to form paragraphs, and how paragraphs are constructed to form a full composition.

Your composition must be your own individual response to the subject. It is important, therefore, not to regurgitate material or to learn compositions off by heart. Nor is it advisable to write a composition simply 'off the top of your head', without any preparation. It can be useful to use fifth year and perhaps some holiday time to read and prepare material on different styles of compositions. Remember, the best compositions are written on topics that you enjoy, so learn to identify your own style and work at cultivating various interests.

PROBLEMS AND PITFALLS

Content

One of the main problems is in knowing what exactly to write. Having to write on an unseen topic at Higher Level can be confusing and unsettling for many people. The content in compositions must reflect a certain maturity of approach and a balance of judgment, particularly when writing on factual topics. Avoid digression or introducing irrelevant information. Avoid repetition of ideas.

The language genres

The different language genres or styles for the English course have certain distinctive features. It is important to be aware of these aspects and to know how to use them.

Writer's block and exam paralysis
Overcoming exam paralysis and starting to put pen to paper is another problem.

Lack of unity and structure
There is also the difficulty of organising ideas – of knowing exactly how to construct a paragraph and how to select relevant information and discard useless ideas. Sometimes pupils have problems writing a suitable opening paragraph.

Poor timing
Time and time management can be a further problem.

Faulty style
Faulty style can be shown in many different ways, such as excessive repetition, poor spelling and bad grammar.

Misinterpreting the question or the title
This can occur from a careless reading of the titles.

Solving these problems

1. Gather ideas from newspapers or magazines that deal with current affairs and keep a notebook in which you can jot down ideas. Identify your style of writing and what genres appeal to you. The advice from your teacher can be invaluable here. For the most part, you write best on subjects that you enjoy or feel strongly about.
2. Study the guidelines on how to write in the different language genres (Chapter 5). Know exactly what is required for each genre. Also, study the sample material provided for each genre, particularly the commentary after each one.
3. The main thing in overcoming exam paralysis is to put pen to paper and simply write until your thoughts become coherent.
4. Some of the pre-writing strategies, such as brainstorming and writing a rough outline, can help you to structure your ideas and organise your thoughts more clearly. The section on paragraphing, especially on introductory paragraphs, offers some guidelines and sample material to help you construct opening paragraphs (see pages 32–40).
5. Set deadlines for yourself when writing throughout the year. Remember, you have approximately 75 minutes in the exam to write the composition.
6. Pay attention to such details as spelling, handwriting and grammar. Correct all spelling errors and check that every word you use is the right one. Read your work aloud if possible – this can alert you to all repetition, not only of words but also of ideas. Study the section on style (page 13) and learn how to eliminate common errors in both grammar and spelling.
7. Read the questions and titles slowly and take account of every word and the possibilities or connotations of each word.

PREPARATION

Pre-writing activities

The success of a finished product depends to a great extent on the preparation that has gone into making it what it is. This also applies to a piece of writing. Some of the more important pre-writing activities include:

- brainstorming
- clustering
- outlines
- free writing.

Brainstorming

This is the process of throwing your imagination into high gear and trying to trigger as many ideas as possible on the topic. It can be useful to use such techniques as 'trigger questions' (why? how? where? what? when?) to generate ideas on the topic.

Look at the following samples of how you can brainstorm a topic.

Topic 1: The modern magazine

What exactly is a magazine?
What qualifies it as modern?
What is the difference between a modern magazine and an old-fashioned one?
Who decides that a particular magazine is modern or not?

Topic 2: The place of colour in life

What exactly is colour?
Why are there different kinds of colours?
What place has colour in life?
How does colour affect us?

Clustering

Draw together all the points you have generated from your brainstorming. Begin by 'clustering' your ideas or assembling them into groups. For example, look at the brainstorming above on the topic 'the modern magazine'. Answer some of the questions, then cluster these answers.

For example, you can discuss the different types of magazines today. You may go on to discuss whatever is modern or popular – clothes, beauty tips, love, favourite types of food or holidays. You could also contrast today's publications and trends with those of the past. When you group these ideas together you will have the basis for an outline.

Outlines

Outlines form another part of pre-writing activities. The use of outlines can be very helpful when you are planning a writing activity, particularly a composition. Outlines are the result of brainstorming and drawing up clusters of ideas before you set about the process of writing. Outlines have the following advantages:

- They organise your thoughts.
- They clarify exactly where you are going in the composition.
- They help to provide a direction for a flow of ideas in the composition.
- They help to overcome exam paralysis. Staring at a blank page can be a daunting experience and the rough outline can be a life-saver here.
- They help you to organise and structure paragraphs.

Rough outlines help you to organise your thoughts; they show what needs to be emphasised and what needs to be eliminated, where repetition occurs, etc. Many common errors can be eliminated through the outline, such as:
- gaps in the logical development of ideas
- excessive repetition
- omission of central ideas and information on the subject
- going off the point
- insufficient evidence and examples.

The following is an example of brainstorming a topic, then clustering the ideas together and finally drawing up an outline. Examine the method closely and try to follow it in your writing assignments.

Topic
Compose a persuasive composition that seeks to establish the need for a greater awareness of sex stereotyping.

Sample brainstorm
Use trigger questions on the topic:
- What is sex stereotyping?
- How is this created?
- Where is this situation most in evidence?
- What can be done to remedy it?

Sample clustering
Answer the questions from your brainstorming session, then cluster or gather together these answers; for example:

The problem consists of stereotyping people because of their sex.
Sex stereotyping can be seen in certain types of advertisements – the helpless woman, the resourceful man.
Some television serials stereotype male and female characters – the slim, tall women, the strong men in fast cars.
There needs to be a more balanced presentation of male and female roles in the media.

Sample outline
Establish greater awareness of stereotyping in society.

Opening paragraph
The images of Mother cooking a meal, Father watching television on Saturday evening. Father objecting to slogan in advertisement on television – 'So simple even he can do it'.

Paragraph 2
Images of chaos when Father runs the house. Order and harmony with the presence of Mother. The recognition of this type of stereotyping in advertising.

Paragraph 3
Discuss how some areas of professional life limit and isolate people. 'Female jobs': secretaries, cleaners, nurses. 'Male jobs': technicians, drivers.

Paragraph 4
The media constantly consolidate these images. For example, in *The Simpsons*, the intelligent and resourceful mother and daughter nevertheless do the housework.

Paragraph 5
The effects of this on society. Friction between men and women as pressures to conform intensify. The typical image that women mechanics or bus drivers have to be resilient and tough to survive.

Concluding paragraph
The need to tackle this issue: men and women to deal with their limitations and transcend the pressures coming from the media. Television programmes need to broaden people's outlook on this issue.

Free writing
Free writing is a helpful method of warming up before you begin the process of writing in a formal and coherent manner. The main idea underlying this activity is to put pen to paper and to get going on the writing process immediately. Simply write about anything you choose and in whatever way you like, not caring about punctuation, spelling or structure. Write without stopping. Don't stop to plan, organise or edit. It can help to concentrate on a topic and to set yourself a time limit. The main idea is to generate as many words as possible on paper.

PLANNING

1. Be decisive with regard to selecting what topic or question you are going to write about.
2. Rephrase the title as a question (if it is not already in the form of a question); this will help to generate ideas on the subject.

3. Brainstorm the topic by using trigger questions such as who? why? how?
4. Cluster ideas that are related. Be clear about what direction your essay is taking. Don't introduce irrelevant material or go off the point.
5. Select material for paragraphs. Fully write out the topic sentence of each paragraph.
6. Your composition must have a general unity of impression. This will be shown in a clear, conclusive and satisfactory ending and in a logical development of thought between the paragraphs.

Ten basic hints on writing a composition

1. Write every day. Write a paragraph on any topic in order to improve your expression and your flow of thought.
2. Cultivate your own ideas on current events. You can do this by having a notebook in which to collect ideas throughout the year.
3. Understand the topic fully, otherwise don't write on it.
4. Always engage in some of the pre-writing activities – brainstorming, clustering, free writing and drawing up outlines – before writing seriously on the topic.
5. Avoid errors made in previous writing work by learning spellings and correcting mistakes in grammar.
6. Identify your strengths and weaknesses in writing. Work at eliminating the weaknesses and improving the strong points.
7. Write simply. Choose a simple word instead of a more obscure expression. Avoid using clichés: 'few and far between', 'in the heel of the hunt', 'to tell you the truth'.
8. Work at writing interesting and arresting openings.
9. Draw up your own list of quotations and clever phrases and use them in written work.
10. Don't make general or global statements without supporting them with clear, specific examples and evidence.

Ten do's

1. Write a paragraph every day on any topic. Leave it to 'cool', then come back later and correct it.
2. Always brainstorm your title and always write rough drafts.
3. Organise your paragraphs, putting the most important ideas first.
4. Write interesting and exciting opening paragraphs.
5. Make your composition a reasonable length – three to four pages of A4 paper is usually sufficient.
6. Make sure the ideas you use are relevant. Use your own ideas.
7. Make your conclusion clear, fairly substantial and non-repetitive.
8. Vary the length and structure of your sentences.
9. Link your literature course to your composition; weave in quotations or ideas naturally and fluidly.
10. Read your composition aloud in order to hear your mistakes.

Ten don'ts

1. Don't go off the point – stick to the topic.
2. Don't use direct speech unless it is necessary.
3. Don't use two different ideas in one paragraph.
4. Avoid self-conscious expressions: 'I hope to prove …' or 'I feel that I have shown …'.
5. Avoid the use of clichés and repetitive phrases.
6. Don't use quotation marks unless you are quoting.
7. Avoid the use of a definition in your opening paragraph.
8. Don't conclude your composition in mid-air.
9. Don't conclude on one sentence.
10. Don't reproduce compositions that have been learned off by heart.

THE PARAGRAPH

Every piece of prose composition is based on knowing how to build sentences to form an effective paragraph. A paragraph is like a miniature composition – it should have a clear beginning, a middle and a conclusion.

Each paragraph deals with one section of your subject. Each paragraph has one main idea or topic sentence, together with support or examples. The paragraph must have unity – all ideas, examples, statistics or illustrations must be related to the main idea.

Paragraphs can be connected by linking or transitional devices, such as 'nevertheless', 'furthermore', 'however', 'if', 'or', 'so'. Paragraphs can be of any length; however, avoid extremes, that is, writing a paragraph that is either very long or very short. Generally speaking, there should be a variety in the construction of paragraphs within the composition.

Features of paragraphs
- Clarity.
- Unity.
- Emphasis.
- Coherence.
- Transitional or linking devices between paragraphs.

Clarity
Good writing aims at communicating effectively to your readers, not merely impressing them. The main idea must be clear to your reader. Generally speaking, the topic sentence usually comes either at the beginning or end of a paragraph.

The following paragraph is an example of clear writing.

When the Black and Tan lorry left the strand road to swing instead towards the centre of the town, the Dummy was lounging at the corner house. All evening he had stood there in the mild warmth of the October sunlight, and though he was startled he did not move. But when the lorry passed close to him, his eyes narrowed and his head inclined slightly towards the wide strand on his left. He counted the turns. The engine slowed, revved, dropped again. It was going towards Freddie's house. By the time it stopped completely he was hammering loudly at one of the small cottages which faced the strand.

(James Plunkett, *The Web*)

Comment

The main or topic sentence is clearly set out in the opening sentence of this dramatic piece of writing. The remaining sentences demonstrate the reaction of the character to the arrival of the Black and Tan lorry in the town.

Unity

Unity occurs in a paragraph when the main idea is clearly stated and all examples or supporting material are related to that main idea.

So great and deep a cave, of course, had to be dark. But it was even darker than François had expected when he crawled through the narrow entrance. Then he could tell from the feel of the sand underneath his hands that he was inside it in depth. He looked carefully all round him but could see nothing to indicate the presence of Xhabbo, Nuin-Tara, and Nonnie. Were it not for Hintza, who, as always, unless ordered away, was close to him, he could easily have thought himself to be alone. The darkness indeed was so dense that it was almost tangible, and as he stood up, silently and slowly, his left hand brushed the air in front of his face as if to clear the black matter from his eyes. It was a most unpleasant feeling, as if this profound darkness around him had found an ally within, inflicted on them all by the tragic events of the day. The whole was not just a sensation conveyed by the senses but a powerful emotion arguing with the voice of despair that the last light was about to be extracted from life on earth.

(Laurens van der Post, *A Far-Off Place*)

Comment

The theme or main point of this paragraph is the extreme state of darkness within the cave. Every sentence relates to the opening sentence here. The writer draws some vivid images of the effects internally and externally on the characters.

Emphasis

Emphasis comes from the position of the key sentence within the paragraph. This sentence can occur anywhere in the paragraph.

The following two paragraphs show the effect of placing the topic sentence in a distinctive position within the paragraph.

Colour tends to be a subconscious element in films. The use of colour in films is strongly emotional in its appeal, expressive and atmospheric rather than conspicuous or

> intellectual. Psychologists have discovered that most people actively attempt to interpret the lines of a composition, but they tend to accept colour passively, permitting it to suggest moods rather than objects. Lines are associated with nouns, colour with adjectives. Line is sometimes thought to be masculine; colour feminine. Both lines and colour suggest meanings, then, but in somewhat different ways.

COMMENT

The opening sentence here is the topic or main sentence. Every other sentence is developed from this main sentence and illustrates an example of how colour is accepted as a subconscious element of films.

Coherence

Coherence means the logical flow of thought between ideas. All the sentences in a paragraph must relate to the topic sentence and to one another. There must be a link between one sentence and another in such a way that the reader will clearly see a logical progression and development in thought within the paragraph.

There are different ways of achieving coherence within a paragraph. A writer can use linking or transitional words, such as 'moreover', 'but', 'furthermore'. The writer may also use the repetition of the same word, phrase or sentence to link the ideas within the paragraph. The following paragraph is an example of the smooth and logical flow of thought from one idea to another.

> Michael Gill and his wife came last. Gill had begun to reap with the slow methodic movements of a machine driven at low pressure. He continued at exactly the same pace, never changing, never looking up to see where his opponents were. His long lean hands moved noiselessly, and only the sharp crunching rush of the teeth of his reaping-hook through the yellow stalks of the rye could be heard. His long drooping eyelashes were always directed towards the point where his hook was cutting. He never looked behind to see had he enough for a sheaf before beginning another. All his movements were calculated beforehand, calm, monotonous, deadly accurate. Even his breathing was light, and came through his nose like one who sleeps healthily. His wife moved behind him in the same manner, tying each sheaf daintily, without exertion.
>
> (Liam O'Flaherty, *The Reaping Race*)

COMMENT

This is an example of a coherent and fluid stream of thought between one idea and another. The writer cleverly registers each of Gill's movements as he carries out the task of reaping the sheaves of rye. Each sentence is linked to the preceding one, and each flows effortlessly and fluidly along to give a striking image of two people caught up in a reaping competition.

Remember, in order to achieve coherence within a paragraph:
1. Clearly establish your topic sentence.
2. Do not introduce two topic sentences or two different ideas in one paragraph.

3. Make sure that every point made in the paragraph has some relation to this topic idea.
4. Every sentence must develop or advance the preceding ideas or build up to a climax if the topic sentence comes at the conclusion of the paragraph.
5. Do not digress or introduce irrelevant statements into the paragraph.
6. Use linking devices to help provide a smooth and logical continuity within the paragraph.

Linking devices

The use of transitional words or phrases not only serves the function of linking ideas within the same paragraph, but can also serve as a link between the different paragraphs. Linking devices can elaborate and develop a writer's argument.

Look at the following examples of how linking devices can be used in different ways.

To show contrast between ideas:
    But,
    Nevertheless,
    Still,
    Although,
    Conversely,
    Yet,
    On the contrary,

To emphasise a point:
    For example,
    For instance,
    In fact,
    Indeed,

To show cause and effect or the consequences of something:
    Therefore,
    Thus,
    As a result,
    Accordingly,

To show relations of time and sequence:
    Then,
    Later,
    Afterwards,
    Next,
    Meanwhile,
    Soon,

To sum up or conclude:
    In conclusion,
    Finally,
    To sum up,

Examine the following two extracts, which are on different subjects and have clear linking or transition devices, both within and between them. Then carefully study the commentary.

Passage 1

Dare to be dangerous by embracing the hottest colour of the season – red – in shades veering from poppy to plum. On the catwalk, red mixed boldly with tamer neutral tones to create a sophisticated look. Even Prada, the most minimalist of designers, included a bold red knee-length coat in the autumn-winter collection. For those without dominatrix tendencies there was a more subtle offering from Valentino, who showed a beautifully delicate yet stunning bodice-style dress that fell just above the ankle.

If you're wary of red, then embrace it with caution. This season leather is one of fashion's most basic allies because it never goes out of vogue. If leather does not appeal to you because you think it requires too much attitude to wear it, then think again.

The main thing to keep in mind is contrast. Match it with cool jerseys or delicately soft wools for maximum appeal. For most of us, the only thing standing in our way of going hell for leather is cost. If you want to get a leather effect without getting into ferocious debt, then the only way to do it is with PVC.

COMMENT

This extract is from a newspaper account of the latest colours and style in clothes. It is written for a general audience and, obviously, for women. Note how the linking word 'if' is used to offer an alternative to the colours and styles that are mentioned. Also, such terms as 'for those' and 'for most of us' are clearly persuasive and designed to win the reader around to accepting the idea that is being expressed.

Passage 2

Watching Irish politics over the last fifteen years has been like practising deep-space astronomy. It used to be that astronomers watched the skies and noted what they could see. Now, trying to work out what is going on in the wider universe, they pay as much attention to what they cannot see. By observing the motions of heavenly bodies they guess at the forces that must be operating on them. From the way known objects behave, they can be pretty sure that bodies they cannot yet see are affecting them. Eventually, as they look harder, they get clear images of where those bodies are buried.

So it has been with political life. It's been obvious to anybody looking at it with half an eye that invisible forces have influenced its movements. Decisions have been made, actions taken that are simply inexplicable unless we assume the presence of some unseen force, some hidden pull.

We have to conjecture that this force is corruption. But, until the McCracken Tribunal, we couldn't see it with the naked eye, name or place it.

Even now we haven't got the clear, sharp images of our political universe that would allow us to understand exactly how it has worked. However, we still have to work on the assumption that there are many black holes, uncharted but discernible by their effects.

COMMENT

In this article several clear transitional devices are used to signal a relation between the different ideas. The writer proceeds to develop the argument by using certain linking terms, such as 'it used to be', 'by observing' and 'now it is'. The use of certain words and phrases, such as 'eventually' and 'so it has', shows the reader what the results of such findings have been. The writer draws a contrast between the ideas by using the linking words 'but' and 'however' and the phrase 'even now we haven't got'.

The introductory paragraph

The introductory and the concluding paragraphs are the two most important paragraphs in your composition. The introductory paragraph has two main functions:
- to capture your reader's attention
- to introduce your material and demonstrate your stance or approach to the subject.

The opening paragraph of your composition must be interesting and arresting for your reader. Avoid openings that are predictable and dull, for example, definition-style openings:

Fashion may be defined as …

This technological age may be seen as …

'This great stage of fools' is a saying that is true because it is all round us …

Make sure your opening paragraph is original or takes an original slant on the topic. It can help to use an anecdote, a quotation or a surprising statistic. Look at the following paragraph:

The new youth

If the whole point of each fresh generation is to moult, revolt and supplant its parents, to crash through the creaky barriers of the establishment – quite simply, to inherit the earth – then it must be disconcerting to be young right now. The old battles are over. And the new ones, whatever they might be, have not yet taken shape – aside from the sense of helplessness that the very earth the young are inheriting is increasingly damaged. There is no world war; there is no cold one either. For many people in their twenties that good fortune is offset by a yawning lack of common purpose: even the horrors of the Balkan wars did not generate the solidarity of common conflicts. And so the battle cry of the young, 'Do it yourself, for yourself', sounds suspiciously like a Nike ad.

COMMENT

This paragraph takes an interesting and original angle on the subject. A variety of sentence structures and vocabulary is used and the images used are relevant and punchy.

Now study the following paragraphs (taken from pupils' actual work) and examine the commentary following each one.

Hairstyles

I glance at the mirror illuminated by tiny white lights which make you look frighteningly pale and pudgy and just as quickly averted my eyes. This mirror does absolutely nothing for one's appearance, I thought grimly. My hair dripping wet was stuck to my face and there was a big white patch on my forehead where my make-up used to be until some over-eager employer decided to herself that I didn't need make-up on that part of my anatomy. This is too humiliating. I decide that I'll do it myself in future. The future always turns into the next time, though. Vanity and pressure from my friends prevail. It's unfashionably long, look at your split ends, and don't you know that rubber bands break your hair? were constantly being hurled at me, so after one particularly spirit-crushing evening of abuse I made an appointment at the hairdresser's. The 'Guillotine'. How appropriate, I think, as I make the phone call with a certain amount of dread.

COMMENT

This is an example of a weak opening. No real statement is made and no topic sentence is established. The sentence structure is too long and confusing. The writer here seems to be unpacking the contents of her mind onto paper in a disorderly and confusing manner. There is no clear topic sentence and there is poor organisation of thought within the paragraph.

REWRITTEN VERSION

I glanced at the mirror, illuminated by tiny white lights, which make one look frightfully pale and pudgy. I quickly averted my eyes. I began to think grimly: This mirror does absolutely nothing for one's appearance. I stood before the mirror. My hair, which was dripping wet, stuck to my face. There was a big patch on my forehead where my make-up had smudged. I felt humiliated and decided to do it myself next time. But personal vanity, combined with pressure from my friends, prevailed over everything. Comments such as 'It's unfashionably long', 'Look at your split ends' and 'Don't you know that rubber bands break your hair?' had been hurled at me repeatedly. So, after one of these sessions of abuse from my friends, I made an appointment with a hairdresser called the 'Guillotine'. How appropriate, I thought as I made the phone call, not without a certain amount of dread.

The advertising jungle

The world in which we live today seems intent on bombarding us with images of ultra-shining cars that are so clean you can see yourself in them.

Image after image jumps off our television screens out of our radios in through our car windscreen, off roadside hoardings, in a desperate attempt to force us into buying products we don't need and if we really thought about it don't even want. Tempting us to part with our hard earned money so that we can build up more and more material goods which will in turn make us all much better people, because don't forget the more we have and the more we own the better we are, forget about the man down the road who has no money for food.

Comment

There is no clear direction in this paragraph. The punctuation is weak and the paragraph has no clear topic sentence. The writer uses excessive repetition. The words 'advertising' and 'jungle' are not even mentioned.

Rewritten version

> Today's world of advertising seems to bombard us from all angles with numerous images, from those of ultra-shiny cars to the latest trends in clothes or that super-modern gadget for your kitchen. Images assault us from everywhere, be it the television screen, the radio or on hoardings. All are united in the fact that they represent an attempt to manipulate us into buying products we do not need or even want. These images are designed to tempt us to part with our hard-earned money in order to accumulate more material goods. Furthermore, we are enticed into buying more, under the illusion that the more we have, the happier and more fulfilled we will be. Of course, these advertisements do little for the man down the road who has not even got the money for food.

The concluding paragraph

Your concluding paragraph is your final statement on the topic of your composition. It is the last impression left on your reader and therefore it is vitally important.

A good conclusion has two purposes:
* to round off the main points or ideas in your composition satisfactorily
* to provide a general unity of impression.

Avoid conclusions that repeat the main ideas of your composition in the same words. On the other hand, you should avoid going to the other extreme by introducing a different approach or new ideas in your conclusion, which will only serve to frustrate your reader. One happy medium between the two extremes is referring back to the introductory paragraph and developing the anecdote or statistic or simply the point that was made there. This method can ensure that there is a unity in your composition. If, for example, a composition on 'European Union: Where to go to from here?' begins like this:

> Ever since the term 'European' was first used, in the time of Charlemagne, its interpretation has been disputed. What does it mean to be European today? For those in other continents it simply means the people who live in this one. And there are an awful lot of people living here, from Austrian farmers to Norwegian taxi drivers, who don't identify themselves as European …

the conclusion could consist of the following:

> A European Union in the future would be a world mode of what I call 'liberal order'. By this I mean an order without a single dominant power, flexibly open to different alliances of states on different issues and ultimately committed to the peaceful resolution of all

> conflicts between its members. It is only in this way, I believe, that the hopes and fears of the three different kinds of Europeans will possibly be reconciled in a way that has never been achieved since the days of Charlemagne. This is the Europe we need and this is the Europe I urge on my fellow Europeans.

Examine the concluding paragraph of the following composition on 'Isn't it time to limit the use of private cars?'.

> Until the time when responsibility is taken for this problem, the situation will only continue to worsen. Those who sit alone each morning in their cars and complain about the traffic must realise that they play a role in creating the problem itself. The public transport services too, while complaining about the difficulties they face, must realise that the inadequacy of their systems also contributes to this problem. If the problem is left unaddressed we may reach the time when limiting the use of private cars will be necessary. To avoid this situation, we must take co-operative action now and eliminate 'urban gridlock'.

COMMENT

This is an example of a concluding paragraph that makes a clear statement on the issues raised in the title. The writer here ties up certain ideas and presents some solutions in a clear and vigorous manner.

Remember that your conclusion must show that you have complete control over your subject.

Rules for a good style

1. Write to communicate, not to impress. Know exactly what you want to say, then go ahead and say it.
2. Put your statements in a positive form. Make your statements or ideas clear and definite.
3. Choose a specific and concrete word. Avoid the use of vague or abstract expressions.
4. Use an active verb rather than a passive one. Your writing is more effective and forceful when you use active verbs.
5. Avoid repeating yourself in the same words. Repetition has to be used correctly, otherwise it can weaken the writing.
6. Vary the length and structure of your sentences.
7. Every sentence must have a subject, a verb and an object.
8. Always consult a dictionary when you are not sure how to spell a word or to check the meaning of a word.
9. Get used to writing and rewriting.
10. Learn the basic rules of correct punctuation thoroughly.
11. Know how to link your paragraphs correctly. The section on paragraphs (pages 32–40) gives examples of transition or linking devices and how to use them correctly.

CHECKLIST FOR WRITING COMPOSITIONS

Before you begin writing compositions, consider the following questions.

Content
- Are you presenting original and interesting ideas?
- If you are writing in the 'language of argument', have you presented the arguments in a balanced way and supported all statements made with sufficient evidence?
- Have you commented on the significance of quotations or examples in the development of your argument?
- Have you arrived at your own conclusions or relied too heavily on the interpretations of other people?

Organisation
- Does your introduction give a clear idea of what your composition is about?
- Does each paragraph fit into the pattern of your composition and advance the main point, or are there gaps in the development of ideas or digressions that sidetrack your points?
- Are the transitions between the paragraphs effective? Do they unify a paragraph and provide a logical development of thought between each paragraph?
- Does your conclusion link to your opening and tie in all the ideas in an interesting way? Is the conclusion positive? Is there a strong unity of impression from your conclusion?

Language
- Is the language used appropriate to the subject?
- Have you used the exact word to convey the precise meaning?
- Have you used language that is clear and comprehensible and avoided ambiguous expressions?
- Have you avoided slang and jargon?
- Are your sentences varied in length?
- Are the tenses of verbs consistent throughout?

Mechanics
- Have you avoided grammatical errors?
- Is your composition properly punctuated?
- Are all words correctly spelled?
- Are quotations or dialogue introduced correctly?
- Is there any unnecessary repetition of ideas, words or phrases?

The Language Genres

5

Study the notes below on the different language genres. In each section there are notes and guidelines on how to understand and write in the different genres; use these to guide you through the exercises.

THE LANGUAGE OF NARRATION

In the language of narration, or *narrative writing,* the writer is telling a story. Narrative writing is to be found in novels and short stories, plays, poems, histories, letters, some expository essays and reviews. Non-fictional narrative includes biography, autobiography and travel literature.

In an autobiography the writer narrates an account of his or her own life and experiences. Generally these events are narrated in chronological sequence. A biography is the study of one person's life and achievements written by another person. Travel literature records details of journeys and the writer's impressions of places visited in a way that lends a distinctive shape to the narrative.

Features of the language of narration
1. The ability to tell a story that has an effective narrative shape, with a beginning, a middle and a conclusion that are all clearly defined. There must be a distinct arrangement in the sequence of events presented.
2. The story must have a fairly definite location and context.
3. The story should be interesting and original. Clichés and stereotyping are avoided.
4. In a good narrative, the writer introduces some personal commitment or experience.
5. All description must be both vivid and realistic.
6. Sometimes an anecdote can be used as part of a narrative. Here a single incident is told in the form of a short story. The incident almost always contains a definite point.
7. The characters presented must be realistic.
8. The story must have atmosphere. There has to be a certain setting; this can be a country, a certain type of house or a distinct period in history.

Sample passages

I lived in Portstewart, one of the small villages on the coast. I rented a small room at the top of an old dank two-storey Victorian terrace house. The house was the last one in the terrace, and from its window I could look out on the grey, ever-restless ocean. I can still remember the view from the window and the constant changes in the sea. The weather in that part of the north of Ireland was never the kindest, though when the summer came, the landscape round us, the easy access to Donegal and to the remoter parts of the North gave the area its own particular delight.

An old retired couple who owned the house lived in two rooms on the ground floor. Mr Paul was in his eighties, and I remember him going for his nightly walk accompanied by his walking-stick and his small mongrel dog. His bent figure would brave even Portstewart's weather as he walked along the sea front. I never saw the old man at any other time apart from these walks. I heard him occasionally in his own room. His wife, his second, would sit quietly in the kitchen beside the old range, constantly knitting and offering us cups of tea as we came in from the pub or back from studying. She never bothered us much, was always friendly, and enjoyed a cup of tea with those of us who would sit and chat with her.

Mr Paul became ill very suddenly. We were not surprised, aware even then that age can be cruel. But what moved me most was his rapid decline, the fact that I never saw him walking bent double against the wind, and the sight of his walking-stick always lying in the hall. It became a strange kind of symbol. Late into the night I could hear him coughing and throwing up. The fact that we were only aware of this man's illness through his rasping cough and his wife's ministrations lent the house a kind of ominous gloom.

One evening I came in from the cold and straight to the kitchen to heat myself at the range. Mrs Paul sat alone. There was a silence I couldn't understand. I recall now that her knitting-needles were for once not in evidence. There was no steam coming out of the old kettle normally kept simmering on the hot plate. Her face was very still. It took her some time to look up, to acknowledge me coming into the room. 'Would you like a cup of tea?' I asked. She looked up slowly, and I remember her old, lined but still quite beautiful face as she said calmly and without emotion: 'My husband is dead.'

(Brian Keenan, *An Evil Cradling*)

COMMENT

An Evil Cradling describes Brian Keenan's experience as a hostage in Lebanon. This extract recounts an incident in his life and is written in an autobiographical and narrative style. The passage is built around a series of small, effective devices, all of which are a hallmark of good narrative writing. The use of the autobiographical 'I' adds an air of realism to the writing. The imagery and language are precise and homely, and this quality of simplicity lends an arresting impact to the writing.

Question A
1. Show how the writer builds up atmosphere in the passage.
2. Identify several details that contribute to drawing vivid descriptions in the passage.

Question B

Write a short narrative description of some experience that affected you greatly. In your description concentrate on drawing some realistic details of character.

When the news of my birth reached Dr Xia he said: 'Ah, another wild swan is born.' I was given the name Erhong, which means 'second wild swan'.

Giving me my name was almost the last act in Dr Xia's long life. Four days after I was born he died, at the age of eighty-two. He was leaning back in bed drinking a glass of milk. My grandmother went out of the room for a minute, and when she came back to get the glass she saw that the milk had spilled and the glass had fallen to the floor. He had died instantly and painlessly.

Funerals were very important events in China. Ordinary people would often bankrupt themselves to lay on a grand ceremony – and my grandmother loved Dr Xia and wanted to do him proud. There were three things she absolutely insisted on: first, a good coffin; second, that the coffin must be carried by pallbearers and not pulled on a cart; and third, to have Buddhist monks to chant the *sutras* for the dead and musicians to play the *suona*, a piercing woodwind instrument traditionally used at funerals. My father agreed to the first and second requests but vetoed the third. The communists regarded any extravagant ceremony as wasteful and 'feudal'.

Traditionally only very lowly people were buried quietly. Noise-making was considered important at a funeral, to make it a public affair: this brought 'face' and also showed respect for the dead. My father insisted that there could be no *suona* or monks. My grandmother had a blazing row with him. For her, these were essentials, which she just had to have. In the middle of the altercation she fainted from anger and grief. She was also wrought up because she was all alone at the saddest moment of her life. She had not told my mother what had happened, for fear of upsetting her; and the fact that my mother was in the hospital meant that my grandmother had to deal directly with my father. After the funeral she had a nervous breakdown and had to be hospitalised for almost two months.

(Jung Chang, *Wild Swans*)

COMMENT

One of the features of good narrative is describing a specific time and location. Here the writer concentrates on certain significant events that occurred when she was born, how her grandfather died and the small details about the funeral ceremony. We also learn about her communist background and about certain customs in China.

Question A

1. Sum up in your own words the main points you have gathered about the tradition of funeral ceremonies in China.
2. What is the tone of the extract? Support your answer by reference to the passage.

Question B
Rewrite the passage in the form of a dialogue. In writing your dialogue concentrate on registering some striking features of the characters represented.

Writing in the language of narration

The skills of good narrative composition come from practice. Writing a narrative composition essentially requires the ability to write a short story. The story should have one point of view and there should be a definite arrangement of ideas. A story must be original and interesting for your reader. A good story springs from your own experience.

How to write a narrative composition

1. Tell the story in one tense; the past tense is generally best.
2. It can help to put your own experience into the narrative – personal experience authenticates the flavour of a narrative.
3. The structure of your story can be straightforward and in chronological sequence or it can be told in flashback. Remember, your story must have a shape – a clear beginning, middle and conclusion.
4. Use the first-person or third-person narrator to tell your story. Avoid the use of too much dialogue, as it can break up the flow of thought. Remember, dialogue needs to be written well in order to read well.
5. Understand the terms 'plot', 'character' and 'dialogue' when writing a narrative composition and know how to use them correctly.

Plot

A plot can be defined as the series of events that make up a story.
- The plot must move forward towards a definite conclusion.
- The plot must include some element of change. The situation depicted at the beginning of the story must change as the story unfolds.
- All events of the plot must carry the narrative forward.
- There has to be a pace in the plot. Balance your beginning, middle and conclusion carefully to give your story a shape.

Remember when planning your plot to have:

- change in the story
- pace and movement in the narrative
- general shape at the conclusion.

Characters

Because stories are about people, your characters must be real, recognisable figures. Your readers must be able to recognise the characters in your story; if not, they will not arouse any interest. You can reveal the true nature of your characters through dialogue and description. Concentrate on one or two significant features of a character when describing them rather than on several points.

When you are describing a character, don't tell everything at once – use implication or suggestion instead. For example, look at the following descriptions.

> The sister, Catherine, was a slender worldly girl of about thirty, with a solid, sticky bob of red hair, and a complexion powdered milky white. Her eyebrows had been plucked and then drawn on again at a more rakish angle, but the efforts of nature towards the restoration of the old alignment gave a blurred air to her face. When she moved about there was an incessant clicking as innumerable pottery bracelets jingled up and down upon her arms. She came in with such a proprietary haste, and looked around so possessively at the furniture that I wondered if she lived there.
>
> (F. Scott Fitzgerald, *The Great Gatsby*)

COMMENT

Here the writer concentrates on registering some small details in the picture given to us of this character. Note how the writer describes the woman's hair as a 'sticky bob of red hair'. The image of the bracelets jangling up and down her arms is striking and clear.

Look at the effect achieved in the following description of a character.

> Mrs Reed was a woman of robust frame, square-shouldered and strong limbed, not tall, and though stout, not obese: she had a somewhat large face, the under-jaw being much developed and very solid; her brow was low, her chin large and prominent, mouth and nose sufficiently regular; her skin was dark and opaque, her hair nearly flaxen; her constitution was sound as a bell, illness never came near her; she was an exact clever manager, her household and tenantry were thoroughly under her control.
>
> (Charlotte Brontë, *Jane Eyre*)

COMMENT

The writer concentrates on drawing a clear and animated image of a certain type of person. The physical appearance of the woman is registered vividly through a series of small and precise points, such as her robust frame and the fact that she is strong-limbed but not obese. Remember, good description concentrates on making the reader clearly see what is being drawn.

Dialogue

Learn to master the art of writing effective dialogue before beginning a narrative composition. The function of dialogue is to reproduce live speech. Never allow dialogue simply to slip into a conversation – it must have a purpose. Remember that one of the main features of effective dialogue is the ability to convey conflict in a realistic manner. Conversation or good dialogue can add pace and variety to an otherwise dull story.

Learn how to punctuate dialogue correctly. Use quotation marks at the beginning and end of each section of direct speech. Separate the dialogue from the narrative by means of commas. The first word in every piece of direct speech begins with a capital letter. Use a new paragraph each time there is a change of speaker.

Study the following examples of the use of dialogue in composition, then read the commentary.

'How would you like to go to school then, child Alexander, hey?'

The question took me completely by surprise, but anyway my mother answered for me. 'Frederick.' Her voice had a warning in it.

He smiled briefly in her direction. 'Hey then, my boy?'

'I hadn't really thought about it, Father.'

'Well, think about it. Now's the time. Meet a few chaps of your own age. Broaden. Polish you up a bit. Games,' he said, without any enormous conviction. 'Pass the celery, please. And things.'

I passed him the celery.

'Mr Bingham is more than adequate.' Her voice was north-north-east cold.

'Perhaps a widening of outlook would do no harm. There are other subjects which Mr Bingham …'

'He is delicate, Frederick. You must not put his health at risk.'

'In your eyes he is delicate, my dear. I see few signs of it. He has just eaten a most remarkable lunch.'

'Dr Desmond …'

'Dr Desmond is an ass.'

'Frederick, *pas devant …*'

'My dear good woman, you know perfectly well that Dr Desmond will say anything you want him to say.'

(Jennifer Johnston, *How Many Miles to Babylon*)

COMMENT

This extract depicts the strain in the relationship between husband and wife. The dialogue conveys in a terse manner the primary features of these two characters.

Mood and atmosphere

Note the difference between the terms 'mood' and 'atmosphere'. Mood is the way the writer feels; atmosphere is how the place and setting are described.

Every story needs an atmosphere. Atmosphere is created in a narrative by a careful blending of people, events and setting. Your atmosphere must help to draw your reader into your story. While the use of imagination can help to build up an atmosphere, remember that the imagination must be controlled in writing. This is necessary in order to make your writing more realistic and authentic.

STATE EXAMINATIONS COMMISSION CRITERIA FOR ASSESSMENT

The tasks set for candidates in both Paper I and Paper II will be assessed in accordance with the following criteria:
- **Clarity of purpose (P):** 30 per cent of the marks available for the task.
- **Coherence of delivery (C):** 30 per cent of the marks available for the task.

- **Efficiency of language use (L):** 30 per cent of the marks available for the task.
- **Accuracy of mechanics (M):** 10 per cent of the marks available for the task.

Clarity of purpose (P)	Engagement with the set task, e.g. relevance, focus, originality, freshness, clear aim, understanding of genre.
Coherence of delivery (C)	Ability to sustain the response over the entire answer, e.g. continuity of argument, sequencing, management of ideas, choice of reference, use of examples, engagement with texts, control of register and shape, creative modelling.
Efficiency of language use (L)	Management and control of language to achieve clear communication, e.g. vocabulary, syntax, sentence patterns, paragraph structure, punctuation appropriate to the register, use of lively and interesting phrasing, energy, style, fluency – all appropriate to the task.
Accuracy of mechanics (M)	Spelling and grammar, e.g. appropriate levels of accuracy in spelling, grammatical patterns appropriate to the register.

Sample composition

The following composition is written in the language of narration. It is taken from actual pupils' work and is graded according to the standards required at Higher Level. Study it carefully and pay particular attention to the commentary that follows.

The exercise was: 'Write on some experience that left a deep impression on you. Use a narrative or imaginative style in your composition.'

Awakenings

Even now, thirty years after experiencing the bullfight at San María, my pulse still races when it calls to mind
The rippling lengths of bleached canvas overhead
The golden glimmering bullring far below.
I presumed that by sitting half way up the crowded amphitheatre we would be safe,
To a certain extent removed from it all,
Protected from the ferocious intensity below.
We were not.

That summer Pat, Kilty, John Drennan and myself were enjoying a cycling tour of the Iberian Peninsula. Three young students; none older than twenty. We had been in the country for three weeks and had not yet succeeded in understanding the Spanish mind-set. All we had ascertained was that they were tanned, aloof, beautiful and gibbering.

The breakthrough came on a bright Sunday afternoon in late July. It so happened that my bicycle became punctured a few miles outside a modest uphill village called San María. Because of the severity of the puncture we had to venture into the town for an unscheduled stop.

The wife of the local garage owner – an olive, leathery-skinned woman – explained to us that he was at the bullfight, of course. Glad of a temporary respite, we all wheeled our bicycles to the stadium. We were all country boys and therefore had gone hare-coursing and hunting at home. Our voices grew to an animated pitch of feverish excitement as we neared the giant theatre.

Nearly all the seats had been taken half an hour before the event began. Luckily we managed to find three seats half way up the bustling amphitheatre.

Our hungry eyes and ears scanned the onlookers. There were people of all ages and both sexes, delight and excitement clearly visible on their faces. The hushed, reverential noise of the crowd was unlike anything I had previously experienced at hurling matches at home. It was strange and unsettling.

Only when the bull entered did I understand the reason: the close, undeniable presence of death among us. I was in no way prepared for my utter dread of the bull – a gruesome, malevolent presence. He lashed out at the crowd in general, thundering left and right. His red nostrils flared, and the muscles of his silky sweat-covered trunk contracted uncontrollably into spasms.

To my left a samba band announced the arrival of *el matador.* He was a man of twenty-two years – only slightly older than us, a local from a neighbouring upland village. As usual, his father was also a matador before him. It was said that he was a fine fighter, already in a few short years having exceeded the skill, grace and creativity of his father.

To my unaccustomed eye he was short and of slight build. Yet his puny presence had already managed to dissipate some of the bull's choking and stifling sense of menace.

The matador walked towards the bull, the crowd fell quiet, he stopped. Beast and matador silently studied each other. The bull seemed to recognise who exactly he encountered, both the purpose and significance of the encounter. This mutual appraisal lasted no more than fifteen seconds. The bull charged.

Closer and closer the ton and a half of agitating muscle charged. The matador remained motionless. His guttural growl grew to fever pitch. The matador clicked the heels of the delicate dust-covered shoes, recognising a distant face in the crowd.

Then at the last possible instant the matador stepped sideways, totally unconcerned. The crowd erupted.

Amidst the dizzying heat and deafening roars of 'Toro, toro,' a strange thing happened. Choked with fear, I experienced the most potent sense of humanity that to this day I have ever felt. Every sinew in my body pulsed with an immense feeling of pride of race. Every deft little side kick and neat little blow increased my pride in belonging to the human race.

The matador's complete superiority over the bull held me spellbound. Like everybody else, I was far too caught up in the celebration of the matador's prowess even to notice the brutish suffering of this animal. That was it. The breakthrough.

It all now made sense to me. The scenario before me had framed the idea: who exactly these people were. At first I had been horrified by the Spaniards and how lightly they weighed the life of an animal, too cosmopolitan and blasé to care for the suffering of a simple beast. I had missed the point entirely. They understood death more than I. They recognised their own place within nature as humans. They moved within nature, a powerful force with a profound understanding and respect for her.

When the time came to leave and seek out the mechanic, my whole body shook with a vibrancy and energy. It lasted for days, but the lesson learned returned with me to Ireland, the brutal lesson that I had learned amid the heat and bleached canvas, a lesson that eroded my prejudices and gave me a deeper insight into my humanity and even my own soul.

P: 25 C: 25
L: 23 M: 8
Total: 81 **Grade B1**

COMMENT

This composition has an effective narrative shape. It has a clear beginning, middle and conclusion. Furthermore, the narrative is given a distinct location and time. Both the language and description used are original and clear. The story has a dramatic immediacy. There is a wide variety of sentence structure. The terse sentence structure conveys an energy and pace to the narrative. The loose and informal paragraph structure contributes to the flow of the narrative. There is a strong sense of unity in the viewpoint.

The writer is perhaps trying to do too much in too short a space. He wishes to convey the powerful impact on him of having experienced a bullfight and to draw the conclusion that it has left a mark on him forever. However, this is not achieved in enough detail or depth. The conclusion is somewhat abrupt. The characters in the narrative need to be developed in greater detail.

The first page is too formal. Perhaps the writer is trying too hard to impress. Phrases such as 'because of the severity of the puncture', 'I presumed' and 'having ascertained' are awkward and stiff. The use of the term 'gibbering' to describe a language the writer does not understand is offensive. However, the style of the narrative begins to flow steadily as the story develops.

Exercises on writing in the language of narration

1. Write a suitable conclusion to the following paragraph, which is written in a narrative style: 'The village to which our family had come was a scattering of some twenty or thirty houses down the south-east slope of a valley. The valley was narrow, steep and almost entirely cut off; it was also a funnel for winds, a channel for the floods and a bird-crammed, insect-hopping sun-trap whenever there happened to be any sun. The sides of the valley were rich in pasture and the crests heavily covered in beechwoods.'
2. Write a narrative composition on the experience of being a refugee.

3. Write on one of the following topics, using a narrative style:
    'A new millennium'
    'My first job'
    'Fragile Earth'
    'My experience of visiting the home of a pop star'.
4. Take each of these opening sentences and write a narrative-style composition:
    'They began to move up just at dusk, and by the time night fell and the first flares became visible ...'
    'His hat had rolled a few yards away, and his clothes were smeared with the filth and ooze of the floor on which he had lain ...'

THE LANGUAGE OF ARGUMENT

Argument is a form of rational persuasion. The 'language of argument' attempts to prove a particular point by using logic or evidence.

It is important to understand the difference between argument and persuasion. Argument assumes that a reader is objective, is able to follow a logical train of thought, to weigh up evidence and will not be prevented by emotion from accepting the conclusions to which the logic or the evidence points. Argument differs from persuasion in that it appeals to reason and logic rather than to emotion or feelings.

Writing that uses the language of argument includes legal documents, scientific and medical journals and newspaper reports.

Features of the language of argument

1. In a well-constructed argument, claims must always be supported. A claim is a statement that is arguable. Claims can be supported by:
    *   providing data or evidence
    *   facts
    *   examples
    *   statistics, where information is presented in the form of numbers.
2. Good argument must be supported by evidence that is valid. An argument is valid when the conclusion follows logically from the premise or the preceding statements. To test the validity of an argument, assess the truth of:
    *   the premise
    *   each argument
    *   each sub-argument.
3. Argument is effective when evidence and reasoning are both presented in a persuasive manner so as to convince the reader that certain opinions are preferable to others.
4. In understanding the language of argument it is important to distinguish between a fact and an opinion. A fact is something that really exists or occurs – it can be verified or proven by an objective or detached observer. The process of confirming that a statement is true is known as verification.

A fact differs from an opinion because facts can be *verified,* whereas opinions must be *supported.* An opinion is a judgment or a belief regarding something that is held by a person. It can be based on a logical inference from the facts. The following statements are examples of facts:

> The weather has got warmer over the last few years.
> The Leaving Certificate examination brings with it a great deal of pressure on pupils.

We can add some opinions to these facts; for example:

> The weather has got warmer over the last few years, therefore we need to do something about global warming.
> The Leaving Certificate examination brings with it a great deal of pressure on pupils, so perhaps it should be abolished.

To test factual statements we must examine the evidence. To test statements of opinion we must examine:
- the evidence of fact
- the inferences drawn from it.

An *inference* is an interpretation of a fact – it is the product of a subjective reasoning process. We make inferences about things many times without realising it. For example, we meet someone we know very well but they don't greet us, so we may infer that we have done something wrong or that they are in bad humour. The reality may be quite different – they may simply be distracted or tired.

The following example will illustrate more clearly the difference between a fact (or argument), an opinion and an inference:

Fact
All the planets in the solar system are spheres.

Inference
As the planets in the solar system are spheres, the Earth must be a sphere.

Opinion
All the planets in the solar system are wonderful.

Comment
The first statement is a fact. The second statement is an inference that proceeds from the first one, and in this case it is true. The third statement is merely an opinion – not all people will agree with it.

The processes or stages of argument
There are different processes or stages of reasoning in argument:
- deductive reasoning
- inductive reasoning
- *a priori* reasoning
- *a posteriori* reasoning.

Deductive reasoning

Deductive reasoning begins with a general law and moves to a particular case.

All the planets in the solar system are spheres.
The Earth is a planet in the solar system.
Therefore the Earth is a sphere.

The first two statements are called *premises*. They lead to the conclusion in the third statement. These three statements add up to a logical structure, which is called a *syllogism*. However, not all deductive arguments are true.

All tigers are cats.
Our pet is a cat.
Therefore our pet is a tiger.

Though the first two premises are true, the concluding premise is false and therefore the argument is false. For an argument to be valid, all premises or statements must be true.

Inductive reasoning

Inductive reasoning begins with observing individual phenomena and from them arriving at a general law.

John is a man.
John is mortal.
Therefore all men are mortal.

The structure of inductive reasoning is based on establishing certain evidence about something and then drawing a conclusion. Inductive argument can be false; for example:

Joan is a woman.
Joan is a teacher.
Therefore all women are teachers.

A priori *reasoning*

A priori ('from the former') reasoning goes from known causes to imaginary effects; it is a form of deductive reasoning.

They have been working all day, so they must be tired.
He crashed his car, so therefore he will buy a new one.

A posteriori *reasoning*

A posteriori ('from the latter') reasoning moves from known facts to probable causes.

She suffers from migraine, so she must be stressed.
The meat is not cooked, so the oven must be broken.

Fallacies in argument

A fallacy is faulty reasoning or a false or misleading argument. It is important to recognise unsound ways of reasoning or fallacies in argument, such as the following:

- faulty generalisation
- glittering generalities
- begging the question
- ignoring the question
- *non sequitur*
- false dilemma
- emotional appeals.

Faulty generalisations

These occur through drawing the wrong conclusions from certain information. Such generalisations can be unqualified. In most cases the statement 'killing is wrong' can be considered true; however, killing in self-defence may be justifiable, so this statement could be considered an example of an unqualified generalisation.

Hasty generalisations or jumping to conclusions is another example of a faulty generalisation. For example, an article that claims that most rock stars commit suicide would be an example of a hasty generalisation.

Generalisations about things involve reaching a conclusion on the grounds of certain facts or evidence. For example, if pollution causes certain animal and plant life to die, then scientists could draw up a valid or true generalisation about the negative effects of pollution.

Glittering generalities

This is a method of obscuring an argument by deliberately keeping it vague. Glittering generalities usually involve making sweeping statements or extravagant claims about something. Some examples can be the use of certain phrases or expressions:

The best you can get

Tremendous value

For tens of thousands of pupils, exams are approached with total apprehension

Statements of this type are vague and abstract. Examine what the facts are here – what is the writer saying?

Begging the question

Begging the question means taking the point that is being disputed for granted – using the claim to support itself. In this type of argument a statement or idea is presented in such a way that presumes to be true what still has to be proven.

We must believe that God exists because it says so in the Bible, which is the word of God.

Here proof for the existence of God is based on an assumption of His existence and so amounts to no proof at all.

We have to accept change because without change there is no progress.

This statement presupposes that change and progress are synonymous, something that is not necessarily true.

Ignoring the question

In this type of argument the question or issue being discussed is ignored altogether.

Non sequitur

A *non sequitur* ('it does not follow') is a conclusion that cannot validly be inferred from the premise or assertion.

All rats eat rice.
All rice is good.
Therefore all rats are good.

John is an Irishman.
All Irish people are rich.
Therefore John is rich.

The conclusions here are examples of generalisations that do not follow from the preceding statements.

False dilemma

This offers a choice between only two answers or two courses of action, ignoring alternative possibilities.

The Taoiseach should abandon the budget or else resign.
Either you welcome all immigrants to Ireland or you're a racist.

Emotional appeals

Emotional appeals include name-calling, labelling and using loaded terms.

They're very traditional in their beliefs.
She's fanatical about politics.
He's a red.

Emotional appeals invariably lead to *non sequiturs*.

Sample passages

Study the following article, which makes use of the language of argument.

'It was like something straight out of *The Godfather*,' said the taxi driver, appalled at the circumstances in which Sergeant Andy Callanan died in Tallaght this week. And so it was, horrible almost beyond belief, the kind of thing we thought could happen only in a film.

Now we know differently. And the taxi driver's comment is sickeningly relevant, given the belief, firmly held in some quarters, that our cinema and television screens are awash with mindless violence and that this has dreadful social implications.

And the awful manner in which the garda lost his life again raises questions about our culture, how and why it is being influenced by fictional images of violence and the links between screen violence and violence in real life. This is made all the more real by suggestions that the perpetrator of the appalling incident in Tallaght may have been influenced by a recent episode of the television series *The Bill*, featuring a scene in which a policeman was doused with petrol by someone who had a grudge against the force.

The questions and the debate about them are not new. In the United States – the home of Hollywood – the director Oliver Stone is still embroiled in controversy over his film *Natural Born Killers*. The best-selling novelist John Grisham (author of *The Firm* and *The Pelican Brief*), one of whose friends was shot by a couple claiming they had been inspired to carry out the shooting by *Natural Born Killers*, insists that Stone should bear some of the responsibility.

Are films, television plays and videos capable of influencing people to carry out acts of violence? The debate has been joined on this side of the Atlantic by Audrey Conlon, the deputy film censor, who outlined her thinking in a television interview yesterday. 'People tend to have very strong views on censorship and classification. And very often you find yourself in a corner – perhaps not trying to defend your situation but certainly trying to explain what your job is about.'

So what is the most criticism a film censor gets? Do people think the censors today are too lenient or too tough? 'Both. In one corner you can have someone saying, "You can see anything now in the cinema; you can watch anything on video." And then the next day you'll meet someone who'll ask, "Why do we need censorship? Given that the whole media environment has changed so much, are you relevant?" The fact is that it is an area that a lot of people are interested in, particularly parents, who are concerned about what children are viewing.'

When the Video Recordings Act (1989) was introduced it meant that extra staff had to be appointed to the Film Censor's office to deal with video classification, and Ms Conlon was appointed by the Minister for Justice, Máire Geoghegan Quinn. Ms Conlon says she didn't have particularly strong views about films before becoming a censor. 'But I was always very interested in media. I'm a bit of a media junkie. When I go to a hotel somewhere the first thing I do is click on the television to see what's on CNN, and I've always been a reader of newspapers.'

In an age in which technological developments in broadcasting will very soon give us access to two or three hundred television channels, is there still a role for the censor and a place for censorship? 'Yes. But I would prefer not to use the word censorship. People's ideas and perceptions of censorship were probably formed by what they heard about what happened here in the 1940s and 50s. That's not the way the system operates at the moment. Censorship now works with a fairly light hand. Very few mainstream films are banned; but there very definitely is a need for censorship, and it's a need supported by over forty years of research.'

In other words, even in the 1990s there's a need, in Ms Conlon's opinion, to regulate in some way the material that we as a society view, especially the material that our children view. 'What the censor's office now is essentially doing is classifying material.' Which of course means that a lot of the control and responsibility is being handed back to the home. 'Certainly in the home the responsibility is being handed to the parents; but what we are giving them through the classification system is good guidelines – good consumer advice. And we're saying to them that in our opinion, based on our experience, if we classify this as 12 we are encouraging you not to let your six-year-old see it.'

Apart from the awful business in Dublin, that concern was reinforced by reports this week that two boys were motivated to try to murder a friend as a result of watching the horror film *Scream*. Little wonder that Ms Conlon would say that violence is now the main concern of the censorship office, with particular concern for its potential effects on younger people. 'This concern is not just something that we concocted ourselves. It is supported by about forty years of research, and it's research that has been done all over the world. And the conclusion is – and there will always be dissenting voices – that the mass media do bear some responsibility for contributing to violence. That's it in a nutshell.'

Does this exclude real events, like war coverage? 'No. What we see on our screens – all mediated images of violence – all contribute.'

So are we becoming desensitised to violence? The research would certainly suggest that we are and this conclusion appears to have the support of serious researchers, meaning in the end that we are all in danger of being desensitised. 'It drips into our culture. And it appears to have done so this week with horrific consequences.'

COMMENT

In this article on violence in our culture, the writer begins by using a piece of anecdotal evidence on the taxi driver's reaction to Sergeant Andy Callanan's death in Tallaght.

The writer goes on to use references to current events such as popular television shows and films to illustrate and develop his points. He also cites factual evidence when referring to the Video Recordings Act (1989).

Question A
1. What devices has the writer used to support his arguments? Refer to anecdotal evidence, factual information, classification and possible use of statistics in your answer.
2. Are the points made in this article convincing? Has the writer made use of personal opinion or invalid or unsubstantiated claims? If so, give examples.

Question B
Write an article for a local newspaper commenting on some violent videos that you believe have a harmful effect on young people. In your article make some suggestions about how to remedy this situation.

Writing in the language of argument
When you are writing in the language of argument, the emphasis is on being able to write in a discursive manner – presenting facts and argument on a certain topic and arriving at a conclusion. In this type of writing you are trying to convince your reader that your argument is valid.

How to write in the language of argument:
1. Begin by defining or establishing the meaning of your topic in order to set boundaries or limits to your argument.
2. Take a definite stance or position on your topic. You may decide to agree or disagree with the topic. You are free to take whatever position you want.
3. Identify your target audience. For example, are you writing for your own peer group, professional people or children?
4. Decide on what tone(s) you will use.
5. Use some deductive and inductive arguments when writing up your points.
6. Use one or two short anecdotes (short stories with a point) to support your points.
7. Use linking devices between your paragraphs. You can repeat a sentence that went before, or use words such as 'furthermore' or 'therefore' to develop your points.
8. Write in a balanced way. Do not give a one-sided vision of a situation or idea.
9. Try to support every point you make with evidence or statistics.
10. Remember to put only one topic sentence into each paragraph.

Remember, good argument writing is clear and concise. It is structured on original ideas, organised thought and a balanced and logical presentation of facts. For that reason:

- use language that is formal and precise
- express ideas in a logical manner
- use transition words to link your ideas
- anticipate the reader's opposing views
- defend your own ideas in a forceful and clear way
- avoid the use of clichés, repetition, emotional or offensive language, euphemisms and double-speak.

Sample composition

The following composition is written in the language of argument. It is taken from actual pupils' work and is graded according to the standards required at Higher Level. Study it carefully and pay special attention to the commentary that follows. The task was to write an article for a serious journal in which you challenge or support the statement 'There are actually people who take pride in their race. This is stupid.'

As we celebrate the beginning of a new century, the desire to reflect on our history and actions is at a peak. This is a unique time to learn from our mistakes and take pride in our achievements. In the twentieth century the human race advanced in some areas more than it has in the entire course of its history. However, for all our vast and wonderful achievements, the dark and destructive stain of racism remains as a reminder that in some ways we still remain almost at the same level of civilisation as the animals. This inhumanity and injustice to our fellow humans overshadows our greatest achievements and reminds us too clearly of the savage and primitive state that remains latent within.

The idea that a particular race of people could be superior to others is an absurd belief. In the words of Kofi Annan, Secretary-General of the United Nations, 'We may have different religions, different languages, different-coloured skin, but we all belong to the one human race. We all share the same basic human values.' Undoubtedly there are many things that we can take pride in: the first landing on the moon or the first transatlantic voyage. Yet is it possible that such events can compensate for the brutal reality of two world wars and the mindless violence perpetrated in places such as Africa and Europe, and all carried out in the name of racism? Indeed, the few moments of glory in humankind's achievements are nothing compared with some of the grave atrocities that have been committed on our fellow humans.

Undoubtedly racism today takes on many different aspects, from antagonising a group of Travellers at their halting site to barring someone from entry to a club because of their social status or depriving people of educational or welfare benefits due to them.

We may ask the question, what is it that makes a person believe they are superior to another race? We are all cast from the same mould, though decorated differently. Perhaps this mistaken belief in one's superiority could stem from our past, when competition was fierce and indeed competition was the name of the game. The survival of the fittest may still survive in our subconscious thoughts today. If this is the case, then we differ little from our savage ancestors in lacking the spirit of open-mindedness to see the human race in its entirety.

While racism has been a blot on the pages of history for decades, it was only during the colonial years, when thousands of African slaves were traded like cattle between the white settlers of America, that the topic came to the forefront. To this day a rift divides the two cultures and it has seen the growth of terror groups such as the Ku Klux Klan. Up to the sixties African-Americans had little or no rights and were still slaves to society. However, through the painstaking efforts of such people as Martin Luther King, enormous developments and inroads have been made. All this bitter hatred and animosity could have been avoided, however. It is totally unjustifiable and incomprehensible to believe that a person should consider themselves to be superior because of the colour of their skin. In fact, it defies logic.

Extremist views pose the greatest problem in this particular area. Pride in one's achievements becomes converted into a brutal and radical form of racism, and in turn this is translated into profound hatred for different ways, whether the difference is manifested in religion, culture, background or beliefs. Underlying this intransigent attitude is fear – fear of whatever is different. This fear becomes channelled into hatred and can be seen most strikingly in groups such as Combat 18 and neo-Nazism.

In these cases, violence and intimidation become the only method of communication. Diplomacy is non-existent. The results generated by such regimes are devastating. Humankind must learn that violence and injustice produce only suffering and sterility.

Adolf Hitler is an example of one such extremist. The name itself is enough to send a shiver along the spine of any humane individual. Yet he is worshipped as a god for many others. Hitler managed to find a scapegoat for the problems he confronted, both personal and political, in just about anybody, from Jews to Communists. Under his brutal 'final solution', six million Jews and up to twenty million Russians became victims of Nazi concentration camps and were butchered and slaughtered by the malignant SS. His vision of an all-dominant 'Aryan' race that would triumph over humankind and last for centuries ultimately failed. Hitler has earned the unique title of having carried out more murders than any other being in history, all in the name of pride and a wilful blindness to the supposed superiority of one's race.

Racism today is deeply entrenched in the heart of our society. It is evident in all walks of life, from international politics to the area of the media. The recent move to elect Jörg Haider – a well-known master wordsmith for racism and xenophobia – in Austria sent a chill reminder across the world. It may be an interesting irony that Hitler himself was born in the same place. Many people began to fear that history would repeat itself, having borne witness to Haider's strong adherence to Hitler's views. Some people began to fear the consequences of Hitler's legacy in the wake of such political manoeuvring. In the light of this fact, Austria was politically isolated around the world. Public opinion made the statement that his beliefs are not acceptable at the start of a new century, since we know exactly what they led to in the thirties and forties. It is vitally important that a marker be put down, that when extremism is mainstreamed, something profound is happening in Europe today.

As we look back on our past we begin to realise how racism and the belief in one's superiority over another person have proved to be a disastrous combination. We are all members of the same human race. We are all entitled to the same rights and treatment because of our status as human beings. Basic unwillingness and an inability to accept this point inevitably causes conflict and war. The bloodstained history books are a colourful enough reminder of the utter pointlessness of racist beliefs. It is only when we undertake to unite and combat the various limitations within our own nature and within life in general that we can truly begin to become masters first of all of ourselves, and then perhaps we will attain some form of control over this world of ours.

P: 26 C: 26
L: 25 M: 8
Total: 85 **Grade A2**

COMMENT

This composition on the topic of racism is written in the form of an argument. It is clearly structured into a series of paragraphs, all of which deal with the subject in a factual and logical manner. The material used in the article has been well researched, and the examples and supporting evidence are both relevant and topical. The points that are made are clearly supported with evidence. Remember, good argument requires evidence and support to sustain it. The conclusion is effective and there is a distinct unity of thought throughout the composition.

POINTS FOR DEVELOPMENT

The topic of racism has been broadened to include many other types of discrimination. The tendency to blur the meaning of 'racism' by using it as an all-purpose term for prejudice is reflected in its use here to describe discrimination against Travelling people and even discrimination on grounds of social class, while the references to the slave trade and the causes of two world wars reflect an unawareness of colonialism as distinct from racism. The scope chosen by the writer is very wide and it may not be possible to treat all of it in sufficient depth.

Perhaps the language and style could have more energy, contrast and colour. Some of the sentences are a little too weighty and the argument lacks clarity at times. Always remember that good writing is clear writing.

Writing exercises

1. Write a speech for a group of business people on how you consider they could help eradicate some of the injustices in 'Third World' countries.
2. Write the speech you would give at a seminar entitled 'The power of the media'. Clearly describe your views on how the media has been either a positive or a negative influence on society.
3. Write an article for a magazine using the language of argument on the topic 'The greatest of evils and the worst of crimes is ignorance'.
4. Write a letter to a local newspaper using the language of argument on both the positive and the negative changes you have seen in Ireland over the last few years.

THE LANGUAGE OF INFORMATION

The objectives of this type of language can be to:
* convey information in a succinct or terse manner
* give instructions or make requests
* persuade or influence the reader to adopt an attitude or act on a certain issue or matter.

The language of information is to be found in reports, journalism (newspaper, television and radio), instructions, memos and letters, summaries, bulletins, forms and questionnaires. Each of these forms has different objectives. Reports give a factual account of a situation or set of circumstances. Media accounts usually give a report of events in a clear and factual manner. Instructions offer a clear, concise explanation of how to do something. Memos are short messages written in an informal style. Summaries give a condensed account of information. Forms and questionnaires request information in a plain, compact manner.

Features of the language of information

1. There is clear organisation of information. All arguments and information must be presented in a logical and coherent manner.
2. The content is relevant. Do not digress from the main point in what you are writing; avoid introducing useless or irrelevant information.
3. Use an appropriate style and expression. In general, the style required for functional writing is clear and factual. Avoid the use of colourful language and images, such as:

   Performance has plummeted unexpectedly and with increasing force because of a catastrophic lack of in-service training of staff in this area.

   Use simple, factual language instead, for example:

   The lack of in-service training for staff has caused performance to fall greatly.
4. Use short sentences. Convey the information as briefly as possible.
5. Use the precise number of words. Avoid verbose or long-winded statements.
6. Use concrete words rather than abstract ones.
7. Use each word in a way that clearly illustrates its meaning. For example, look at the following sentences.

   Check L's report.

   Does this mean check the report that L has completed or check the report on L? What does 'check' mean anyway?

   Record sales figures for last year.

   Does it mean write down the sales figures for last year or that the sales figures for last year exceeded those of other years?
8. Avoid the use of slang, jargon, buzzwords and commercialese. *Slang* is very informal language. *Jargon* is the inappropriate use of the terminology of a specialised profession. *Buzzwords* are fashionable terms often used in advertising or

informal conversation. *Commercialese* consists of dated or stereotyped formulas of a kind once popular in business correspondence:

Enclosed herewith [I enclose]
Your letter is to hand [I have received your letter]
With reference to same [With regard to …]
I trust this will meet your expectations [I hope this is agreeable]

In addition, good informative writing has the following features.

• It must be simple, clear and concise.
• The information presented must be comprehensive – it must deal with all aspects of the subject.
• It must be appropriate for the intended audience.
• The tone of the language must be objective.

In this section we will examine the different features of reports, instructions, letters and memos, etc. and study how to write them for examination purposes.

Sample composition

The following composition is written in the language of information. It is taken from actual pupils' work and is graded according to the standards required at Higher Level. Study it carefully and pay particular attention to the commentary that follows it. The task was: 'Write an informative newspaper article about your home town or parish, concentrating especially on the qualities that make it unique or memorable.'

Lying south of Limerick rests the parish of Donaghmore. With a present population of approximately 2,600 and an area of 8,500 acres, this parish has evolved over the centuries as one of the most distinctive and distinguished areas of County Limerick.

Since its beginnings as a parish in the thirteenth century, the area has undergone considerable change and its inhabitants have witnessed and participated in some of the important events in local history. From the arrival of St Patrick to this land in the fifth century to the War of Independence in 1921, this parish has contributed greatly to the rich heritage of the south of Ireland.

What makes the chronology of this parish so monumental and atypical has been the consistent involvement in both cultural and sporting activities. Rich architectural features are a striking hallmark of this parish. These bear witness to some of the more impressive changes that have been a constant feature of this region. As you saunter along the road or drive through the narrow laneways, you will see the ancient ruins of castles and churches nestling snugly alongside more modern structures.

This particular parish has played a large part in our history. The Great Famine of 1845 brought about considerable change for the Irish people at that time. Community spirit was at a low ebb, with the brutal reality of emigration rampant everywhere. It is ironic that precisely at a time of profound neediness and suffering the parish managed to construct one of the richest churches in the region, magnificently decorated with some outstanding stained-glass windows and fronting a large and elegant roof – an undoubted architectural achievement!

A singular feature of Famine times was the famous Mass paths, and of course my parish boasts several – those secret paths where many local people stole silently along in early morning time, in spite of the danger involved, and attended their Mass gathered around a rock in a large bare field. Such are the strong remnants of a deep Christian community, which still remain in evidence today.

One of the clearest documented facts is that some people from my parish participated in the Boer War of 1899.

Clearly, some of the most memorable achievements of the people from this region will be in the area of sports. One of the greatest moments in history is recorded on the first Sunday of September 1973, when Éamon Grimes of Rootiagh captained Limerick to win the All-Ireland senior hurling title, a feat that has yet to be repeated by any Limerick man. Undoubtedly this was one of the proudest and most extraordinary events in the lives of many parishioners. Some other strong links in the sporting scene include Dromore Celtic and Glenview FC, which figure predominantly in the Limerick soccer scene. Indeed, my parish is home to one of County Limerick's oldest and most well-established GAA clubs, South Liberties, which has attained numerous trophies over the years.

One of the striking features of some of the buildings bears witness to the existence of that strong feature of Irish educational life, the hedge school. In a corner of a large field lie the ruins of one of the most famous hedge schools in the country, a place that testifies to the eager attempts of the Irish to overcome oppression and struggle to retain some vestige of their identity by keeping the Irish language alive.

No parish would be complete without a focal point for its young people and my parish stands foremost in providing a large hall, which is well endowed with stage and dance floor. Our local group may not be the outstanding rock metallers but they do supply our lively youth with some good entertainment every weekend.

One of the most striking achievements of my community has been the establishment of a strong community centre, situated in the heart of the parish. It is here that the various social and educational activities take place, and it is here that many young people find an outlet for their various talents, from tap-dancing to disco dancing, and from community work to teaching arts and crafts.

Spearheaded by some students and a keen drama teacher, Youthbrief, a popular drama group, has set the parish on the map. Not only has this drama group been at the centre of a national festival, but they have managed to entertain the local community on many long winter nights with various performances of *Riders to the Sea* and *The Playboy of the Western World*. This universally popular entertainment has become one of the most organic and dynamic initiatives undertaken in recent years.

In addition, there are voluntary projects that are organised and run by some young people of my parish. These embrace different activities, from visiting the old people, helping with odd jobs and shopping to teaching literacy skills to the local Travelling community.

The community centre provides a rich forum for organising and sustaining these varied activities. Every Saturday the organisers of this community, who work voluntarily, run a disco for young and old alike to finance the different projects. Classes are held every Tuesday and Wednesday morning for all mothers. Here they have an opportunity to develop and improve various skills, from cookery to guitar, to acquiring another language or brushing up an already rusty one. To facilitate their lives, an extension has been added on to the centre where crèche facilities make it easy to relax and enjoy the morning in peace and perhaps engage in gossip and chat about the local news.

There are a host of various activities and areas of interest in this exciting community. This is an area that is characterised by a striking sense of good will, an area that is unique in the support and consolidation offered by its members to the old and disadvantaged. Truly my community is both unique and noteworthy.

P: 26 C: 26
L: 25 M: 8
Total: 85 **Grade A2**

COMMENT

In this piece the writer has structured the information clearly into separate paragraphs, all of which deal with a distinct aspect of the subject. Each of these paragraphs gives a graphic and detailed insight into some particular feature of this parish that makes it noteworthy.

Remember, good informative writing has to be both clear and concise. This composition has hints of a personal touch, which prevent the subject from becoming boring. The whole article is comprehensive – it gives a thorough insight into the more striking features of this community and covers the central aspects of its life. The writer uses a variety of sentence structure and vocabulary to communicate the points effectively. The subject is handled confidently; this is evident in the style, which is smooth flowing and lucid.

Exercises on writing in the language of information
1. You are the secretary of a city youth club. Write a report that you will submit to the Department of Education and Science with an application for a grant. Include details of all the activities of your club and the numbers who attend.
2. You are the manager of a small restaurant. Write a list of instructions for your employees on the procedures to be followed in the event of a fire.
3. You wish to object to an advertisement that you consider to be unsuitable for viewing on television. Write a letter to the Advertising Standards Body clearly setting out your objections.
4. As a journalist for a local newspaper, write a factual report on an All-Ireland rugby match.

THE LANGUAGE OF PERSUASION

The language of persuasion is used by writers to try to influence the way in which a person may think or act. Its primary purpose is to influence how a reader thinks. This is the type of writing that forms the framework of political speeches, advertising writing and marketing.

Persuasion can be achieved in different ways:
- by manipulation
- by appealing to emotions
- by argument.

The language of argument and that of persuasion are quite similar; however, the techniques used in both are distinctive. Because the aim of the persuasive writer is to manipulate feeling and emotion, there is a heavy reliance on emotive vocabulary and on using feeling and emotion to elicit agreement or acquiescence. Persuasive writing can be found in letters, political speeches and addresses, film reviews, some newspaper reports and advertising.

Features of persuasive writing
Because persuasive writing has as its aim convincing you about something, most of the techniques used are directed at the emotions or the senses rather than the intellect. The language of persuasion relies on emotive argument to communicate its message more forcefully to the reader.

All types of persuasive writing use the same tactics. It is worth examining the following features of persuasive writing, in particular in the area of advertising, to persuade or convince:
- slogans
- repetition
- statistics
- imperatives and commands
- rhyming
- rhetorical questions
- buzzwords
- tones.

Slogans
A slogan can be described as a point made without any support, often in the form of a short, punchy phrase. Advertisements usually contain slogans.

> If you ache when you wake …
> When it pours, we reign.
> You can with a Nissan.
> Every Rolex takes twelve months to make; no wonder time is so valuable.
> When you're healthy on the inside, it shows on the outside.

The purpose of a slogan is to fix an image in your mind, so the writer will use graphic images and perhaps a play on words wherever possible.

Repetition
Repetition is a hallmark of persuasive writing, particularly of advertising.

> Introducing PURE COLOUR nail lacquer with a treat at the House of Fraser.
> Pure impact. Pure luxury. Pure colour. Pure treat.

The following extract from an article on drugs is a clear example of how repetition can be used effectively in persuasive writing:

> We know that good education and good training policies work. We know that strict regulation is much more effective in keeping drugs such as alcohol and tobacco away from children than the anarchic market in illegal drugs has ever been. We know, above all, that what we're doing now is, by any objective standards, a failure so disastrous that no change could ever make things worse.

The repetition of the phrase 'we know' gives a strong and emphatic punch to the ideas here.

Statistics

Statistics are also used by persuasive writers. The use of statistics may lend an air of authority to an otherwise dubious claim.

> A nationwide study by a team of doctors has demonstrated that in 97 per cent of headaches, X works to give relief.
> Up to 80 per cent sleep better on the Tempur mattress.
> Syndol gives relief in half an hour.
> Now 82 per cent of people in the country have opted for the Maxi central heating system.

Imperatives and commands

These are also a feature of persuasive writing. Imperatives demand immediate action:

> Buy now ...
> Use this coupon to send for our free brochure ...
> Send in this form and you will receive ...
> Order today ...
> Pay in the next ten days and you will receive ...
> All you have to do is ...

Rhyming

Persuasive writing often uses words that rhyme, which can give a sense of movement to the piece of writing.

> A flawless look ... imperceptible, undetectable.
> Firm up your flab in five weeks.

Rhetorical questions

A rhetorical question is one to which an answer is not really expected – the question usually implies the answer and is used merely as a persuasive device.

> Have you problems getting your wash white?
> Would you believe there are bikes that cost more than this car?
> What really kills weeds?

What gas heating is more simple than ...?

Why not enjoy life with a Sunrise Scoota?

What other cereal will provide a better balance of the things your body needs?

Buzzwords

Buzzwords are fashionable, often pseudo-technical terms that are usually meaningless – 'empowerment', 'cyberspace', 'out there', 'in terms of', 'the bottom line'. They are widely used in persuasive writing to impress the reader.

Tones

Tone is the relationship a writer establishes with the reader. It is an important ingredient of effective persuasive writing. A writer wishing to persuade can adopt any number of tones, including:

* humorous
* ironic or satirical
* didactic or instructive
* oratorical.

HUMOROUS TONE

A writer can use humour to illustrate a point, as in the following paragraph about computers.

> Bugs are the usual excuse for computer breakdown, but a London company had a particular problem with rats that liked to eat the insulation around the cables. Rodent exterminators were brought in and laid tubs of poison underneath the floorboards. The rats just dragged the dishes out of the way to get at the insulation. The ratters then spread special spy-dust, which, instead of laying a trail to the rats' nest, got swept into the air-conditioning system and made the staff sneeze.

The humour here mocks the attempts of humans to deal with computer breakdown.

IRONIC TONE

Both irony and satire can be used for purposes of ridicule or mockery. Irony can also be used to hammer home a point effectively. In the following paragraph, the writer makes clever use of irony to condemn the growth of 'warlords' in eastern European countries.

> Much of the former Yugoslavia is now ruled by warlords. Their vehicle of choice is a four-wheel-drive Cherokee Chief with a policeman's blue light to flash when speeding through a check-point. They pack a pistol but they don't wave it about. They leave vulgar intimidation to the bodyguards in the back, the ones with shades, designer jeans and Zastava machine-pistols. They themselves dress in the leather jackets, floral ties and pressed corduroy trousers favoured by German television producers. They bear no resemblance whatsoever to Rambo. The ones I met at the check-points on the roads of Croatia and Serbia were short, stubby men who in a former life were small-time hoods,

small-town cops or both. Spend a day with them touring their world and you'd hardly know that most of them are serial killers.

SATIRICAL TONE

In satirical writing the folly of human nature is exposed to ridicule. Dickens possesses the remarkable gift of drawing an exquisitely satirical portrait in some of his characters. The following passage is an example of humorous satire that describes Pip eating his Christmas dinner as a child.

> Among this good company I should have felt myself, even if I hadn't robbed the pantry, in a false position. Not because I was squeezed in at an acute angle of the table-cloth, with the table in my chest and the Pumblechookian elbow in my eye, nor because I was not allowed to speak (I didn't want to speak), nor because I was regaled with the scaly tips of the drumsticks of the fowls and with those obscure corners of pork of which the pig, when living, had had the least reason to be vain. No; I should not have minded that if they would only have left me alone. But they wouldn't leave me alone. They seemed to think the opportunity lost if they failed to point the conversation at me, every now and then, and stick the point into me. I might have been an unfortunate little bull in a Spanish arena, I got so smartly touched up by these moral goads.
>
> (Charles Dickens, *Great Expectations*)

The following description is an example of how character portrayal can be used effectively to gain maximum satirical effect.

> The worst of it was that that bullying old Pumblechook, preyed upon by a devouring curiosity to be informed of all I had seen and heard, came gaping over in his chaise-cart at tea time, to have the details divulged to him. And the mere sight of the torment, with his fishy eyes and mouth open, his sandy hair inquisitively on end, and his waistcoat heaving with windy arithmetic, made me vicious in my reticence.

The description of Pumblechook's physical appearance is based on a series of small graphic details – 'gaping over in his chaise-cart at tea time', 'fishy eyes', 'mouth open', 'sandy hair inquisitively on end'. The combination of these striking and effective details with a distinct tone of satire makes this piece a splendid example of ironic satire.

DIDACTIC TONE

Didactic writing sets out to instruct or teach the reader about something. The writer uses the imperative 'must' or 'have to' and a dogmatic tone in this type of writing.

> I have learned that many people who take astrology seriously were first attracted to the field by reading horoscopes in the newspapers. It is deplorable that so many newspapers now print this daily nonsense. At the start the regular reading is a sort of fun game, but it often ends up as a mighty serious business. The steady and ready availability of astrological 'predictions' can, over many years, have insidious influences on a person's

> judgment. Faith in astrology and other occult practice is harmful in so far as it encourages an unwholesome flight from the persistent problems of real life. Other solutions must be found by people who suffer from the frustrations of poverty, from grief at the death of a loved one or from fear of economic or personal insecurity.

The purpose of this passage is to persuade the reader against falling victim to astrology. The tone is an explicit condemnation of reliance on astrological predictions. The writer uses a dogmatic tone to point out the fact that faith in such practices results in an unwholesome escape from the problems that are a part of daily life.

ORATORICAL WRITING

Oratorical writing is also used by the persuasive writer, though it is more suited to the spoken than to the written word. Some features of this type of writing are:
- a magnificent flow of thought
- the use of rhetorical questions
- a fine command of expressions and language.

Examine the following speech of St John Rivers to Jane Eyre, all in an oratorical tone.

> I am the servant of an infallible master. I am not going out under human guidance, subject to the defective laws and erring control of my feeble fellow-worms: my king, my lawgiver, my captain, is the All-perfect. It seems strange to me that all round me do not burn to enlist under the same banner – to join in the same enterprise.
>
> Humility, Jane, is the groundwork of Christian virtues: you say right that you are not fit for the work. Who is fit for it? Or who that ever was truly called, believed himself worthy of the summons? I for instance am but dust and ashes. With St Paul I acknowledge myself the chiefest of sinners: but I do not suffer this sense of my personal vileness to daunt me. I know my Leader: that he is just as well as mighty; and while he has chosen a feeble instrument to perform a great task, he will, from the boundless stores of his providence, supply the inadequacy of the means to the end. Think like me, Jane – trust like me. It is the Rock of Ages I ask you to lean on: do not doubt but it will bear the weight of your human weakness.
>
> (Charlotte Brontë, *Jane Eyre*)

In this extract, St John Rivers is urging Jane to leave everything and become his wife out on the missions. The tone is emotive. Examine the use of repetition and rhetorical questions: these are effective rhetorical devices in moving an audience over to your side and are hallmarks of oratorical writing.

The following is an example of a political speech written in an oratorical tone.

> Ladies and gentlemen, I would like to talk to you for a moment about the present situation. Never before has this country faced such a crisis and what is now needed is a great deal of courage and honesty. Should we fail to deal with the economic crisis at once, the situation could be disastrous. It is at moments such as this that the true character of a nation shines through. I believe that the right action taken now will resolve the

problems that have faced us so menacingly. What we must all realise is that the way ahead is hard and sacrifices must be made, but on no account and in no circumstances must our resolve be shaken. It is obvious that those who do not firmly believe as I do that this is so are mistaken. Were we to act as they suggest we would face a situation from which we might never recover and this must not be allowed to happen. I sincerely hope that you will join with me in saying 'Yes' to what I am proposing, because saying 'No' would mean not only that I was defeated but that I was wrong.

This is an example of a speech that relies for its effect on arousing the emotions of the audience. Note the reliance on emotive vocabulary in the sentence beginning 'Should we fail to deal …'. In oratorical writing there is a certain degree of exaggeration, which is also a hallmark of persuasive writing. Phrases such as 'never before has this country faced such a crisis' and 'were we to act as they suggest' rely for their effect on exaggeration and drama.

Writing in the language of persuasion
A good persuasive writer must be able to:
*   express their views clearly and logically
*   foresee all possible angles of opposition and be able to tackle them effectively.

Before you begin any type of persuasive composition, be aware of the following points:
*   know your audience
*   know your subject
*   establish the correct tone with your audience
*   state your purpose clearly and confidently
*   use persuasive techniques.

Know your audience
Have a good knowledge of who your reader or audience is. A rousing talk on drug dependence is hardly likely to stimulate a group of pensioners. Similarly, an excellent article describing the advantages of pension schemes will not attract the attention of a group of teenagers. Identify as clearly as possible who your readers are, what level of knowledge they have about the subject and their motivations and interest in reading the composition. Know what type of persuasion will affect your reader.

The following headlines are taken from different magazines and are written in a persuasive style. Identify the intended audience in each case.

When pop stars have to talk love, they only talk to their fave mag, *TV Hits*
They're the cutest twosome in pop – but what makes Marvin and Tamara tick?
Why we adore Dior

These headlines are obviously taken from magazines that are aimed at young people. Naturally this type of approach could not be adopted in an educational publication or a medical journal.

Know your subject

It makes no sense to start writing about something you know nothing about, particularly when you are trying to persuade somebody to adopt your viewpoint. Consider the following two paragraphs on how fashion in clothes is the deliberate creation of waste.

> Fashion today is nothing more than creating a lot of waste. People buy clothes they do not need and so waste them. This is particularly the case with women, because they are in a sense more slaves of fashion than men. Thus clothes designers produce new designs each year and they in turn contribute to this development of waste.

There is very little in this argument that will make you adopt any serious viewpoint. On the other hand, look at the following passage on the same theme.

> Over the years, the great majority of men have successfully resisted all attempts to make them change their style of dress. The same cannot be said for women. Each year a few so-called top designers in Paris or London lay down the law and women the whole world over rush to obey. The decrees of the designers are unpredictable and dictatorial. This year they decide, in their arbitrary fashion, that skirts will be short and waists will be high; zips are in and buttons are out. Next year the law is reversed, and far from taking exception, no one is even mildly surprised.
>
> If women are mercilessly exploited year after year, they have only themselves to blame. Because they shudder at the thought of being seen in clothes that are out of fashion, they are annually blackmailed by the designers and the big stores. Clothes that have been worn only a few times have to be discarded because of the dictates of fashion. When you come to think of it, only a woman is capable of standing in front of a wardrobe packed full of clothes and announcing sadly that she has nothing to wear. Changing fashions are nothing more than the deliberate creation of waste. Many women squander vast sums of money each year to replace clothes that have hardly been worn. Women who cannot afford to discard clothing in this way waste hours of their time altering the dresses they have. Hemlines are taken up or let down; waislines are taken in or let out; necklines are lowered or raised and so on.

The writer here gives examples to support the argument and the examples chosen are graphic and relevant. Remember to research your subject before beginning the process of writing.

Establish the correct tone with your audience

Once you have identified your audience, adapt your message and tone accordingly. You cannot use a lofty or philosophical tone with a group of schoolchildren; neither can you use a colloquial tone in a speech to the board of management of your school. Similarly, do not use formal language if you are writing on pop music for a teenage magazine.

It can sometimes help to introduce a note of humour or irony into your writing in order to gain the attention of your reader more readily.

State your purpose clearly and confidently
Outline clearly in your opening paragraph what your intention is.

Use persuasive techniques
Some examples can be the use of effective images or anecdotes to support your viewpoint. These can also serve the function of arousing certain emotions about your topic in readers and getting them on your side.

The following paragraphs are an excellent example of how humour and the anecdote work together to communicate a point effectively.

> As everyone knows, 'getting away from it all' involves a lot more than just physical distance. For me, though, it has to be shoes: one hint of even the shortest weekend break and I feel I should get into shoes so comfortable I could conceivably sleep in them. I have a particular antipathy to flat shoes because the stupid things make me feel short, fat and flat footed.
>
> This antipathy to flatties took on a more sinister note on a recent trip to Galway, when, as usual, I took the first, quavering step to really relaxing by donning my old school trainers. They're made of canvas with three bright blue stripes and they're flatter than a glass of Seven-Up left in the sun. They go down very well in trendy night clubs and at casual brunches in friends' back gardens when everyone usually has a good chat about how they don't make trainers like that any more. This is all very well, but after two days of short wanders to the beach and back to the pub I was practically bed-ridden, with legs bent like nutcrackers. It didn't take an Einstein or even a Dr Scholl to work out that this complete seizure in the leg department was the result of wearing flat shoes for the first time in – oh, dear – seven years. The tendons in my calves were used to being made tight by two inches of heel and were complaining loudly about being stretched to their natural length.

The writer of this passage uses a familiar and homely vocabulary that is accessible to the ordinary reader. The humorous tone makes it a lively piece of writing. The writer also varies the structure of the sentences.

Remember
Bear in mind the following guidelines when writing a persuasive composition or article.
1. Avoid making sweeping statements or vague and broad generalisations, such as:

    All pupils suffer from extreme examination pressure.
    All governments are corrupt.
    All teenagers take drugs.
    All women are victims.

2. Don't make unsupported statements. Support each point you make with sufficient evidence or effective illustrations.
3. Avoid using an aggressive or bitter tone, as it will only alienate your reader.
4. Don't distort the truth. While a certain amount of hyperbole or exaggeration is permissible in persuasive writing, it is never acceptable to distort or pervert the truth or to tell a lie in your writing.

Sample composition

The following passages are written in the language of persuasion. They are taken from actual pupils' work and are graded according to the standards required at Higher Level. Study them carefully and pay particular attention to the commentary that follows.

The task here was: 'Write a persuasive article for a teenage magazine on the subject of dieting and weight.'

Lighten up – you'll never get stuck in the aisle

You're walking down the aisle of a crowded bus and straight ahead you see the last vacant seat. Approaching it in slow motion, you realise that there are steel bars on each side of the seat. Everyone is watching as you sit down. Squeezing against the bars of the seat are your bulges of fat and they're multiplying by the second. Wide-eyed passengers point and stare as you struggle to get out of your seat and walk back down the aisle in sheer terror. Oh, the relief when the alarm wakes you up to the Divine Comedy's 'National Express'.

A few weeks ago our transition-year class in St Jude's was busily discussing ideas for our magazine, *Voice from the Well*. We all got distracted and started to talk about weight. Within minutes we were heatedly deploring the emaciated appearance of Monica in *Friends*.

Women through the ages have wasted their time worrying about their weight and their appearance and I think it's about time we confronted our fears. We might feel tempted to blame anorexic actors, gaunt girl-groups or the supercilious models of today for making size six a figure. We could say that women's magazines are the cause of such mass misery, bombarding us as they do with revolutionary diets that just don't work. But the simple truth is that women were concerned about their weight and appearance long before such things even existed.

According to a tour guide in Bath, a lift built to honour Queen Victoria in one of the finest hotels in the city made no difference to her lifestyle. She overheard a peasant saying something like 'Oh, my goodness, would you look at the Queen's flat ankles', and she fled the city in a huff, never to return. I can't help but feel a little sympathy for the petulant queen because, in the words of Julian Browne, obesity is a condition that proves that the Lord does not help those who help themselves.

Imagine having to ask your sister to help you crush your lower chest cavity with a corset every morning and you would wonder how any woman could ever have inflicted those elephant-tusks of discomfort on herself. Yet women once chanced breaking the odd rib to gain some control of their figure.

Today dieting seems to have replaced the corset. After all, it takes a lot of self-discipline to stick to a diet consisting of a rice cake for breakfast, a cup of tea for lunch and no dinner at all. Lots of women would be quite happy to be a little less pear shaped, but successful control freaks, like Courtney Cox and Calista Flockhart, go much further and, not surprisingly, have been accused of being anorexic.

Scientists have proved that a woman with Barbie Doll proportions could not survive, yet many women strive for what they see as perfection.

'All the other reindeer used to laugh and call him names ...' If you ever really thought about that jolly Christmas song, you'd realise that it isn't so jolly after all. You might even say that Rudolph epitomises our cultural over-emphasis on physical appearance. Poor old Rudolph was stigmatised for having a red nose and was accepted only when it dawned on the other reindeer that he might come in handy because of it. Being fat is also highly stigmatised and women tend to use their weighing scales to evaluate their physical attractiveness. The average female was dismayed when *Titanic* star Kate Winslet was described as 'too fat to be attractive'.

On groggy-eyed days, when you sit sluggishly at the back of the classroom and feel your hair, you suddenly realise that the strange shampoo you used that morning must have been conditioner. Then you feel as if you had poured petrol over yourself before coming to school. And just as you were forgetting about your facial volcanoes you're asked to analyse the Prince of Morocco's line in *The Merchant of Venice* – 'Mislike me not for my complexion.' By the time you get home and collapse in front of the telly nauseated with self-pity you're simply in no form for irritating Special K advertisements.

If you compare yourself with others you may become vain and bitter, for, as the 'Desiderata' says, 'there will always be greater and lesser persons than yourself.' You might never be a Naomi Campbell or a Kate Moss, but the chances are too that you'll never realise your recurring nightmare and make headlines for getting stuck in the aisle of a bus. I suggest that we all lighten up and become more like Rudolph. Do something useful, like buying a nice cream bun. Perhaps some shops and bakeries might even think of putting up a little sign saying 'Thank you for not dieting.'

P: 26 C: 26
L: 25 M: 9
Total: 86 **Grade A2**

COMMENT

This is a witty and light-hearted piece of writing on the topic of weight and dieting. The opening anecdote is entertaining and catches the reader's attention immediately. The language and style are both vibrant and humorous. There are some light-hearted yet clever hints of satire and sarcasm. The examples that are used are familiar and topical. There is clear identification of the audience – the article is written for a teenage magazine and the examples and illustrations used are interesting and relevant. There is an energy and vibrancy in the ideas presented; it is clear that the writer is enthusiastic about the topic. The writer here seems to be very much in control of her subject at every stage. The writing is immediate and accessible, as the writer constantly addresses the reader.

Perhaps some of the references could be developed in more detail and depth to gain that higher mark. Also, the narrative moves on a bit too abruptly at times.

For the next composition the task was to write a persuasive article for a teenage magazine on the topic 'Beauty is only skin deep.'

Angelina Jolie, Posh Beckham, Gwyneth Paltrow...the list goes on and on and on. Yes, readers, the infamous celebrities. Those people we fall asleep dreaming we'll become some day. The people we gossip about at the hairdresser's, the people who decorate the backs of our buses and star in our favourite movies. Those people who cause us near-despair by creating an unreal stereotype of apparent perfection.

Perfection? I hear you professors of psychology scoff. Because they know that the idea of perfection is a load of proverbial codswollop. And yet the knowledge that Angelina has the perfect face, Jennifer Anniston the perfect hairstyle or Elle McPherson the perfect body is continuously being shoved down our throats by the media. We are being taught to associate Hollywood with perfection.

Well here is one person who has had enough. This stereotype is one that should be destroyed.

As a little girl I used to prance around my house wearing a pink feather boa. I believed I was going to be famous. Not a soap star or a pop star (God forbid), the next Audrey Hepburn. The style, the glamour were all waiting out there for me. I was going to see my name in lights and hear my voice on advertisements worldwide 'because I'm worth it'.

Then one day the earth-shattering truth hit home. Fame, that deranged vision, is merely a competition measuring aesthetic standard. Talent? Poise? Elegance? No good if you haven't the bone structure, darling. This is all due to the stereotype presented by the media creating an almost unachievable standard for wannabes.

Can you think of those memorable mornings when you stumbled out of bed humped over, bedraggled with bloodshot eyes, matted hair and looking like a monster or a crab? You can bet your bottom dollar that the same fate has fallen on our famous celebrities at some stage.

Because of media manipulation celebrities have become the gods and goddesses of our society. Magazines such as *OK*, *Hello!* and *Now* have become our bibles, while Hollywood seems to be an altar from where we worship their glory and splendour. Unfortunately the stereotypical celebrity becomes the standard against which we measure ourselves.

And the implications of this stereotyping on us poor mortals? The list is endless – bulimia, anorexia, drug abuse, and addiction to plastic surgery…

In society today where values seem to have become rather warped, our average person needs to prepare themselves with some standard survival techniques. So the next time you are reading *Hello!* and you become riddled with the green-eyed monster, simply stop and ignore him. Look up and remember you are free, babe, free, and with that freedom you can conquer the world! So get going!

P: 28 C: 27
L: 25 M: 8
Total: 88 **Grade A2**

COMMENT

This is a good piece of persuasive writing. It is suitable for a teenage magazine and uses current example to support the points made. There are some spelling and grammatical errors.

Exercises on writing in the language of persuasion

1. Write a short, persuasive article for a local newspaper on the value of having sport as a compulsory part of the curriculum. Aim your article at a general readership.

2. Compose a persuasive article for a popular magazine on the topic 'Is it now time for men's liberation?'
3. Compose a persuasive composition for a teenage magazine that seeks to establish the need for a greater degree of selectivity in the viewing of television programmes.
4. Write out an advertisement for your favourite make-up, aiming it at members of your own class. In the advertisement include price, special offers and the imperative use of language.
5. Write a persuasive letter to a local newspaper about ways in which the environment could be kept cleaner.

THE AESTHETIC USE OF LANGUAGE

The emphasis here is on the use of language as an artistic or creative medium, in order to create a beautiful picture of something.

Writing in which language can be used aesthetically includes fiction, drama, films and poetry.

Features of the aesthetic use of language

1. The use of imagery, i.e. the capacity of words to create pictures. Imagery can also be defined as word pictures; it is the way a writer uses words to conjure up a picture or image of something. Imagery is the basis of all writing, but in particular in the writing of poetry, drama, certain types of fiction and, in a different way, in films.
2. A stress on how language can be used in an artistic way.
3. The different ways in which words can be used to create concepts of beauty and harmony.

Read the following descriptive passage, then study the commentary that follows.

Smoke was rising here and there among the creepers that festooned the dead or dying trees. As they watched, a flash of fire appeared at the root of one wisp, and then the smoke thickened. Small flames stirred at the bole of a tree and crawled away through leaves and brushwood, dividing and increasing. One patch touched a tree trunk and scrambled up like a bright squirrel. The smoke increased, sifted, rolled outwards. The squirrel leapt on the wings of the wind and clung to another standing tree eating downwards. Beneath the dark canopy of leaves and smoke the fire laid hold on the forest and began to gnaw. Acres of black and yellow smoke rolled steadily towards the sea. At the sight of the flames and the irresistible course of the fire, the boys broke into shrill, excited cheering. The flames, as though they were a kind of wild life, crept as a jaguar creeps on its belly towards a line of birch-like saplings that fledged an outcrop of the pine rock. They flapped at the first of the trees, and the branches grew a brief foliage of fire. The heart of flame leapt nimbly across the gap between the trees and then went swinging and flaring along the whole row of them. Beneath the capering boys a quarter of a mile square of forest was savage with smoke and flame. The separate noises of the fire merged into a drum-roll that seemed to shake the mountain.

(William Golding, *Lord of the Flies*)

COMMENT

This passage is highly dramatic and vivid. The effect here is achieved through a series of energetic verbs and vocabulary: 'a flash of fire appeared', 'the smoke increased, sifted, rolled outwards'. The writer is intent on conveying movement and energy. Through the expert combination of certain techniques, such as the use of intense imagery, splendid descriptions and energetic language, he paints a highly effective image of the whole scene.

Now look at the following extract, which has many examples of the figurative use of language.

> As the sun set, its light slowly melted the landscape, till everything was made of fire and glass. Released from the glare of noon, the haycocks seemed to float on the aftergrass: their freshness penetrated the air. In the far distance, hills with woods up their flanks lay in light like hills in another world – it would be a pleasure of heaven to stand up there, where no foot ever seemed to have trodden, on the spaces between the woods soft as powder dusted over with gold. Against those hills, the burning red rambler roses in cottage gardens along the roadside looked earthy – they were too near the eye.
>
> The road was in Ireland. The light, the air from the distance, the air of evening rushed transversely through the open sides of the car. The rims of the hood flapped, the hood's metal frame rattled as the tourer, in great bounds of speed, held the road's darkening magnetic centre streak. The big shabby family car was empty but for its small driver – its emptiness seemed to levitate it – on its back seat a coat slithered about, and a dressing case bumped against the seat. The driver did not relax her excited touch on the wheel: now and then while she drove she turned one wrist over, to bring the watch worn on it into view, and she gave the mileage marked on the yellow signposts a flying, jealous, half-inadvertent look. She was driving parallel with the sunset: the sun slowly went down on her right hand.
>
> (Elizabeth Bowen, 'Summer Night')

COMMENT

This is a splendid example of how language can be used in a highly creative and aesthetic fashion. In the extract, the writer gives us some beautiful images of nature. Note, for example, her reference to colour: 'everything was made of fire and glass', 'the woods soft as powder dusted over with gold', the 'burning red rambler roses'. All the images used are rich and sensuous and serve the function of painting a powerfully clear picture of an Irish landscape in summer.

The following extract, from the verse play *Murder in the Cathedral*, is a good example of how language can be used aesthetically.

> *Chorus:*
> Numb the hand and dry the eyelid,
> Still the horror, but more horror
> Than when tearing in the belly.
> Still the horror, but more horror

Than when twisting in the fingers,
Than when splitting in the skull.
More than footfall in the passage,
More than shadow in the doorway,
More than fury in the hall.
The agents of hell disappear, the human, they shrink and
dissolve
Into dust on the wind, forgotten, unmemorable; only is here
The white flat face of Death, God's silent servant,
And behind the face of Death the Judgment,
And behind the Judgment the Void,
more horrid than active shapes of Hell;
Emptiness, absence, separation from God;
The horror of the effortless journey, to the empty land
Which is no land, only emptiness, absence, the Void,
Where those who were men can no longer turn the mind
To distraction, delusion, escape into dream, pretence;
Where the soul is no longer deceived, for there are no objects, no tones,
No colours, no forms to distract, to divert the soul
From seeing itself, foully united for ever, nothing with nothing,
Not what we call death but what beyond death is not death
We fear, we fear. Who shall then plead for me,
Who intercede for me, in my most need?

(T. S. Eliot, *Murder in the Cathedral*)

COMMENT

This passage is written in a highly poetic style, which is also a feature of the language of aesthetics. The vocabulary is rich and poetic; images are lyrical and emphatic. The writer uses splendid and fluid rhythms, together with effective repetition, to conjure up some frightening images of Hell and loss.

Writing in the language of aesthetics

The ability to write in order to demonstrate the aesthetic quality of language involves a capacity to use images. Language that is aesthetic is rich in beautiful imagery and description. Learn the art of writing description well. Good descriptive writing concentrates on giving a clear, vibrant picture and on involving all the senses.

Method of writing descriptive composition

1. Select details of what you are describing with great care and concentrate on registering a few small points.
2. Be selective in what you write about when describing. Do not include every feature, but concentrate on one or two.
3. Refer to location in some way. This can be the geographical context, the country or

region, the landscape or the time, season or historical period.
4. Remember, effective imagery is created through the association of words. This can be achieved by:
    *   similes, metaphors or rhythm
    *   direct description.
5. Use images and language that appeal to the different senses. Visual images can include features of colour or shape and size. The use of images that appeal to the ear create a deep and lasting impression on your reader.

> The scullery was water, where the old pump stood. And it had everything else that was related to water: thick steam of Mondays edgy with starch; soapsuds boiling, bellying and popping, creaking and whispering, rainbowed with light and winking with a million windows. Bubble bubble toil and grumble, rinsing and slapping of sheets and shirts, and panting Mother rowing her red arms like oars in the steaming waves. Then the linen came up out of the pot like pastry or woven suds or sheets of moulded snow.

The effect of this description is to conjure up a vivid picture of the scullery and how the washing was done. The writer draws on all the senses – the sense of smell by the starch and the soapsuds and the sense of touch in the references to slapping the sheets and 'rowing her red arms like oars in the steaming waves.'

Describing people
The ability to draw effective description of character requires:
*   drawing an image of their inner character, motivations, moods or situation
*   painting a picture of the background, age, professional situation or emotional state.

Sometimes a writer will use the actions of a character or their particular environment to depict internal dispositions.

> Towards the end of her day in London Mrs Drover went round to her shut-up house to look for several things she wanted to take away. Some belonged to herself, some belonged to her family, who were by now used to their country life. It was late August; it had been a steamy showery day: at the moment the trees down the pavement glittered in an escape of humid yellow afternoon sun. Against the next batch of clouds, already piling up ink-dark, broken chimneys and parapets stood out. In her once familiar street, as in any unused channel, an unfamiliar queerness had silted up; a cat wove itself in and out of railings, but no human eye watched Mrs Drover's return. Shifting some parcels under her arm, she slowly forced round her latchkey in an unwilling lock, then gave the door, which was warped, a push with her knee. Dead air came out to meet her as she went in.
>
> (Elizabeth Bowen, 'The Demon Lover')

The following passages show how language can be used in an aesthetic way. They are taken from actual pupils' work and are graded according to the standards required at Higher Level. Study them carefully and pay particular attention to the commentary that follows.

The first assignment was: 'Compose an imaginative series of reflections on the topic "autumn".'

September and October can be the very worst months of the year. Look at the weather: rain, wind, mist and damp; wind blowing in relentlessly from the Atlantic, heralding the first onslaughts of winter. Fog and mist roll in and sometimes for days on end the countryside is enveloped in a thick blanket of grey. It clings to river banks, shrouds mountain tops, nestles in valleys and between the folds of hills. It deadens sound, obscures sight and creates an eerie, ghostly atmosphere.

There is dampness everywhere. On walls! On windows! On floors! Housewives become irritated and drivers frustrated as the damp of their windscreens lessens visibility. There is mud and mire on city paths and country lanes and as you walk you hear the squelch as the water and mud ooze up around your shoes. Old people tread warily as all around 'moist green leaves rest in rotting rust.' Everywhere shoes make a lovely crunching, crackling, rustling, popping sound as you walk on the carpet of leaves underfoot.

Then again you may awake some October morning and the world appears transformed. You swish back your curtains and lo! you look out into a dazzling world, your eye marvels at the dizzy blue sky overhead and here and there scattered in the high dome of the heavens, clouds like puffballs and torn tufts of cotton-wool glide lazily in the vast expanse of blue. You open your front door and your eye is assaulted and bombarded with glowing, jewel-bright colours. What colour! Hedgerows, wood ditches, forests and fields are clothed in a glorious array of colour: vivid orange, fiery reds, bright yellows, garish mustards, dull browns and sombre black.

Trees, shrubs, flowers are now beginning to wear a tattered, forlorn look. They are no longer clothed in the glossy, green, luxuriant foliage of high summer. Trees are taking a gaunt, skeletal look as they raise brittle, bare branches to the sky. Ominous-looking brown and black spots are appearing like some malignant disease on the ripe blooms of roses and flowers. Leaves look as if they are sickening for some fatal disease: they shrivel up, become crisper and crisper and then in the first gales of autumn flutter gently to the ground, yielding up their fragile, tenuous hold on life and lie decaying on the ground.

Meanwhile, frenzied and feverish preparations go on in both the animal and the human world. Take a walk in your local woods – but tread carefully. Move stealthily through the undergrowth and you may see a sudden flash and a brown bushy tail belonging to a busy squirrel who is hurriedly scuttling out of your way as he clutches a pawful of nuts. You may hear a rustling sound and lo! you may see a mole or badger digging out their winter home in preparation for hibernation. Look overhead and your eye will marvel at the sight of birds congregating on wires, twittering excitedly in anticipation of their annual winter holiday when they migrate to sunny southern climates.

In cosy country kitchens filled with a smell of turf, plump, bustling housewives are sweating as they bend over hot stoves making delicious jams, pickles, mouth-watering pies and potent wines and ales and reminding us only too well of those vivid words of Shakespeare, 'and greasy Joan doth keel the pot.' Out in the straw-strewn farmyard the red-faced farmer is busy bringing in the last of the crops. In both town and country, young folk with long, doleful faces are making last-minute and begrudging preparations for returning to school.

P: 25   C: 25
L: 24   M: 9
Total: 83 **Grade B1**

COMMENT

This article is written in an imaginative and highly descriptive style. There is a strong emphasis on describing colour, movement and shape, which is a hallmark of good, effective description. Some of the images used are rich and sensuous.

AREAS FOR DEVELOPMENT

The opening of this composition is a bit too obvious. Openings have to be dynamic and arresting for the reader. There is an atmosphere of 'purple prose' throughout, a conscious striving for effect, giving the whole piece an unnatural air.

Perhaps the writer could concentrate on developing the description in more detail. Concentrating on the lives of people would perhaps broaden the scope and develop the theme in greater detail. The conclusion needs to be developed in more detail and depth, as it is a bit too abrupt and flat and a little disappointing.

The next passage is from an aesthetic composition on the topic 'Memories'.

'Children of the sun'

The black nannies congregated on the corner of Gillian Road, shouting out greetings of 'Sanibonai' and 'Ngikhona' in their loud, cheerful voices. The coarse sound of their voices was softened by the beautiful musical lilt of their language. Their vibrant exclamations hovered on the still hot air and their infectious laughter lingered over the neighbourhood.

Faint echoes of the carefree chatter floated out over the vast, dry, empty land in front and were carried downwards over the gently sloping field of burnt dry tufts of grass, which crackled underfoot, and sand of almost the same yellowish-brown shade, until they reached the river. The gurgle of the deep brown water mimicked the buoyant giggles and the hadida bird's call from above echoed across the vlei. Children's playful shouting and a dog's excited barking reverberated among the cloud-like rocks bordering the river. Two bluish-white trees, though quite bare, provided the only source of shade from the blazing sun. But the refreshing sound of flowing water made the sun's crude heat more bearable.

The only refuge from a scorching midday sun was beneath the cool, clear blue waters of a swimming pool. Happy and carefree children screamed in delight while splashing around in the water, duck-diving and dodging the bees and wasps that hovered on the surface. Around the edge of the pool, steam rose from the slabs of slate, roasting any feet that ventured out of the pool.

Towards early afternoon little brown bodies lay glistening in the sun, stretched out on towels, shivering with warmth and with the ticklish feeling as each tiny droplet evaporated.

But peace and serenity did not last long. Sharp ears perked up as the familiar tinkling

tune of the ice cream man drifted through the air. And the legs that had been stretched out in the sun sprang to life in anticipation. Money in shrivelled hands and children in swimming costumes with stringy wet hair ran barefoot down the driveway in glee. And it didn't matter that the ice creams melted before they reached their mouths or that the raspberry sauce dropped down onto bronzed feet and made their toes stick together. The children walked slowly back up the driveway, heads bent forward in an attempt to catch as much of the liquid as possible. They sat on the patio's stone steps licking the ice creams, with dots of white on their noses and red sauce smeared around their mouths, happy and content.

Even when empty, the patio held all the voices and memories of the neighbourhood. It was a place where many stories had been told, jokes shared and tears shed. Overlooking the swimming pool and surrounded by luscious green tropical plants, its cold stone floor and cool shade were both refreshing and relaxing. Out in front, the garden sloped down towards the road, bordered on one side by a tall white wall and on the other by the long driveway running adjacent to a boundary of trees, plants and hedges.

Once darkness fell, the lush flowerbeds, trees and shrubs provided an ideal place for 'tip the lantern' and, starting from the bottom of the garden, the children tried to sneak their way up to the top beside the patio without being seen. Scrapes and bruises on bare legs and arms were ignored as little bodies wormed their way through soil and plants like camouflaged snakes.

The rustle of shrubs was covered up by the shrill of the crickets, whose sound was so constant that it was forgotten but would be missed if absent.

Gay chatter drifted across from the adults around the candle-lit patio table, where they still sat hours after the braai was over. Floating candles on the pool created a magical glow and the warm night was softly scented with the mingled fragrances of sweet pea and honeysuckle.

Life revolved around nature and the outdoors. Trees, plants, bushes and shrubbery provided innumerable playgrounds. A forest of tall bamboo supplied rich, cool shade and a soft leafy floor for exhausted children and an ideal storage place for caterpillars in shoe boxes, waiting for them to spin cocoons.

Long scrape marks on the syringa barks all over the neighbourhood marked the struggles of scratched legs' attempts to overcome the initial challenge of the bare tree trunk, before climbing through green leaves and rough branches. The tall sky-rockets were much easier to climb, for the thick coniferous foliage started at ground level. But a challenge was always welcomed and syringas, with their beautiful, sweet-smelling pink flowers, had better-shaped branches for tree-houses.

Grubby children solemnly collected wood, planks and ropes from old compost heaps and fields full of shoulder-height yellow grass. They emerged laden with precious materials and covered in blackjacks. Planks of wood were wedged between branches and tied meticulously, and gradually the tree-houses were erected. These were the sites of many tree parties and secret nocturnal meetings when even the crickets were asleep.

The silent whispers in this magical land of the large trees at night was a stark contrast to the shouting of children at play on the road during the day. BMX bikes skidded in the earth, sending up clouds of dust behind them. The bikes, which were once brightly coloured and shiny, were now almost indistinguishable from one another, for each was coated in the same layer of dry brown dust.

A stranger could not tell which children belonged where, for wooded stiles, built by the gardeners, provided easy access for barefoot children from garden to garden. Sandy children with messy hair, skimpy clothing and dirty bottoms scrambled in all directions.

But every Monday afternoon they all headed in the same direction, muttering Bible verses under their breath that should have been learned over the past week. Children from even further afield than Gillian Road came to Good News Club, and the competition for a perfect memory verse record and the ultimate prize was tough.

But behind all the competitiveness, the love shown and taught among friends and neighbours shone back through the glowing eyes of their happy children.

P: 28 C: 27
L: 28 M: 8
Total: 91 **Grade A1**

COMMENT

This is a highly original piece of writing and approach to the topic. The images and language are vivid and poetic, all of which are strong features of the aesthetic use of language. The whole composition is clearly punctuated with its striking emphasis on colour, sounds and smells. There are some splendid touches of poetry, for example, the sibilance in the lines 'around the edge of the pool, steam rose from the slabs of slate, roasting any feet.' The imagery used is varied, rich and sensuous: 'little brown bodies lay glistening in the sun, shivering with warmth.'

This passage is written to emphasise how language can be used in an aesthetic manner. For that reason the subject matter does not have to be developed or analysed in a deep or weighty manner; instead there is a heavy reliance on the aesthetic use of language, harmony, the use of images, sound patterns and poetic touches.

Exercises on writing in the language of aesthetics

1. Write a descriptive article for a holiday magazine on a city scene preparing for a new millennium.
2. Compose a sketch or dramatic scene for a play on any topic you are interested in. Concentrate on drawing out specific features of the characters you are presenting.
3. Write a poem or a short story, paying particular attention to the use of imagery or description, on any scene from country life or nature that has impressed you.
4. Write a series of diary entries on your experiences in settling in another country.

Answering Question B, Paper I

6

Question B on Paper I usually involves a writing exercise. You must be able to know how to write the following:

- reports
- instructions
- memos
- letters
- notices and bulletins
- interviews
- reviews
- diary entries
- a speech
- a radio talk
- text for a property page
- write on a photograph or a picture.

WRITING A REPORT

A report gives a factual account of something. The main function of a report is to analyse a situation and present it in a clear, objective manner. Not all reports need a detailed layout. Newspaper reports, for example, do not generally have headings but follow the ordinary structure of a report, which is: title and introduction, the investigation carried out in the report and some suggestions.

Use correct headings

- **Title:** Give a name to the report.
- **Introduction:** A short paragraph on what the report is about.
- **Work carried out:** This involves what was done to gather the information for the report.

- **Findings:** These are the findings from the research carried out during the report.
- **Suggestions:** This means any suggestions for areas of improvement.
- **Recommendation:** This is the writer's own personal ideas on how the situation being studied in the report can be improved.

Features of a report
- Use objective language, for example, 'More bins must be put into the school to prevent the litter problem.'
- Use the correct layout, either bullet format or simply numbers.
- Reports must be clear.

Sample report
This is an example of a report using some of the headings described above.

Report on television viewing by pupils aged between 15 and 18

Introduction

At the request of the Minister for Education and Science, a report on television viewing by young people has been authorised. The number of hours and the types of programmes watched will be studied. A list of recommendations will be drawn up.

Procedures

A detailed questionnaire on the amount of time spent watching television and on the types of programmes watched was issued to all secondary schools in the country. This questionnaire was aimed at the 15–18 age group.

Findings

Pupils generally watched between ten and twenty hours of television a week. Among the more popular types of programmes were serials, such as *Friends*, *Neighbours* and *Home and Away*. Boys generally watched more sports programmes than girls. Boys also spent more time on the internet than watching television.

Conclusions

Very few pupils engaged in selective viewing of television programmes. More than 80 per cent of viewing has little educational content. Many of the programmes watched were sentimental serials with little or no substance. The literary ability of pupils in this group has declined, perhaps in part because of the decreased amount of time spent reading and writing.

Recommendations

1. More programmes with an educational or informed content should be broadcast in the evenings.
2. Parents should take a more decisive part in monitoring television viewing.
3. Local libraries should provide more video and internet facilities to stimulate young people to carry out research, read and study.

COMMENT

A good title helps to provide a clear focus on what the report is about. The introduction sums up all aspects of the report – the reasons why the report is being undertaken, time limits, details of those carrying out the report and who authorised it.

Remember that the style of report writing must be factual and objective. Avoid the use of emotive and ambiguous language. Also remember to sign and date a report.

How to write a report

Before you begin, ask yourself the following questions:
- What is the purpose and the theme of this report?
- What objectives am I hoping to achieve?

Preliminary work

Because reports have very different objectives, it is necessary to put in a great deal of work in preparing the material before beginning the process of writing it. This preliminary work will determine the quality of the result and will enable you to structure and organise your material more effectively.

1. Establish the purpose or objective of the report. Is it to describe or evaluate a situation or set of circumstances? Is the report explaining a procedure or situation?
2. Once you have established the purpose of the report, decide on a title; this will help you to concentrate more clearly on what exactly the report is about. You may be asked to write a report on how secondary school girls use their free time at weekends. You could use a title such as 'The use of free time at weekends by schoolgirls aged 14–17'. Establishing a title will help you to limit the topic and to concentrate more clearly on what exactly you must write.
3. Find out who will read the report. This will affect the style of your report. Writing a report for the school committee will demand a different style from one for the managing director of a company.
4. Establish whether the report has a time limit, and if so, what this is.
5. Look at the resources at your disposal. What budget have you been allocated? What equipment have you got? What materials will you need?
6. Study how to structure your report. Will your report be structured in sections with sub-headings? Will the report be a summary?

Checklist for reports

1. Does the title clearly indicate the nature of the report?
2. Are the objectives of the report clearly stated?
3. Are all the terms used in the report clearly defined?
4. Is the report written in the correct tense? (Generally, reports are written in the past tense.)
5. Is the language of the report clear? Are there obscure phrases, evidence of bias, emotive terms or intemperate language in the report?
6. Are all the claims made substantiated clearly by facts?
7. Are the conclusions based on evidence?

8.   Are the recommendations feasible?
9.   Is the report signed and dated?

Media accounts

Media accounts of some event or happening generally give a factual and objective description of what they are reporting. However, such accounts are often influenced by a number of things – the type of publication, the readership aimed at or the writer's own viewpoint on the event.

INSTRUCTIONS

Instructions can be written on technical or human subjects. Technical subjects involve giving detailed guidelines on certain procedures, such as changing a fuse, fixing the plug of a hairdryer or changing the bag on a vacuum cleaner. These types of instructions will use specialised vocabulary and perhaps a series of numbered stages or steps.

On the other hand, instructions can be written on human subjects, such as 'How to increase your self-confidence', 'How to benefit from the points scheme' or 'How to cope with exam stress'. In these type of instructions, the use of generalised vocabulary and illustrations will help a great deal. The style will be more relaxed and informal.

In writing instructions, as in all writing situations, take into account:
• your subject matter
• your audience
• the best techniques that can be used to communicate that subject matter to the audience.

Examine the following set of instructions on 'taking your children out of the rat race', then study the commentary that follows it.

> **Taking your children out of the rat race**
> Quality bus corridors, rising house prices, corrupt politicians, lack of child care facilities, the cost of the latest football strip – has your blood pressure shot up yet? If not, you're in a minority. It seems that stress levels for most of us have increased at a similar pace to economic growth. Have you noticed how aggressive other drivers have become? Or how casual and dismissive shop assistants are? Perhaps it is all symptomatic of the negative aspects of prosperity. The outcome of our new-found status is a population that appears less caring and more interested in promoting self-interest. In the middle of all this material mayhem, it is important for parents not to lose sight of core values. How many of the following do you do regularly?
> • Talk to your children. Do you know what your children did at school today? If not, why not?
> • Play with your children. There can surely be no more rewarding experience for a parent than getting lost in the child's world. Your child likes nothing more than spending time with his or her parents – no toy or bag of sweets is more cherished.

- Tell your child about your own experiences. Younger children love to hear about what life was like when Mammy and Daddy were the same age. This is also a useful strategy if you suspect that your child is experiencing some difficulties. For example, if you suspect that your child is being bullied, talking about when you were young can be a useful way of getting your child to open up.
- Listen. It's not an easy skill. Go for a walk and let the child do the talking. Sit and simply shoot the breeze. Try to say nothing. Let your child lead the conversation.
- Be yourself. There is no such thing as a perfect parent or a perfect child. Being trendy or over-generous will not enhance the relationship with your child; being yourself will. That means getting into the habit of leaving work outside the front door and tuning into the home environment as you find it.
- Inform your child about what is happening in the world.
- Watch your child. Children like nothing better than having their parents watching their activities. Whether this involves cringing as your child rides a bicycle with no supports for the first time or freezing on the sideline of a football pitch for an hour, your child will appreciate it.
- Be present. Stress makes us spend all our time reflecting on the past and planning for the future. It means we miss the most important time of all. Try to come into the present and enjoy the magic and beauty of your children as they are today.
- Say 'no' sometimes. There is a temptation to make up for lost time with material goods. This can lead to frustrations on both sides when it becomes impossible to supply all your child's desires.

COMMENT

This passage is written in an information format. Note the informal, almost chatty style of introduction. The layout is clear and unambiguous; all points are signalled and no excessive information is used.

Writing instructions

1. Work out exactly what you want to achieve. What is the purpose of the instructions? Are you trying to teach children how to cook, to outline the stages of a game or to instruct people how to operate a machine?
2. Instructions must be clear. Make your statements specific.
3. Make sure there is a logical sequence in the stages of your instructions. Each stage should follow logically from the preceding one.
4. Say one thing in each sentence and make sure your different stages are manageable.
5. Put the most important item in each sentence at the beginning.
6. Use the imperative form of the verb.
7. Use short sentences and short paragraphs.
8. Avoid jargon.

Sample instructions
Study the layout of the following set of instructions.

Tableware care

Detergents

Many different automatic dishwashing detergents are available. Choosing the correct one is vitally important because some detergents with a high alkaline concentration can cause permanent damage to your tableware. Whenever possible, choose a detergent that can provide a good hygienic result without damaging your tableware and never use more than the recommended quantity.

Temperatures

A washing temperature of 60°C (140°F) is accepted as the most suitable for the effective removal of food particles while minimising the risk of damaging the glaze or decoration. Excessively high temperatures will reduce washing efficiency and may damage your tableware.

Scraping

Use a plastic or rubber scraper to remove food residues. Do not use metal utensils, which can cause marking. Ideally, also spray with water before washing.

Racking

Make sure that racks and baskets are plastic or plastic coated. Replace damaged baskets immediately, as exposed metal will cause marking. Avoid the use of metal scourers. Rack your tableware correctly to ensure that items do not vibrate against each other during the wash cycle. Avoid placing cups of differing heights in the same basket.

Cutlery

Always wash cutlery separately in specially designed cutlery baskets to prevent marking of the tableware.

Microwave ovens

Tableware with metallised decorations, for example gold, is not suitable for use in microwave ovens.

Thermal shock

Ceramic tableware is not designed to withstand thermal shock, so avoid moving your tableware from a freezer to a hot oven or hob, or from a hot oven to a cold surface. Do not place tableware on or near a naked flame.

Staining

If glaze staining is a problem, use a recognised destainer or soak the tableware in a weak solution of bleach or washing soda crystals. Avoid using abrasives to remove staining.

MEMOS

A memo can be defined as a brief and informal letter. The main differences between a letter and a memo are:
* a memo is informal
* the message is immediate
* memos are written in offices or other workplaces.

In general, both letters and memos involve:
* getting the reader's attention
* making a claim
* supporting the claim by justification or explanation
* calling for action; this may include what you want the reader to do, what you will do or both.

Memos generally explain or outline all details in a short, compact form. Avoid long sentences and pompous words. Use information that is relevant; avoid digressing. Maintain a polite and courteous tone.

The following layout can also be used when writing a memo.

To: Religion Department
From: Punchier Press
Subject: Senior Level, Textbook

Dear Teacher,
Our new publication for Senior Level Religion will be in the shops in August. Phone Punchier Press to reserve a complimentary copy for your department.

Religion for Life, Volume I:
* A combined textbook/workbook with lots of examples.
* Illustrated guides covering all aspects of the syllabus.

Special features:
* Sample answers to exam-style questions provided.
* Perfect guide to time management in exam.

LETTERS

There are different kinds of letters. *Formal letters* include business letters, letters of complaint, job applications, sales letters and letters to the newspaper. *Personal letters* include letters of condolence and letters to a friend or pen-pal.

When writing any kind of letter:
- know what you want to say
- set out your information logically and in paragraph form
- use the correct layout and the correct tone.

Examinations on the writing of letters and memos are testing:
- the coherent organisation of information
- the use of appropriate expression
- accepted standards of layout.

Features of a letter
1. Use the correct layout and make it pleasing to the eye.
2. The sender's address is usually written in the top right-hand corner. (A letter on behalf of an organisation or a company will be on printed letterhead that includes the name and address.)
3. Write out the date fully, e.g. 23 January 2008. All letters must be dated, as they constitute a written record of a transaction.
4. Reference numbers are usually written either above or below the recipient's address.
5. Begin the letter by addressing the person by name or alternatively 'Dear sir/madam'.
6. The first sentence contains the main point of your letter.
7. Conclude your letter with either 'Yours sincerely' or 'Yours truly'. Remember, 'Yours' begins with a capital letter; 'sincerely' has an *e*; 'truly' has no *e*.
8. Use the correct tone for the context. Use a formal, tactful and courteous style, especially if you are conveying unwelcome information.
9. Choose appropriate language. Avoid clichés, wordy statements and jargon. The language should be clear and simple.

How to write a letter
1. Decide what you want to say.
2. Set out your information logically and organise it into paragraphs. In a letter, paragraphs are signposts for the reader that enable him or her to follow your message more clearly.
3. Choose a suitable tone when writing letters. Remember to be factual and not emotional in letters.
4. Use correct spelling and punctuation.
5. Choose the correct vocabulary for the person who is being addressed.
6. Avoid verbose language and clichés. Choose fresh, concise language that is free from jargon.
7. Write the main point of your letter in the first sentence.

Sample letters
Read the following letters, then study the commentary carefully.

Letter of application for a summer job

14 Moygrave Park
Cork

13 May 2008

Mr John Naughton, Personnel Manager
Bel Computers Ltd
Cloneen Industrial Estate
Cork

Dear Mr Naughton,

I wish to apply for the position of computer operator advertised in the *Cork Examiner* on Thursday last. I am a fifth-year pupil at Crescent Comprehensive College, Cork, where I have just completed a special course in computers. I also spent some time during my transition year working in a computer firm as part of my work experience.

I feel that I would be capable and proficient in carrying out this job. I would be available to start work from 1 June until September.

I enclose a copy of my CV and I will supply you with two recent references should you require them. You can contact me by telephone at (021) 6372334.

Yours sincerely,

Neil Dolan

COMMENT
This letter clearly sets out the important details concerning this applicant. The writer makes use of short sentences and short paragraphs, which contributes to making the points striking and clear.

Letter to a newspaper

> 4 Carew Park
> Blakestown
> Killarney
>
> 6 January 2008

Letters to the Editor
Irish Times
11 D'Olier Street
Dublin 2

Dear sir,

In recent weeks your paper has carried negative articles about Travelling people. As a Traveller and a member of the Irish Association of Travelling Women, I would like to invite the writers of these articles to live for a week in a Travellers' site so that they can experience for themselves what it means to live without running water, toilets or refuse collection.

Your articles imply that Travellers cause dirt and litter, which they leave to the local authority to clean up. I would challenge the writers to keep a site clean with no bin collections, no running water and no toilets, not to mention settled people dumping their own rubbish in skips on Travellers' sites. Many of these sites are indeed a disgrace, but whose fault is it?

Mr Davis states that Travellers refuse to work, even when there is a labour shortage. I would like them to tell me who will give Travellers a job, when they are followed by security people even as they go innocently into shops.

Finally, Traveller parents have been criticised for making their children beg, subjecting them to 'emotional and physical slavery'. Yes, there is a minority of Traveller children who beg – usually because of severe hardship at home – but anyone passing along any city street knows that the majority of people begging nowadays are settled people and are mostly adults.

It does not befit your paper to allow space for articles and letters such as those of Mr Graham and Ms Moore, which contribute to anti-Traveller prejudice and make the work of Travellers' organisations much harder.

Yours sincerely,

Margaret Rushe

COMMENT

This letter is a complaint against unjust claims and statements made about Travelling people. The style is clear and to the point. The sentence structure is short and the vocabulary used is precise.

Remember, when writing a letter of complaint you must:
* concentrate clearly on the results you want, rather than on the incompetence of the

people involved
- describe your problem clearly without giving way to anger; control of emotion is essential to get the desired result
- keep a record of all contacts and transactions made
- make sure you are complaining to the right person
- keep letters of complaint short.

NOTICES AND BULLETINS

Notices place the emphasis on layout and attracting the reader's attention through short, catchy phrases and words. Their main aim is to attract the attention of different people. For that reason, their position on a noticeboard must be:
- well positioned for all to see
- big and attractively laid out
- up to date.

INTERVIEW

You may be asked to write an interview with someone who is famous or a popular TV personality.

Start by giving your reader a clear picture of who you are representing (a radio or TV show) and who exactly you are interviewing.

Sample extract of an interview
You are a disc jockey in a popular radio show. Write out an interview you had with a famous model or actor.

Hi! Roddy Stewart here from Radio Dublin. This is your early morning show and here with me today is the beautiful Kate Moss on a short trip to Dublin.

Roddy: Hi Kate, welcome to Dublin and especially to our show this morning. It's great you managed to make it to our studios. We know you're here for a big fashion show in the RDS. How are things going?

Kate: Great, Rod. And thanks for inviting me on your show. We launched the show last night, so things were pretty busy.

Roddy: I notice you're bringing your baby with you now everywhere. It's so cute. You and Pete must be delighted.

Kate: Yes, things are definitely looking up. Myself and Pete are moving on in spite of all the media talk and hype, which certainly can get you down.

COMMENT
This is just a short extract of an interview. The important thing to note is to give each speaker a new line for their conversation. Write the name each time and follow this with a colon, as is done above.

It can help to know something about the person and to use this as material in your interview.

REVIEW

You may be asked to write a review of a restaurant, CD, film, book or popular soap.

Reviews at Leaving Cert level do not need strict, formal headings. However, it can help to follow the usual format of a review without the headings.

Sample review of a restaurant

I recently took it upon myself to visit the new gastro pub off Fletcher Street. Sarnium can be found next to the AIB. Upon entering, one is exposed to black leather chaise lounges, diamond-encrusted tabletops and dim lighting. These hints of post-Celtic Tiger materialism can seem daunting and intimidating. However, I managed to convince my somewhat uneasy partner to scan the menu.

I gingerly opened the leather-bound menu while cradling a glass of house wine in my hand. I opted for the feta cheese salad drizzled with an opulent brandy sauce and served on a bed of crisply tossed lettuce. Don opted for the safe fillet steak with pepper sauce.

Our meal arrived forty minutes later. Both dishes were superbly presented and Don's steak looked scrumptious. Both meals were very pleasant, even if the salad had a slightly settled air to it.

Dessert consisted of a wide choice of death by chocolate, baked pears in red wine and Bailey's homemade ice cream. I chose the Bailey's while Don decided on the pears. Both were very good.

The damage came to €64, not bad, really, considering we had a bottle of fairly decent house wine. Service was quite slow and the background music was a bit too loud. All in all, Sarnium did live up to its reputation of being a good restaurant with quite good food.

COMMENT
*   Start a review by naming the book, restaurant or CD you are reviewing.
*   Give a short description of the place, plot or content of what you are reviewing.
*   Write a short paragraph evaluating or weighing up the merits/demerits of what you are reviewing.
*   Conclude by recommending (or not) the suitability of the price or age of what you are reviewing.
*   Write up your review in series of short paragraphs.

DIARY ENTRIES
*   You may be asked to write a series of diary entries or simply one diary entry.
*   Diary entries are short and personal.
*   Generally, the sentence and paragraph structure of diary entries are quite short.
*   List a date and a time when you start the diary.
*   It is not necessary to write 'Dear Diary' each time.

The following is an example of three diary entries written by a famous celebrity on a very special day.

> Thursday, 4 June, 5 p.m.
> Am really tired after that photo shoot, and certainly will be exhausted when today is over. I was delighted with the premiere of the film this evening. I could not believe that we won the top prize in the Cannes festival for our film.
>
> Friday, 5 June, 3 p.m.
> Am looking forward to the banquet, which is taking place in Powerscourt Castle. It is going to be crowded, with lots of exciting people. I am really looking forward to meeting Pierce Brosnan, who is here on holidays for a few days.
>
> Monday, 8 June, 2 p.m.
> Everything is going great. I have just had a phone call offering me another job in a big film starting in November. I am so excited. It means working with Richard Gere and Sandra Bullock. I think I may take it even though I had been intending to take a break that month. Life is so exciting.

COMMENT

The main point to note about diary entries is that they should give the reader an insight into the type of person who is writing them.

SPEECH

You might be asked to write a speech to your class or a more formal speech about a topic.

Begin by addressing your audience and introducing yourself to them, e.g. 'Fellow classmates, I would like to speak to you today about a fund-raising event which we hope to orgnanise at senior level in the school.'

Write your speech in paragraphs. Conclude by going back to your audience and thanking them, e.g. 'Thank you all for listening and I hope that together we can manage to achieve something really worthwhile in the area of raising money for our beloved school.'

SCRIPT FOR A RADIO TALK

You might be asked to write a short talk as part of a radio programme. Make sure to mention the name of the radio show and who exactly you are, your name and function.

Sample opening paragraph of a script for radio

> Good morning, listeners, Heidi Smith here in 67 FM studios. In today's programme we'll consider a key emotion in our society today, and that is anger. Is anger a destructive emotion? Though it pains me to admit it, yes it is. Why else are we hearing countless

reports of rape, murder and violence on our streets? There seems to be an uncontrollable amount of rage out there, between angry drivers on the roads, irate teenagers on Saturday night binges or housewives getting beaten up.

This morning we have here in our studio Professor Good from the University of Toronto, who is an expert on anger and the disorders it causes. Good morning, Professor Good, we're delighted to have you here with us today.

COMMENT

As you can see, this is only an extract from a radio talk. The opening begins by establishing the context and the name of the presenter. The rest of the talk can be structured into short, clear paragraphs. Use language that is accessible to a general audience when writing a script for radio.

TEXT FOR THE PROPERTY PAGES OF A NEWSPAPER

Sometimes you will be asked to write an advertisement for selling a house or a piece of property. In this case, use persuasive language.

Sample extract of a text on selling property

'Something extra nice in Nice'

Stretching across the Cote D'Azur of the Mediterranean, Nice is one of the most illustrious and captivating cities in France. Miles and miles of golden coastline span the city, where sandy beaches and aquamarine waters play host to millions of sun worshippers annually.

Located about 500 metres from Nice's most popular beach, La Langue Plage, this new apartment development, Apartments Du Soleil, offers top-range facilities in an idyllic location. The development consists of 214 three-bedroom apartments, all en suite and all facing the sunny south. Each apartment has a stunning view of the sparkling Mediterranean and each comes complete with modern facilities and furnishings.

Some of the attractive selling features of these apartments are the large swimming pools which adjoin the complex. In addition, there are two restaurants and a pool-side café.

Families with small children would find these apartments ideal. There is a club for kids running from May to August, where children from as young as six months can be entertained by responsible carers.

Apartments Du Soleil will be completed in May of this year. They will range in price from €280,000 to €350,000, depending on size and facilities.

These apartments are ideal for a family who would like a second home in sunny France and for all those people yearning for an idyllic pied-à-terre.

All those familiar with the literary works of Gerard Didier will remember his words on Nice: 'Nice has taught me to love, to laugh and to live.'

Details can be obtained from Hynes Ltd or by e-mail at niceapart@goodmove.com

COMMENT

The text of a property advertisement is written in language designed to persuade. The above extract mentions the special features of these apartments as well as prices and contact details.

Structure your answer into short paragraphs. Adding a small homely detail about the place can also increase the appeal of the advertisement. Even if you are not asked to write a title, it is helpful to make up an appealing or catchy title or headline to market your property better.

WRITING ON A PHOTOGRAPH OR A PICTURE

- Begin by summing up the subject matter of the photo or picture, e.g. 'This is a photograph of a rural landscape in winter' or 'This is a picture of an abandoned orphan in Africa.'
- Write on the background, foreground and middle ground of the photo/picture.
- Concentrate on small details, either in the person or place in the photo/picture.
- Look at unusual camera angles or positioning in the photo/picture.
- Look for any examples of contrast in the photo/picture and explain why this is used.
- Write on what you think may be the purpose of the picture/photo.

7

Samples of Paper I with Model Answers

STRUCTURE OF PAPER I

Study the following samples of Paper I. They follow the same layout as the examination at Higher Level. In each paper there are four different comprehension texts. Some of these texts may include a photograph or an advertisement. Each text is followed by a number of questions, which correspond to the type of questions that will be asked in the examination.

Suggested answers are provided for the comprehension questions on each text (see pages 123–37). The purpose of these answers is to suggest a method of approaching a particular question. None of these answers are definitive – a variety of approaches may be adopted.

To improve your technique in answering comprehension questions, try answering the questions yourself first, then compare your own answers with the suggested answers provided.

- Time allowed for Paper I: 2 hours and 50 minutes.
- This paper is divided into two sections: Section I COMPREHENDING and Section II COMPOSING.
- This paper contains *three* texts on a general theme.
- Both sections of this paper (COMPREHENDING and COMPOSING) must be attempted.
- Each section carries 100 marks.

Section I: Comprehending
(100 marks)
- Read each of the texts carefully a number of times.
- Two questions, A and B, follow each text.
- You must answer a question A on one text and a question B on a different text. You

must answer only one question A and only one question B. These questions carry equal marks.

• N.B. You may NOT answer a question A and a question B on the same text.

Section II: Composing
(100 marks)

Write a composition on *any one* of the topics provided.

The composition assignments are intended to reflect language study in the areas of information, argument, narration and the aesthetic use of language.

FIRST SAMPLE PAPER: CULTURE AND TRENDS

This paper contains *three* texts on the general theme of culture and trends.

Section I: Comprehending
(100 marks)

Text 1

Hellfire and hyperdrive: the Gospel according to *Star Wars*

'I am trying to bring up my children with Jedi values' – so wrote an earnest Christian recently in a discussion on an internet site devoted to modern culture. The combination of Christianity and *Star Wars* may seem one of the more bizarre bits of merchandising in the hype around *The Phantom Menace*, but now a Methodist university chaplain in Liverpool has written an entire book on the subject. 'I'm not into buying light-sabres, running around pretending to be Princess Leia or anything like that,' said the Rev. David Wilkinson, who worked for six years as an astrophysicist before his ordination. He claims to be only a moderate fan, though he has already seen *The Phantom Menace* twice in the line of duty. But, he says, this is the way that schoolchildren and students get their moral discussions nowadays. 'I went to a school the other day and spoke to a group of around a hundred people. Half of them had already seen it on pirate video, even before the official release.'

Though *The Phantom Menace* has been generally panned, Wilkinson sees it as in some respects the most theologically interesting of the films, because it centres on a character changing sides. 'How does the boy Anakin Skywalker turn into the evil Darth Vader? What is it that conspires within us to produce evil?' That the answers to this question are not necessarily Christian ones does not bother him, though conservative Christians around the world have complained that *Star Wars* spreads New Age heresies.

In the climactic scene of *Return of the Jedi*, where Darth Vader returns to his original team and chucks the evil Emperor into the glowing maw of the hyperdrive, Wilkinson sees an echo of the Christian theme of redemption through self-sacrifice. He sees the Force as a sign of hope: 'It's not a picture of God, but it's raising the question of God. There is a tension in the films between the scientific-materialistic world view and the transcendence – the good guys rely on the Force and the bad guys rely on the Death Star. They even use a robot army in *The Phantom Menace*, which is an illustration of a Western technological society trying to stamp out any sense of the transcendent.'

On the other hand, to most people the Force is nothing like the idea of a Christian God. The interesting bits of Christianity, from the Book of Job onwards, are adaptations to the fact that the spaceship does not rise miraculously from the swamp, even when the good guys want it to, really badly. This does not worry Mr Wilkinson. It seems to him that *Star Wars*, though it is one of the greatest consumerist phenomena of the age, opens up a vision of a world beyond technological consumerism. It is designed to appeal to the kind of characters – 'a small boy and a whiny teenager' – who would never have anything to do with normal church life.

It's all an imposing theory and will make an interesting companion to an earlier book he published on *The Spirituality of The X Files*. Both phenomena, he says, show evidence of a tremendous need to believe in the reality of stuff outside our narrow imaginations and to anchor myth with detailed reality. There is a key difference, he insists. Christianity's gospel stories weren't made up in the way that those about Skywalker and Darth Vader were. *Star Wars* fans, of course, might not agree.

QUESTION A

1. Briefly explain the arguments the writer uses to draw a parallel between Christian ideas and those underlying the presentation of *Star Wars*.
2. What techniques does the writer use to back up or substantiate the claims made in the above passage?

QUESTION B

Write a short review of a film you enjoyed watching.

Text 2

Eating at Mama's

For the first time since the decline of Dadaism we are witnessing a revival in the fine art of meaningless naming. This thought is prompted by the film *Trainspotting* and by the opening of a new play on Broadway called *Virgil Is Still the Frogboy*. The play is not about Virgil: no frogs feature therein. The title is apparently taken from a Long Island graffiti, to whose meaning the play offers no clues. This omission has not diminished the show's success.

As Luis Buñuel knew, obscurity is a characteristic of objects of desire. Accordingly, there is no train-spotting in *Trainspotting*, just a predictable, even sentimental movie that thinks it's hip. (Compared with the work of, say, William Burroughs, it's positively cutesy.) The film has many admirers, perhaps because they are unable to understand even its title, let alone the fashionably indecipherable slang of the dialogue. The fact remains that *Trainspotting* contains no mention of persons keeping obsessive notes on the arrival and departure of trains. The only railway engines are to be found on the wallpaper of the central character's bedroom. Whence, therefore, the choo-choo moniker? Some sort of pun on the word 'tracks' may be intended.

Nowadays, dreary old comprehensibility is still very much around. A new film about a boy-man called Jack is called *Jack*. A film about crazed basketball fans is called *The Fan*. The new version of Jane Austen's *Emma* is called *Emma*.

However, titular mystification continues to intensify. When Oasis sing 'You're my wonderwall', what do they mean? I intend to ride over you on my motorbike, round and round at very high speed? Surely not.

And *Blade Runner*? Yes, I know that hunters of android replicants are called 'blade runners'. But why? And yes, William Burroughs (again) used the phrase in a 1979 novel and, to get really arcane, there's a 1974 medical thriller called *The Bladerunner* by the late Dr Alan Nourse. But what does any of this have to do with Ridley Scott's film? Harrison Ford runs not, neither does he blade. Shouldn't a work of art give us the keys with which to unlock its meanings? Perhaps there aren't any; perhaps it's just that the phrase sounds cool, thanks to those echoes of Burroughs, 'Daddy Cool' himself.

In 1928 Luis Buñuel and Salvador Dali co-directed the surrealist classic *Un Chien Andalou*, a film about many things but not about Andalusian dogs. So it is with Tarantino's *Reservoir Dogs*. No reservoir, no dogs, no use of the words 'reservoir', 'dogs' or 'reservoir dogs' at any point in the film. No imagery derived from dogs or reservoirs, or dogs in reservoirs, or reservoirs of dogs. Nothing; or as Mr Pink and co. would say, '. . . nothing'.

The story goes that when the young Tarantino was working in a video shop his distaste for fancy European writer-directors such as Louis Malle manifested itself in an inability to pronounce the titles of their films. Malle's *Au Revoir, les Enfants* defeated him completely ('Oh reservoir les . . .'), until he began to refer to it contemptuously as – you guessed it – 'those, oh reservoir dogs'. Subsequently he made this the title of his own film, no doubt as a further gesture of anti-European defiance. Alas, the obliqueness of the gibe meant that the Europeans simply did not comprehend. 'What we have here,' as the guy in *Cool Hand Luke* defiantly remarked, 'is a failure to communicate.'

But these days the thing about incomprehensibility is that people aren't supposed to understand. In accordance with the new *zeitgeist**, therefore, the title of this piece has in part been selected – 'sampled' – from Lou Reed's advice – 'Don't eat at places called Mama's' – in the diary of his recent tour. To forestall any attempts at esotericism, I confess that as a title it means nothing at all, but then the very concept of meaning is now outdated.

Welcome to the new incomprehensibility: gibberish with attitude.

* *Zeitgeist*: spirit of the times.

QUESTION A
1. What is the main thrust of the writer's arguments in this passage?
2. Comment on:
    i)   the writer's use of reference in the above passage
    ii) the style of the passage.

QUESTION B
'Welcome to the new incomprehensibility: gibberish with attitude.' How apt a conclusion to the passage is this statement? Give reasons for your answer.

Text 3

QUESTION A
1. What type of lifestyle is suggested by this picture? Support your answer by reference to details in the photograph.
2. What kind of statement is this photograph making?

QUESTION B
Compose a short introductory paragraph that might accompany this photograph.

(For suggested answers on the first sample paper see pages 123–6.)

Section II: Composing
(100 marks)

Write a composition on *any one* of the following.

1. Write a narrative composition on your experience of making a film or of an interview that you carried out with a film star.
2. Write a letter to your local newspaper on what you consider to be the advantages of health food shops.
3. Choose an exotic region that you would like to visit. Write a descriptive account of your trip and the particular cultural experiences that impressed you.
4. Write a persuasive speech for a debate entitled 'Discrimination is still rampant today.'
5. '*Star Wars*, though it is one of the greatest consumerist phenomena of the age, opens up a vision of a world beyond technological consumerism. It is designed to appeal to the kind of characters – "a small boy and a whiny teenager" – who would never have anything to do with normal church life.' Compose a series of arguments on what you consider the relationship between religion and ordinary life should be.
6. Imagine that you are working on the set of a film being made about your locality. Compose an imaginative account of your experiences of working with the film crew.
7. 'Vitamin pills increase the risk of lung cancer and heart disease among smokers, according to a report to be published by the World Health Organization (WHO).' Write an informative article for a teenage magazine on the importance of healthy eating.
8. Write the speech you will deliver for a debate on the topic 'Young people today are slaves of fads and fashions.'

SECOND SAMPLE PAPER: VIOLENCE AND DESTRUCTION

This paper contains *three* different texts on the general theme of violence and destruction.

Section I: Comprehending
(100 marks)

Text 1

Animal cruelty and mass murder

Shortly before the killings at the US Capitol building in Washington, the chief suspect in the case shot sixteen cats with his father's revolver. This vitally important incident was barely mentioned in reports of 'the assault on the front door of democracy'. It should have received banner headlines.

In England a few years ago the 'Butcher of Hungerford', Michael Ryan, tested his vast array of weapons on cats and wildlife before blowing away his neighbours. At the age of fourteen he had set animals alight just to watch them burn. Yet the police never considered him a threat to society – not until Michael declared open season on humans.

Recently two schoolchildren in Arkansas made world headlines when they shot their teacher and several pupils. As it happened, the children had been taught from an early age to hunt and kill animals – and to enjoy doing it. Video footage showed them pumping bullets into deer at point-blank range, with smirking adults standing over them.

After the murders a local policeman was quoted as saying, 'We just don't understand how something like this could happen in our small, peaceful, deer-hunting community.'

In Britain, neighbours had seen two children who abducted and killed a younger child cutting the heads off live pigeons. Gangsters Bonny and Clyde tortured livestock on a farm before embarking on their killing spree. In one of Ireland's most gruesome murder cases, the killer admitted in court that exposure to cruelty in a meat plant where he worked had brutalised him. After watching pigs die without being stunned, which his co-workers found amusing, he 'hadn't the slightest remorse' about using a butcher's knife on his victims.

The people involved in these and similar crimes had different motives, backgrounds and psychological profiles. But they all had one thing in common – ill treatment of animals had made them insensitive to human suffering.

For example, one study found that sport hunters in the US were seven times more likely to beat their wives than non-hunters. This disturbing tendency was attributed to an 'excessive need among hunters to control and dominate their environment'.

In Ireland firearms abound. Our gun culture is getting out of hand. Parts of the countryside have become a virtual battlefield, with bird and animal corpses littering the woods and fields. We should tackle this issue before 'harmless' taking of life spawns a major tragedy. One effective measure would be to have all weapons electronically tagged. Police could then monitor their use and whereabouts. Sadistic or over-zealous gunmen could be given the same treatment, depending on how the situation developed.

It is, after all, a matter of life and death.

QUESTION A

1. Do you consider this passage to be an example of effective writing? Give reasons for your answer.
2. Distinguish the facts from the opinions in this passage.

QUESTION B

Write two paragraphs, using a descriptive style, on a street scene at night.

Text 2

What is it possible to say about the loss of lives resulting from the Northern troubles? This. That so far it has all been in vain, quite purposeless. No cause was advanced in any way which would have not been better served by peaceful means. Who can say what this island would have been like if the depraved culture of violence had not once again taken root? Aside from the 3,600 lives lost, how much else has been lost? What opportunities to learn, to be civilised, to create art and order were squandered in the cretinous squalor of war?

If we had listed the dead of 1916–22, described who they were and how they died, if we had studied the barbarous injustice of their fate, if we had dwelt on the sufferings of their families, if we had made the immorality of political violence a keystone of our political culture, we would not have tolerated the violation of law and life of the last thirty years.

Catalogue

There might be an excuse for being ignorant of the events of 1916–22. There is no excuse now for ignorance over the events of 1966–99. The definitive catalogue of those who died in our troubles, how, where and when they died, who their families were and how else their families might have suffered, has been produced by David McKittrick and published by Mainstream Publishing. It is the saddest, most sobering, most heartbreaking book I have ever read. Not a page of it is without an almost unbearable tragedy; each tragedy is real, each one was lived by actual people, each one spread vast repercussions through family, friends and the broader community to which they belonged.

Numbers numb. Very soon after one starts counting deaths they lose meaning. Three hundred, four hundred, five hundred; people become ciphers, their identity, their purpose in life, the people they loved and the people who loved them in return vanish behind the metronome ticking of digits passing through our minds. That is how we have been able to bear the unbearable during these troubles. We let the shutters of statistics conceal the mountain range of human suffering behind them.

In the greatest single piece of historical scholarship in either journalism or historical studies that has ever been conducted in this country, David McKittrick has liberated the dead from the limbo of statistics. The unliving live again. He has followed up each death, back to the first killings in 1966, and up to the most recent, that of Charles Bennett last year – the numbered corpses and their poor bereaved families come back to life on the page. And in their merely literary resurrection they serve as a terrible indictment of the culture of political violence that finds so many apologists throughout Irish life.

Utter futility

A page of David's masterpiece should convince any civilised person that a resort to violence to solve the communal problems of Ireland is no more than a celebration of idiot-barbarism. And it is not enough to say this is the case today. The resort to violence in the name of the Republic has been marked by two enduring features. The first is the enormous suffering it has caused, the second is its utter futility. The war for a united Irish republic has been going on intermittently now for nearly eighty-five years. It is no closer to achievement today than it was when the violent accounts were opened in Dublin in 1916 and two unarmed police officers – Constables Lahiffe and O'Brien – were murdered in the centre of Dublin.

How are these murders commemorated today? They are not. Children are not taught about these poor men butchered while doing their duty. They are not taught about Countess Markievicz capering around the body of the policeman she had just shot in St Stephen's Green joyfully shrieking, 'I shot him, I shot him.' There is a statue to her not far from where she gunned down this blameless man; he has vanished from history, as have the hundreds of others who died that Eastertide.

Those who are ignorant of the realities of the Easter Rising and of the violence of 1919–22 could be forgiven their ignorance. The issue is not about individual atrocities. The issue is violence itself. That is the atrocity. It is the atrocity which we have had to live with for the greater part of this century, an atrocity which in each generation has re-emerged. But until the publication of *Lost Lives*, it has always been possible to hide the true evil of violence. Not any more. There can be no more searing indictment, not merely of the individual deeds of violence but of the political culture which justifies it, than this book.

Monstrosity

I defy anyone to browse through the pages of *Lost Lives* without being stunned by the sheer monstrosity of all that we have done, or allowed to be done, over the last thirty years. Evil, unspeakable evil, rose in our midst and we as a people were too weak, too indecisive, too pusillanimous to deal with it. And here now is a record of the consequences; in its encyclopaedic detail, in its towering integrity and in its moral compassion it could be the most influential study of Irish history that has ever been presented.

I know of no work which can alter behaviour as this one can, should, must. The argument it presents against the use of violence, for all that it is implicit, is compelling and complete.

Nothing more needs to be said. Buy *Lost Lives*. Nobody on this island can have an excuse for not knowing about the evils of violence. Nobody who can work through the 1,600 pages of murder it covers will ever find an excuse or a pretext for political violence again.

QUESTION A
1. Consider this passage as an example of effective persuasive writing.
2. In what type of publication would you read this type of article?

QUESTION B
Write a speech for your class, of about 200 words, outlining the reasons why you think they should read this book.

Text 3

Photograph A

Photograph B

Photograph C

Photograph D

Photograph E

QUESTION A
1. Study photographs A–E and briefly describe what comment is being made in each case.
2. Pick one photograph and identify three different techniques that are used to communicate its particular message.

QUESTION B
Write a headline that could accompany each photograph.

(For suggested answers on the second sample paper see pages 126–129.)

Section II: Composing

(100 marks)

Write a composition on *any one* of the following.

1. 'There might be an excuse for being ignorant of the events of 1916–22. There is no excuse now for ignorance over the events of 1966–99.' Write out a speech for a debate in which you would either challenge or support this statement.
2. Write a narrative composition on your experience of seeing a street fight.
3. 'In Ireland firearms abound. Our gun culture is getting out of hand. Parts of the countryside have become a virtual battlefield, with bird and animal corpses littering the woods and fields.' Write a letter to the newspaper on your own views of the hunting and shooting of wild animals.
4. 'The lightning now was the colour of silver, and gleamed in the heavens like a mailed army.' Use this statement as the starting point for a short story. Concentrate on using vivid, descriptive language.
5. Compose a series of arguments on the subject 'Violence has become a hallmark of our society.'
6. Write the dialogue for a screenplay on the subject 'Peaceful solutions'.
7. In an article intended for a serious magazine, write a persuasive account of your own experience of the horrors of war.

THIRD SAMPLE PAPER: COMMUNICATION

This paper contains *three* texts on the general theme of communication.

Section I: Comprehending

(100 marks)

Text 1

Does anywhere on Earth sound more exotic? Or does the name Bali evoke an image long since past of a Mecca for artists in the1930s and hippies in the 1960s? Does it offer adventure, romance, peace and quiet, spiritual rejuvenation? Well, yes. Bali has volcanoes, jungles, elephants, wild monkeys, amazing birds, vistas of rice paddies, azure seas, gleaming sands, colourful culture and captivating music and dancing. It also has bungee jumping, go-karting, paragliding, white-water rafting, paint balling and an internet café – this last lot are present because Bali is to Australians what Torremolinos is to British and Irish people.

The views of the jungle and rice paddies opposite are luscious. At night the sound of the stream at the bottom of the gorge and the clatter of insects provide an auditory environment just as compelling.

Plenty of tours will take you on a boat to a desert island or bird park. In any of these places you will come across the monkeys. As well as being charming, they are adept pickpockets, but can usually be bribed with food to return whatever they have purloined. Who is to say whether or not the nearby vendors who sell you the titbits of food are in league with the monkeys?

QUESTION A
1. Do you consider this to be an effective piece of persuasive writing? Give reasons for your answer.
2. Identify the facts in this passage.

QUESTION B
Write out an advertisement that would accompany this article. Include a slogan and an arresting caption and concentrate on using some persuasive techniques in the language you use.

Text 2

The wind blew the smell of rain down the valley ahead of the rain itself, the smell of wet earth and aromatic plants. The old woman pulled in her washing and fetched the cane chairs off the terrace. The old man, Anton Hahn, put on boots and a waterproof and went into the garden to check that all the catchments were clear. The peon came over from the barn with an empty bottle and the woman filled it with apple *chicha*. He was drunk already. Two red oxen stood yoked to a cart, bracing themselves for the storm.

The old man walked round his vegetable garden and his flower garden bright with annuals. Having seen that they would get the full benefit of the rain, he came inside the house. Apart from its metal roof nothing distinguished it from the houses of a southern German village, the half-timbering infilled with white plaster, the grey shutters, the wicket fence, scrubbed floors, painted panelling, the chandelier of antler tines and lithographs of the Rhineland.

Anton Hahn took off his tweed cap and hung it on an antler. He took off his boots and canvas gaiters and put on rope-soled slippers. His head was flat on top and his face creased and red. A little girl with a pigtail came into the kitchen.

'Do you wish your pipe, *Onkel*?'

'*Bitte*.' And she brought a big *meerschaum* and filled it with tobacco from a blue-and-white jar.

The old man poured himself a tankard of *chicha*. As the rain slammed on the roof, he talked about the Colonia Nueva Alemania. His uncles settled here in 1905 and he had followed after the Great War.

'What could I do? The Fatherland was in a bad condition. Before the war, no family could have enough sons. One was a soldier. One was a carpenter, and two stayed on the farm. But after 1918 Germany was full of refugees from the Bolsheviks. Even the villages were full.'

His brother lived on the family farm on the borders of Bavaria and Württemberg. They wrote letters once a month but had not met since 1923.

'The war was the biggest mistake in history,' Anton Hahn said. He was obsessed by the war. 'Two peoples of the Superior Race ruining each other. Together England and Germany could have ruled the world. Now even Patagonia is returning to the *indígenas*. This is a pity.'

He went on lamenting the decline of the West and, at one point, dropped the name Ludwig.

'Mad Ludwig?'

'The King? Mad? You call the King mad? In my house? No!'

I had to think fast.

'Some people call him mad,' I said, 'but, of course, he was a great genius.'

Anton Hahn was hard to pacify. He stood up and lifted his tankard.

'You will join me,' he said.

I stood.

'To the King! To the last genius of Europe! With him died the greatness of my race!'

The old man offered me dinner, but I refused, having eaten with the soprano two hours before.

'You will not leave my house until you have eaten with us. After that you may go where you will.'

So I ate his ham and pickles and sun-coloured eggs and drank his apple *chicha*, which went to my head. Then I asked him about Wilson and Evans.

'They were gentlemen,' he said. 'They were friends of my family and my uncles buried them. My cousin knows the story.'

The old woman was tall and thin and her yellowing skin fell from her face in folds. Her hair was white and cut in a fringe across her eyebrows.

'Yes, I remember Wilson and Evans. I had four years at the time.'

It was a hot, windless day in early summer. The Frontier Police, eighty of them, had been hunting the outlaws up and down the Cordillera. The Police were criminals themselves, mostly Paraguayos; you had to be white or Christian to join. Everyone in Río Pico liked the North Americans. Her mother, Doña Guillermina, dressed Wilson's hand, right here in the kitchen. They could easily have gone over into Chile. How could they know the Indian would betray them?

'I remember them bringing in the bodies,' she said. 'The *Fronterizas* brought them down on an ox-cart. They were here, outside the gate. They had swelled up in the heat and the smell was terrible. My mother sent me to my room so I shouldn't see. Then the officer cut their heads off and came up the steps, here, carrying them by the hair. And he asked my mother for preserving alcohol. You see, this *Agencia* in New York was paying five thousand dollars a head. They wanted to send the heads up there and get the money. This made my father very angry. He shouted them to give over the heads and the bodies and he buried them.'

The storm was passing. Columns of grey water fell on the far side of the valley. Along the length of the apple orchard was a line of blue lupins. Wherever there were Germans there were blue lupins.

By the corral a rough wood cross stuck out of a small mound. The arching stems of a pampas rose sprang up as if fertilised by the bodies. I watched a grey harrier soaring and diving, and the sweep of grass and the thunderheads turning crimson.

The old man had come out and was standing behind me.

'No one would want to drop an atom bomb on Patagonia,' he said.

(Bruce Chatwin, *In Patagonia*)

QUESTION A
1. Good narrative writing depends for its effect on vividly recording small details. In the extract above, identify how the writer has drawn some vibrant description by means of small details.
2. From your reading of this extract, comment on the type of person you think the narrator is. Give reasons for your answer.

QUESTION B
1. Sum up in your own words the anecdote given above and say how much it contributes to the power of the passage.

Text 3
QUESTION A
1. Identify the target audience of the advertisement on page 116.
2. Do you consider this to be an effective advertisement? Give three reasons for your answer.

QUESTION B
Write a short paragraph on your reaction to this advertisement.

An angel In search of a guardian.

Please send me further details about sponsoring a child, or call 01460 23 8080.

I'm interested in sponsoring in:

☐ Africa ☐ Asia ☐ Where need is greatest

Mr/Mrs/Miss/Ms _____

Address _____

_____

Postcode _____

Tel (Day) _____ (Eve) _____

170012

I can't sponsor a child now, but enclose a gift of:

☐ £200 ☐ £100 ☐ £50 ☐ £25 ☐ £_____

Make cheques / POs payable to ActionAid, and send to:
ActionAid,
FREEPOST BS4868,
Chard, Somerset TA20 1BR

ACTIONAID

The thought that someone cares about your everyday welfare can be a very comforting one.

Especially in the developing world where poverty and ill health are so much a part of growing up.

By sponsoring a child like Joshi through ActionAid you can offer a community a way forward.

With your support we can help provide children and their families with access to safe, clean water, healthcare and education.

These essentials make a difference to their everyday lives now and are vital in their fight to become self-sufficient in the future.

As a sponsor, you'll see how your money is working through regular updates from local field workers and messages from the child you sponsor.

Contact us today and we'll send you an information pack with a photo of a child awaiting your sponsorship.

Fill in the coupon and become a much needed guardian angel.

Section II: Composing
(100 marks)

Write a composition on *any one* of the following.

1. 'By the corral a rough wood cross stuck out of a small mound. The arching stems of a pampas rose sprung up as if fertilised by the bodies. I watched a grey harrier soaring and diving, and the sweep of grass and the thunderheads turning crimson.' Compose a descriptive account of some particular scene in nature that impressed you. Concentrate on using some original images and small details in your descriptions.

2. 'But there they were this week, lining the front rows at the final Paris *haute couture* showings, picking their frocks for the party to end all parties.' Write a review for a magazine on a fashion show you attended.

3. 'Or does the name Bali evoke an image long since past of a Mecca for artists in the 1930s and hippies in the 1960s?' Compose an article, using a persuasive style, on what you consider to be the advantages of taking holidays abroad.

4. 'Apart from its metal roof nothing distinguished it from the houses of a southern German village, the half-timbering infilled with white plaster, the grey shutters, the wicket fence, scrubbed floors, painted panelling, the chandelier of antler tines and lithographs of the Rhineland.' Write a narrative account of your experiences abroad. Include some details of your impressions of the people, food and culture.

5. 'Travelling broadens horizons.' Taking this topic as the subject for a debate, write out the arguments you would use in your speech.

6. Compose a series of diary entries by a person who is engaged in working on a Third World project. Include details of the people, their lifestyle, food and culture.

7. Write a letter to a local newspaper on your opinion of modern culture.

FOURTH SAMPLE PAPER: HOME AND IDENTITY

This paper contains *four* texts on the general theme of home and identity.

Section I: Comprehending
(100 marks)

Text 1

The Westernisation of the world

A traditional scene

In Singapore, Peking opera still lives, in the back streets. On Boat Quay, where great barges moor to unload rice from Thailand, raw rubber from Malaysia or timber from Sumatra, I watched a troupe of travelling actors throw up a canvas-and-wood booth stage, paint on their white faces and lozenge eyes and don their resplendent vermilion, ultramarine and gold robes. Then, to raptured audiences of bent old women and little children with perfect circle faces, they enacted tales of feudal princes and magic birds and tragic love affairs, sweeping their sleeves and singing in strange metallic voices.

The performance had been paid for by a local cultural society as part of a religious festival. A purple cloth temple had been erected on the quayside, painted papier mâché sculptures were burning down like giant joss-sticks and middle-aged men were sharing out gifts to be distributed among members' families – red buckets, roast ducks, candies and moon-cakes. The son of the organiser, a fashionable young man in an Italian shirt and gold-rimmed glasses, was looking on with amused benevolence. I asked him why only old people and children were watching the show. 'Young people don't like these operas,' he said. 'They are too old-fashioned. We would prefer to see a high-quality Western variety show – something like that.'

He spoke for a whole generation. Go to almost any village in the Third World and you will find youths who scorn traditional dress and sport denims and T-shirts. Go into any bank and the tellers will be dressed as would their European counterparts; at night the manager will climb into his car and go home to watch television in a home that would not stick out on a European or North American estate. Every capital city in the world is getting to look like every other, and not just in consumer fashions – the mimicry extends to architecture, industrial technology, health care, education and housing.

Perverting development

The Third World's obsession with the Western way of life has perverted development and is rapidly destroying both good and bad in traditional cultures, flinging the baby out with the bath water. It is the most totally pervasive example of what historians call cultural diffusion in the history of mankind. Its origins lie in the colonial experience, in which a variety of European conquerors suffered from the same colonial arrogance. Never a doubt entered their minds that native cultures could be in any way – materially, morally or spiritually – superior to their own and they firmly believed that the benighted inhabitants of the darker continents needed enlightening. And so there grew up, alongside political and economic imperialism, that more insidious form of control – cultural imperialism. It conquered not just their bodies but the souls of its victims, turning them into willing accomplices.

Reference-group behaviour

The most insidious form of cultural imperialism works by what sociologists call reference-group behaviour, found when someone copies the habits and lifestyle of a social group they wish to belong to or to be classed with and abandons those of their own group. This desire to prove equality surely helps to explain why Kwame Nkrumah of Ghana built the huge stadium and triumphal arch of Black Star Square in its capital, Accra. Why the tiny village of President Houphouet-Boigny in Côte d'Ivoire has been graced with a four-lane motorway, starting and ending nowhere, a five-star hotel and an ultra-modern conference centre. The aim was not to show the old imperialists but to impress other Third World leaders in the only way everyone would recognise: the Western way. Fashions and dress codes have also fallen victim to this compulsion to Westernise. In post-war Turkey a ruthless policy was pursued which saw the replacement of the Arabic script with the roman alphabet, while the wearing of the traditional hat, the fez, became a criminal offence. Launching this campaign the president declared: 'The people of the Turkish Republic must prove that they are civilised and advanced persons in their outward respect also. A civilised international dress is worthy and appropriate for our nation and we will wear it. Boots or shoes on our feet, trousers on our legs, shirt and tie, jacket and waistcoat – and of course, to complete these, a cover with a brim on our heads. I want to make this clear. The head covering is called a hat.'

QUESTION A

1. Briefly describe the writer's views on the impact the 'obsession with the Western way of life' has made upon the people of the Third World.
2. Do you consider this passage to be an example of effective writing? Give reasons for your answer.

QUESTION B

Write a descriptive passage of between 150 and 200 words for a holiday brochure, describing what you consider to be the ideal holiday. In preparing your writing, pay careful attention to the way the author of the above passage uses detail in the opening two paragraphs.

Text 2

Pioneers: A view of home

I'm just a little picky about what I take pride in. There are actually people who take pride in their race. This is stupid. Not that anyone should be ashamed of his or her race, it's just that when you think about it you had nothing to do with it. Not your race, not your age, not your nationality. Not even your name.

Family feud

Recently I was watching a repeat of a television show called *Family Feud*, in which two families compete in guessing the answers to the silliest questions. The 'right answer' was the one that had been given earlier by a fabled 'one hundred people'. (We asked a hundred people to name a friendly neighbourhood bird and the families had to guess what this one hundred had said – 'buzzard'.) Whichever family reached 350 points first was the winner. A black family consisting of father, mother, two daughters and a son-in-law were playing a white family of father, mother and three sons in uniforms. As luck would have it the black family won. The show's presenter went over and shook the hands of the white family and thanked them for coming. Then one of the sons piped up with: 'Well, we can still fly.' I guess they were Air Force, but mostly that was a racist remark: you blacks may know what one hundred people think, but hey – we whites can fly. Totally unnecessary. And tacky. I don't object to the boys being proud of flying – if I could fly I'd be proud of myself when I board a flight! No. It was the context in which the remark was made. As if 'Well, after all, we're still white' could make up for the fact that they lost.

We are not so important after all
It's so clear, now that we have photographs from the moon and man-made satellites even farther away, that Earth resembles nothing so much as a single cell in the human body. What a concept – that the planet on which we live is no more than a specimen on a slide. We, who think humans are nature's invention, may well turn out to be no more than the life we see swimming in an ordinary drop of water. What is really important then? What does that do to our notions of race, fatherland and home?

Where is home?
They say home is where when you go, they have to take you in. I rather prefer the idea that home, when you could go anywhere, is where you would prefer to be. The true joy of being a black American is that we really have no home. Europeans bought us, but the Africans sold. We might not have come to America of our own volition, but that is true of so many of the people who have come here from the overcrowded, disease-ridden cities of Europe. And what of those who had to flee religious persecution, or the unspeakable Catholic Inquisition, starvation in Italy or the black rotten potatoes lying in the fields of Ireland? No one came to the New World in a cruise ship; they all came because they had to. They were poor, hungry, criminal, persecuted individuals who would rather chance dropping off the end of the earth than stay inert, knowing that both their body and spirit were slowly having the life squeezed from them. A pioneer has only two things – a deep desire to survive and an equally strong will to live. Home is not the place where our possessions and accomplishments are deposited and displayed – it is this earth that we have explored, the heavens we view with awe, these humans who, despite the flaws, we try to love and those who try to love us. It is the willingness to pioneer the one trek we all can make, no matter what our station or location in life – the existential reality that wherever there is life, we are at home.

QUESTION A
1. In your own words, characterise the attitudes of the writer of this passage to questions of identity and belonging.
2. Consider this passage as an example of predominantly persuasive writing.

QUESTION B
Write a short letter (100–150 words) to the television company which produces the show *Family Feud*, commenting on the behaviour of the families as described in this passage.

Text 3

In this passage taken from *How to Write a Novel*, the English novelist, John Braine, establishes a link between the appearance and atmosphere of places and the people who live in them.

Writing about home

People are places, and places are people. This isn't to dazzle you with its originality; it's simply another working rule. Whenever you write about places you also write about people. It isn't always that you mention the people when you write about the place. Sometimes it's necessary, sometimes it isn't. On the whole the best way is to concentrate on making the reader see the place.

The most revealing place of all is the home. Imagine yourself suddenly in the home of a complete stranger. Within five minutes you'll have an accurate general picture of what sort of person he is. There are obvious guides, like the kind of books or, for that matter, the absence of books, and the pictures and ornaments, and the quality of the furniture. There are different kinds of tidiness, from the house-proud to the clinically obsessive; different kinds of untidiness, from profusion to squalor. There is, over and above all, the atmosphere of a home. Some people have the gift of creating comfort, some have not. But be careful about this. If you describe a home properly, if you see it accurately, there's no need to say anything about the atmosphere. Or, to be more precise, your reader instantly makes the inference of falling between a shot of a man swaying on a windowsill ten storeys up and the same man sitting on the ground.

This isn't to say that we are exclusively the creatures of our economic environment. We aren't, for instance, made what we are by our homes (using the word in its narrowest sense). We make our homes. We were there first, so to speak. We even make impersonal places, like offices and factories, bear the imprint of our personalities: pin-ups on the walls behind the workbench, trendy executive toys, gold pens, silver mounted portraits on the executive's desk (or, equally revealing, nothing at all).

QUESTION A
1. Describe accurately and concisely the author's illustration of his opening statement: 'People are places, and places are people.'
2. Do you think he states his argument well? Support your points by detailed reference to the text.

QUESTION B

Imagine yourself in the home of some well-known figure from the world of entertainment or political life. Write a short account (150–200 words) for a popular magazine of what you imagine this home to look like and give some indication of what you have chosen to include as significant detail.

Text 4
QUESTION A
1. What lifestyle is suggested to you by the collection of images on page 122?

2. How is this lifestyle suggested?
3. In what type of publication would you expect to find images such as this? Refer to the images in support of your point of view.
4. Compose an introductory paragraph of about 200 words that might accompany this image in the publication you have chosen in response to question 3.

QUESTION B

Imagine you are employing a graphic designer to compile such a photo gallery of your own life. Write a brief letter to him or her in which you outline the kind of images or objects you would include, giving the reasons for their inclusion.

Section II: Composing
(100 marks)

el Klaui

Write a composition on *any one* of the following.

1. 'Home, when you could go anywhere, is where you would prefer to be.' 'Home is not the place where our possessions and accomplishments are deposited and displayed.' In an article intended for a serious journal, present a case for or against one of these views of home.

2. 'There are actually people who take pride in their race. This is stupid.' Write an article in which you challenge or support these views.

3. 'Tales of feudal princes and magic birds and wars and tragic love affairs.' Compose a fable or fairytale suggested by one or more of the details in this quotation. You may, if you wish, give your composition a modern setting.

4. 'If you describe a home properly, if you see it accurately, there's no need to say anything about its atmosphere.' Write an informative newspaper article about your home town, parish or locality, concentrating especially on the qualities that make it unique or memorable.

5. 'Fashions and dress codes.' Compose a persuasive article or a speech for a debate that discusses the issue 'We are what we wear.'

6. 'The most revealing place of all is the home.' Compose a series of thoughtful diary entries of a person returning to their native country after an absence of some years.

7. 'Days in my life.' Imagine you are working in the household of the person in the images under Text 4. Compose an autobiographical sketch or dramatic scene in which you characterise your experience in the house and comment on your relationship with the householder.

MODEL ANSWERS TO COMPREHENSION QUESTIONS

First sample paper (pages 100–104)
Culture and trends: Text 1
ANSWERS TO QUESTION A

1. The writer begins by referring to a Methodist university chaplain in Liverpool who has written a book on the subject of linking the film *Star Wars* with Christianity. This man – Rev. David Wilkinson – states that the film *Star Wars* is one of the most interesting films theologically because it centres on a character changing sides. He goes on to pose the question: what is it in us that produces evil? He draws a parallel between the situation in the film where the evil Emperor is thrown into the glowing maw of the hyperdrive and the theme of redemption through self-sacrifice. He goes on to claim that the Force is a sign of hope. While it is not a picture of God, it is raising the question of God. The tension in the film is based on a scientific-materialistic world

view and the idea of transcendence. In the film, we are told, the good guys rely on the Force and the bad guys rely on the Death Star. Rev. Wilkinson maintains that *Star Wars* is one of the greatest consumerist phenomena of the age, as it opens up a vision of a world beyond technological consumerism.

2. The writer uses the following techniques in order to develop the arguments in the passage. The passage opens with reference to words expressed by 'an earnest Christian' on how they are trying to bring up their children with Jedi values. The writer moves on to outline how there exists a direct correlation between some of the values of Christianity and those underlying the film *Star Wars*. He uses some words expressed by Rev. David Wilkinson in order to substantiate this claim.

The article develops by illustrating the clear correlation between certain Christian ideas, such as the theme of redemption and self-sacrifice, and those that are shown in the film.

ANSWER TO QUESTION B

One of the films which I have truly enjoyed watching is *Life is Beautiful*. The film consists of two parts, which are closely related. In the first part, Guido (played by Roberto Benigni) falls in love with a school teacher in the town of Arezzo. The second part of the film takes place five years later and deals with the Nazi occupation. Guido, his wife and son are taken to a concentration camp because Guido is part-Jewish. Here, Guido uses all his wit and ingenuity to keep his son alive. For me the striking effect of this film is its ability to show the triumph of the human imagination over adversity. Guido pretends to his son that the death camp is a resort and that all the inhabitants are engaged in a game and the best players will win an enormous prize.

Some people have objected to the fact that this film trivialises the Holocaust. However, I disagree with this view. For me, the film portrays death and suffering in a highly realistic manner. The effect of this serves the purpose of identifying more clearly the enormous horror of the Holocaust. This becomes very obvious for me when Guido himself is compelled to face the ultimate horror in the picture of the piled-up bodies.

I enjoyed this film very much, as it gives a very realistic and human portrayal of characters who suffered from the horrific effects of war and genocide.

Culture and trends: Text 2
ANSWERS TO QUESTION A

1. The writer begins his argument by stating that we are witnessing a revival in the art of giving names which are totally meaningless to things. To support this statement he uses several examples from films, for example *Trainspotting*, *Blade Runner* and *Reservoir Dogs*. The stories of these films have nothing whatsoever to do with their titles.

To illustrate his argument more clearly, the writer uses a humorous and almost ironic anecdote. In this anecdote we learn how Tarantino supposedly got the title *Reservoir Dogs* for his film because of his inability to pronounce the title of the film *Au Revoir, les Enfants*.

The writer concludes his argument by claiming that nowadays things are not meant to be understood; the more incomprehensible they are, the better. The concept of meaning has become outdated.

2. (i)   The writer's references mainly deal with cinematic allusions. He supports his main argument about the revival of the 'fine art of meaningless naming' by referring to a play, *Virgil Is Still the Frogboy*, and the films *Trainspotting* and *Blade Runner*. He also refers to several film directors, among them Luis Buñuel and Louis Malle, and to William Burroughs. He mentions the actor Harrison Ford in order to comment humorously that in the film *Blade Runner* he neither runs nor blades and to emphasise the fact that the title has nothing whatsoever to do with the film's content.

Then, to demonstrate the fact that dreary comprehensibility does still exist, the writer makes reference to the films *Emma* and *The Fan*.

(ii)   A number of very effective features of style are used in this passage to support the writer's main points. The tone of the entire passage is ironic and humorous. The writer uses colloquial expressions that would be familiar to the American reader, such as 'positively cutesy', 'hip' and 'Daddy Cool', all examples of the writer's use of colloquial language and his mocking use of buzzwords.

The writer makes effective use of illustrations to support his argument. For example, the reference to the title of the film *Trainspotting* illustrates his main point that incomprehensibility is popular nowadays. In addition, there are copious references to various film directors and their films. The use of the colourful anecdote also illustrates very effectively how the young Tarantino got the name for his film *Reservoir Dogs*.

The sentence structure is varied; most of the sentences are brief, snappy statements that are in keeping with the colloquial or informal tone that is used. The writer also uses a series of short paragraphs that are clearly linked.

Answer to question B

The conclusion of this passage is very suitable for the preceding argument and the tone used in it. The whole thrust of this article, conveyed by a series of striking examples, is how we are now confronted with a culture of incomprehensibility. The examples the writer uses throughout are taken from popular films and the work of modern artists. The writer also shows how directors give their films names that have nothing to do with their content. The examples he gives include films such as *Reservoir Dogs* and *Trainspotting*.

The conclusion is very effective. It succinctly sums up the writer's central arguments in a neat, effective and compact manner.

Culture and trends: Text 3

Answers to question A

1. The lifestyle suggested to me by this photograph is one of poverty and need. The clothes of the two boys are old and torn. The bigger boy has no shoes and the ground is rough and seems to be filled with rubble. In addition, the cart is roughly made: it seems to be made of a cardboard box and wiring and the wheels are broken. The metal bar propelling this old car is also rough-and-ready. The boys, however, seem to be happy. We can tell this from the smile on the face of the older boy and the fact that they are united in the picture.

2. The statement that seems to be made in this photograph is of a sense of initiative on the part of the boys. Even in conditions of poverty these two boys can find something to smile about – the older boy is happy as he pushes the younger boy along in this home-made cart. There is a strong sense of unity between the two, shown in the small detail of both boys holding the one pole and driving forward.

ANSWER TO QUESTION B

Even in the midst of extreme hardship and poverty, Kiko and Yami can still find something to smile about. Born and bred in the Kikuyo tribe in the North Kenyan mountains, both boys were left destitute at an early age. Their father abandoned their mother and ran to the mountains and later on their mother died from disease and starvation. These two boys survived and now live with their uncle, spending their time entertaining each other and the kids from the nearby village by giving each other joyrides in the local BMW.

Second sample paper (pages 105–11)

Violence and destruction: Text I
ANSWERS TO QUESTION A

1. This passage is a dramatic example of persuasive writing. The writer's contention is that cruelty to animals is closely allied to cruelty and violence against people. The passage opens with a series of short anecdotes that illustrate the main point – how certain people who inflict cruelty on animals become dominated by a thirst for violence, which is then used on humans. Each point made by the writer is clearly laid out in a series of neat, concise paragraphs, which make it easy to follow the writer's train of thought.

The writer uses language that is accessible and effective. Phrases such as 'pumping bullets', 'gruesome murder cases' and 'the countryside has become a virtual battlefield' serve the function of hammering home more forcefully the writer's message about the profound impact of violence on human consciousness.

The writer concludes by using an authoritarian tone in order to motivate the reader to do something about the problem: 'We should tackle this issue', 'It is, after all, a matter of life and death.' This tone is a hallmark of effective persuasive writing.

2. The following are examples of facts used in the article. (i) The chief suspect in the killings at the Capitol in Washington shot sixteen cats with his father's revolver. (ii) Michael Ryan, also called the 'Butcher of Hungerford', tested his weapons on cats and wildlife before shooting his neighbours. At the age of fourteen he had set animals alight. (iii) In Arkansas two schoolchildren, who had been taught by adults to hunt and kill animals, shot their teacher and several pupils. (iv) Neighbours in Britain had seen two children who abducted and killed a younger child cut off the heads of live pigeons. (v) Bonny and Clyde tortured livestock before they embarked on a killing spree. (vi) In Ireland a murderer claimed that exposure to cruelty in a meat plant had brutalised him. (vii) Research shows that sport hunters are seven times more likely to beat their wives than non-hunters.

The following are examples of opinions expressed in the article. (i) The killings at the Capitol in Washington should have received banner headlines. (ii) The violence in sport hunters is attributed to an excessive need among hunters to control and dominate their environment. (iii) Our gun culture is getting out of hand. Parts of the country have become a virtual battlefield. (iv) We should tackle this issue before the killing of animals spawns a major tragedy. (v) One effective measure would be to have all weapons electronically tagged so that police could monitor their use. Sadistic or over-zealous gunmen could be given the same treatment.

ANSWER TO QUESTION B
A street scene at night
It is almost three hours since the black veil of darkness covered the city. Now and then a sliver of moonlight penetrates through the smog and illuminates the streets below. The screeching of tyres – scarcely audible above the booming noise of nightclubs – fills the air as two stolen cars race each other down the main street, driven by teenage joyriders. A lone drunk stumbles along the footpath, using parked cars for handrails.

Across the street in a dark and gloomy alleyway two wretched tramps huddle in a doorway begging for money. One of them covers the scars of a lifetime of pain and suffering beneath a coarse, wrinkled face and dull beard. Drops of rain slowly trickle down an old rusty drainpipe. At the side of the disco a young man deals drugs to his clients before they enter the club. Other people pass by in fancy clothes eager for a night of enjoyment.

Violence and destruction: Text 2
ANSWERS TO QUESTION A
1. This is a very good example of writing as propaganda. The writer opens the article with a number of rhetorical questions: 'What is it possible to say about the loss of lives?', 'Who can say what this island would have been like?', 'How much else has been lost?'. Rhetorical questions are a hallmark of such writing and are a powerful device for gaining the reader's attention.

The writer makes use of emotive vocabulary in order to present his controversial views and images, such as 'the most sobering, most heartbreaking book . . . not a page of it is without an almost unbearable tragedy'. This type of language is very effective, as it serves the function of involving the reader on an emotional level.

Another feature of persuasive writing is the use of repetition. This device illustrates a writer's points or arguments in an emphatic way. The following examples of emphatic repetition illustrate the writer's arguments very well: 'each tragedy is real, each one was lived by actual people, each one spread vast repercussions through family, friends . . .'.

Another feature of persuasive writing is the use of metaphor and images. The writer of this article makes abundant use of images, particularly metaphors, to express an idea more forcefully through such images as 'we let the shutters of statistics conceal the mountain range of human suffering behind them', 'liberated the dead from the limbo of statistics'.

One effective device in persuasive writing is the technique of reinforcing a positive or affirmative statement by means of a negative. The writer of this article succeeds in doing this in a highly effectual and striking way in statements such as 'The issue is not individual atrocities. The issue is violence itself' and 'Not a page on it is without an almost unbearable tragedy; each tragedy is real, each one was lived by actual people'.

The most arresting feature of this passage is the one-sided view it presents of complex and controversial events, which are reduced here to a simple emotional level, the purpose of which is to undermine the legitimacy of any alternative point of view.

The writer concludes the article by making use of the imperative: 'Nothing more needs to be said. Buy *Lost Lives*. Nobody on this island can have an excuse . . .'.

2. This article would probably appear in a newspaper aimed at a readership already inclined to agree with such opinions. The views put forward are expressed in such a provocative manner that there is little likelihood that they would convince an objective reader at the level of rational argument. The article uses highly selective facts and dubious analogies, such as equating the Northern violence with the War of Independence, all aimed at rousing the reader to an emotional involvement that will make them more ready to accept the writer's extreme views.

ANSWER TO QUESTION B

I would like to inform you about a book called *Lost Lives*. My purpose in addressing you today is to put forward a number of reasons why you should buy this book. *Lost Lives* addresses itself directly to our own history. It deals with all the deaths arising from political conflict in this century, from 1916 up to the events of the last thirty years. There can be no excuse for not knowing about the history of these events. This book describes the enormous suffering experienced by a huge number of families because of these deaths. Many negative as well as positive acts characterised the struggle for national independence and the negative ones must be confronted honestly. Some people use these facts to put forward a one-sided view that gives the impression that the recent campaign of violence was not only wrong but happened for no reason. They try to ignore the years of sectarian discrimination and repression that led large numbers of people – wrongly, in my opinion – to resort to violence. We must study the causes as well as the effects of political violence if we are serious about making certain that it never happens again.

Violence and destruction: Text 3

ANSWERS TO QUESTION A

1. Photograph A shows someone who is engaged in a parachute jump. He is being helped by two other people who are sitting in a plane. The main comment that is made in this photograph seems to be that this man is trusting absolutely in his two friends. It shows his dependence on other people and what can be achieved by people working together in harmony. In addition, the photograph seems to be suggesting the enormity of the world of nature and how small we humans seem to be within it.

Photograph B shows the football champion Jack Charlton playing with a schoolgirl and attempting to paint her face. It is a situation of fun, as can be seen from the stance of the girl, who is turning away and laughing. The expression of the other girl in the picture is also one of amusement. In some ways this photograph could represent the need for heroes and a type of hero worship.

Photograph C shows two elderly women studying an old cannon. The comment that seems to be made by this picture is how fascinating antique things can be. The fact that they are looking at a cannon, which has a pile of cannonballs beneath it, could also make a statement about the grim reality of war.

Photograph D shows a family at the seaside with their young son. He has made friends with a dog and is obviously fascinated by it. The photograph shows the power and meaning of friendship and communication.

Photograph E shows a man standing on a rough, rocky surface with his face hidden. In the distance stand two donkeys. The man appears to have climbed, as he is leaning on the stick and wears what appear to be walking boots. The significance of this photograph could be that the man is reflecting deeply on something, perhaps in a spirit of prayer or repentance.

2. Photograph A: This is a very effective image in depicting how humans engage in the art of flying. Two men seated in an aeroplane are holding a rope that is attached to another man, who is in mid-air. This serves the function of emphasising the unity of the action and how they can achieve so much when working together in unison. In addition, a contrast is drawn between the man and the enormity of the landscape behind him. The face of the man who is in mid-air shows a sense of satisfaction at a feat that has been accomplished.

ANSWER TO QUESTION B
Photograph A : 'A leap of faith'
Photograph B : 'Picasso Jack'
Photograph C : 'The way we were'
Photograph D : 'Man's best friend or kid's worst enemy?'
Photograph E : 'The pilgrim'

Third sample paper (pages 112–15)
Communication: Text 1
ANSWERS TO QUESTION A
1. This is a very effective example of persuasive writing. The article opens with several rhetorical questions, a hallmark of persuasive writing: 'Does anywhere on earth sound more exotic? Or does the name Bali evoke an image long since past of a Mecca for artists . . . Does it offer adventure, romance, peace and quiet . . .?'

The article develops by answering the question using a colloquial tone: 'Well, yes.' The writer gives a list of attractions offered by this exciting place, among them 'volcanoes, jungles, elephants, wild monkeys, amazing birds'. The writer gives a list of the activities that can be engaged in, such as go-karting, paragliding, white-water rafting, paint balling and an internet café. To illustrate Bali's popularity the writer makes use of a simile: 'Bali is to Australians what Torremolinos is to British and Irish people.'

The writer makes use of richly sensuous images, for example: 'The views of the jungle and rice paddies opposite are luscious. At night the sound of the stream at the bottom of the gorge and the clatter of insects provide an auditory environment just as compelling.' The function of such imagery is to attract the reader on an emotive level.

The article concludes by drawing a humorous illustration about the monkeys and the food vendors. This technique adds a sense of colour and interest to the writing.

2. (i) Bali was a Mecca for artists in the thirties and sixties. (ii) There are volcanoes, jungles, elephants, wild monkeys, birds, rice paddies, seas, music and dancing in Bali. (iii) In Bali there is bungee jumping, go-karting, paragliding, white-water rafting, paint balling and an internet café. (iv) Tours will take you by boat to a desert island or a bird park where there are monkeys.

Answer to question B

Want that perfect paradise?
You have it now in BEAUTIFUL BALI.
Escape to the blissful beaches of Bali, where you can have the time of your life
* wallowing on the golden sandy beaches
* soaking up the glorious sunshine
* lying by cool mountain streams.

Bali has an amazing mixture of adventure sports, magnificent views of the jungle, exotic boat tours and delicious and exciting food.
All you have to do is *book now* for that perfect holiday.
No better value than Bali –
Book your holiday today!

Communication: Text 2
Answers to question A

1. The writer opens this section by appealing to the different senses: we can almost smell the rain as it blows down the valley, with 'the smell of wet earth and aromatic plants'. We gain an insight into the habits of this community as they prepare for the oncoming storm. We can visualise the old woman gathering up her washing and the old man putting on his boots and waterproofs before he goes out to the garden. The writer also registers colours vividly with a series of adjectives: 'two red oxen', 'the half-timbering infilled with white plaster, the grey shutters', 'the painted panelling', the 'tobacco from a blue-and-white jar'. As he leaves the house at the conclusion he notes that there is a line of blue lupins, a favourite of German people. There is an emphasis on delineating small details in a vivid and economical way, for example, Anton Hahn takes off a tweed cap and hangs it up on an antler. Features of the characters are shown very vibrantly: 'a little girl with a pigtail', 'his head was flat on top and his face creased and red', the old woman's 'yellowing skin fell from her face in folds', her hair was 'white and cut in a fringe across her eyebrows'.

From the use of small detail we gain an insight into the type of characters represented. We learn that Anton likes his tobacco and *chicha*. We also learn from his conversation that he is bitter about the war and that he is loyal to the former king,

Ludwig. In a headstrong gesture he compels the writer to drink to the health of Ludwig and he forces him to stay to dinner in spite of his protestations. It is also clear that these people were humane from their reaction to the death of the two Englishmen. Anton's father had insisted on giving them a proper burial, and before leaving, the writer notes this in the small detail of the rough wooden cross that lay beside the corral.

2. The narrator is observant. This can be seen from his expert and skilful registering of small details in both character and the environment. The old woman is described as 'tall and thin', her skin is 'yellowing' and 'falling from her face in folds'. Anton wears a tweed cap which has its own place: it hangs on an antler. The writer also carefully notes certain customs and habits, such as Anton putting on his rope-soled slippers before he settles down with his pipe and tankard of *chicha*. As the narrator leaves the house he notes the beauty of nature: the arching stems of a pampas rose, the grey harrier soaring and diving. He also observes the small cross over the graves of the two Englishmen who were killed.

The narrator is also fast and resourceful. He makes the mistake of calling the former king 'Mad Ludwig', but is quick to qualify this by claiming 'he was a great genius'.

The narrator is sensitive. He registers the details of the anecdote about the two people who were victims of the frontier police with a great deal of insight and sensitivity. He is also courteous. At the insistence of Anton, he eats what is put before him even though he maintains that he just had a meal with the soprano. He also joins Anton in a toast to King Ludwig out of respect for Anton's view.

ANSWERS TO QUESTION B

1. Wilson and Evans were friends of the Hahns. They were betrayed to the frontier police, who claimed their heads in order to get money. However, the father became angry and insisted on burying them. The anecdote contributes to the power of the passage by showing more clearly the type of people the Hahns were. Though they were Germans and had apparently suffered because of the war, they retained a great deal of humanity and sensitivity, as is evidenced by their reaction to the murder of the two men.

2. The story begins with the narrator coming down into the valley as the rain is starting. It recounts how he meets Anton Hahn and his wife and how he is invited to dinner. He then develops the narrative by giving us an insight into the character of Anton. Through the conversation we learn that Anton is bitter about the Great War – he believes that the war was the biggest mistake in history. We also see Anton's loyalty to the former German king, Ludwig. The reference to the Englishmen shows us another side to Anton's family – the humanity and generous spirit of his father, who insisted on giving the two men a proper burial. The passage concludes with the writer noting the passing of the storm and the blue lupins, which are a favourite of German settlers. Hahn's philosophical comment that no one would want to drop an atom bomb on Patagonia concludes this passage. The narrative has a distinct shape – a definite beginning, middle and conclusion.

There is also a realistic insight into the characters present in this narrative – a hallmark of good narrative writing. The dialogue is immediate and clearly shows the more striking features of these characters, in particular Anton, who is more dominant and headstrong. The style and manner of the narrative shows us different features of the narrator – his capacity for observation, his love of nature, his sensitivity and ability to record small events in a dramatic manner.

Another feature of effective narrative is the ability to draw realistic description. Here, by focusing on a series of details – on colour, movement and shape – we can almost visualise the whole scene before us. Images such as 'So I ate his ham and pickles and sun-coloured eggs and drank his apple *chicha*, which went to my head' and 'The *Fronterizas* brought them down on an ox-cart . . . They had swelled up in the heat, and the smell was terrible' bring the whole situation alive.

Communication: Text 3
ANSWERS TO QUESTION A
1. The intended audience for this advertisement is the ordinary reader. The advertisement addresses itself to the reader who is in a position to help an underprivileged person in another country more effectively.
2. The advertisement is very effective, in the following ways: (i) The photograph of a young boy is highly effective in attracting the attention and sympathy of the reader. The boy's eyes and facial expression suggest someone who is desperately in need and who would greatly appreciate some small help. (ii) The heading at the top of the photograph is arresting and vivid. The underlying idea is one of helplessness in the young boy and his need for effective help, with a clever play on the term 'guardian angel'. (iii) The use of a coupon is a good way for people to find out how to help. In addition, the logo of the organisation Actionaid is clearly positioned and makes it obvious that help is being sought.

ANSWER TO QUESTION B
My reaction to this photograph is an immediate impression that the boy is in urgent need of help. His eyes and the position of his hand convey a strong impression of a cry for help. The whole image is one of vulnerability and helplessness. This image is reinforced by the words at the top of the photograph: 'An angel in search of a guardian'.

Fourth sample paper (pages 117–123)
Home and identity: Text 1
ANSWERS TO QUESTION A
1. The writer of this article makes several powerful points about the consequences of the Third World's obsession with the Western way of life. He believes it has stunted development and destroyed both the good and the bad in traditional cultures. He contends that this obsession is a striking example of 'cultural diffusion', the roots of which lie in colonialism. He maintains that colonialism, blinded by its own sense of superiority, imposes its culture while ignoring that of the country it has conquered. The writer concludes that cultural imperialism has become a hallmark of such societies and that it controls both the body and the soul of its victims.

The writer identifies the most insidious form of this type of dominance as 'reference-group behaviour', with the imitation of the habits and lifestyle of another culture and the simultaneous abandonment of one's own. He illustrates this by referring to Ghana and Turkey. In both instances the Western lifestyle was adopted to impress other Third World leaders and to show them that this was superior to their own culture.

2. The passage is a clear example of effective argument for the following reasons.

The writer begins the article with a colourful anecdote to illustrate his argument that adherence to traditional culture in Third World countries is maintained mostly by older people, while younger people prefer to see a performance from the Western world.

The topic sentence in each paragraph stands out clearly and is supported by graphic examples. The writer defines the term 'reference-group behaviour' and then cites examples to support this definition. This method of supporting his points with evidence makes the argument coherent and effective.

The passage concludes very effectively. The writer uses direct reference to an imposition made by the Turkish authorities, which made it compulsory to wear Western dress. The language and tone of the quotation communicate the point with added effectiveness.

ANSWER TO QUESTION B

We are living in a material world, but you are not a material thing. Even if you were that bony bathing goddess lying on a Mediterranean beach, you know you wouldn't be happy. Sometimes the brochures with the blue skies and the even bluer seas serve only to give you the blues. It's a change of mind that you really want, not a change of scenery. But how do you get what you want, what you really want?

Sri Nisargadatta Maharaj, a guru in India, tells you what you already know: 'You are living in a dream world – seek the truth!'

Enlightenment awaits when you conquer the body and mind. This all-inclusive holiday to India offers you not just a superficial tan, but enables the sun to shine from your very soul as you wallow in a form of eternal bliss. You've heard the message, but the empirical knowledge is the only one of value. Seek!

This magazine also offers you tape-recorded conversations with Sri Nisargadatta Maharaj in the best-selling book *I Am That* for the special price of €10.99.

Home and identity: Text 2

ANSWERS TO QUESTION A

1. The writer speaks about the subject of identity and belonging in the following points: he draws attention to the moral obtuseness underlying racist behaviour in the anecdote about the television programme *Family Feud*. He goes on to question the importance of our identity by commenting on the size of the planet Earth, which 'resembles nothing so much as a single cell in the human body'. Having stated that the planet on which we live may be little more 'than a specimen on a slide', the writer proceeds to ask the question: How does this affect our notions of home and race?

The writer goes on to contend that home is where you would prefer to be when you are in a position to go anywhere in the world. He concludes by stating that home is the place we belong and where we find our identity. Home is the earth we explore, the people we live with and try to love in spite of their faults, the ability to pioneer the road we have undertaken no matter what situation we are in and the realisation that 'wherever there is life, we are at home'.

2. The passage is an effective example of persuasive writing. The tone of the passage is subjective. The writer uses personal references together with the subjective 'I' to show his objection to people who espouse racist views. The use of the personal pronoun 'we' is a subtle persuasive device which presupposes the reader's acquiescence in what the writer is contending. For example, phrases such as 'Home is not the place where our possessions and accomplishments are deposited and displayed: it is this earth that we have explored, the heavens we view with awe . . .' take for granted that the reader is agreeing with the arguments or points being made.

The writer uses a colloquial tone in order to address the reader more directly. The passage is structured clearly into a series of sub-sections, which make it easy to follow the writer's train of thought. The use of the anecdote about the television programme is a vivid method of illustrating his point about the destructive impact of racism. The writer also uses several rhetorical questions, another useful device to persuade the reader.

The conclusion of this passage is very effective. The writer first of all presents a negative statement, then reinforces this with a series of affirmations in order to hammer home his point more effectively: 'Home is not the place where our possessions and accomplishments are deposited and displayed – it is this earth . . . it is the willingness to pioneer . . .'. This is a very valuable technique for use in persuasive writing.

Answer to question B

> Mallow Road
> Cork
> 13 July 2008
>
> Dear sir,
>   I would like to draw your attention to the recent edition of *Family Feud* that was broadcast at 8 p.m. on 9 July.
>   I consider the incident involving the two families to be in very poor taste. It was shocking to see that there are people who can behave with such blindness and arrogance towards another group of people. Programmes and references like this serve to do nothing other than undermine the dignity and integrity of the person. In this particular case the people who came out badly were the white family. A programme of this type only highlights the innate ignorance and insensitivity of some people with regard to the real truth about the human person.
>   Perhaps, in the event of being unable to show such issues in a balanced and mature manner, you would refrain from dealing with them in any future programmes.
>   Yours sincerely,
>   Mary McMahon

Home and identity: Text 3
ANSWERS TO QUESTION A

1. The writer illustrates his argument that 'People are places, and places are people' by maintaining that whenever you write about people you also write about a place. He maintains that the best way to describe a place is to make the reader see it.

He goes on to make the statement that the most revealing place of all is the home. He uses the idea of imagining yourself in the home of a complete stranger. He declares that within five minutes you will know what type of person lives there. This will be revealed clearly through the way objects are positioned: the books (or absence of books), furniture and ornaments. The different kinds of tidiness or untidiness will tell you a lot about the person. The writer claims that if you can describe a home correctly you will not need to talk about the type of atmosphere in it because the description will have done this for you. To illustrate the power of accurate description he uses a graphic image, showing how your reader will be able to make an inference between the image of a man swaying on a windowsill ten storeys up and the same man sitting on the ground.

The writer concludes by stating that we are not 'exclusively the creatures of our economic environment'. It is people who make a home and not the opposite. He cites some familiar examples to support this statement. We make impersonal places, such as offices and factories, bear the imprint of our personality by putting pictures on the wall or by displaying gold pens or 'executive toys'.

2. Yes, I believe that the writer argues his position clearly. He begins with a short, terse sentence that introduces his main argument: 'People are places, and places are people.' A variety of sentence structure is used to develop the argument that we can determine the atmosphere of a place from its description.

Each paragraph is clearly laid out and easy to follow. The writer sets out the topic or main sentence at the beginning of each paragraph. The first paragraph develops the argument by addressing the reader directly in a colloquial tone: 'This isn't meant to dazzle you with its originality: it's simply another working rule.' In the following paragraphs the topic sentences are developed and expanded by means of effective and apt analogies. The second paragraph opens with the statement that 'The most revealing place of all is the home.' To develop this statement the writer uses the argument about being in the home of a complete stranger and how we can make a judgment on what type of person he or she is. The examples used are simple and accessible – the novel description of different types of tidiness and untidiness, the positioning of material things. The concluding paragraph also makes use of familiar and relevant examples, such as the type of accessories one can accumulate in a place of work, whether pictures on the wall, gold pens or 'trendy executive toys'.

ANSWER TO QUESTION B

Hello, and welcome to this special edition of *Empire*. Today we are going to take a peek into the private life and home of none other than Jack Nicholson. The world-famous actor now lives in Los Angeles, where his new three-storey villa is some sight!

Let's start with the outside. The front gates form part of an enormous electric fence, with two security cameras and a tough-looking bodyguard. The long drive up to the house is interesting, filled with exotic plants and luxurious smells. The garden looks like something from ancient Rome, with its two Jacuzzis and its enormous pool surrounded by magnificent marble statues.

Inside this large and lavish house we gain another insight into the type of man Jack Nicholson is through the existence of a small but significant detail: a striking oak cabinet in the front hall. Here we are confronted with not one but two Academy Awards and numerous Golden Globes for Nicholson's many starring roles.

The hall and dining room are filled with prestigious masterpieces, such as works by Van Gogh and Picasso.

The large drawing room contains an amazing view over the lake and in the centre of the parquet floor lies a large leopard-skin rug. The seats are made of black Italian leather and make it enormously difficult to emerge from them once you sink into their luxurious folds. Certainly this home is worth a visit to see how the other half lives!

Home and identity: Text 4
Answers to question A

1. The lifestyle suggested to me by this collection of images is one of wealth. The image of the old mansion, together with the pictures of antiques and a horse, suggest a country estate of grandeur and elegance.

2. This lifestyle is suggested by the various pictures, such as the horse, the binoculars which are obviously old and precious and the two dogs that lie indolently on each side of the picture. The picture of the woman with pearls suggests a person of wealth.

3. The type of publication that would show such images is a 'country life' magazine such as *Town and Country* or *Horse and Hound*. Such publications are aimed at a very selective readership, including rich landowners, aristocratic families and other wealthy people.

4. Introductory paragraph for the magazine *Horse and Hound*:

Set in the heart of Connemara, the ancient castle of Ballyglunin Park lies secluded on its own grounds of several thousand acres. The River Cloon flows through the grounds. Stretching out beyond the huge grounds at the back are the splendid stables, which shelter many of the finest thoroughbreds this area has ever seen. The castle itself is famous for its distinctively wide hallway, containing a splendid stained-glass window. This carries the date 1415, the year in which it was taken over by its previous owners, the Butlers. The present owners, the O'Brien family, are renowned for their great love of animals. Once a year Ballyglunin Park opens its doors to host the annual Antique Fair, an event that draws people from all over the country. This castle and its heritage are something we can all take pride in.

ANSWER TO QUESTION B

9 Laurence Terrace
Huntstown
Co. Limerick
14 December 2008

Ms Marie Heraughty
Graphic Design Centre
Arch Row
Belfast

Dear Ms Heraughty,

I am planning to compile a photo gallery of things that are important to me and that I have accumulated throughout my life.

I have been given your name by a friend of mine who has praised your expertise in this area. I wish to include some pictures that would show an image of happiness and success. For that reason, perhaps you could include some large maps of the world to show that I have travelled a great deal. I would also like you to include pictures of my home and family, in particular a picture of my youngest daughter.

Could you contact me at the above address or by phone (061) 2276893 to let me know whether this is possible?

Yours sincerely,
Joan Dunne

Paper II

Paper II, the literature paper, is divided into three sections: fiction, drama and poetry. Each of these sections is dealt with separately below.

Examination Technique in Paper II

8

Students are required to study:
1. *One text* on its own from the following texts:

AUSTEN, Jane	*Pride and Prejudice*
BRONTË, Emily	*Wuthering Heights*
KINGSOLVER, Barbara	*The Poisonwood Bible*
MILLER, Arthur	*Death of a Salesman*
SHAKESPEARE, William	*Macbeth*

   All these texts are discussed in this book.

2. *Three other texts* from the list below, in a comparative manner, according to the comparative modes prescribed for this course.

   Any texts from the list below, other than the one already chosen for study on its own, may be selected for the comparative study.

   A film may be studied as one of the three texts in a comparative study. The comparative modes for examination in 2007 at Higher Level are:

   (i) general vision or viewpoint

   (ii) theme or issue

   (iii) cultural context.

Texts prescribed for comparative study for examination in 2007
(texts marked with an asterisk are discussed in this book)

ATWOOD, Margaret	*Cat's Eye**
AUSTEN, Jane	*Pride and Prejudice**

BRANAGH, Kenneth (Dir.)	*Henry V* (film)*
BRONTË, Emily	*Wuthering Heights**
CAREY, Peter	*True History of the Kelly Gang*
CHEVALIER, Tracy	*Girl with a Pearl Earring*
COETZEE, J. M.	*Boyhood: Scenes from Provincial Life*
DEANE, Seamus	*Reading in the Dark*
DESAI, Anita	*Fasting, Feasting*
DEVLIN, Anne	*After Easter*
ELIOT, George	*Silas Marner**
FRAYN, Michael	*Spies*
HADDON, Mark	*The Curious Incident of the Dog in the Night-time*
IVORY, James (Dir.)	*A Room with a View* (film)*
JOHNSTON, Jennifer	*How Many Miles to Babylon?*
JOYCE, James	*Dubliners*
KEANE, John B.	*Sive*
KINGSOLVER, Barbara	*The Poisonwood Bible**
LEE, Laurie	*A Moment of War*
LIVELY, Penelope	*Moon Tiger*
LUMET, Sydney (Dir.)	*Twelve Angry Men* (film)*
McCABE, Eugene	*Death and Nightingales**
MILLER, Arthur	*Death of a Salesman**
MOORE, Brian	*Lies of Silence*
NAIPAUL, V. S.	*An Area of Darkness*
O'BRIEN, Kate Cruise	*The Homesick Garden*
O'CASEY, Seán	*Juno and the Paycock*
PATCHETT, Ann	*Bel Canto*
RADFORD, Michael (Dir.)	*Il Postino* (film)*
SHAKESPEARE, William	*Macbeth**
	*Twelfth Night**
	*As You Like It**
SHERIDAN, Jim (Dir.)	*My Left Foot* (film)*
TAYLOR, Mildred	*The Road to Memphis*
TÓIBÍN, Colm	*The Blackwater Lightship*
TYLER, Anne	*A Slipping-Down Life*
WEIR, Peter (Dir.)	*Witness* (film)*
WILDE, Oscar	*The Importance of Being Earnest*
YOSHIMURA, Akira	*Shipwrecks*

3. Shakespearean drama
    At Higher Level a play by Shakespeare must be one of the texts chosen. This can be studied on its own or as an element in a comparative study.

4. Poetry
   A selection from the poetry of the following eight poets is prescribed for the Higher Level examination in 2007:
   BISHOP
   DONNE
   ELIOT
   FROST
   KAVANAGH
   MONTAGUE
   PLATH
   YEATS
   Students will be expected to have studied at least six of the prescribed poems by each poet.

Prescribed texts for examination in 2008

Students are required to study:

1. *One text* on its own from the following texts:

BRONTË, Emily	*Wuthering Heights*
ISHIGURO, Kazuo	*The Remains of the Day*
McCABE, Eugene	*Death and Nightingales*
MILLER, Arthur	*The Crucible*
SHAKESPEARE, William	*Othello*

   All these texts are discussed in this book.

2. *Three other texts* from the list below, in a comparative manner, according to the comparative modes prescribed for this course.
   Any texts from the list below, other than the one already chosen for study on its own, may be selected for the comparative study.
   A film may be studied as one of the three texts in a comparative study. The comparative modes for examination in 2008 at Higher Level are:
   (i) theme or issue
   (ii) cultural context
   (iii) literary genre.

Texts prescribed for comparative study for examination in 2008
(texts marked with an asterisk are discussed in this book):

BRANAGH, Kenneth (Dir.)	*Much Ado About Nothing* (film)*
BRONTË, Emily	*Wuthering Heights**
CAREY, Peter	*True History of the Kelly Gang*
COETZEE, J. M.	*Boyhood: Scenes from Provincial Life*

DEANE, Seamus	*Reading in the Dark*
DESAI, Anita	*Fasting, Feasting*
DEVLIN, Anne	*After Easter*
FRAYN, Michael	*Spies*
FRIEL, Brian	*Philadelphia, Here I Come!*
HADDON, Mark	*The Curious Incident of the Dog in the Night-time*
HAMILTON, Hugo	*The Speckled People*
HARDY, Thomas	*Under the Greenwood Tree*
ISHIGURO, Kazuo	*The Remains of the Day**
JOHNSTON, Jennifer	*How Many Miles to Babylon?*
JOYCE, James	*A Portrait of the Artist as a Young Man*
KINGSLOVER, Barbara	*The Poisonwood Bible**
LUHRMANN, Baz (Dir.)	*Strictly Ballroom* (film)*
LUMET, Sydney (Dir.)	*Twelve Angry Men* (film)*
MACLEOD, Alistair	*No Great Mischief*
MARTEL, Yann	*Life of Pi*
McCABE, Eugene	*Death and Nightingales**
MILLER, Arthur	*The Crucible**
MONK KIDD, Sue	*The Secret Life of Bees*
MOORE, Brian	*Lies of Silence*
NAIPAUL, V. S.	*An Area of Darkness*
O'CASEY, Seán	*The Plough and the Stars*
O'CONNOR, Frank	*My Oedipus Complex and Other Stories*
PATCHETT, Ann	*Bel Canto*
SHAKESPEARE, William	*Othello**
	*Hamlet**
	*As You Like It**
SHERIDAN, Jim (Dir.)	*My Left Foot* (film)*
SHIELDS, Carol	*Unless*
TÓIBÍN, Colm	*The Blackwater Lightship*
TORNATORE, Guisseppe (Dir.)	*Cinema Paradiso* (film)*
WEIR, Peter (Dir.)	*The Truman Show* (film)*
WILDE, Oscar	*The Importance of Being Earnest*
WOLFF, Tobias	*Old School*
YOSHIMURA, Akira	*Shipwrecks*

3. Shakespearean drama
    At Higher Level, a play by Shakespeare must be one of the texts chosen. This can be studied on its own or as an element in a comparative study.

4. Poetry
    A selection from the poetry of the following eight poets is prescribed for the Higher Level examination in 2008:

BOLAND
DONNE
FROST
LARKIN
MAHON
MONTAGUE
PLATH
RICH

Students will be expected to have studied at least six of the prescribed poems by each poet.

PRESCRIBED TEXTS FOR EXAMINATION IN 2009

Students are required to study:
1. *One text* on its own from the following texts:

ATWOOD, Margaret	*Cat's Eye*
BARKER, Pat	*Regeneration*
BRONTË, Charlotte	*Jane Eyre*
MILLER, Arthur	*The Crucible*
SHAKESPEARE, William	*Macbeth*

All these texts are discussed in this book.

2. *Three other texts* from the list below, in a comparative manner, according to the comparative modes prescribed for this course.
    Any texts from the list below, other than the one already chosen for study on its own, may be selected for the comparative study.
    A film may be studied as one of the three texts in a comparative study. The comparative modes for examination in 2009 at Higher Level are:
    (i)   theme or issue
    (ii) general vision and viewpoint
    (iii) cultural context.

Texts prescribed for comparative study for examination in 2009
(texts marked with an asterisk are discussed in this book):

ATWOOD, Margaret	*Cat's Eye**
BANVILLE, John	*Kepler*
BARKER, Pat	*Regeneration**
BARNES Julian	*Arthur and George*
BECKETT, Samuel	*Waiting for Godot*
BINCHY, Maeve	*Circle of Friends*
BRONTË, Charlotte	*Jane Eyre*

CHATWIN, Bruce	*In Patagonia*
DESAI, Anita	*Fasting, Feasting*
FRAYN, Michael	*Spies*
FRIEL, Brian	*Philadelphia, Here I Come!*
GAGE, Eleni	*North of Ithaka*
HADDON, Mark	*The Curious Incident of the Dog in the Night-time*
HAMILTON, Hugo	*The Speckled People*
HARDY, Thomas	*Under the Greenwood Tree*
JOYCE, James	*The Portrait of the Artist as a Young Man*
LESSING, Doris	*The Grass is Singing*
LONCRAINE, Richard (Dir.)	*Richard III* (film)*
LUHRMANN, Baz (Dir.)	*Strictly Ballroom* (film)*
MACLEOD, Alistair	*No Great Mischief*
MALOUF, David	*Fly Away Peter*
MARTEL, Yann	*Life of Pi*
McDONAGH, Martin	*The Lonesome West*
MILLER, Arthur	*The Crucible* *
MONK KIDD, Sue	*The Secret Life of Bees*
NGOZI ADICHIE, Chimamanda	*Purple Hibiscus*
O'CASEY, Seán	*The Plough and the Stars*
O'CONNOR, Frank	*My Oedipus Complex and Other Stories*
O'DONNELL, Damien (Dir.)	*Inside I'm Dancing* *
PATCHETT, Ann	*Bel Canto*
REED, Carol (Dir.)	*The Third Man* *
SEIERSTAD, Åsne	*The Bookseller of Kabul*
SHAKESPEARE, William	*Macbeth* *
	The Tempest *
SHIELDS, Carol	*Unless*
TORNATORE, Guisseppe (Dir.)	*Cinema Paradiso* (film)*
TWAIN, Mark	*The Adventures of Huckleberry Finn*
WEIR, Peter (Dir.)	*The Truman Show* (film)*
WOLFF, Tobias	*Old School*

3. Shakespearean drama
   At Higher Level, a play by Shakespeare must be one of the texts chosen. This can be studied on its own or as an element in a comparative study.

4. Poetry
   A selection from the poetry of the following eight poets is prescribed for the Higher Level examination in 2009:
   BISHOP
   KEATS

LARKIN
LONGLEY
MAHON
MONTAGUE
RICH
WALCOTT

Students will be expected to have studied at least six of the prescribed poems by each poet.

EXAMINATION TECHNIQUE IN PAPER II

1. The total number of marks required for Paper II is 200, or 50 per cent.
2. The time allowed for Paper II is three hours and 20 minutes.
3. You must answer from four different sections:
   - one question on a single text (total marks: 60)
   - one question on a comparative study of texts (total marks: 70)
   - one question on prescribed poetry (total marks: 50)
   - questions on an unseen poem (total marks: 20).
4. Divide your time in the following way:
   - the single text: 60 minutes
   - the comparative study of texts: 70 minutes
   - the prescribed poetry: 50 minutes
   - the unseen poetry: 15 minutes.
5. Give yourself five minutes to read back over the paper and to check your answers against the questions asked. *Do not exceed this time.* Remember, good time-keeping in an examination is essential in order to gain the necessary marks. *You will not receive extra marks by writing beyond the time.*
6. Attempt all sections of the paper.
7. Remember, you must answer a question on Shakespearean drama, either as a single text or as part of a comparative study.

ANSWERING LITERATURE QUESTIONS

1. Do the question that you find easiest first. This will cause you to peak; it will boost your confidence and help you with the other sections.
2. Do not rush at answering questions. Spend time working out the implications of the question. Make sure you clearly understand what is being asked in the question. To do this, analyse or decode every aspect of the question.
3. Know the difference between such terms as 'justify', 'analyse', 'discuss', 'compare', 'contrast', 'evaluate', 'assess', 'comment', 'paraphrase'.
4. Remember, you don't have to agree with the question that is asked. Clearly show what stance you are taking on the question. Use evidence from your text(s) to support your stance on the question.

5. Rephrase the question in your own words. It can help to formulate it as a direct question: for example, '*Silas Marner* explores the effects of obsession for money and the need for human love' can be rephrased as 'How are the issues of obsession with money and the need for human loved developed in the novel *Silas Marner*?'

6. Draw a circle around the main points of the question and begin to organise a rough draft.

7. Brainstorm the topic. Use trigger questions: how? why? where? when?

8. Begin by *answering* the question asked. Your opening paragraph should simply make a *firm* and *clear* statement on the question that is asked.

9. Use the present tense in your answer. Use modern English as much as you can.

10. Give yourself time to look back over the answers. Check your answer for irrelevant statements, incoherent argument and repetition of ideas.

11. Before you construct a paragraph in your answer, consider:
    - What is the topic sentence or main idea of this paragraph?
    - What relationship does this paragraph have to the question?
    - Are the ideas in the paragraph given support through evidence or quotation?
    - Does the concluding paragraph tie up all the ideas and refer back to the question?

Remember in each paragraph to refer to what is being asked in the question and remember that each paragraph in your answer has to advance your argument to another stage. Each paragraph is a logical stage in a coherent and developing argument. If the paragraph doesn't have a bearing or relationship to the question, then discard it.

Features of a good answer on literature

1. A unity of impression. All paragraphs relate to one another and to the topic in general. The concluding paragraph must synthesise or tie up all the preceding ideas and arguments.

2. Answers that focus on what is asked, that don't beat around the bush, digress or introduce material that is irrelevant.

3. A style that is familiar and clear to your reader. Remember that you are communicating with, not impressing, your reader. Avoid:
   - awkward syntax
   - long-winded sentences
   - repetition
   - the self-conscious 'I think', 'I hope to prove that', 'I feel I have shown that'. These are redundant and weaken your argument. A good literature essay does not need such statements – it should speak for itself.

4. A clear understanding of the question asked. The opening paragraph must focus your position on the question and show the direction your answer will take.

5. An individual or personal response. Don't rehash notes or critiques – make the answer your own. Support what you say by reference to or quotation from the text.

6. A maturity of response. Answers in the literature section must show that you have evaluated all sides and are presenting an objective, balanced and coherent answer.

7. A structured and organised argument, with supporting evidence that leads logically to a conclusion. Good essays make progress – they advance an argument, explore an issue and arrive at a conclusion.

Incorporating quotations in answers

Every question on the literature paper requires reference to or quotation from the text. Quotations must be positioned in such a way that they play a central role in advancing your argument. The length of quotations must be appropriate to the point being made – give as many words from the text as are strictly relevant to your point – no more and no less. You must explain the relevance of a quotation, i.e. how this quotation relates to the point or points being made.

Use a colon or comma to introduce a quotation. 'The novel *Dubliners* represents many instances of male violence. For example, in one story, 'Counterparts', we learn that Farrington, a young man, "aches to revel in violence" and that "the indignities of life enrage him".'

THE STUDY OF A SINGLE TEXT

The questions in the exam will take for granted that you have acquired a thorough knowledge of the novels or plays you have studied. This means you must:
- know the main features or characteristics of the central characters well
- study the plot and how it develops in the text
- know how language and imagery are used to serve the writer's purpose
- study the principal quotations that describe the motivation of the characters, and the attitude of the writer to the characters and to the issues that are treated in the text.

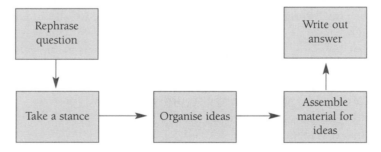

How to answer the question on the study of a single text

HOW TO ANSWER A QUESTION ON THE STUDY OF A SINGLE TEXT

1. Rephrase the question. Sometimes it can help to formulate the task as a direct question.
2. Take a definite stance on the question. Decide clearly whether you agree, partly agree or disagree with the question. You are free to take whatever stance you like, as long as you support it clearly with evidence and reference to the text.

3. Your opening paragraph should state clearly, in one or two sentences, your position on the question and the direction your essay will take.

4. Begin to organise your ideas before you start to write the essay. Jot down several points – six or seven – in note form. These will deal with different aspects of the question and will be constructed in paragraphs. The diagram on the previous page illustrates these points more clearly.

The Comparative Study of Texts

9

A comparative study of texts (play, novel or film) means the ability to focus on similarities or differences between texts, under such headings as:
- the genre and techniques used by the writer
- the treatment of different issues or themes
- the social or cultural background or context
- the general vision or outlook of the text.

The genre of a text (2008 exam)
Is the text:
- a tragic play?
- a romantic novel?
- an autobiography?
- a travel book?

Plot and sub-plot
A plot is the sequence of events that happen in a story. A sub-plot is a lesser story within it, which may reflect the central action of the text.

Soliloquy
A soliloquy is a speech made by a character when alone; it is often an insight into the soul of a character.

Narrative technique
This is the way the story is told in the text. A story can be told in the *first person* or *third person*. In first-person narration the story is told from the point of view of the writer or narrator ('I'). In third-person narration the writer has an overview of the whole story,

like an uninvolved outsider who observes events.

Themes or issues (2007, 2008 and 2009 exams)

This is the central message presented by the writer, for example the themes of evil and the supernatural world in *Macbeth* or the theme of revenge and passion in *Wuthering Heights*. At Higher Level you must examine how a theme is developed in the text and what the writer's approach to it is.

Cultural context or social background (2007, 2008 and 2009 exams)

The setting of a text includes the physical or geographical background, for example rural Ireland in *Death and Nightingales* or the moors in England in the novel *Wuthering Heights*.

Under the heading 'cultural context or social background', study the text with regard to:

*   its cultural situation
*   social customs, particular traditions or rituals
*   national or class differences
*   beliefs and values held by characters
*   the role of women and men
*   the importance of work in that society
*   religious beliefs and practices
*   power structures and political issues.

Some examples of cultural context are the witch trials in Salem in the 17th century in Miller's play *The Crucible* and England prior to the Industrial Revolution in the novel *Silas Marner*.

The general vision or viewpoint (2007 and 2009 exams)

You should be able to compare and contrast the different ways of looking at life in the text and see whether there is a coherence or lack of coherence between these viewpoints.

ANSWERING A QUESTION ON THE COMPARATIVE STUDY OF TEXTS

1. Know exactly what your three texts for this section are. Take one of these as your main text.
2. Spend time choosing your question. Clearly identify what exactly you are asked in the question: is it a question on themes or issues, genre, or on cultural context and social background?
3. Begin by working on a rough draft. Work with the main text first. Jot down five or six different points related to the question based on that text. In each point make sure to have a quotation or reference related to that point.
4. Write out your answer in draft form, using the main text only.
5. Look at the other two texts and draw in the main points of each text, showing how they compare or contrast. You can do this in two ways: add on some ideas from the two texts to each paragraph or simply write a separate paragraph on each text,

outlining how it is related to the question.

6. All the material from your texts must be tied in to your answer in a fluid and natural way. Don't divide your answer into sub-headings with the title of the texts at the top. The main thing is to link or weave in the texts naturally and to show how they relate to the question, jotting down all points of comparison or contrast between the texts.

7. Organise your points into paragraphs and make sure you have used quotation from or reference to the texts as much as possible.

8. Prioritise and order your points and make sure each point refers in some way to the question asked.

9. Start writing the answer and stop at the end of each paragraph to examine what relevance it has to the question.

DRAFT QUESTIONS AND SAMPLE ANSWERS

In the following examples, the method of organising and assembling material for an answer on the comparative question is shown in rough draft form. There are sample questions on cultural context, literary genre, theme and general vision or viewpoint. Study the method carefully and try to apply it to the possible types of questions on the comparative section, which you are studying.

The following is a short extract from a sample question on cultural context. Even though you may not be studying these actual texts for your examination, pay close attention to the *method* used in this answer and in particular the commentary at the conclusion.

Sample question and answer on cultural context

Compare the societies in each of the texts you have studied for your comparative question from the viewpoint of the degree of personal freedom allowed to its members.

Opening paragraph
The texts I propose to discuss for this answer are: *The Remains of the Day*, written by Kazuo Ishiguro, the film *My Left Foot*, directed by Jim Sheridan, and the Shakespearean play *Macbeth*.

Paragraph 2
The societies represented in the three texts are all noticeably different. There are people within the different societies of each text who use their freedom in a particular way. In all instances, this freedom within the individuals is conditioned and affected by the particular society or environment which surrounds them.

Paragraph 3
On the one hand, the society which is represented in the novel *The Remains of the Day* is England in the period spanning 1922–1956. It is a time when the large old English houses with their lords and ladies flourished. **In contrast**, the type of

society represented in the film *My Left Foot* is working-class Dublin in the early twentieth century, **while** the particular society which is shown in the play *Macbeth* is war-torn Scotland in the early seventeenth century.

In the case of the novel, *The Remains of the Day*, narrated by Stevens, a butler, we gain an insight into life inside a large British house in the early twentieth century. Life revolved around the walls of this house for Stevens. As he frequently states in the novel, he has had the privilege of seeing the best of England from within these walls. Undivided loyalty and service to Lord Darlington is the primary motivating factor for Stevens. **On the other hand,** working-class society of Dublin in the 1950s forms the background of the story in the film *My Left Foot*. Christy Brown is born into a large family and forced to live in extremely cramped conditions as well as having to deal with physical disability in the form of cerebral palsy. He spends much of his early years huddled under the staircase and moving in a confined space. **In contrast to both texts**, the play *Macbeth* shows us a man who is governed by the latent ambition to become king. Macbeth attains enormous and undoubted prestige because of his loyalty and valor in serving Scotland as a soldier. However, it is clear that in spite of his success and achievements, Macbeth is not free. His mind hungers for kingship.

COMMENT

This is *not* a complete answer to a comparative question – it shows how to structure the opening paragraph and how to develop the points in the following two paragraphs. A full answer would need about five or six paragraphs with a clear conclusion.

Sample question and answer on genre

Compare and contrast the ways in which the stories are told in the different texts on your comparative course.

The three texts I have studied as part of my comparative course are *Witness*, directed by Peter Weir, the novel *How Many Miles to Babylon?* by Jennifer Johnston and the play *Philadelphia, Here I Come!* by Brian Friel.

The genre of each text is different as one is a film, another is a novel and the third text is a play. Each text is written through a different medium and makes use of different techniques to convey the central purpose of its creator, whether director, novelist or playwright.

In my opinion, Weir has the most freedom and makes the best use of his chosen medium to tell his story. Because *Witness* is a film, it is not as reliant as the other two texts on dialogue only. Weir makes maximum use of such techniques as music, lighting, camera angles and symbols to tell the story in this text. **In contrast to** the film, the play uses different episodes to narrate the story of Gar O'Donnell's attempts to leave Ballybeg for Philadelphia. Dialogue and stage directions are used to tell the story in the play and **these contrast** with Weir's techniques.

On the other hand, the novel is told through extended flashback. In fact,

Johnston uses the opening chapter as the conclusion of her story. This method **contrasts with** the other two texts.

Similarly, symbols become a powerful method used in each of the texts. **All three texts are linked** in the way in which they use symbols to develop the story.

COMMENT

This answer is only an extract of a full answer on genre. The important thing to note is that every time you make a point about the genre of a particular text, you **must** use a linking device or phrase. The linking devices used in this extract are highlighted in bold.

Sample question and answer on theme

Discuss how a certain theme has played an important part in the texts you have studied as part of your comparative course.

The three texts I have studied as part of my comparative course are the film *Witness*, directed by Peter Weir, the novel *How Many Miles to Babylon?* by Jennifer Johnston and the play *Juno and the Paycock* by Seán O'Casey.

The theme that plays a dominant part in all three texts is war and violence. From the outset, the novel *How Many Miles to Babylon?* introduces the reader to a situation where the narrator, Alec, is facing his imminent execution for disobedience. **In the same way,** violence looms large early on in the film *Witness*. Samuel, a young Amish boy, is exposed to the brutal murder of a police officer in the bathroom of a train station. **Similarly,** in the opening scene in *Juno and the Paycock*, we hear about the Irish Civil War and how Mrs Tancred's son was found on the road riddled with bullet wounds.

War and violence are frightening realities **in all three texts**. Casey introduces his audience to a true Irish patriot in the figure of Johnny Boyle, who has lost an arm in battle and still possesses a burning desire to fight for his country: 'Ireland only half free will never be at peace.' **Contrasting sharply with this** is the apathy about the war shown in the figure of Alec in *Babylon*. He is being forced to fight for a cause he 'neither understands or cares about'. **The same** anti-war attitude is shown in *Witness* when Eli blatantly condemns war as being wrong: 'It is wrong to take life, only for God to do.' Eli is adhering to the regulations of his faith, **while** Johnny is driven by a love for his country. Alec, **however,** neither cares for country nor religion and yet suffers profoundly as a result of war and violence.

COMMENT

Note that each text makes a different comment on war and violence. The extract above links the points by means of different linking words, which are all highlighted in bold.

Sample question and answer on general vision or viewpoint
Compare and contrast the general vision in the texts you have studied for your comparative course.

> The three texts I have studied as part of my comparative course are the film *Inside I'm Dancing*, directed by Damien O'Donnell, the play *The Crucible* by Arthur Miller and the novel *The Remains of the Day* by Kazuo Ishiguro.
>
> **All three texts differ greatly** in their general vision or viewpoint. The film represents a situation of two modern young boys who fight against their disability and try to express their freedom in society as young men. It is a positive outlook on life and shows the deep need for friendship and love in human beings. **Similarly,** the novel shows the same desire to be loved and understood. In the figure of Stevens, the stiff British butler, we see how emotional regression causes a great deal of anguish, but at the same time he acknowledges his need for love and companionship. **In contrast to these two texts**, the general vision inherent in the play *The Crucible* is deeply negative and sombre. In the small, biased community of Salem, there are connotations of deep prejudice and injustice. This vision permeates the whole text and **contrasts with** the warmth and humanity which colours the other two texts at various stages.

COMMENT
Note the linking devices above. These must be used to draw a point of similarity or difference between your texts.

It is important to note that general vision is not the same as theme or issues. General vision is the overall attitude of the writer or director to human life and humankind in the text. This attitude can change within the text, but it must be identified as either positive or negative or even both at some stages.

Finally, clearly mention the names of all three texts together with the author/director in your opening paragraph.

POSSIBLE TYPES OF QUESTIONS ON THE COMPARATIVE STUDY OF TEXTS

Literary genre (2008 exam)
1. Take three different texts on your course and show how each writer uses a different method to tell the story.
2. Compare three different texts under one of the following headings:
   * tragedy
   * social realism
   * romance.
3. With regard to three different texts on your course, discuss the various methods used by each writer in the opening of their texts. In your answer, concentrate on the relationship between the opening and conclusion in each one and discuss which you consider to be most effective.

Themes or issues (2008 and 2009 exams)
1. Show how your understanding of a particular theme or issue has been deepened or changed from the study of three different texts on your course.
2. Compare and contrast the issue or theme of self-discovery in any three texts on your course.
3. In three different texts on your course, take one central theme or issue treated by the writer. In the case of each text, show how this theme or issue has been developed or treated by the writer.

Cultural context (2007, 2008 and 2009 exams)
1. With regard to three different texts on your course, show the difference between the value system presented by each writer. State which text you consider to be the most effective and why.
2. 'Racism forms part of the cultural background of many of the texts on your course.' In the case of three different texts, discuss how this issue is treated.
3. Take one central character from three different texts on your course. In the case of each one, outline how the cultural context of each text has influenced that character. Which text do you consider to be the most effective? Give your reasons why.

General vision or viewpoint (2007 and 2009 exams)
1. Show how the general vision or viewpoint in the texts you have studied as part of your comparative course is or is not related to the actual events which occur in the texts.
2. Compare the general vision or viewpoint in the texts you have studied for your comparative course under one of the following headings:
   * optimistic
   * pessimistic
   * unexpected.
3. Identify the general vision in the texts you have studied as part of your comparative course. In your opinion, which of these was the most interesting? Give reasons for your answer.

10

Notes on Some Prescribed Texts

CAT'S EYE
Margaret Atwood

(2007 exam, comparative study only, and 2009 exam)

The story

The painter Elaine Risley returns to Toronto to attend an art exhibition where her own paintings are on display. When she returns, she begins by wondering what she would tell Cordelia about herself were she to meet her again. Elaine lives in an ordinary house in British Columbia. Her husband, Ben, runs a travel agency that specialises in trips to Mexico and was married before. Elaine has been married twice. Her first husband is called Jon, who is now married again. Jon is an artist who spends some of his time doing special effects for movies. On this visit, Elaine stays in Jon's flat.

The story is told through mingling the past with the present. Atwood is dealing with the past but uses the present tense throughout when she recalls the past.

Elaine announces that she was happy until she moved to Toronto. She recalls how she spent time camping with her brother, Stephen, and her parents before the war. She grew up in the 1940s and remembers details about the war. She also remembers moving to a new house in Toronto, a bungalow built of yellow brick and surrounded by raw mud.

Her father was a university professor in zoology. She attended the Queen Mary Public School and she speaks about how they walked through the freezing mud to school. She made friends with Carol and Grace and talks about growing up and playing games in each other's houses. They spent time fishing with her brother, swimming in the lake and camping.

She remembers the first time she met Cordelia and how she was shy because she felt grubby. Cordelia lived in a two-storey house. Her mother had a woman who cleaned the house for them. Cordelia had been to plays and ballet.

She mentions how Cordelia had endless power over her, and how even now she scans the faces of her own daughters for traces of any bullying they might be experiencing.

Her friends, including Cordelia, begin to tell her she is not normal and that they are doing this for her own good. She comments on the fact that hatred would have been easier to feel, as it's clearer. She got sick more often because of the 'so-called friends'. After a time, she moved away from them for the summer when her family went to a rented cabin in Lake Superior and began to relax.

In the chapter entitled 'Cat's Eye', she mentions how she did a series of paintings about her mother, entitled *Pressure Cooker*, before she died, describing the way her mother cooked in the 1940s.

When she returned from holidays in September, Cordelia had become more ruthless and relentless.

Elaine kept the cat's eye (a marble) in her pocket, as valuable as a jewel. Cordelia's bullying ways have become subtler. Elaine's mother begins to notice things and tells her to 'stand up for herself, to have backbone'.

Elaine mentions a visit from Princess Elizabeth and says she saw her as brave and heroic. People waved their Union Jacks.She began to learn art in school but she felt that her drawings were inadequate. At this stage she is only ten.

Her mother told her about Catholics and the Blessed Virgin and doing something rebellious, such as praying to the Blessed Virgin. Elaine knows that telling the truth about Cordelia is unthinkable for her. She gets sick one day when she is forced into a gorge to collect her hat and nearly gets frostbite. She has an image of the Blessed Virgin calling her in a motherly voice and protecting her. After this incident, Elaine decides not to have the three girls as friends. She stops going to Sunday school, refuses to play with them and takes the long way home. She finds a new friend and no longer hears them in her life. At the end of the section entitled 'Our Lady of Perpetual Help', she mentions how she found the strength to stand up to Cordelia.

Elaine moved to Burnham High School and she meets Cordelia again. This time the relationship has changed. Elaine gets on better with boys than girls. Cordelia fails her zoology when she is in her final grade. She does not care. She is forced to move to another school. During the exam, Elaine realises she wants to be a painter. She goes on to study art and architecture in the University of Toronto. She wins a scholarship to the university.

Her art teacher, Mr Hrbik, is a refugee from Europe. She speaks about how the war is far away enough now to be romantic. She speaks about the various characters who are doing the art course with her. Elaine discovers that one of her friends, Susie, is having a love affair with Mr Hrbik. It transpires that Hrbik is a divorced man from Hungary. Elaine lives at home while she is in the university. Her brother, Stephen, gets arrested. He is studying astrophysics in California University. He chases butterflies into a military zone and they think he is a spy.

She begins an affair with Hrbik, even though he is still seeing Susie. Elaine is afraid Susie will find out about the affair. Cordelia has run away from home. Cordelia has got a job in Stratford working in small parts in plays.

Elaine does not want to remember the past. She says it has become discontinuous, like 'stones skipped across water, like postcards.' As she continues the affair with Josef Hrbik, he begins to speak a bit about his past life and how he shot a man in the head and that he comes from a country that no longer exists. He speaks about going to the United States to direct films.

As she moves back to present-day Toronto, she notices the changes in the environment. There are now lots of opulent restaurants, designer jean emporiums and expensive boutiques in places that were formerly semi-hovels. Susie calls her one night on the phone and Elaine later finds her lying unconscious in bed, covered in blood. She has had an abortion. Elaine abandons Josef shortly after this in contempt. She has her own apartment and Jon lives there two days a week. She discovers she is pregnant. She is upset and contemplates having an abortion, but then thinks of Susie and rejects the thought. She has a child called Sarah. She marries Jon because of the child. Jon is a lapsed Lutheran from Niagara Falls. They are unable to face their adult responsibilities, so they fight. Jon supervises at a co-op graphics studio. He is no longer painting. She begins to paint the Blessed Virgin. They begin to throw things at one another. She organises a show of painting and sculpture with other women.

She meets Cordelia again and finds her much older. She is in the Dorothy Lyndwich Rest Home. She tells Elaine how she took pills and had to have her stomach pumped. She asks Elaine to help her get out of the place. Elaine refuses to help her, but Elaine still has nightmares about Cordelia after this encounter. That was the last time Elaine spoke to Cordelia.

She mentions how she saw Josef's name on a film by accident. Going back to the past, she records Jon's infidelities and how girls made phone calls to him. She is filled with suppressed anger and evasion. Jon fails to come home one night, so she attempts suicide with a knife, slashing her wrists. She decides to leave the city and also leave Jon at the same time. She leaves for Vancouver. She puts Sarah into a pre-school and she does some freelance work. She goes to a shrink for a short time. She begins to meet other women artists and starts painting again. Many of the women in the group are lesbians. She rejects these types of women and refuses to attend their meetings. It reminds her of earlier times when she rejected Cordelia. Eventually she divorces Jon. Her parents come to visit her and they are disappointed. She records how she meets Ben for the first time in the supermarket. She states how years ago she would have considered him too dull and too simple minded. He has made his money in real estate. Shortly after this, she marries him. He is ten years older and also divorced. They have a daughter, Anne.

On the morning of the show, she travels along the row of houses where she grew up with Cordelia. She recalls how her brother, Stephen, died five years ago when the plane he was travelling in was hijacked and he was thrown out by one of the hijackers, and how her parents died within a year of one another.

She begins to speak about one of the paintings called *Cat's Eye*, which is in the exhibition. She describes it as a self-portrait. It includes a half portrait of her head with grey hair and another, younger picture. There are also three small figures of her childhood friends forty years ago against a field of snow. She wonders again about Cordelia and what she would say to her if she were to meet her. Elaine is greeted by a young artist at the exhibition who congratulates her on one of her paintings, called *Falling Women*, and tells her how it summed up an era. Elaine feels relegated to the dust heap with that remark. She gets drunk. She awakes with a hangover and misses the plane. She sees a bridge and remembers the place where she fell into the water and the bank where she scrambled up, and where she heard the voice of the Blessed Virgin. Then she sees the image of Cordelia in her grey snowsuit jacket and green wool knee socks with bangs hanging into her eyes. She sees her defiant face, and Elaine feels the same shame, the same knowledge of her own wrongness and weakness, the same wish to be loved, and the same fear. But she now acknowledges that these are no longer her own emotions but Cordelia's, and it was Cordelia who had the problems, not Elaine herself. Elaine is the older and stronger one now.

The story concludes as she is returning on the plane beside two old ladies. She wonders how old they are. She comments on how they are carefree, and responsibilities have fallen away from them for a short while. Elaine ends by describing a full, clear, moonless night filled with stars which she claims are not eternal.

Themes
Memories
Many of the memories that occur to Elaine in the novel revolve around Cordelia. She is a powerful force in the life of the artist. Cordelia exercised a strong influence on Elaine as a child and managed to bully her successfully. Elaine's memories fluctuate between the past and the present reality of her life in Canada as a famous and successful artist. Through all these memories, she is obsessed by the image of Cordelia, who even in later life exercises an influence over her.

Bullying/childhood
Most of the novel deals with her experiences and relationships as a child. The main memory is that of her relationship with Cordelia and how much she suffered in that relationship. Yet they were both similar and got on very well in later life. Ironically, the relationship reversed. While Cordelia was clearly a bully as a child, Elaine managed to challenge her and in later life was able to be the strong one in the relationship. Elaine never actually confronts Cordelia about the reality and truth of her character and personality and this is what haunts her for a good deal of her life.

Women
Feminism and the desire to express her own individuality through relationships and her art is a central issue in this text.

There are many different types of women represented in this novel. There is the whimsical and fickle picture of Susie, who is involved in an affair with the faithless Hrbik and who later has an abortion, which goes badly wrong.

Then there is the powerful and manipulative Cordelia, who loses her power and influence as she gets older and also loses her focus in life. She ends up as a failure, having been thrown out of many colleges and having achieved nothing with her life. When Elaine meets her for the last time, she is recuperating in a home, having attempted suicide by taking too many pills.

Elaine stands out as the most heroic woman, who courageously faces her past with all its shortcomings. In addition, she faces herself, her own limitations of character, her failed relationships, her misjudgments and her artistic failures or shortcomings. Yet she manages to salvage herself amidst all this self-analysis and self-questioning and at the conclusion she acknowledges how she has overcome the ghosts of her past, particularly the one of Cordelia.

Genre

This is a novel of social realism, which deals with the past. The narrative is interspersed with continuous flashbacks. Atwood repeatedly interrupts the narrative and returns to the present. The effect of this technique is to help Elaine make sense of her past life and to integrate it more fully into her present experiences as a mature artist living in Vancouver.

One of the most striking symbols used in the novel is that of the Cat's Eye. Atwood uses it in different ways. It becomes a means of trying to deal with the difficult areas of her past life, and in particular her experiences with Cordelia. The image of the Virgin Mary is also used symbolically in the novel. She is seen as a maternal and protective force in the life of Elaine as a child.

Cultural context

Twentieth-century Canada forms the backdrop of this novel. Elaine gives an insight into Canada, past and present. She moves back to Canada forty years from the start of her narrative, which is mid-twentieth-century, post-war Canada. We gain an insight into the fact that they sang certain British songs, which shows their allegiance to Britain in that time.

In the figure of Hrbik, she shows the image of the post-war European who had suffered in his native Hungary from war and poverty.

The Canada she returns to visit is changed – there is much more affluence and prosperity. This is evident from the fancy restaurants that she visits, the expensive designer shops and the elaborate types of food and drink. The art world forms an important part of the cultural atmosphere of this novel. In her young days, art was associated with a bohemian lifestyle and a laissez-faire attitude towards convention and order. The present-day art world of Elaine Risley is elegant, wealthy and exclusive. Social convention and lifestyle have changed.

General vision or viewpoint

The general vision and viewpoint gradually unfolds throughout the story. Because the novel is told through a continuous blending of past and present experience, the general vision develops slowly in this text.

Elaine's perceptions about her life, her relationships and her work are largely positive. Even though her experiences have been painful and involved a good deal of suffering, she manages to knit these together and accept them as the story develops. She faces her fears and sufferings from the bullying and even manages to see how

Cordelia, the one who inflicted pain by bullying, was really the empty one who embodied insecurity and fear. The novelist's vision of life and humankind is positive. She shows the need for healing and self-help in our lives, and through the experiences of her leading protagonist, the artist Elaine Risley, Atwood manages to show us how the human spirit can triumph over adversity, even if it takes many years to do so.

SILAS MARNER
George Eliot

(2007 exam)

Historical and literary background
The historical background of this novel is just before the Industrial Revolution in England in the early nineteenth century.

The story
The opening chapter moves from the past to the present by showing us the attitude of the Raveloe people to the profession of the weaver. It also records Marner's treatment by the brethren in Lantern Yard and how he was banished from that community because he was accused of stealing money from an old parishioner. The community in Lantern Yard was a strict Puritan group who judged his guilt on the basis of drawing lots. Marner's best friend, William Dane, a member of this community, betrays him by slandering his reputation and later goes on to marry Marner's girl.

Marner settles on the outskirts of Raveloe, a small village in the heart of England. There he becomes a recluse for fifteen years and spends his time accumulating money by weaving for the local people. In Raveloe there is a rich family by the name of Cass. Squire Cass is an arrogant man who has two weak and dissolute sons, Godfrey and Dunstan. Godfrey is secretly married to a drug addict and they have a child. Dunstan bribes Godfrey and manages to get his horse. He has an accident outside Marner's cottage and steals his gold. Dunstan later dies when he falls into the quarry near the cottage.

Meanwhile, Molly, Godfrey's wife, decides to pay a visit with her child to Raveloe. It is New Year's Eve and Godfrey is having a party to honour Nancy Lammeter, whom he hopes to marry. Molly dies on the way and her child accidentally crawls into Silas's cottage while he is having a cataleptic fit. Silas discovers the child and thinks that it is his gold returned. He decides to adopt the child and bring it up as his own. He christens it Eppie. A local woman, Dolly Winthrop, helps him to manage Eppie.

Godfrey marries Nancy. They are unable to have a child. Eppie grows up and becomes engaged to Dolly's son, Aaron Winthrop.

Dunstan's body is discovered in the quarry with Marner's gold. Godfrey is forced to tell Nancy about his wife and child. They decide to adopt Eppie but she refuses to leave Marner. At the conclusion Eppie marries Aaron.

Themes

- The power of love to redeem.
- Deception and betrayal.
- The strict and rigid nature of Calvinism.
- The self-destructive quality of isolation.

Genre

The novel *Silas Marner* belongs to the genre of social realism. It gives a realistic insight into rural life in England before the onslaught of the Industrial Revolution. Under this heading, also study the following.

The structure of the novel

The first chapter blends past and present and gives us an insight into the reasons why Marner has settled on the outskirts of the village of Raveloe.

The novel is divided into two parts. There is a time lapse of sixteen years between Part I and Part II. This serves the function of showing the development of the plot: Squire Cass is dead, Nancy is married to Godfrey and Eppie is eighteen years old.

There are two plots: a main plot (Marner's story) and a sub-plot (Godfrey's story). These stories parallel one another.

Eliot makes use of the cataleptic fits to develop the plot. It is significant that in Part II, when Marner has attained happiness in loving Eppie, the fits disappear.

Style

The style of the novel is richly symbolic. The names and locations of places are used as symbols. Raveloe, an easy-going place, lies in the rich central plain of Merry England. Lantern Yard is used ironically. It prides itself on being a strong religious community, yet it is a place that offers no light, and significantly at the conclusion when Eppie and Marner return to look for it, it has disappeared.

Eliot makes use of a didactic or moralistic style to teach or instruct on certain issues, such as duty and personal responsibility for one's actions. She also uses this tone to articulate her views on society at that time. For example, when Dunstan goes to tell his father, Squire Cass, about the accident with his horse, we are told how 'Fleet the deer-hound consumed enough bits of beef to make a poor man's holiday dinner.'

The writer makes use of gold as a symbol of love. There are repeated references to Eppie's golden hair, which is obviously intended to replace the stolen gold. Many fairytale motifs are used – the accumulation of the gold by the miserly weaver, the loss of the gold, the recovery of the loss in the form of a child, the villain and the fairy godmother (Dolly).

Cultural context

We gain an insight into the old English way of life before the Industrial Revolution. The novel is set in the days when spinning wheels hummed busily in farmhouses. It celebrates the integrated sense of neighbourliness that was a hallmark of life before the onset of the Industrial Revolution. The whole story spans thirty years of an era of rapid change in England. The conclusion of the story shows the beginnings of industrialisation in England.

The story is set in the period of the Napoleonic wars when the price of agricultural goods was high, so farmers were free to farm badly at their ease. This is particularly the case in the highest social class at that time, the Squirarchy. Eliot attacks this particular class through the figure of Squire Cass and his two dissolute sons, Dunstan and Godfrey.

Class structures are clearly marked out in the novel. Each person has their own place in society and keeps to it. Godfrey, by marrying below his class, has allowed himself to be dragged into mud and slime.

Calvinism is shown in the portrait of Lantern Yard. The insight given in the novel is dark and negative. They profess a belief in revelation and the drawing of lots. This is how justice is exercised within this community. The beliefs and practices of Lantern Yard are shown to be destructive of human fellowship and community.

General vision or viewpoint
The general vision at the conclusion is that the old community life as exemplified in Raveloe is slowly vanishing with the onset of industrialisation. The Industrial Revolution is seen negatively. When Marner and Eppie return to pay a visit to Lantern Yard, they find that everyone is in a hurry. Eppie describes it as 'a dark ugly place. How it hides the sky, it's worse than the Workhouse.' We learn about the cramped conditions of life and the bad smell.

One of Eliot's beliefs was 'as you sow so shall you reap'. Marner sows love and kindness and so he reaps happiness in the figure of Eppie, who in turn is united in marriage to Aaron. Godfrey sows deception and selfishness and so he reaps a marriage that turns out to be childless. The general vision is that one must live with the results of one's deeds and take responsibility for one's actions. The power of love to redeem is also evident at the conclusion.

JANE EYRE
Charlotte Brontë

(2009 exam)

The story
Jane Eyre is an orphan who is thrown upon the protection of relations and living in an out-of-the-way corner of England in a large house called Gateshead Hall. These relatives neglect, mistreat, chastise and abuse her. Jane turns on her persecutors in a fit of rebellion and passion. She is sent to a charitable institution called Lowood. Here in Lowood House she has to prove herself. Through her relationship with Helen Burns and helped by the benign influence of Miss Temple, Jane learns that patience is nobler than passion. She grows up into an independent young woman and takes on the job as teacher in Lowood.

Weary of the monotonous life of a teacher, she advertises for a situation as governess. She becomes engaged as governess to a country gentleman by the name of Mr Rochester who entrusts to her the care of a pretty, frivolous French ward by the name of Adele, the child of an opera dancer. Unknown to Jane, Mr Rochester has kept a lunatic wife on the third floor of Thornfield in the charge of a gin-drinking servant called Grace Poole. The house frequently resounds with demoniac laughter and at one stage the mad wife attempts to burn her husband in his bed. Jane falls in love with Rochester and they decide to get married. On the eve of Jane's marriage, the mad Bertha, as she is called, comes into Jane's room and tears her bridal veil in half.

At the altar steps just before the marriage, Jane discovers that Rochester is already married to Bertha Mason, who lives in Thornfield. She refuses to get married and runs away. She travels across miles of countryside until finally, in a state of exhaustion and near starvation, she drops at the front door of a house. It happens to be the house where three of her cousins live. Shortly after her arrival she discovers that she is the heiress of an uncle who has left her £20,000, which she promptly shares between her three cousins.

One of them, Rev. St John Rivers, is a missionary who proposes settling in India. He urges Jane to accompany him as his wife although clearly he is not in love with her. Jane is on the point of yielding when she hears Rochester's voice calling her. She hastens back to Thornfield where she learns that Rochester's wife has burned it down, killing herself and blinding Rochester. Jane finds Rochester and marries him. He partially recovers his sight and they have a child.

Themes
- The woman.
- Freedom.
- Love.

Genre
The novel belongs to the romance genre. It is written in an autobiographical form and the subjective view of issues presented in the novel firmly sets it within the tradition of romance genre. Brontë constantly parallels inner states and feelings with nature in a highly vivid manner in this novel. Human emotions, moods, internal states and character development are all mirrored in the natural world. She also uses her setting and scenery in a symbolic manner. Jane's character is portrayed from the core of the personality and developed outwards. This development of her inner life and soul is all portrayed against the dynamic backdrop of nature and natural forces.

The novel has elements of the Gothic novel to it, for example, the idea of the mad wife hidden in the attic and the repeated references to supernatural elements, together with the notion of ghosts and goblins, etc.

The structure of the novel
The plot centres on Jane Eyre, the heroine of the book. Strictly speaking the book is divided into five geographical regions:

- Jane's experiences as an orphan at Gateshead Hall.
- Her education at the institution Lowood Hall.
- Her role as governess in Thornfield.
- Her stay at Moor House.
- Her return to Ferndale and her marriage to Rochester.

The plot develops through depicting Jane Eyre's various fluctuations in fortune and how she comes to terms with the difficulties she encounters.

Narrative technique
In the novel Brontë functions as an omniscient consciousness. She controls the entire narrative but her own viewpoint does not intrude. Jane Eyre is the narrator of the story at the same time as being the central consciousness and the heroine. The narrative is told in the first person.

Cultural context
The cultural context of the novel changes because it is set in five different geographical locations. The novel opens in Gateshead Hall, the rich establishment of the Reeds, who have two pampered and spoiled children. There are overtones of a rich indulgence within this house – the rich red draperies, the butler and the footman all depict a pampered and indolent lifestyle. There is a distinct emphasis on social class and it is because of her position as a poor relation that Jane is consigned to the regions of the nursery and made to manage with a candle and the erratic company of Bessie, the nurse.

The cultural context underlying Lowood Hall depicts the enormous harm which was caused by such institutions in Victorian England. We are given some startling insights into the devastation caused by typhus and disease through the number of people who actually died. It is significant that Jane records how things changed in Lowood. The building was reorganised due to the noxious site, corrupt water system, unhealthy food and poor clothing.

We also get an insight into the upper-class system in England through the style of life revealed within Thornfield. The servants' quarters are downstairs while Rochester keeps his mad wife locked away on the third floor of the mansion. There are repeated references to keys and locks, which denote the theme of imprisonment.

When Rochester returns with a company of friends the lifestyle changes. There are dinner parties, riding parties, more fires are lit, new servants are hired and there is a richer abundance of material things in the house. Jane describes some of these guests as similar to 'white plumy birds' because of their attire. These visitors are haughty, elegant, proud, lofty and distinguished, clearly on a different social level from what Jane is used to.

This novel shows us in a realistic way the particular social position of the governess at that time. The governess existed on a mid-point socially between the servants and the middle classes. Thus, Jane is uncomfortable socially during these dinner parties while the Ingrams and such people are presiding. The return to more homely, domestic values is signalled in the portrait given to us of Moor House at the conclusion.

Through vivid depiction of small details we get a look into different cultural levels, from the poor and deprived class to the rich indolence of the upper class, to the sedate and comfortable middle classes. Brontë paints a rich and realistic vision of English life both in the city and country in the early years of the nineteenth century.

General vision or viewpoint

The novel concludes with Jane happily married to Rochester for ten years and the partial recovery of his sight. They also have a child. The general idea here at the conclusion is that after a loveless and isolated existence Jane has eventually found happiness and fulfilment.

Rochester is more humble and less arrogant. He acknowledges that his physical maiming is a just punishment for his earlier deeds. The general vision of both characters at the conclusion is that they have grown and developed. Jane, less dependent on other people now, is totally fulfilled as she offers moral support to Rochester, who, formerly cynical and suspicious of others, is now child-like and dependent.

There is also a commentary given to us about St John Rivers. He zealously pursues his missionary goals and is assured of his salvation having lived a life of faith and charitable works. The implication here is that St John Rivers has not wavered at any stage from his relentless pursuit of what he considers to be good.

WUTHERING HEIGHTS
Emily Brontë

(2007 and 2008 exams)

Historical and literary background

Wuthering Heights was first published in 1847 in England. The Brontës lived in Haworth, Yorkshire. The novel is set against the background of the wild moors of Yorkshire.

The story

The story is told by two narrators, Nelly Dean, the housekeeper at Wuthering Heights, and Lockwood, who takes over as tenant of the Heights. The story spans three generations and is centred on two main houses, Wuthering Heights and Thrushcross Grange. It begins with Old Earnshaw, who has two children, Cathy and Hindley, who live in the Heights. Old Earnshaw returns from Liverpool with a bundle, which turns out to be a boy that he found wandering along the streets. He is called Heathcliff from then on. Hindley and he become bitter enemies. However, Cathy and Heathcliff develop a deep and passionate relationship, spending their time on the moors. One day they accidentally meet the Lintons, who live at Thrushcross Grange. Isabella and her brother Edgar live at the Grange with their parents. Cathy is attacked by their dog and is forced to stay in the Grange until she recovers. Heathcliff is sent home in disgrace.

Cathy returns after several weeks from the Grange a changed woman. She is flattered by the attention from the Lintons, particularly Edgar. She develops a double side to her character. She acknowledges to Nelly Dean that it would shame her to marry Heathcliff and he accidentally overhears a part of her conversation. He leaves the Heights for three years and returns when Catherine has been married to Edgar for three years. Heathcliff is changed. He is filled with revenge. He moves into the Heights, where Hindley lives alone. He gambles and succeeds in gaining all the property from Hindley and robs Hareton, Hindley's son, of his lawful inheritance.

Meanwhile, Isabella develops an infatuation for Heathcliff and elopes with him. Cathy warns her, but in vain. Isabella escapes from Heathcliff shortly after her marriage when she discovers his true nature and settles in London. There she gives birth to a boy who is named Linton. She dies shortly after this. Heathcliff uses young Linton to avenge himself on Edgar and Cathy. Edgar and Cathy also have a child, whom they call Cathy. Shortly after giving birth the elder Cathy dies. Heathcliff tricks young Cathy into marrying young Linton and so gains possession of the Heights. Heathcliff dies at the end a tortured soul who is clearly haunted by the presence of the ghostly Catherine. Lockwood buys the Heights from Heathcliff at the conclusion.

Themes
- Passion and love.
- Betrayal and loyalty.
- Revenge.
- The supernatural.

Genre
This novel belongs to the genre of romance. In the novel Emily Brontë constantly parallels inner states and feelings with nature – human emotions, moods, internal states and character development are all mirrored in the natural world and in particular in the wild moors.

Narrative technique
There are two different narrators: Nelly Dean and Lockwood. Nelly Dean is an ordinary woman who is housekeeper for three generations of the Earnshaws and later on the Linton household. Lockwood is a young man from London with plenty of money and time on his hands who takes over tenancy of the Heights towards the conclusion of the story. Both of these ordinary and readily identifiable narrators tell a story of extraordinary supernatural dimensions. They serve the function of bringing otherwise incredible and unrealistic events within the reader's grasp and understanding. They are used as a means to give this incredible story a foothold in the normal world of everyday affairs.

The narrative technique also makes use of flashback. The first chapter begins at the conclusion and the remainder of the narrative recounts the events of the story through extended flashback. In many respects, the effect of this device in narration is to disorientate the reader and enable them to realise that this story is not dealing with normal life.

Style

The style of *Wuthering Heights* is that of a 'poetic prose'. As Charlotte Brontë, Emily's sister, states in her preface to the novel: 'It is rustic all through. It is Moorish and wild and knotty as the root of heath. Its colouring is of mellow grey and moorland moss clothes; and heath with its blooming bells and balmy fragrance. Her descriptions of natural scenery are what they should be, and all that they should be.'

The novel makes use of many images on a richly symbolic level. Nature is used in a symbolic manner throughout, symbolising strife, discord and moral decay. The storm, thunder and lightning, together with the repeated references to fire, are all used to show the profound depths of violence and heightened passion that dominate the atmosphere.

The actual locations of the two houses mentioned in the novel, Thrushcross Grange and Wuthering Heights, are also used as symbols. The Grange is set in a leafy valley while the Heights is exposed to 'atmospheric tumult' of every kind. The atmosphere within the Heights exudes a profound spiritual degeneration while that in the Grange is civilised and controlled.

Cultural context

The novel is set in nineteenth-century England. We get a vision of two different lifestyles in the Heights and the Grange. The lifestyle in the Heights is wild and uncontrolled. Within the Grange there is rich luxury, 'a splendid place carpeted with crimson, a pure white ceiling bordered by gold, a shower of glass-drops hanging in silver chains from the centre.'

Through the figure of Joseph we gain an insight into the strict harshness of Calvinism. He is a rigid and intransigent figure who spends his time preaching at the children.

Through Nelly Dean we see the role of the housekeeper. In this particular context Nelly is more a mother figure for the children than an actual employee within the house.

General vision or viewpoint

At the conclusion of the novel Heathcliff is ultimately left with power, a power that he finds intolerable and painful. He is consumed with a hell fire, yet refuses to repent. The heaven of others is entirely unvalued and uncoveted by him. His death is explicitly pagan; he wants no minister, no mourners and no prayers to be said for his soul. In Heathcliff's death there is a sense that evil has destroyed itself, that the fire of hatred and destruction that eats its way through his system and through the novel has burned itself out. His power for wickedness has been his punishment, just as his passion for Catherine was a curse, not a blessing. He destroys himself throughout the book, thereby showing how true Isabella's earlier statement is that 'treachery and violence are a double-ended spear, which wound the inflictors more than the sufferers.'

The actual conclusion of the novel gives the reader an image of a happy, harmonious and natural human love. The ending shows the happy marriage of Cathy to Hareton, Heathcliff's revenge plans are frustrated, property is restored to its rightful owners and

Nelly Dean takes delight in her 'children's happiness'. All of this is cleverly juxtaposed with an image of pain, rapture and ghostly phenomena. Two types of love are simultaneously affirmed at the conclusion: the ghostly vision of Heathcliff and Catherine as they wander the moors shows us that in some way they too have attained their heaven, while simultaneously we are given the vision of Hareton and young Cathy in a state of blissful union walking in the moors.

DEATH AND NIGHTINGALES
Eugene McCabe

(2007 exam, comparative study only, and 2008 exam)

The story
The story is set in Fermanagh in the 1880s. It is based on a rich Protestant farmer called Billy Winters. Billy is married to a Catholic woman, but unknown to him their child is illegitimate and not his own. When Billy discovers this fact he abuses his wife and child, Beth. Later on Winters's wife dies. Beth develops into a strong and beautiful woman who becomes attached to a Fenian revolutionary called Liam Ward. She becomes pregnant by him and he persuades her to steal Winters's money and run away with him. Winters discovers her crime and savagely beats her. Beth later on discovers that Liam intends to kill her and steal the money. She prepares to leave with him in a fishing boat. Liam is unable to swim and Beth uses this as a means to revenge herself on him. As they are out in the lake Beth pulls the plug from the bottom of the boat and watches as Liam drowns in front of her eyes. The story concludes with the reconciliation between Beth and Winters. He declares his undying love for her and promises to look after her for the rest of her life.

Themes
- Anglo-Irish relationships.
- Politics.
- Revenge.

Genre
This is a novel of social realism.

Cultural context
The cultural context of this novel is rural Ireland in the 1880s, the time when Parnell ruled in the Ascendency. The novel traces the inbuilt violence between Catholics and Protestants, which was a striking feature of life in that time. There are references to the political volatility and instability of Ireland in the 1880s.

General vision or viewpoint
The general vision of this novel is sombre and grim. Throughout the story there is a strong stress on the divisions within a local community. It is clear that the relationship

between Beth and Winters will never be normal or stable. In many ways, McCabe seems to be using this relationship to show how the various communities in the North will always be divided because of the tragic inheritance from the past.

The Poisonwood Bible
Barbara Kingsolver

(2007 and 2008, comparative study only)

The story

The story is based on one family who settles in the Congo in 1959. The father is a Baptist preacher and they have four girls called Adah, Leah, Rachael and Ruth May. The story deals with the various characters and the experiences each member of the family has during these years in Africa, a time when the Belgians occupied the Congo and did not allow the native Congolese to receive a proper education.

Nathan Price, the father, is a shrill Baptist preacher who dominates his family, particularly his wife, Orleanna. Orleanna Price suffers a great deal in the story. Her youngest daughter, Ruth May, dies shortly after she is bitten by a snake. Nathan is deeply concerned because she was not baptised. The whole story traces the growth and development of each of the family members as well as the corresponding political situation in the country in the years between 1959 and 1986. After eighty years of colonial rule, the Congo celebrates liberation and the corresponding inauguration of a black leader in 1960. We learn about Independence Day and how the blacks regain control of their own country again. Nathan begins to change after the war and becomes a tyrant and conqueror in his own home. He is determined to do the will of God in a strong and mighty way. Orleanna passively submits to him.

Rachael is the first one to leave and settle with a black man called Axelroot, who is involved in a lot of double-dealings and eventually leaves her for another woman. She marries several times and eventually inherits a large hotel called The Equatorial in a place called Brazzaville in the French Congo. She manages to organise and run this in an efficient way for various businessmen. Rachael never marries again and remains there, happy in her job of hotel owner and manager.

Lumumba assumes control as president in the Congo. There is a coup organised to put Mobutu in charge of the entire army. Lumumba manages to escape but is recaptured and badly beaten. He dies shortly after this and Mobutu assumes control in 1961. Things begin to deteriorate in the country, there is little food and the country suffers severely from bad drought. The people begin to change with independence and decide to vote in church about the question of whether Jesus Christ is a personal god. The Congolese are beginning to become used to the whole idea of the democratic process.

Nathan Price is voted out of the church and the people rebel against him. Orleanna leaves with Adah and the father is left alone. He is later attacked by the natives and burned. Leah is brought to a mission run by French nuns. Adah goes to study in Emory University to become a doctor. She remains in Atlanta and continues to do research into unusual viruses. She never marries. Leah marries a coloured man called Anatole and they have four sons. She remains in Zaire, which now has changed its name from the Congo.

Themes
- The family.
- Relationships.
- Religion.
- War.

Genre
This is a historical novel, which is narrated by five different voices. Each of the daughters tells her version of the story and then Orleanna, the mother, gives her own insight into the events that occur during these years in the Congo.

The structure of the book imitates the names of the bible – Genesis, the Revelation, the Judges and Exodus. This particular structure serves the purpose of showing that the story is not anti-Bible, but is one that contains another history and belongs to another place.

Cultural context
The background of this book is post-colonial Congo during the years after independence. It is a volatile time politically and we are given much insight into the turbulent years following French rule and the transition of the country from that of Congo to Zaire. In the book we witness the years under Lumumba's rule and also Mobutu, another black leader.

We gain a vivid insight into a country governed by Belgian rule, which is struggling to regain its own independence and establish its culture. There is a great deal of poverty and insecurity in the economy of the country. The initial assumption of democracy by the native Congolese gives rise to a good deal of fear and strife for the white people in the newly developed Zaire.

General vision or viewpoint
The general vision of this novel is drawn against the backdrop of two different stories: the personal history of the Price family and the historical development of post-colonial Zaire, or what was formerly the Belgian Congo. Through the rigidity of Nathan Price's style of missionary activity, there is a strong sense of how self-destructive the whole process of white colonisation becomes. The two stories develop and in many ways parallel one another. This type of structure serves the purpose of highlighting the main issues more forcibly. Accordingly, as each member of the Price family assumes independence and adopts a different lifestyle, we are exposed to the varying changes in the political situation of the Belgian Congo and the difficulties involved in the assumption of independence and freedom. There is a striking sense of the importance of personal freedom in a country and the corresponding need and preparation for that freedom.

PRIDE AND PREJUDICE
Jane Austen

(2007 exam)

The story

The story is set in England and centres around the Bennet family, who live in Longbourn. The Bennets have a moderate income. There are five Bennet girls and Mrs Bennet is anxious to have her daughters married well. Elizabeth and Jane are the two older girls, who are more rational than the others. Mr Bingley, a man with plenty of money, moves into Netherfield, a large estate near the Bennet family. Mr Bingley falls in love with Jane, but under the influence of another rich gentleman by the name of Mr Darcy he abandons his pursuit of Jane because she does not have enough money.

Mr Darcy is regarded by everyone in the area as proud and arrogant. He falls in love with Elizabeth and proposes to her. She refuses him because she believes he is a snob. In addition, she dislikes his treatment of Mr Wickham, an officer in the regiment. It turns out that Wickham is a fortune hunter who used the Darcy family to get money. Wickham elopes with Lydia, Elizabeth Bennet's younger sister, and Darcy is forced to pay him money in order that he will marry Lydia.

Mr Bingley returns from London and proposes to Jane, who accepts him. Elizabeth changes her mind about Darcy and they get married at the end. Jane marries Mr Bingley.

Themes

Pride

The title of the novel is *Pride and Prejudice* and this pride can be seen in the figure of Darcy. Darcy believes he is superior to everyone and in particular despises Mrs Bennet, Elizabeth's mother. When he initially proposes to Elizabeth she notices that his references to her own family and his possible association with them would be a 'degradation'. Darcy changes throughout the novel and becomes more humble and acknowledges that his pride governed his behaviour and that he is prepared to rectify it.

Marriage

Marriage is a central theme in all of Austen's novels. The plot of this novel is constructed around the relationship between Elizabeth and Darcy. Austen is interested in the complexities of human relations. Marriage was the means by which many of the women characters escaped a life of spinsterhood. Look at the case of Charlotte, who marries the dull and stupid Mr Collins. Her reasons are practical, as she tells Elizabeth: 'I am not romantic. I ask only a comfortable home.' Elizabeth's standards for a happy marriage are based on love. The union between Lydia and Wickham is brought about because, as we are told in the novel, 'their passions were stronger than their virtue'. Darcy ends up assisting Wickham in his profession while Elizabeth helps Lydia out with money.

Money
Wealth and affluence are a hallmark of this society. Darcy is a wealthy landowner whose estate, Pemberley, is large and rich. Many of the characters in the novel are introduced in terms of their social position and wealth. The novel deals with certain characters who are rich and filled with pride and snobbery. This is the case in particular with Lady Catherine de Bourg, who is related to Darcy and who refuses to tolerate his marriage to Elizabeth on the grounds that her family is not wealthy or prestigious enough.

Genre
This novel is written in the third-person narrative voice. Austen uses irony in her narrative as a means of showing the truth about situations and people as well as a means of moral and social judgment. She also makes use of humour as a tool to entertain and sometimes to satirise.

Cultural context
The background of this novel is England in the mid-nineteenth century. Austen's social world is restricted to dealing mainly with the middle classes.

The mode of transport is carriage and horses. Many of the activities carried out by the characters consist in sedentary occupations such as quadrille, backgammon and whist parties.

General vision or viewpoint
Throughout this novel relationships between men and women are a central topic. It becomes evident that the right selection of a marriage partner is a critical and a central choice to be made in life. The novel shows us the development of various relationships between different types of people and how they culminate in marriage. Most of these marriages are happy, while some are simply expedient and practical. Marriage, however, seems to be a key factor determining happiness and fulfilment in life.

Sample answer on Pride and Prejudice
Would you consider the issues that are represented in the novel *Pride and Prejudice* to be relevant to a modern-day reader?

Sample answer
Austen wrote against the background of mid-nineteenth century England and held a mirror up to life. However, this life has a limited and restricted quality to it because many of her issues and concerns were confined mainly to the middle class. While many of the issues she deals with are still relevant in our modern society, she depicts life and human relationships from the standpoint of a woman in this century. It must also be admitted that her subject matter, which is largely marriage, class distinction, snobbery and human relationships, greatly restricts the scope of her work.

However, while the subject matter of her work may be limited, it is still undoubtedly true that her skills as a novelist surpass any limitations in her work and are certainly relevant to modern-day society. Thus, her psychological perception of character and motivation, her constant humour and her faultless control of tone and narrative method are all exemplary and are still relevant today.

Austen was a critical observer of human nature. Her concerns are morals, human happiness, virtue and self-knowledge and not mere abstract ideas or principles. She exposes the follies and idiosyncrasies of her characters with a profound insight and a subtle and clever irony. Through irony Austen exposes sham values and superficiality and penetrates through falsity in the society around her.

In the novel *Pride and Prejudice*, the Bennets are the main family on which the plot centres. They are a respectable, middle-class family made up of marriageable daughters. It becomes clear from the outset, however, that social interaction between the Bennets and other families, such as the Darcys and the Bingleys, is out of the question. Austen is intent on satirising class consciousness and snobbery. Her vision of life is ironic, and irony was part of her method, through which she captured many of the contradictions of life. For Austen, irony is a more truthful mode of communication in a world where she realised that 'seldom does truth belong to any human disclosure'. Irony also served Austen's moral purpose because her vision of life was critical and objective. Therefore, she uses irony as a means of moral and social judgment and through irony she evaluates human behaviour, judges the foibles and follies of her fellow humans, and shows the value of virtue. Much of the irony in the novel *Pride and Prejudice* centres on the two main characters, Elizabeth and Darcy, and how they begin to re-evaluate one another as the story develops.

 Mr Collins becomes another target of irony from the novelist. He is a clergyman who believes he is doing the Bennet family a great favour by proposing marriage to Elizabeth, the eldest daughter. When Elizabeth declines his proposal he justifies this as something that is not ascribed to the 'usual practice of elegant females'. His high opinion of himself is not daunted and he proceeds to ally himself in marriage to Charlotte. Mr Collins spends a good deal of time in the novel cultivating and flattering his upper-class patron, Lady Catherine de Bourg. It becomes clear that these types of people are still recognisable in our society today.

A good deal of the male characters are governed by this type of empty vanity and petty snobbery. Mr Darcy believes in the dignity of his lineage and he becomes a target of attack many times in the novel. Miss Bingley, who dislikes anyone not as socially accepted as she is, becomes another example of a snob, while Wickham, who will do anything he can to get enough money to raise himself into a higher station, is realistically portrayed throughout. It becomes clear as the story develops that the satire directed at Mr Collins is in reality more subtly directed at the entire social hierarchy, with its shallow values and hollow pretensions.

The plot in *Pride and Prejudice* centres on the relationship between Elizabeth and Darcy and the various prejudices, both within the characters themselves and the society around them. Through the Darcy-Elizabeth and Bingley-Jane marriages, Austen shows the power of love and happiness to overcome class boundaries and prejudices.

Marriage has a central importance in Austen's work and this is apparent in the novel *Pride and Prejudice*. All of her novels end in marriage, which she considers to be 'the origin of change'. The power of marriage to bring fulfilment and happiness is stressed more in Austen's work than in modern society. The relationship between the sexes is more dependent in Austen's world than now, and Austen is intent on showing how the heroine in her story begins to grow morally through marriage. Marriage clearly does not have the same power in our society today, with the liberation of the sexes and feminism.

However, other issues, such as the reality of pride, prejudiced views and class consciousness, are still relevant today. *Pride and Prejudice* certainly provides the reader with a realistic and valid insight into nineteenth-century English life.

Comment

This answer begins by clearly addressing the question, which is the relevance of the novel *Pride and Prejudice* to a modern twenty-first-century reader.

The answer develops by showing what particular issues interest Austen and how some of these are shown to be relevant and how others are not as important today.

Particular examples are taken from the text to support the points made in the answer.

The answer concludes by tying all the ideas together and restating how some issues are still relevant while others are not quite so important.

Death of a Salesman
Arthur Miller

(2007 exam)

Historical and literary background
This drama spans a period of forty years from the early twentieth century, a time of dramatic change in lifestyle from an era of abundant job opportunities to one of increasing unemployment because of growing mechanisation. Money and power are primary values in the play.

The story
Willy Loman, the central character of the play, has been a travelling salesman for the Wagner Company for thirty-four years and is now sixty-three years of age. He is married to Linda and they have two sons, Biff and Happy. Biff has been living away from home and is unable to sustain a secure job. The relationship between Biff and Willy has been strained ever since Biff discovered that his father was unfaithful to his mother. Linda and her two sons are worried about Willy's behaviour. Willy decides to approach Howard Wagner, who is the son of the man he worked for thirty-four years ago. Willy wishes to work in New York City, closer to his home. However, Willy learns that he has no job because he has been a failure while working in New England. Willy is devastated at losing his job and goes to Charley, who is an old friend, to borrow more money in order to pay his insurance premium. Charley offers Willy a job but he refuses out of pride.

When Biff tries to communicate with Willy about his failures in finding work and getting a loan, Willy refuses to listen to him. Later on Biff returns home to find Willy planting seeds and talking to his brother Ben, who has been dead for nine months.

At the conclusion, Willy crashes the car and commits suicide. He hopes that he will gain twenty thousand dollars from the insurance. Tragically, nobody turns up for Willy's funeral and he dies a forgotten man.

Themes
- Family relationships.
- Self-deception and self-realisation.
- Personal failure.
- Work.

Genre
The play is a tragedy. The main character, Willy Loman, refuses to face reality and ends by committing suicide, thus destroying any possibility of happiness for himself or his family.

The structure of the play
Under the title of this play the following words are written: 'Certain private conversations in Two Acts and a Requiem'. This play dramatises a mind in turmoil. The structure of the play fluctuates between the past and the present. The time span of the play is only a twenty-four-hour period. There is no logical time sequence in the play. Willy's mind moves to the past twenty years before and focuses in particular on one year – 1928.

The style of the play
Many of the characters, with the exception of Linda, Willy's wife, use clichés and generalisations.

Certain symbols are used, such as the flute, which is connected with Willy's father. The idea of planting seeds suggests that Willy is anxious to reap some fruit in his life, to see something flourish.

Cultural context
The play shows the culture of America in the early twentieth century, a period of dramatic changes in society. After World War I there followed an increase in industrial production, but this was accompanied by a slump in the late 1920s, which resulted in high unemployment and a shortage of money. The increase in high-rise apartments in the city of New York is so intense that Willy feels the city is stifling him.

General vision or viewpoint
The general vision of life at the conclusion of this tragedy is grim and pessimistic. The disastrous failure to communicate basic emotions and ideas seems to be the tragic culmination of Willy's life and efforts. This failure destroys his family life and

relationships. The basic need to be loved and understood is evident from Willy's situation. The conclusion dramatises the tragic lifestyle that results when the individual is unable to feel loved or understood.

THE CRUCIBLE
Arthur Miller

(2008 and 2009 exams)

The story

The opening scene takes place in the bedroom of Rev. Samuel Parris in Salem, Massachusetts. Parris is a man in his mid-forties. He is described by the playwright as 'a villain in life, a widower with no interest in children.' He is praying beside the bed of his daughter, Betty, who is ten years old. The negro slave called Tituba enters the room. Parris throws her out. The niece of Parris, Abigail Williams, aged seventeen, also enters. She is an orphan and is described as having a 'capacity for dissembling'. Susanna, a young girl, comes from Dr Griggs and tells them that the sickness she suffers from is not natural.

They speak about the rumour of witchcraft. Parris is fearful that the community will remove him from the parish, so he pleads with Abigail to tell him what abomination they committed in the forest. He also asks her to tell him why she has been dismissed from Goody Proctor's service. Abigail declares that Goody is a gossiping liar.

Another woman enters, called Mrs Ann Putnam. She is described as 'a twisted soul of forty-five, a death-ridden woman haunted by dreams.' Her husband also comes in and they tell about how their own daughter, Ruth, has not woken that morning. They speak about witchcraft. We are told that Thomas Putnam is a man with many grievances. His brother-in-law, James Bayley, had been turned down as minister of Salem. Putnam is the eldest son of the richest man in the village and regards himself as the intellectual superior of most of the people around him. He is upset that the village turned down his brother-in-law. He feels his own name and his family's honour have been smirched by the village and he intends to right matters.

Putnam is intent on getting revenge on Parris and insinuates that there are spirits taking hold of the child. Putnam's wife and her husband try to convince Parris to declare himself to the community and tell them that he has discovered witchcraft. Their servant, Mercy Lewis, a 'sly merciless girl of eighteen years', enters. We learn that Mercy was the one who was dancing naked in the forest. Parris goes out to lead the congregation in prayer. Betty wakes up and is frightened of Abigail. She mentions that Abigail drank a charm to kill Goody Proctor.

John Proctor comes in. He is a farmer in his mid-thirties who is opposed to the current thinking on witchcraft at the time. Mary Warren is his servant. Abigail begins to flirt with him. He is married to a woman called Elizabeth and he rejects Abigail's advances. The community is below singing a psalm as Betty wakes, screaming. A woman called Rebecca Nurse, aged seventy-two, enters. She is the local midwife of Salem and is a good lady. She stands over the girl, who becomes quiet again. Rebecca is married to Francis. Parris begins to attack the group, including Proctor and Putnam. He explains how he is the third preacher in seven years to take over in the parish and how he is not given enough money to keep himself in firewood. Then Putnam begins to row with Proctor over land. Giles takes Proctor's side.

Rev. John Hale of Beverly enters. He is described as 'a tight skinned, eager eyed intellectual.' He mentions how sex, sin and the devil were linked early on and continue to be in Salem. Rev. Hale's goal is described as 'light, goodness and its preservation and he knows the exaltation of the blessed whose intelligence is called upon to face the…bloody fight with the Fiend himself.' He comes laden down with many heavy books.

Hale begins to ponder over the books while Old Giles speaks about how his own wife, Martha, reads books in a corner at night and how he cannot pray until she stops.

Hale begins to pray over the body of Betty. He interrogates Abigail about what happened in the forest. Tituba is brought into the room and announces that they drank chicken blood. They all begin to accuse Tituba of conspiring with the devil to deceive the girls. They threaten to whip her to death. She denies it all. Hale pleads with Tituba to help him discover who the devil's agents are in the village. Tituba tells them how she heard a voice telling her to kill Parris. Abigail begins to cry out as she becomes enraptured in a pearly light about all the names of people she saw with the devil.

Act II takes place eight days later. The setting is the common room in Proctor's house. Elizabeth, Proctor's wife, is singing in the living room to the children.

They speak about how Mary Warren has gone to Salem as an official of the court. People are being imprisoned and sentenced to hanging on the accusation of being involved in witchcraft.

Elizabeth urges Proctor to go and tell the court how Mary told them it was all lies about the stories of witchcraft. They have a conversation about Abigail and it seems that Proctor thinks Elizabeth does not trust him at all. She maintains that she is not judging him, that 'he is a good man…only somewhat bewildered.' Mary Warren enters and tells them the details about the proceedings in the court that day. She tells them that some of the women have confessed, for example, Sarah Good, on how they made a pact with the devil. Then she tells Elizabeth how her name had been mentioned in court that day and how she had been also accused of being guilty of witchcraft. Proctor orders Mary not to go to court again. She maintains that she is a woman of eighteen and is not to be ordered about.

Elizabeth urges Proctor to go to Abigail and tell her she is a whore. Hale arrives and interrogates Proctor about why he does not attend church regularly on Sundays and the fact that two of his sons are not baptised. He gets him to repeat the commandments. Giles Corey enters and announces that his wife, Rebecca, is in jail. She is charged with the murder of Goody Putnam's babies. Cheever and Marshal Herrick, two men from the community, enter and tell Proctor that his wife is charged in court. They accuse her of keeping poppets. Elizabeth happens to have a poppet with a needle in it. Mary Warren had given it to her. The others believe, however, that Elizabeth intended to murder Abigail with the needle. Herrick and Cheever take Elizabeth to prison in chains. Hale is confused. He is unsure whether or not she is innocent. Act II concludes with Proctor ordering Mary to go with him to the court and tell the truth about the fact that it is all fiction about the witches. She cries all the time that she cannot.

The setting of Act III is the anteroom of the general court. Martha Corey, Giles's wife, is being interrogated by Hathorne, the judge. He is described as 'a bitter remorseless judge'. Danforth, the Deputy Governor, 'is a grave man in his sixties of some humor and sophistication.' Mary Warren arrives with Proctor and tells the court that the whole thing is a lie. Parris is there and he believes they are trying to overthrow the court.

Danforth tells the court that Elizabeth is pregnant and that she will be safe from imprisonment for a year. Then Proctor hands Danforth a petition signed by ninety-one local people who claim that the whole thing is a lie and that the women have been falsely imprisoned. Danforth wants these people to testify in court openly, saying 'a person is either with this court or against it…there can be no road between.' Putnam is summoned by the court and denies the fact that his own daughter fabricated lies about witches. Giles is forced by the court to reveal the names of the local community who signed the petition. He refuses, as he believes they, too, will end up in prison. Hale asks the court to consider the petition before making a decision. The girls are brought in to refute the charges. It is clear that Abigail is the leader. Abigail denies Mary's story and says it is all lies. Proctor tells the court that he thinks Abigail intends to murder his wife. When Mary begins to tell the court about how she fabricated the whole thing and pretended to see witches and to faint, she becomes very weak and feeble. It is also clear that she is deeply influenced by Abigail's reactions. Abigail pretends there is a sharp wind blowing in the court. At one stage Proctor grabs Abigail and accuses her of being a whore. Then he admits to the court that 'he has known her'. They accuse him of being a lecher. He also tells them about how his wife Elizabeth discovered the two of them and how she threw Abigail out of the house. They bring Elizabeth in and question her about the details of her husband's relationship with Abigail. She denies the fact that her husband is a lecher and so they think that the two are lying. Then Abigail pretends to see a yellow bird. Mary begins to change and tells everyone how Proctor told her to do the devil's work and how he forced her to sign the petition or he would murder her. Proctor tells them how this is all fraud and how God damns them all. The scene concludes with Proctor and Giles being put in prison and Hale stating how he denounces these proceedings.

The setting in Act IV is a jail in Salem. Sarah Good and Tituba are in jail. Hale is helping the people who are condemned to hanging by praying with them. Cheever and Danforth have a conversation and we learn that there are many cows wandering the highroads because all the owners are in prison. Parris explains to Danforth that some of the women are thinking of confessing. He asks Danforth to postpone the hanging for a while to give people time to confess. He believes the people are discontented and that rebellion is brewing. Proctor appears, very pale and gaunt. He is in chains and under heavy guard. Elizabeth appears and they plead with her to convince her husband to confess his guilt. She believes this is the devil's argument.

In their conversation, he learns that Rebecca refuses to confess and that Giles died, having been stoned to death. He refused to make any confession he 'would not answer aye or nay to his indictment.' Elizabeth declares that she will not judge John and that he should do what he feels is right. She also acknowledges that he is a good man and she has sins of her own. Proctor tells Danforth that he will confess but he refuses to write it down. He refuses to testify against anyone else, claiming he has no right to judge or make confession on behalf of other people. They want him to sign his confession so that they can nail it on the door of the church for everyone to see. He refuses to have it posted everywhere. Danforth wants good and legal proof. Proctor tells him he has the confession and that he needs no more. He wants to retain his name, having given them his soul. He does not want to deal in lies. He is told he will hang. Danforth wants him to be hanged high over the town for all to see. Hale asks Elizabeth to plead with her husband that 'it is all pride and vanity.' The scene concludes with her words: 'he have his goodness now. God forbid I take it from him.'

The play concludes with a short excerpt, entitled 'Echoes Down the Corridor'. It explains that Parris was voted from office and never heard of again. In March 1712 'the congregation rescinded the excommunications…to all intents and purposes the power of theocracy in Massachusetts was broken.'

Themes/issues
Religion
The type of religion represented in the play is Puritanism. This is seen to be rigid and inflexible. The community is obsessed with the idea of witchcraft and seems intent on destroying itself through this manic witch hunting. Rev. Parris, the embodiment and upholder of this type of religion, is seen to be a hypocrite in his manner and way of dealing with people. His niece, Abigail, the villain of the play, is a hypocrite and a rebel who shows the worst elements of this type of religious espousal.

Power and authority
The embodiment of law and authority lies mainly in the figure of Danforth, the Deputy Governor. He upholds power and authority both in state and church within this small community. He is shown to be an unrelenting and intransigent man whose only concern is the enforcement and maintenance of law and order. He is not interested in the individual.

There are obvious parallels between this play and the era of McCarthyism, which dominated the 1950s in America, when Miller wrote this play, an era of hypocrisy and false allegations. Those who had connections with Russia were forced to answer before a committee of the state to explain their involvement and to name their friends. This has obvious parallels with Proctor's dilemma in the last scene. Miller is satirising the hypocrisy of government departments and the double standards that prevail there. He is also showing the profound impact of this type of behavior on the lives of ordinary people, who are seen as the real victims.

Women
The women in this society are largely seen as victims of the narrow-minded rigidity and hypocrisy of this community. With the exception of Abigail, who seems to be the embodiment of evil, all women suffer death, isolation and slander on account of their

position and the narrow society that encompasses them.

Elizabeth is a clear victim of prejudice and villainy. Her husband, Proctor, has engaged in an adulterous relationship with Abigail, a sly, cunning and evil woman. As a result, Elizabeth becomes the target of Abigail's deeply vindictive intentions in the play. Elizabeth is slandered before the court of Salem and is forced to face the fact of her husband's unlawful imprisonment while she herself is pregnant. In the figure of Rebecca Nurse, the local midwife, we also get an example of courage and heroism. She refuses to testify falsely before the court of Salem at being involved in witchcraft. As a result, she, too, is hanged, as are many of the other innocent women in Salem.

Genre

The genre of this play is one of social realism. It is structured into four different acts – Act I is entitled 'An Overture'. The play operates on the level of allegory. It seems to draw a parallel with another existing situation and in doing so it teaches a lesson on life.

The central symbol in the play is the image inherent in the title, the crucible, which signifies a great test or trial. This is what happens to the members of the small Salem community, who are all accused of being involved in witchcraft.

Cultural context

The play is set against the background of the witch trials in Salem, Massachusetts in the seventeenth century. This was one of the first towns in New England and the predominant religion was Puritanism. It is described as a 'barbaric frontier inhabited by a sect of fanatics'.

We are told early on in the play how a revolution had unseated the royal government in Salem and substituted a junta, which was in power at the time of the play's setting. The people of Salem developed a theocracy, a combination of state and religious power whose function was to keep the community together and to prevent any kind of disunity.

The world of the play is a narrow one, with unexplored land inhabited by marauding Indians. The American forest was the last place on earth not paying homage to God. The people of Salem had failed to convert the Indians.

The mentality is superstitious and backward. People are repressed and haunted by guilt and superstition. It is also a world where people are ready to betray their neighbour for the sake of self-preservation. Miller shows us some good in this world in the figure of Rebecca Nurse, the local midwife who goes to her death telling the truth and refusing to compromise with evil and deception. Proctor also offers another alternative to the world of deceit and hypocrisy, which seems to dominate from every angle.

General vision or viewpoint

From the outset of this play, the overall vision or viewpoint is deeply bleak and grim. Miller shows the disastrous effects within a small puritanical community of rigid, narrow-minded structures. Miller articulates his general vision through the different settings of each act. The setting changes from spring to autumn in the last scene. What Miller seems to be suggesting in these different seasonal settings is how humanity in Salem has receded to its lowest common denominator. The actual word 'fall' could also denote a fall from grace.

Parris, the local upholder of religion in this community, is shown to be a deeply hypocritical and selfish figure. Miller seems to be satirising this type of insincerity and showing its far-reaching effect on the ordinary inhabitants of this community. Overall, the legal systems of government are shown to be corrupt and untrustworthy and cause a great deal of suffering to ordinary people, who are the victims.

THE REMAINS OF THE DAY
Kazuo Ishiguro
(2008 exam)

Historical and literary background
The events in this novel take place in the period spanning 1922 to 1956 in England. In 1956 England experienced the Suez crisis, which represented an attack on her colonial powers abroad. The novel deals with the crisis in Europe prior to and including World War II. The Versailles Treaty has been drawn up with strict measures operating against Germany. Lloyd George is the Prime Minister of Britain during the time of this story.

The story
The novel begins in 1956. Stevens, who is a butler in Darlington Hall in England, tells the story. At the beginning of the story, Stevens is working for Mr Farraday, an American gentleman who now owns Darlington Hall. Stevens undertakes a visit to Cornwall. The journey takes six days, during which Stevens travels through different parts of England. His purpose is to meet a former employee called Miss Kenton. She is now married and has become Mrs Benn. Her marriage has not been happy, however. Formerly she had worked as housekeeper in the Hall while Lord Darlington was alive. Stevens hopes that Miss Kenton may rejoin the staff at Darlington Hall, because he is now getting old and needs staff. During the trip Stevens recalls certain vivid incidents from the past through flashback.

Through Stevens's recollections of the past we learn about his father, who came to work at Darlington Hall when he was already an old man and a long-serving butler. He died of a stroke in the Hall during an important international conference in 1923. We also learn that Lord Darlington was sympathetic to the Nazi cause – Stevens recalls an incident when Lord Darlington sacked two maidservants who happened to be Jews.

It is clear from Stevens's comments and story that he and Miss Kenton had an attachment for one another. However, Stevens was very committed to his work as a butler and to serving Lord Darlington to the best of his ability. Eventually Miss Kenton leaves the Hall and marries Mr Benn. Several people hint to Stevens that Lord Darlington is mistaken in his political views but Stevens refuses to listen to them. Lord Darlington's efforts to serve the German cause turn out to be misguided and as a result he dies an isolated and broken man. Mr Farrady, an American, buys the Hall. The staff is reduced. Stevens, however, remains in the Hall working as a butler.

Stevens recalls how he met Miss Kenton, now Mrs Benn, on a bench at the pier. She tells him that she has learned to accept the limitations of life and has grown to love her husband after many years. It becomes clear from her conversation that she was truly in love with Stevens. He is heartbroken. Eventually she leaves on a bus.

At the conclusion Stevens meets a retired butler on a bench beside the pier. Stevens tells him that he feels his life has been a waste. The man, however, advises him to stop looking back at the past and adopt a positive attitude; to enjoy the remains of the day. Stevens decides to follow the man's advice and stop lamenting the past. The novel concludes as Stevens plans how he can improve his bantering skills in order to surprise his employer, Mr Farrady, on his return from the States.

Themes and issues
* Loyalty.
* Self-deception.
* Relationships.
* Professional work.

Genre
This novel belongs to the genre of social realism. It gives a realistic insight into the large houses in England in the early twentieth century preceding World War II.

Narrative technique
The novel is told in the first person by Stevens, the central character. This is a limited point of view and therefore has many implications. We are given a very subjective view of events. This is apparent in such things as Stevens's description of the relationship with Miss Kenton. It is clear that Stevens fails to realise the power and depth of her feelings for him. Through this type of narration we gain an insight into the central character, Stevens. We see underlying motivations governing his decisions about things. We understand deeply his dreams, desires, shortcomings and blind spots. The narrative voice could also be described as part-memoir, part-travelogue.

Flashback
During the six-day journey to Cornwall there are various uses of the device of flashback. One effect of the sustained use of flashback in the novel is to highlight the strong link between the past and the present. Stevens is intent on justifying to his reader (but mainly to himself) the motivations for acting as he did throughout his years of service under Lord Darlington.

Much of Stevens's memories cover the period of the 1920s and 1930s.

Style
The landscape in the novel is used as a metaphor to parallel the striking sense of calmness and restraint in the English countryside and in Stevens's character.

Cultural context

The cultural setting is that of the great lords and houses in England post World War II. Dignity and professional competence are primary values for Stevens. Lord Darlington spends a great deal of time engaged in political meetings and entertaining eminent politicians. We gain an insight into the role of the butler in England in the mid-twentieth century. The novel is also narrated in the wake of World War II when Nazism had become a powerful force.

Relationships between men and women are formal and restrained. There is a strong emphasis on sustaining correct social codes of behaviour and etiquette.

General vision and viewpoint

The novel concludes on a positive note. Stevens faces reality fully. He recognises that he has sacrificed a lot by serving Lord Darlington so faithfully. He also recognises that a real attachment existed for Miss Kenton. He acknowledges that Lord Darlington was a tragic victim of circumstances and still forgives him his errors. Stevens learns to face the limitations of his own life and to stop looking back at the past and lamenting. He decides to adopt a positive attitude and dedicate himself to the task of serving his new employer, Mr Farrady, in the best manner possible. The general vision of this novel is to struggle to make the best of the particular limitations and shortcomings of this life and move out towards other people.

REGENERATION
Pat Barker
(2009 exam)

The story

The story opens with the poet Siegfried Sassoon's anti-war Declaration, which is dated July 1917. Rivers is a pioneering psychologist, neurologist and anthropologist who operates from Craiglockhart War Hospital in Scotland. The hospital engages in nerve regeneration treatment and then decides whether or not the men are fit to return to fight in the war. He is speaking to his colleague, Bryce, about Sassoon's Declaration, which will be read before the House of Commons. Sassoon is coming to stay in Craiglockhart, supposedly suffering from a severe mental breakdown. Sassoon is on the train on the way to the hospital and begins to think about his earlier conversation with Robert Graves, a fellow officer, and how Graves had told him he would be court-martialled on account of the Declaration. Sassoon maintains that it has been the hardest thing he has done about the war.

On his arrival in Craiglockhart, Rivers is impressed with his interviews of Sassoon, whom he believes is anti-war as a matter of honour. Graves arrives at the hospital to tell Rivers how he convinced the Board that Sassoon was suffering from a nervous breakdown on account of his experiences in the trench. He wants to save Sassoon from a court martial and so he is lying. He believes Sassoon is right in his ideas about the war, but he also knows that his methods are wrong. Rivers reads some of Sassoon's anti-war poems.

The novel mainly deals with Rivers's perceptions of the patients in Craiglockhart, who are all war veterans and are suffering from various types of post-traumatic shock. Rivers is a very humane man who takes time to understand and empathise with his patients. The novel gives an insight into many different types of men who come for treatment to Craiglockhart and who are patients of Rivers. Among them is a young man called Burns, who is suffering from extreme shock, having been hit by a bomb and spent several days lying on a German corpse whose insides had ruptured.

Another soldier called Prior arrives. He suffers from post-war trauma and severe asthma, and initially he is very hostile towards Rivers. When Rivers meets Prior's parents, he begins to understand the reasons for Prior's rough and abrupt behavior. Prior wants Rivers to use hypnosis on him in order to help him recover. Rivers initially refuses, as he wants the men to recover in as natural a way as possible. When Rivers begins hypnotic therapy on Prior, he recalls all the horrors of life in the war. Prior finds it difficult to face the fact that he had a breakdown. Prior meets a girl called Sarah and he begins to have an affair with her.

It also becomes clear as the story develops that Rivers is governed by an internal conflict about the war. He wonders about its necessity for the sake of succeeding generations and yet he is appalled at the horror that such events cause such suffering.

Sassoon meets Wilfred Owen in the hospital, a man who writes poetry and is clearly in awe of Sassoon. Sassoon encourages Owen to write more poetry and include references to the war. Owen is editor of the *Hydra*, which is the hospital magazine. Sassoon has nightmares about the front. He begins to dream about Orme, a soldier who fought with him on the front. Sassoon spends his time in Craiglockhart playing golf.

After a while, Rivers begins to find everything in the hospital to be too much. He wakes up one night with a bad pain in his chest. He realises it is on account of all his work with the patients and the subject of war neurosis. Bryce, another doctor, orders him to take a break.

While Rivers is taking a break from Craiglockhart, he is offered a new job at the Central Hospital in London as a psychologist with the Royal Flying Corps. Rivers pays a visit to Burns, who is now living with his family. Burns still suffers from nightmares and has periodic fits. At one stage Burns becomes deeply upset when he accidentally comes across some carcasses of animals in the woods. Rivers is forced to conclude that 'nothing justifies this, nothing, nothing, nothing.' It is clear that Rivers is becoming deeply anti-war from his experiences with his patients.

Shortly after this, Rivers returns to Craiglockhart, knowing that when he takes up his new job he will miss Craiglockhart deeply. Sassoon informs Rivers that he is returning to the war in France. Sassoon reminds Rivers that 102,000 corpses were lost in one month alone to Germans and not to forget that. Rivers realises that the Board will not have a court martial for Sassoon because the casualty lists are too 'terrible to admit any public debate on continuing the war.' Instead, the Board will declare him to be insane. Sassoon wants to visit another doctor called Mercier so that the Board will be unable to say that he had a relapse if he happens to continue with the protest on his return to France.

The narrative is interspersed with some conversations of Sarah, Prior's girlfriend, and her friends. Prior gets Permanent Home Service. Shortly after this, Prior apologises to Rivers and tells him how he has helped him a lot. Prior develops his relationship with Sarah and it seems that they are deeply in love. He wants to meet her mother, Ada.

Before Sassoon leaves Craiglockhart, he exchanges poems with Owen. Sassoon has given up hope about influencing events and so he is putting all his anger and grief into his poetry.

Rivers leaves Craiglockhart and moves into lodgings near the Central Hospital, where he takes up his new post as psychiatrist to the Royal Flying Corps. Rivers pays a visit to the National Hospital, which also rehabilitates war veterans and is run by Dr Yealland. This hospital uses different methods from those used in Craiglockhart. When Rivers arrives in the hospital, he begins to feel very ill. He meets a 'creature', a man who is in a wheelchair in an unnatural position. Rivers also carries out a ward round with Yealland, whose contact with the patients is cold and even brutal. There are no personal questions about their psychological state; instead Yealland is a bully. The men are subjected to a brutal shock treatment of electrodes on their body and then released within a week. Rivers decides to witness first-hand the electric shock treatment of one man called Callen, who refuses to speak. This is a particularly cruel section, where Rivers himself begins to feel sick and uncomfortable. The whole treatment carried out by Yealland is similar to a torture chamber. After this event, Rivers is exhausted by what he feels has been a confrontation with Yealland. He has a bad nightmare after this and ironically thinks it was an air raid that woke him up.

Rivers begins to realise that while the methods used by himself and Yealland to cure patients are different, their role is the same. They both operate as controllers of these men. He and Yealland are locked into the system as much as the patients. Rivers acknowledges that both he and Yealland's encouragements to their men to go back to war are really activities that are 'not merely self destructive but positively suicidal.' Rivers begins to realise now that what Yealland did was not getting Callan to speak as much as to silence him on the whole subject of war. In Yealland's own words to Callan, 'You must speak, but I shall not listen to anything you have to say.' They are both silencing their patients, whose terrors, nightmares, memory lapses and paralysis are all unwitting protests against war.

Rivers makes a short visit to Craiglockhart and realises that the attempt to run a psychiatric hospital 'on parade ground lines has been briefly tried and then abandoned.' He meets Sassoon, who has finished a book called *Counter Attack*. Rivers recommends Sassoon for general services overseas. Sassoon's case goes before the Board. He is given permission to return even though he clearly reiterates that his position on the war has not changed. He still suffers from nightmares. Rivers acknowledges that he himself has been changed by his patients in all this time. Formerly he had been deeply politically conservative; now the sheer extent of the 'mess' is forcing him into conflict with the authorities over a whole range of issues, both medical and military. He also realises that 'a society that drowns its own young deserves no automatic or unquestioning allegiance.'

The story concludes with Rivers realising that Sassoon is simply going back to

France to be killed in the war in order to show them all. Rivers closes Sassoon's file, on which is written 'Nov. 26 1917 discharged to duty'.

Themes

War trauma

Much of the story deals with the post-war trauma experienced by a huge number of British soldiers as a result of their experiences in the trenches in France during World War I. Barker, the novelist, uses her main protagonist in the story, Rivers, to articulate some very damning condemnations of war and its total failure to achieve anything constructive. All the horrors of war and the sufferings experienced there are shown through the different reactions in the various patients in Craiglockhart. Yet there is a profound similarity in the experiences of each nightmare, memory lapse and physical and mental trauma. Through the humanity of Rivers and his approach, Barker manages to make many statements about war and its self-destructive quality. One of the most explicit condemnations of war comes from Rivers's realisation that 'a society that drowns its own young deserves no automatic or unquestioning allegiance.' War is seen as anything but glorious in the story. Instead, it is shown to be profoundly destructive of human life and relationships.

Recovery

The setting is Craiglockhart, a hospital dedicated to healing British soldiers who have suffered war trauma and physical disintegration as a result of war. In Craiglockhart, the patients are treated very much as human beings who have a free will and a rational faculty. This contrasts greatly with the insight given in the novel of the treatment carried out in the National Hospital under Dr Yealland. Here the system is brutal and unnatural. Yealland does not treat the patients as free human beings with a will of their own. The atmosphere here is similar to a brutal concentration camp where the patient experiences all the traumas of a torture chamber in the name of recovery. The method here is not only brutal, but deeply inhumane. Perhaps Barker is outlining the similarity between this type of barbaric practice and that waged in the trenches. Rivers rejects this type of treatment and sees it as totally destructive to the individual who is subjected to it. He himself is tortured by nightmares as a result of his exposure to Yealland's methods. Recovery in the story is shown to emerge when the individual is able to face the truth about war and its squalid reality, just as Sassoon does at the end.

Genre

This is a novel which contains a mixture of historical fact and fiction. It is structured into four different parts. The story is told mainly from the perspective of Rivers, the main character in the novel.

The author makes striking use of realistic dialogue to develop the narrative.

Cultural context

The novel is set in a Scottish hospital during the years of the World War I, 1914–18. Many of the soldiers being treated in the hospital come from very ordinary backgrounds with ordinary middle-class families.

The poet Sassoon is seen to be a different type of character in so far as he has made a defiant anti-war stance, which has reached the House of Commons. He is admired by many of the patients in the hospital and held in high esteem largely because of his stance and his fame as a poet.

Rivers, the army psychologist, is a clever man who is a very successful and prestigious neurologist. He is able to enter the lives of the men and empathises greatly with their various dilemmas. Furthermore, he can relate to their families very well.

There are various references to working-class culture in the different conversations carried on by Sarah, who is Prior's girlfriend, and her friends.

When Rivers visits the National Hospital in London, he encounters a cold and clinical atmosphere in Yealland's mode of working. This culture is inhumane and deeply destructive of human life.

In the nightmares and memories of the men, there are some very graphic images of all the full horrors of life in the trenches during World War I.

General vision or viewpoint

The general vision or viewpoint in this novel speaks about the brutality and horror underlying war. From the outset, the novel opens with Sassoon's strong denunciation against war. Barker uses the figure of her chief character, Rivers, the army psychologist, to articulate some very strong condemnations of war.

War is seen to be very complex. At the beginning of the story, Rivers and the other army psychologists take it for granted that war is a reality and that the men must be treated as quickly as possible in order to return to the battle. Through his various reactions and the fact that halfway through the story Rivers is forced to take a leave of absence from his work in the hospital, it becomes evident that this attitude towards war is not quite so simple. As Rivers moves away from the ambience of Craiglockhart, he has more time to ponder the implications of his particular treatment of his various patients. After his experiences with Yealland and exposure to his brutal methods, Rivers comes to acknowledge that both he and Yealland are silencing their patients through their different methods. He comes to acknowledge that the patients' nightmares, paralysis, memory lapses and stammering are simply 'unwitting protests' against war.

Through Sassoon's firm stance and his retention of his position, Rivers is forced to reassess all that he has believed about war and to change his position. The ultimate statement about war seems to hover over the entire narrative and certainly shows war as a horrifying and brutal reality totally destructive of human life and relationships.

11

Notes on Shakespeare Drama

In this chapter we will study the main techniques Shakespeare used in his tragedies. There are also notes on *Macbeth*, *Hamlet*, *King Lear* and *Othello* under the headings 'themes and issues', 'genre', 'cultural context' and 'general vision or viewpoint'.

TRAGEDY IN SHAKESPEARE

Tragedy in Shakespeare involves a central figure who is an exceptional person, a hero of high stature, whose sufferings are extreme. This person is invested with qualities that raise him above his fellows. In Shakespearean tragedy this situation of loss or catastrophe results in recognition by the hero of the consequences of his mistakes or flaws; this is usually accompanied by a state of moral growth and finally death, which must arouse the sympathy and pity of the audience.

Primary features of a Shakespeare tragedy

1. The hero is a person of high status, such as a king, prince or a military leader.
2. This hero is endowed with a fatal flaw, which brings about an exceptional degree of suffering or calamity.
3. The flaw in the character is a form of evil that triggers off the tragic events of the play. These generally lead to the death of the protagonists.
4. Evil in Shakespeare is self-destructive – it annihilates itself.
5. The supernatural forms a part of the structure of his plays, for example, the storm in *King Lear*, the ghost in *Hamlet*.
6. Chance or accident plays a part in developing the plot. In *King Lear*, Edgar meets his father, the Earl of Gloucester, at opportune times, for example, when he is filled with despair and wants to commit suicide. Edgar manages to save his life. In *Hamlet*, there are many instances of the use of chance and coincidence, such as when young Hamlet discovers the letters which contain a plot on his life or when he encounters pirates who manage to escort him safely back to Denmark.
7. The conclusions of Shakespeare's plays are distinctive. They always dramatise a

qualified form of redemption with the restoration of good, harmony and justice, but this is always of a mitigated kind. In other words, it is achieved at the expense of death and destruction of the good. The example of Cordelia in *King Lear*, together with the number of deaths in this play alone, qualifies the complete triumph of good over evil.

To sum up, a Shakespeare tragedy is a story of exceptional suffering experienced by a person of high status and culminating in death.

When you are studying the Shakespeare play:
- examine the central scenes that contribute to the development of the action and plot in the play
- examine the main features of the central characters or protagonists and in particular take note of their flaws or shortcomings
- examine how these flaws or defects contribute to the tragic events that occur in the play
- study the main characters' recognition of their flaws and how they grow in self-awareness towards the conclusion of the play
- examine the soliloquies; remember that soliloquies are an insight into a character's soul and give us a deep knowledge of what they are thinking and the reasons for their actions.

Examine soliloquies under the following headings:
- Where do they occur?
- What gives rise to them?
- What do they tell us about the character?
- What do we learn about the plot?
- What images are used and why?

Study the summaries of all the soliloquies at the end of the notes on *Macbeth*.

Historical and literary background

The literary and historical background of Shakespeare's plays is late sixteenth-century and early seventeenth-century England. The tragedies *Hamlet*, *Macbeth* and *King Lear* were written in the same period, 1600–1608.
- This was a time of conflict between a traditional way of life and the new.
- The political framework of sixteenth-century England was hierarchical.
- Rulers at that time, whether king, prince or general, were regarded as divinely appointed. Usurpation of kingship was considered to be an act of sacrilege.
- The audience came from all strata of society.

HAMLET

(2008 exam, comparative study only)

The story

Claudius is king of Denmark when the play opens and he has recently married Gertrude, his late brother's wife. Gertrude has one son, Hamlet. He is a student in the University of Wittenberg and his closest friend is Horatio. Denmark has been at war with Norway over land lost by Fortinbras, king of Norway. His son, young Fortinbras, is raising an army against Denmark in order to reclaim these lands.

A ghost appears to two soldiers, Marcellus and Bernardo, while they are on guard duty outside the palace of Elsinore (Helsingør); it is dressed like Old Hamlet, the late king. The two guards tell Horatio, who decides to inform Hamlet. The following night Hamlet meets the Ghost, who informs him that he is his father and that he was murdered by his brother, Claudius. He orders Hamlet to avenge this deed.

Hamlet tells no one but instead adopts an 'antic disposition' – pretending to be mad – to deal with this predicament. Meanwhile, Claudius has successfully averted a war with Norway and has drawn up a peace treaty.

Polonius is the principal advisor to Claudius. He has a son, Laertes, who goes to France, and a daughter, Ophelia, who is in love with Hamlet. Polonius warns Ophelia to stay away from Hamlet, because they are not socially compatible.

Some players arrive at the palace and Hamlet takes this opportunity to organise a play, called *The Mousetrap*, wherein he hopes to 'catch the conscience' of Claudius – he wants to test his reaction as he watches the play in order to confirm his guilt.

Rosencrantz and Guildenstern, two old school friends of Hamlet, have been hired by Claudius to spy on Hamlet. He realises this and constantly makes fools of them.

When the play is put on before the court, the king reacts by calling for lights and disappears to his chapel to try to repent. Hamlet decides not to kill him then – he would rather catch him in the commission of a sinful act so that his soul would be lost forever. Hamlet confronts his mother; here he accidentally kills Polonius, who is spying behind the arras (a hanging screen or tapestry), thinking it is Claudius.

Hamlet is dispatched to England in the care of Rosencrantz and Guildenstern, who are supposedly responsible for his safety but in fact have orders to kill him. Hamlet reads the letter containing their orders, substitutes another one arranging that Rosencrantz and Guildenstern be killed instead and returns to Denmark to confront Claudius.

Ophelia goes mad from unrequited love and the death of her father and she commits suicide.

Laertes has returned from France because of his father's sudden and strange death. Claudius manipulates him and organises a duel in which Laertes will kill Hamlet with a poisoned sword. He also arranges that a chalice of wine will be poisoned in case his plot should miscarry. By accident, Laertes is pierced with the poisoned sword at the same time that he wounds Hamlet with it. Before he dies he repents and tells Hamlet that Claudius is the villain. Hamlet kills Claudius with his sword and forces him to drink from the poisoned chalice. Gertrude has also drunk some wine from this chalice and she dies.

When Hamlet dies, young Fortinbras becomes king of Denmark and Horatio survives to expose the truth.

Themes
- Revenge.
- Deception or false appearance.
- Woman and frail womanhood.

Genre

Hamlet belongs to the category of revenge tragedy. This revenge is initiated by the injunction from the Ghost to revenge the 'foul and unnatural' deed of Claudius. A young, sensitive prince receives a commission from a ghost to carry out the deed of revenge. Adopting 'an antic disposition' as a weapon to deal with the corruption around him, he delays the deed of revenge for different reasons. Finally, he obtains an opportunity in the concluding scene, having banished Ophelia and driven her into a state of madness and attacked his mother for her sinful deed.

The tragedy concludes with the death of the main protagonist and many of the leading characters.

The structure of the play

The main plot centres on Hamlet and the task he is compelled to carry out as a result of the Ghost's revelations and specific injunction to revenge Claudius's 'foul and unnatural' deed. The sub-plot is structured around the family of Polonius and his two children, Laertes and Ophelia.

The whole play *Hamlet* centres on revenge. Hamlet is faced with a wicked but superficially attractive uncle whose evil is poisoning the state (the body politic). Hamlet cannot appeal to law, as Claudius is the law.

Act I is made up of five scenes. By the conclusion of Act I the details of the plot have been set in motion. Hamlet has met the Ghost and has been informed of his need to avenge. All the main characters have been introduced and we have been given an insight into their main characteristics. The conclusion of Act I reveals Hamlet in a state of profound perplexity and confusion with the deed he is compelled to execute. Both his words and actions from now on show a profound disintegration. This could stem from the fact that his conscience is in revolt against the task and thus his mind is divided:

> The time is out of joint. O cursed spite,
> That ever I was born to set it right!
> (Act I, Scene v)

Act II deals with the interaction of the main plot and the sub-plot. We see Polonius's hypocrisy as he sends a servant to spy on his own son, Laertes. The king employs two old school friends, Rosencrantz and Guildenstern, to spy on his nephew, Hamlet. The players arrive and they provide Hamlet with an idea for his revenge plan.

The two central events in Act III consist of the play within a play scene and the closet scene. Hamlet has verified the authenticity of the Ghost and forced his mother to acknowledge that she is guilty.

In Act IV, Laertes returns from France and Hamlet is shipped to England. Both Laertes and Hamlet grapple with each other in the graveyard scene. Ophelia goes mad and commits suicide.

In Act V, the final scene concludes with the resolution of the conflict in the deaths of the leading protagonists.

Some of the scenes have titles and these have a particular bearing on the structure of this tragedy. Shakespeare cleverly introduces a play within a play, as it were. This is the scene (Act III, Scene ii) where Hamlet verifies the words of the Ghost, thereby catching the conscience of Claudius.

This scene is significant for the following reasons: Claudius sees his own act of poisoning. Gertrude sees a mirror of her own distasteful behaviour. Hamlet sees a nephew killing an uncle, i.e. himself and the deed he is called upon to do. Thus, Hamlet obtains the evidence he needs in Claudius's reaction after this play.

Both the nunnery scene and the closet scene (Act III, Scene i) deal with the theme or issue of woman. Both scenes are similar in so far as they both show Hamlet overwhelmed with a profound and powerful sense of emotion.

Another scene which has structural significance in the development of the plot is the scene called the graveyard scene (Act V, Scene i). This is a richly ironic scene. It is also structurally important, as it comes before the death of the leading protagonists and it speaks in ironic terms about life after death. While the two gravediggers are clowns who are meant to provide a type of comic relief, there are unmistakable notes of grim irony permeating this scene. One of the first statements made is that the gravemakers' houses last till doomsday. This powerfully reinforces the permanence and power of the grave.

Another aspect of the structure of these tragedies is Shakespeare's use of the soliloquy, which forms an integral part of a Shakespearean tragedy. Most of the soliloquies show the characters analysing and speculating on the consequences of their own or other people's actions. Claudius's first two soliloquies show his complete acknowledgement of guilt and disgust with his life of insincerity and hypocrisy:

> How smart a lash that speech doth give my conscience!
> The harlot's cheek, beautied with plastering art,
> Is not more ugly to the thing that helps it
> Than is my deed to my most painted word:
> O heavy burden.
>
> (Act III, Scene i)

After he has seen his own deed of murder enacted in the play within a play scene, Claudius rushes in guilt to his private chapel and begins his prayer with the words:

O, my offense is rank, it smells to heaven;
It hath the primal eldest curse upon't,
A brother's murder!

> (Act III, Scene iii)

However, Claudius may possess the capacity to feel guilty and in need of repentance, but his ambition for power is far greater. His final soliloquy in Act IV, Scene iii reveals an attitude where he has coarsened his conscience and ruthlessly suppressed any openness to repentance or amendment of his behaviour:

And England …
                    thou may'st not coldly set
Our sovereign process, which imports at full,
By letters congruing to that effect,
The present death of Hamlet.

> (Act IV, Scene iii)

The queen's aside, which is the only one in the play, also reveals a sensitivity of conscience:

To my sick soul, as sin's true nature is,
Each toy seems prologue to some great amiss,
So full of artless jealousy is guilt.

> (Act IV, Scene v)

Most of Hamlet's soliloquies reveal a character who is deeply sensitive and is possessed with a refined moral conscience. The Hecuba soliloquy and his speech in Act III, Scene ii after the performance of *The Mousetrap* play are the only soliloquies which specifically show his plan of attack and the development of the plot:

the play's the thing
Wherein I'll catch the conscience of the king.

> (Act II, Scene ii)

After he has proven the Ghost's authenticity, Hamlet announces his intention with respect to his mother, which he will execute in the closet scene: 'I will speak daggers to her, but use none'.

Many of the soliloquies reveal a dilemma within the character and with their conscience in particular. Overall, Hamlet's soliloquies reveal a deeply reflective and philosophical nature that is endowed with an acutely sensitive moral conscience.

Imagery and language in the play

Early on in the play, Polonius tells Claudius that he would 'find truth even if it is within the centre' (Act II, Scene ii). In many ways this statement could sum up the essence of Hamlet's motto underlying his use of language and imagery in the play. Hamlet needs imagery for his 'antic disposition'. His language and imagery are all designed to unmask people, to strip them of their false appearance and to expose them in their true nature. It also reflects his real ability to penetrate to the real essence of things, to break down the barriers erected by hypocrisy.

Through the simile of the pipe he shows Rosencrantz and Guildenstern that he has seen through their intent:

> You would play upon me you would seem to
> know my stops, you would pluck out the heart of my
> mystery ...
> (Act III, Scene ii)

The protective mask of his assumed 'antic disposition' enables him to communicate basic truths in some strikingly colourful ways. For example, he tells Rosencrantz and Guilenstern that they are 'sponges' that 'soak up the king's countenance, his | rewards, his authorities' (Act IV, Scene ii). He wishes to ridicule their hypocrisy and corrupt ambition. The sponge metaphor unmasks their deception and reveals how they have become willing dupes in Claudius' hands.

Hamlet seeks to lead his mother to the truth by means of images, 'a mildewed ear blasting his wholesome brother ...', 'a cutpurse', 'a king of shreds and patches'.

The poison symbol becomes the leitmotif of the imagery in the play, where imagery and action reflect one another. The corruption of Denmark and its people is seen as an insidious poison. The graphic details of Claudius' murder are not enacted on the stage, but instead are depicted in terms of vivid images of corruption, such as 'the leprous distilment', 'vile and loathsome crust'.

Poisoning becomes the means whereby all the main characters die. This powerful imaginative pattern built up of poison, decay, corruption and sickness depicts the unwholesome moral condition of Denmark. The image of an ulcer infecting and eating away the body becomes the central image in the play.

The unnecessary fighting between Norway and Poland is a kind of tumour which grows from too much prosperity:

> This is the imposthume of much wealth and peace,
> That inward breaks ...
> (Act IV, Scene iv)

Hamlet's mother and her association with Claudius takes off the 'rose from an innocent love and sets a blister there.'

Claudius' use of disease images has different implications. The health of Denmark and its security is related to Claudius' security. All is governed by self-interest. Hamlet's free reign in the kingdom is seen as a distinct threat to Claudius' security and life; it is like

> diseases desperate grown
> By desperate appliances are relieved ...
> ... like the hectic in my blood he rages.
> (Act IV, Scene iii)

Images operate on different levels in the play. On the one hand they can depict truth for Hamlet and help him to expose and strip away false appearance. On the other hand, imagery gives him the freedom he needs to cloak his real purpose behind ambiguity, puns, word play, quibbles and ambiguities. To those people he distrusts and dislikes he deliberately misconstrues them and attaches irrelevant and dubious meaning to what they say. He particularly treats Polonius in this manner because he sees through the fact that Polonius is a meddlesome and prying old fool. At one stage Hamlet tells Polonius that he is a fishmonger and when he denies it Hamlet cynically claims:

> Then I would you were so honest a man.
> (Act II, Scene ii)

Thus, Hamlet's hostility for a character is revealed through his use of ambiguous language, for example, his repeated use of misleading comments to Claudius. Our first insight into the relationship between both Claudius and Hamlet reveals these undercurrents of bitterness, when Claudius asks Hamlet:

> How is it that the clouds still hang on you?

to which Hamlet bitterly replies:

> Not so, my lord. I am too much in the sun.
> (Act I, Scene ii)

Later on Claudius greets Hamlet with the words:

> How fares our cousin Hamlet?

to which Hamlet replies:

> Excellent i'faith of the chameleon's dish: I eat
> the air promise-crammed, you cannot feed capons so.
>
> (Act III, Scene ii)

Hamlet finds such evasion essential as a weapon of self-defence because he finds himself in a world where he does not know who to trust, surrounded by people who use deceit and lies to probe and uncover the truth about other people.

Much of the language and imagery used in the play is richly symbolic and serves the primary function of depicting the central issues and themes.

Cultural context

The particular cultural context of the play *Hamlet* must take into account certain attitudes towards the following:
* kingship/aristocracy and the political landscape
* marriage
* the role of women
* the particular system of values at that time.

The type of kingship that forms the background of the tragedies is monarchy. The king was God's representative on Earth; no person had a right to kill him. Claudius himself echoes this idea when he hypocritically tells Gertrude:

> There's such divinity doth hedge a King,
> That treason can but peep to what it would,
> Acts little of his will.
> (Act IV, Scene v)

Therefore, to murder a lawfully elected king amounted to sacrilege. Furthermore, to marry a brother- or sister-in-law was tantamount to incest in this society. Thus, at the opening of the play the reigning king, Claudius, is guilty of both regicide (the murder of a lawful king) and incest because of his marriage to Gertrude, his brother's wife. When the Ghost appears, he brings with him an injunction to Hamlet, the young prince of Denmark and the next in line to the throne, to exercise the code of morality and revenge this foul deed.

The political panorama is one of peace except for Fortinbras' attempts to mount an army against Poland. We learn from Hamlet that this action is the result of excess wealth and corruption which has been experienced by Norway and Poland. Claudius is an effective and adept politician who knows how to manage any threat on peace to his kingdom swiftly and adroitly.

We get a distinct impression that marriage is not held in very high esteem by either Gertrude or Claudius. From the Ghost's words, we learn that Claudius is guilty of adultery as well:

> Ay, that incestuous, that adulterate beast ...
> (Act I, Scene v)

The Court of Elsinore is therefore corrupt. This corruption is rooted in both Claudius and Gertrude, king and queen of Denmark, and seeps out like a poison corrupting the culture, the value system and the people involved in this society.

The role of women in this society is largely seen in a negative manner. Both of the women in the play, Ophelia and Gertrude, are seen as weak and frail. They allow themselves to be used by men and in general they are treated with contempt and cynicism by the men in the play. Both Polonius and Laertes treat Ophelia as a child – described as a 'green girl', they patronise her and intrude into her private life and relationships.

The value system which is shown to be upheld by the characters seems to be contradictory at times. Shakespeare presents some distinctly Christian values, particularly within Hamlet's mode of behaviour. However, this value system seems to conflict and clash with a more barbaric and primitive mode of reasoning in Hamlet. Early on in the play, Hamlet will not commit suicide because it is a mortal sin:

> Or that the Everlasting had not fixed
> His canon 'gainst self-slaughter!
> (Act I, Scene ii)

Yet later on in the play he seems to have no problem with murdering Claudius and wanting to catch him in an act where his heels will kick at heaven and his soul will be as damned and black as hell.

At the conclusion of the play, Hamlet sees himself and his future in the hands of God:

> There's a divinity that shapes our ends,
> Rough-hew them how we will.
> (Act V, Scene ii)

Although Hamlet can speak with great conviction about heaven and God's plans for men – 'there's a special providence in the fall of a sparrow' – he can still organise the murder of Rosencrantz and Guildenstern with 'no shriving time allowed'.

Hamlet is quick to preach about marriage and the sacred character of matrimony to Gertrude. Her marriage to Claudius has made all marriage contracts void, religion is a mockery and a rhapsody of words. Her deed of incest has 'taken off the rose from an innocent love and set a blister there' instead.

Yet in action Hamlet seems to have no qualms at the conclusion in stabbing the king and forcing him to drink from the poisoned chalice with the words 'thou incestuous, murderous, damned Dane'.

Murder, revenge and punishing evil with evil are fundamentally opposed to the Christian ethic; these are contradictions that are not resolved at the conclusion of the play. They could stem from the fact that for a great deal of the play Hamlet was governed by conflicting emotions, and this could have clouded his rational faculty and prevented him from acting in a consistently sound fashion.

General vision or viewpoint

This play begins with darkness, uncertainty, questioning, falsehood and selfishness and ends with certainty restored, self-sacrifice vindicated and justice restored through the medium of Horatio, who has never concurred with evil, and is compelled by Hamlet to remain alive in order to bear witness to the truth. Treachery is seen to breed treachery, murder to breed murder. Evil is seen to destroy itself. The conclusion is the redemption of society from corruption and deceit and the peaceful death of the tragic hero:

> Good night sweet prince:
> And flights of angels sing thee to thy rest!
> (Act V, Scene ii)

In all Shakespeare's tragedies, evil is shown to be self-destructive. Through the logic of events, Shakespeare shows that there is a universal moral law that one transgresses at one's peril.

Summary of the soliloquies

Hamlet's soliloquies

In many of Hamlet's soliloquies we gain an insight into a character whose mind seems to be divided. This may stem from the enormous task of revenge imposed on him by the Ghost. In his soliloquies Hamlet also shows a profound philosophical capacity.

1. Act I, Scene ii. This is Hamlet's first appearance in the play. He professes a belief in

God and an avoidance of suicide because of that belief. He shows disgust at his mother's hasty remarriage and expresses a desire for revenge. *Imagery*: Classical images show his scholarship and learning: his father is a Hyperion, Claudius is represented as a satyr and his mother is like Niobe. Disease images, such as 'unweeded garden' and things 'rank and gross in nature', reflect this theme of moral corruption.

2. Act I, Scene v. This soliloquy occurs after the Ghost's disclosures as an expression of Hamlet's moral shock at the Ghost's revelations. He has to lock this horror inside: 'thy commandment all alone shall live … volume of my brain, | Unmixed with baser matter'. *Imagery*: The 'smiling damned villain' reflects the theme of insincerity and false appearance.

3. Act II, Scene ii. This is the Hecuba soliloquy. The tears of the players as they enact the drama of Hecuba lead to this soliloquy and make Hamlet realise his inaction. He condemns himself for his tardiness in acting against his uncle. For the first time in the play he articulates the fact that the Ghost may not be authentic: 'the spirit that I have seen may be a devil' (line 587). He announces his plot: to 'catch the conscience' of Claudius by staging a play.

4. Act III, Scene i. This soliloquy occurs just before the nunnery scene and is the one that has earned Hamlet the title of 'prince of philosophical speculators'. He engages in some profound reflections on life, death and the meaning of suffering. He claims that his indecisiveness and lack of resolution stem from too much thinking.

5. Act III, Scene ii. This soliloquy occurs after the play within a play scene, when Claudius' guilt has been exposed. Hamlet ironically announces that 'I could drink hot blood' (line 372–3) and 'do such bitter business as the day would quake to look on.' He announces his intentions regarding his mother: 'I will speak daggers to her, but use none' (line 377).

6. Act III, Scene iii. This soliloquy occurs in the prayer scene, when Hamlet fails to kill Claudius in the chapel. He offers reasons why he will not kill him: he wants to catch him in an act that will damn his soul. These reasonings contradict his earlier beliefs as a Christian.

7. Act IV, Scene iv. Fortinbras is passing through Denmark on his way to capture a small tract of land in Poland. This is similar to the Hecuba soliloquy, as Hamlet compares himself to Fortinbras and again reproaches himself on his delay in setting about his revenge. Spurred on by Fortinbras' spirited activity, he steels himself to perform bloody deeds.

Claudius' soliloquies

Claudius' first two soliloquies show that he has a moral conscience. The third shows how he has become more deeply immersed in guilt and evil-doing.

1. Act III, Scene i. This is Claudius' first acknowledgment of his guilt. It reflects the fact that he has a conscience and shows the burden of his life of deceit and hypocrisy. *Imagery*: The 'harlot's cheek, beautied with plastering art' conceals her ugliness, reflecting the theme of duplicity and insincerity.

2. Act III, Scene iii. This soliloquy occurs in the prayer scene, where Claudius is

struggling with himself to repent. He acknowledges his crime: 'My offence is rank'. He enumerates the reasons why he committed the murder: 'My crown, mine own ambition, and my queen.' The priorities here are interesting: 'his queen' figures last on his list.

3. Act IV, Scene iii. Claudius, now fully immersed in evil-doing, has organised the murder of Hamlet. *Imagery*: 'like the hectic in my blood he rages'. The disease imagery reflects the threat on Claudius' peace and security while Hamlet lives.

Ophelia's soliloquy

Act III, Scene i. This soliloquy occurs at the conclusion of the nunnery scene and is an ironic soliloquy. Ophelia laments the destruction of Hamlet's splendid qualities and blames it on madness. In her next appearance in the play she will be the one to be stricken with madness because of her treatment at the hands of Hamlet.

Gertrude's aside

Act IV, Scene v. Here Gertrude has just learned of Ophelia's madness. Like Claudius, she acknowledges that she is guilty of sin: 'to my sick soul as sin's true nature is …'.

AS YOU LIKE IT

(2007 exam and 2008 exam, comparative study only)

The story

The story opens with the fact that Duke Frederick has taken over the dukedom from his brother, Duke Senior, and banished him to the Forest of Arden. There Duke Senior lives like Robin Hood with some noblemen. Rosalind, Duke Senior's daughter, has stayed with her cousin Celia, Duke Frederick's daughter. They are both good friends and do not want to be separated from one another.

Orlando is the youngest son of Sir Rowland de Boys, who was a good friend of Duke Senior. Oliver is Orlando's brother. He is jealous of Orlando and wishes evil against him. He even states himself that he is 'full of ambition … a secret and villainous contriver' (Act I, Scene i). Oliver castigates Orlando to Charles, who is a good wrestler, and arranges a wrestling match between both in the hope that his brother will be defeated.

However, Orlando defeats Charles and is immediately banished from the kingdom by Duke Frederick. At this stage Orlando has met Rosalind and they have fallen in love. Duke Frederick banishes Rosalind from the court with the penalty of death if she disobeys. Celia decides to join her in her banishment. They adopt disguises and false names. Rosalind disguises herself as a young boy and assumes the false name of Ganymede, while Celia takes the name of Aliena.

Touchstone is a clown who meets Audrey, a peasant goatherd, and they decide to get married.

In the meantime, Adam, who is Oliver's servant, warns Orlando about his brother and warns him to leave. Adam offers to protect Orlando and offers him gold. Orlando flees to the Forest of Arden, where he meets the exiled Duke Senior. Orlando appeals to the Duke to give them food and bases his appeal on the customs and courtesies of a civilised society, even though he is now living in the middle of the forest. Rosalind and Celia meet Orlando in the forest and the disguised Rosalind begins a conversation with Orlando about the authenticity of his love. There is a great deal of comic and ironic humour governing this part of the play.

Oliver has been commanded by Duke Frederick to find Orlando and capture him. Oliver meets with Rosalind and Celia and tells them that he has repented of his evil intentions against his brother and is sorry. Oliver and Celia fall in love with one another. Jaques de Boys enters to tell them all how Duke Frederick has repented and become converted, and in addition he has returned all the lands stolen to his exiled brother.

The play concludes happily with the marriage of four couples – Orlando and Rosalind, Oliver and Celia, Touchstone and Audrey and Phebe, a shepherd, and Silvius, a shepherdess.

Themes
- Romantic love and loyalty.
- Deception.
- Relationships.
- Women.
- Contrast between the court and the country.

Genre
A comedy in five acts. A good deal of the dialogue in this play is based on ironic humour.

Cultural context
There are two different cultural contexts in this play. We get an insight into the values of court life in Act I. The remainder of the play is based in and around the Forest of Arden. The values that are represented in the forest have a dual nature – we are exposed to an ideal pastoral world on the one hand and an actual forest where people are afflicted with fatigue and hunger on the other. There are continuous contrasts drawn in the cultural world of the play between the realities of forest life and the flatteries that dominate the court.

In the Forest of Arden there is also a good deal of respect for the values of the civilised court, such as respect, gentleness, courtesy in speech and action, respect for status and rank, etc. The play manages to highlight how a creative compromise can exist between the two different worlds.

General vision or viewpoint
The general vision or viewpoint inherent in this play is based on the idea of celebrating certain values in life, such as love and friendship. Romance and intrigue govern the plot of this play and it becomes apparent that friendship and loyalty between various characters are important values. The conclusion gives us a happy vision of the unity of four couples in marriage. What appears to be dominant throughout this play is that

certain ideals, such as courtesy and love, that have permeated the play's structure are neither sentimentalised nor destroyed at the end.

OTHELLO

(2008 exam)

The story

Othello is a Moor and is the Commander-in-Chief of the Venetian army, which has been commanded to carry out the job of defending Cyprus against the Turks. Cassio has been appointed as his lieutenant. Iago is an 'ancient', or type of advisor to Othello. He is the villain of the play who hates Othello for having promoted Cassio in his stead, and so he plots to revenge himself on Othello. Othello has married Desdemona, daughter of Brabantio, one of the Senators in Venice. Roderigo, a friend of Iago, is being manipulated by Iago into giving him money so that Iago can win the hand of Desdemona for Roderigo.

Iago organises things so that Cassio gets drunk and is expelled from his position as lieutenant in the army. Then he subtly insinuates to Othello that Cassio is having an affair with Desdemona, Othello's wife. Iago uses his own wife, Emilia, to facilitate his plot. She provides Othello with proof that Desdemona has been unfaithful, in the form of a handkerchief which belongs to Desdemona, which was supposedly found in Cassio's apartment. Meanwhile Iago wins the confidence of Cassio and advises him to use Desdemona to intercede on his behalf to regain his position.

Bianca is a prostitute who is having an affair with Cassio. She is used by Iago and is implicated in the attempt to murder Cassio. Iago's plot fails when his attempt to murder Cassio backfires. Iago kills Roderigo because he is afraid of being exposed. Othello yields to the devious suggestion about his wife told to him by Iago and, consumed with rage, he decides to murder his wife. He smothers her in bed. After Desdemona's murder Emilia exposes her husband's villainy. Iago kills her. Othello kills himself. Iago is captured and punished.

Themes and issues

Some of the themes and issues which will be dealt with here are:

- Women.
- Racial prejudice.
- Dissimulation or false appearance.
- Jealousy.

The theme of women

All the female characters are unwitting victims of deception, guile and intrigue. They all inadvertently act as instruments of evil. Take, for instance, Bianca's affair with Cassio, Emilia's thoughtlessness in handing over the handkerchief to Iago which furnishes him with proof of Desdemona's supposed infidelity, and Desdemona herself, unable to discern the corrupt plotting undermining her innocence. There is a striking contrast drawn throughout the play between the characters of Desdemona and Emilia.

Desdemona's moral rectitude is integral, inviolate and pure. Emilia, on the other hand, is more worldly; her moral reasoning in the face of infidelity is tenuous and weak. She would 'venture purgatory to make her husband a monarch.'

The conversations which take place in Act IV, Scene iii between Desdemona and Emilia about marital infidelity and betrayal on the part of spouses serve the function of confirming and consolidating Desdemona's absolute marital integrity in the eyes of Emilia. This scene also functions to contrast the different standards of values professed by the two women. Emilia has weaker moral standards; standards which are corruptible and more worldly. For this reason, it is fitting that Emilia becomes the woman to stand up and vindicate the purity and integrity of Desdemona's virtue when her husband has murdered her.

It is ironic that Emilia becomes the one to expose the villainy of Iago. Despised repeatedly by her husband for being a strumpet, she emerges at the conclusion of this tragedy as a heroine who vindicates truth and honour. It is the love and loyalty of Emilia, the two virtues which Iago tries to erode in the play, which finally destroy him. Emilia's love and loyalty to Desdemona at the end become the means to reveal the full evil of Iago's manoeuvrings.

The general idea left with us by the play is that 'women must be circumstanced'; they must put up with the state of affairs and do their best with the position of things while men can do what they like.

The theme of racial prejudice

As a Moor from another culture, Othello is an outsider in this society and hence is regarded with suspicion and distrust. His position as a stranger to this culture intensifies his vulnerability and facilitates Iago's devious plot.

From the opening scene we are confronted with the issue of racial prejudice. Iago's resentment and spite rouse Roderigo, who in turn provokes the superstitious Brabantio with the words, 'an old black ram is tupping your white ewe…', 'Your fair daughter has been transported to the gross clasps of a lascivious Moor…' (Act 1, Scene i). Later that night when Brabantio takes up the issue in the Venetian senate, he condemns Othello for having 'abused her delicate youth with foul charms…' (Act 1, Scene ii). This attack is directed at Othello who, in the words of Brabantio, has bewitched his daughter to such a degree that 'she ran from her guardage to the sooty bosom of such a thing as thou…' (Act 1, Scene ii).

Prior to this, Brabantio entertained Othello in his house, paying tribute to him as a high-ranking military general. However, the marriage of his beloved daughter to this Moor – this outsider – is an entirely different matter. It leads him to make the statement to Roderigo, whom in fact he despises, 'O, that you had had her…' (Act 1, Scene i).

Othello is deeply insecure because he lacks essential knowledge of issues such as marriage, social relations between men and women and certain customs and traditions peculiar to Venice. It is this lack of knowledge and experience which leaves him an open target for exploitation. Look, for example, at Iago's words in the temptation scene: 'In Venice they do not let God see the pranks, They dare not show their husbands…' (Act III, Scene iii).

Subtly setting his perverted mind to work on Othello's weak nature, Iago suggests that perhaps the cause of Desdemona's infidelity has to do with race and colour:

> Ay, there's the point: as, to be bold with you,
> Not to affect many proposed matches
> Of her own clime, complexion and degree, ...
>   one may smell in such, a will most rank,
> Foul disproportion, thoughts unnatural...
>   I may fear
> Her will, recoiling to her better judgment,
> May fail to match you with her country forms
> And happily repent   (Act III, Scene iii)

That Iago succeeds in undermining Othello's faith in himself and his own wife becomes saliently clear from his soliloquy, which follows immediately after the above lines.

It is Othello himself who articulates how vulnerable and how defenceless he is because of his colour:

> Haply, for I am black
> And have not those soft parts of conversation
> That chamberers have...   (Act III, Scene iii)

His tragedy lies in the fact that he is unable to transcend these limitations within his own nature and arrive at the real truth. Instead, he consolidates his weaknesses even more by acting on impulse and executing judgment on Desdemona.

There is no doubt that the issues of racism and the underlying prejudice generated by it contribute to the precipitation of a good deal of the tragedy in this play.

Theme of dissimulation or false appearance

This theme of dissimulation finds expression in the character of Iago. Described as a 'demi-devil', he rests confidently on the assurance that people, and in particular Othello, believe him to be honest. He possesses an exterior glitter which is, in reality, sinister, and which misleads everyone in the play.

Cassio turns to him for advice, ironically addressing him as 'Honest Iago', and stating in full sincerity 'I never knew a Florentine more kind and honest' (Act III, Scene i). When Othello turns on Desdemona in a fit of passion, asking her to produce the handkerchief immediately, she beseeches Iago with the words, 'O, good Iago, good friend...'.

Othello repeatedly leans on the 'honesty' of Iago, frequently addressing him as 'Good Iago', 'Honest Iago', 'My life upon her faith: honest Iago'.

Iago handles every situation with tremendous skill and dexterity. He deftly manipulates every person in the play with cynicism and ironic contempt, and speedily turns everything to his own advantage.

Iago's ability to control Othello is supreme. Using several tactics, Iago strategically manages to erode Othello's faith in his own wife. Through this sustained use of devious and ingenious tactics Iago shows how the issue of evil or dissimulation can be compatible with outstanding human powers. His human strengths are potent: a keen energy and vitality, massive or prodigious powers of self-control, together with a highly superior intelligence. One of his main weapons is his ability to weigh up all the flaws of the chief characters, which he uses to further his own advantage. It is ironic that in his soliloquies he demonstrates a more astute and correct apprehension of Desdemona's strengths and weaknesses than her own husband.

It is interesting that Iago fools everyone, even his own wife Emilia. While Emilia is projected as a foolish and superficial bawd-type of woman, at no stage is she remotely aware of the depths of evil inherent in Iago's nature. This is because his capacity for dissimulation or duplicity are astounding. In the final scene, her words reveal this fact:

Disprove this villain...
He says thou told'st him that his wife was false.
I know thou did'st not, thou'rt not such a villain.
Speak, for my heart is full.

Shakespeare uses irony to dramatise this theme of false-seeming or dissimulation. Irony is an ideal technique to project such a theme, involving, as it does, the discrepancy between what is said or implied and what is really the case. The root of much of the irony in this play lies in the basic misconception by everyone that Iago is 'honest'.

And so a network of ironies, from situational to dramatic to verbal irony, illustrates this theme. For example, when Emilia informs Iago of Othello's attack on Desdemona in the words

The Moor's abused by some most villanous knave,
Some base notorious knave, some scurvy fellow... (Act IV, Scene ii)

we get a splendid example of irony of situation.

The play abounds in similar examples of the clever use of irony, all of which demonstrate how effective Iago has been in embodying this particular ability to pretend to be something he is not. His ability to deceive everyone triumphs and wreaks havoc as the conflict develops and the events unfold. It is only when Othello has murdered his wife and caused chaos in Venetian society that the full reality underlying Iago's plausible appearance of honesty is finally and ultimately cracked. His smooth veneer of honesty and plausibility is stripped bare by Emilia's staunch defence of the truth and her fearless denunciation of his villainy.

The theme of jealousy

This is an issue which permeates much of the play. There are overtones of jealousy in the opening lines of the play. These stem from the jealous references and disparaging comments that Iago makes about the character of Cassio:

A fellow almost damn'd in a fair wife;
That never set a squadron in the field,
Nor the division of a battle knows
More than a spinster…
mere prattle, without practise,
Is all his soldiership   (Act I, Scene i)

The root of his envy is anger at Cassio's military expertise and the fact that he has been promoted in lieu of Iago.

Iago's jealousy is pervasive. He himself acknowledges that he is jealous of Cassio:

He hath a daily beauty in his life
That makes me ugly.   (Act V, Scene i)

Iago works off this jealousy by creating counter-jealousies. Othello becomes his primary target. Iago announces in an early soliloquy how

I will put the Moor
At least into a jealousy so strong
That judgment cannot cure…(Act II, Scene i)

He manages to achieve this with consummate success. Othello's concluding words before he dies confirm the truth of this, and the success of Iago's warped intrigues:

Speak of me…
Of one not easily jealous, but, being wrought…   (Act V, Scene ii)

Othello's whole nature is indisposed towards jealousy or envy of any kind, but once it dominates him, it consumes and finally destroys him. The disposition of his temperament is to act rashly and impulsively, to seek immediate proof and resolve his doubts without stopping to reflect on the consequences of his actions. Of course Iago perceives all this thoroughly. Halfway through the temptation scene, when he is handed the handkerchief, Iago is able to fully assess the state of Othello's inner nature:

…trifles light as air
Are to the jealous confirmations strong
As proofs of Holy Writ   (Act III, Scene iii)

Iago appraises completely that Othello's soul is animated by an uncontrolled, 'an unbookish jealousy'.

It is perhaps significant that both Emilia and Iago provide us with definitions of jealousy in the play.

Iago warns Othello to be wary of jealousy in the temptation scene:

O! beware, my lord, of jealousy;
It is the green-ey'd monster which doth mock
The meat it feeds on.   (Act III, Scene iii)

And later on Emilia tells Desdemona that Othello's ill-treatment of her may be due to jealousy, and proceeds to echo her husband's earlier words:

...It is a monster
Begot upon itself, born on itself.   (Act III, Scene iv)

The deliberate echo by both characters of the theme of jealousy could certainly say a great deal about their marriage.

Within the context of this play and the ensuing events, jealousy does turn out to be a monster that breeds on itself, an evil that is self-destructive. The conclusion of the play dramatises this point only too clearly. Othello destroys the bonds of his marriage, the beautiful Desdemona, and then kills himself. Iago's destructive plot is overturned and his devilry unmasked at the conclusion.

Literary genre

Othello is a tragedy of incomprehension. The tragic experience is concerned with a loss of faith. Othello, who is a Moor from another culture, allows himself to be deceived into believing his wife has been unfaithful. His tragedy is rooted in his inexperience of this culture and his unqualified trust in the honesty and loyalty of Iago. He accepts Iago's insinuations as truth, and acts on them by murdering his wife. Only after the murder is the full truth of Iago's wickedness exposed, and Othello then kills himself.

The structure of the play

The plot is the character of Iago in action. This action depends largely on his knowledge of character and in particular the way in which he assesses the vulnerabilities of each of the characters. This plot finds expression in Iago's soliloquies. In these soliloquies he fabricates his plot and outlines reasons for his revenge.

He weighs up each one of his victim's strengths and weaknesses and shows how he will use the weaknesses to further his own evil ends. A great deal of the plot depends on Iago's knowledge of character together with the occurrence of accident or chance. The plot revolves around the image of a net in which people are caught and from which there is no escape. In Iago's own words:

And out of her own goodness make the net
That shall enmesh them all.   (Act II, Scene iii)

The time sequence of the play is very short; the whole play lasts approximately four or five days. In terms of what actually happens, this time-span is incredibly short.

Act I opens on Othello's wedding night. That same night he is dispatched to Cyprus.

Act II opens with the arrival of all the main characters, including Othello, in Cyprus three days later. The night after the arrival in Cyprus, Cassio is sacked.

The next day in the temptation scene, Act III, Scene iii, Iago poisons Othello's mind about his wife's infidelity. That same day, the handkerchief is lost by Desdemona, found by Emilia, given to Iago and planted in Cassio's chamber. Cassio's death is planned to be carried out within the next three days. Othello himself undertakes to kill Desdemona. All of this occurs in one complete scene, which is the day after Cassio is dismissed. The time-span is unbelievable.

In Act IV Othello is recalled to Venice. Othello humiliates Desdemona publicly by striking her, and later by treating her as a strumpet.

Act V concludes with the conversation between Emilia and Desdemona about marital infidelity. The last scene is the death of the leading protagonists.

The style of the play
Imagery
Imagery reflects some of the major themes in this tragedy. Dramatic contrast forms the pattern for much of the imagery of the play.

Because the play depicts a world of creation set against a world of destruction, contrast lies at the essence of the style. Othello radiates a world of romance, heroic and picturesque adventure. He reflects through his poetic speeches the qualities of soldiership in all its glamour of romantic adventure. On the other hand, Iago is colourless and ugly. He gnaws at the roots and values of this world. With his unfounded suspicions and ambiguous language, he worms his way into its solidity and finally poisons it.

Colour contrast dramatises the difference between certain characters. Desdemona is repeatedly reflected in terms of religious symbolism, for example 'Divine Desdemona', 'white ewe', 'fair devil', 'white sheets'. These are all symbols which show her striking purity, innocence and goodness. On the other hand, dark or black images suggest evil. All the surreptitious manoeuvrings of Iago take place at night. The opening scene is a night scene and serves the function of revealing the dominance of evil, of negation and of malignancy in the atmosphere of the play. This is reinforced by the two concluding scenes, both of which take place at night and have death as their theme.

Another example of contrast in the network of imagery used in the play is in the diabolic and celestial imagery. The use of celestial imagery mainly finds expression in the character of Desdemona. Cassio vehemently declares that the 'grace of Heaven surrounds her'. Her last words have rich religious connotations: 'I never loved Cassio, But with such general warrenty of heaven, As I might love.'

Emilia, in her chastisement of Othello's action, is quick to declare:

O! the more angel she,
And you the blacker devil...
Thou art rash as fire to say
That she was false: O! she was heavenly true.

This type of imagery forms a striking contrast to the dark pattern of diabolic and black symbolism which dominates the play.

The patter of diabolic or demonic imagery is woven about the character of Iago and all his motives, manipulations and manoeuvrings. Iago refers to his own plans as hellish: 'Hell and night, Must bring this monstrous birth to the world's light.' Iago sees himself under the patronage of hell:

> Divinity of Hell!
> When devils will their blackest sins put on,
> They do suggest at first with heavenly shows
> As I do now...

This kind of language and imagery is first used by Iago in the play, but as the events proceed and develop, it begins to form the content of much of Othello's language patterns. Othello begins to apply images of hell and damnation to Desdemona: 'Damn her lewd minx, fair devil', 'She is a liar gone to burning hell.'

A significant change occurs in the application of diabolic imagery on Desdemona's death. Emilia, who now realises the full truth, applies this kind of imagery to Othello: 'the more angel she, and you the blacker devil'.

Othello, in his sense of retribution and self-chastisement at the wrong action he has committed, cries out the following words of repentance:

> Whip me you devils,
> From the possession of this heavenly sight!
> Blow me about in winds! Roast me in sulphur!
> Wash me in steep-down gulfs of liquid fire!   (Act V, Scene ii)

Damnation, evil and the subsequent diabolic connotations are all synonymous in this play. The general impression left at the conclusion of Iago's character and operations is that of a nature who is damned and satanic in intent. He is repeatedly referred to as a 'demi-devil', a 'damned slave'. At the conclusion, when Othello, in an overwrought state for what he has done, declares in perplexity

> I look down towards his feet; but that's a fable.
> If that thou be'st a devil, I cannot kill thee.

in many senses these words are a chilling conclusion to Iago's career.

Another type of image used in the play is disease or poison imagery. This is seen in the corrupting effect of Iago's intrigues. Iago himself acknowledges that his plot is 'pestilence in Othello's ear'; that the effort to defame Othello's reputation before Brabantio is 'poison'. Othello refers to the handkerchief as a 'ravan over an infected house'. In his soliloquy, Othello depicts life with an unfaithful wife in terms of 'a forked plague' and 'a horned beast'.

Shakespeare uses a rich variety of images to project his themes. Images also identify certain things about each character as well as showing the gradual deterioration of the moral atmosphere in this play.

Cultural context

Venice and Cyprus are the two areas which are shown in this play. These places have very different value systems. Othello is a Moor and therefore his culture is rooted in North Africa. The predominant culture of this play is rooted in Venice. Venice is seen as a rich and powerful place, with its value system resting firmly on power, possession and control. Control here does not just mean power over people but also the supremacy of reason over emotion and passion. Venice is not just a place, it is an influence. Its mores or standards are implanted firmly in all the characters.

Venetian society has a superficially smooth and civilised veneer, seen in, for example, the noble senator, the competent and well mannered lieutenant and the conventional gentlewoman.

The Venetian senate

The senate in Venice embodies order, reason, justice and concord. Ancient laws and established customs control violence and ensure the safety and well-being of the individual and society. The ideal of this culture is control. In this culture, self-control is desirable and highly valued in soldiers. Othello shows a profound degree of self-control. He is calm and reasonable and knows that his lineage is as royal and as wealthy as any Venetian. Even under threat of attack from Brabantio, he remains serene and in control.

The scene in the senate depicts the values of honour, lawfulness, decorum, knowledge and power. Brabantio's grievances are examined here in a court of law. They are judged by reason and the verdict is enforced by civic power.

Here also in the senate the actions of the Turks are examined, their true purpose is penetrated, sense is made of the frantic and contradictory messages which pour in from the fleet and the necessary defence is arranged.

The two lovers, Desdemona and Othello, are surrounded by the governors of Venice who control passions and enforce law and reason. In this context they are forced to explain how they fell in love and to justify their love for one another.

However, there are anarchic forces at work threatening traditional social forms and relationships. These forces centre on Iago. Iago's discontent with his own rank and his determination to displace Cassio endanger the orderly, military hierarchy. Iago's attempts to create civic chaos in Venice are frustrated by Othello's calm management of affairs and by the orderly proceedings of the senate.

Cyprus stands on the frontiers between barbarism, as represented by the Turkish attack, and the city. Cyprus is not the secure fortress that Venice is. It is an outpost far out in the raging ocean; the immediate object of attack by the enemy. Here passions are more explosive than they are in Venice. Cyprus lacks the ancient order and established government of Venice. Othello the Moor is the one man to control violence and defend civilisation. In Cyprus, however, society is less secure and Othello alone is responsible for exposing the truth about things and for the maintenance of order.

Iago's poison works effectively in this society and he succeeds in manufacturing the riot and chaos that he failed to create in Venice. Disruptions occur both in society and in human relationships. Through his unfounded suspicions of his own wife, he endangers marriage. He tries to subvert the operation of law and justice by stirring up the dark, anarchic passions within Roderigo. The general is set against the officer, husband against wife, Christian against Christian, servant against master. Manners disappear as Othello strikes his wife publicly and, later, treats her as a whore.

Venetians cut one another down in a dark Cyprus street; men are murdered from behind. The quality of life deteriorates.

Another feature of the value system underlying the Venetian culture is the attitude towards women. Not only are women themselves treated with contempt and disdain, but also certain qualities such as loyalty, fidelity and purity are not expected of a woman. Women are largely seen as puppets or pawns to satisfy the male. Women in this culture are trivialised; the bonds of marriage and relationships are abused.

Othello's values are those of the aristocratic Venice, while Iago holds the values of the lower edge of that culture. Iago has contempt for women and all that femininity represents. He believes in control, power, possession and individualism. Significantly, he opens the play and dictates the terms of the action throughout. He speaks of money, hate, jealousy and women.

It is Othello's lack of familiarity with this culture which enables Iago to undermine his faith in his wife, Desdemona. Othello is unfamiliar with Venetian customs, in particular the pattern of infidelity and adultery which seem to be rife. Infidelity among the gentry is a commonplace occurrence and it is this particular feature of Venetian culture which erodes Othello's confidence in his wife and makes him a ready tool for exploitation.

General vision and viewpoint

Emilia plays a large part in the vindication of Desdemona's virtue and honour. It is she who heroically defends Desdemona's purity and virtue and steadfastly confirms her innocence. She dies in this act of defence and vindication.

The play concludes with the death of the tragic hero and the restoration of harmony in society. Iago is captured and it is presumed that he will be punished for his crimes. The general impression left to us is that his evil is of an ambiguous nature; the motivation underlying his actions is deliberately left obscure.

The general vision at the conclusion of this play is that evil is punished, but not before it has done a great deal of harm in the play. The power of the woman to change and grow in moral stature and to reveal the underlying corruption within this society can be seen in Emilia's attack on Othello and her corresponding defence of Desdemona.

Othello's repentance, together with the execution of judgment on himself, is an affirmation of loyalty to Venice.

Sample question and answer on Othello

What do you consider to be the importance of Bianca in the play *Othello*?

Bianca is part of the pattern of womanhood and of the analysis of women in love in this drama.

As a prostitute, she is a marginalised social figure, very much an outsider, at a polar extreme from the aristocratic Desdemona, daughter of a Venetian magnifico. Bianca is also distanced from Emilia, who, though a commoner, is a respectable married woman and part of the middle-class element in Venetian society, aspiring to establishment status.

All three women are involved in the theme of sexual jealousy, which is a dominant issue in the play, but Bianca's situation contrasts with that of the other women since she herself is jealous in relation to the man she loves, and the other two are victims of their husbands' jealousy.

Bianca is what Othello supposes Desdemona is. Thus each character contrasts with each other in terms of the theme of appearance versus reality, which is one of the dominant elements in the play. Desdemona cannot even bear to repeat the name which Othello uses for her, that name which defines Bianca: 'I cannot say whore | It does abhor me to speak the word | to do the act that might the addition earn | Not the world's mass of vanity could make me.'

On a plot level, all three women are involved with the handkerchief as a result of Iago's manipulation of them and it is Bianca, who quarrels with Cassio over it.

There are some elements of stereotype in Bianca's depiction. She rants and raves, venting in vulgarly strident words when angered, as prostitutes were supposed to do: 'A likely piece of work, that you should find in your chamber,' she vociferously protests to Cassio and then works herself up into a fine rage as she gives vent to her jealousy and her sense of being exploited as she berates him: 'this is some minx' token…I must take out the work…'.

However, Bianca is no mere stereotype; she is genuinely in love with Cassio. It is Iago who comments cynically on the irony of the fact that the prostitute has fallen for one of her clients: 'A creature that dotes on Cassio…tis the strumpet's plague…is beguiled by one.' She may flaunt her sexuality on the stage and be rancorously angry the next minute, yet she is not essentially different from the other women in the play on an emotional level.

Like the other two women, she is emotionally bound to the man she loves, and precisely because she loves Cassio she gives him the power to hurt her, to make her feel neglected and rejected. Thus her position not only parallels the other two women in the play, but oddly enough, parallels Othello's relationship to Desdemona. When Bianca says resignedly to Cassio, 'I must be circumstanced', she is clearly speaking for all the women who figure in the male-dominated world of the play, accepting what they cannot alter, while at the same time acknowledging their need to be loved.

It is wrong to dismiss Bianca's role as that of a foil or a polar opposite to Desdemona. She does love Cassio with more than a harlot's mere empty profession of affection. Thus when she insists in answer to Emilia's angry outburst that 'she is no strumpet but of life as honest | As you that thus abuse me', she is speaking the truth and there is dignity in her response.

The theme of appearance and reality is constantly highlighted in relation to the depiction of each woman. The ugliness of the brothel episode in Act IV, where Othello treats Desdemona as 'the subtle whore of Venice' that he believes her to be, sufficiently underlines the sordidness of the prostitute's lifestyle. Cassio's fear of being found in public with Bianca – 'would not have him see me womaned' – makes it clear that he is ashamed of this liaison, however flattering to his vanity the fact that Bianca is patently in love with him might be.

Cassio is incredulous at the idea that anyone would imagine even for a moment that he might marry her: 'I marry her! what? a customer? Prithee, bear some charity to my wit.' Obviously he realises that he must break with her, but up till now he has been too weak and too self-indulgent to do so.

Bianca's status as a social outcast is again highlighted when Iago seizes the opportunity to try to incriminate her in relation to Cassio's wounding: 'Gentlemen, I do suspect this trash | To be a party in this injury…'. Here he is obviously relying on the fact that few will be prepared to believe anything Bianca says in her defense.

The parallel with the falsely accused Desdemona is obvious; Othello will believe nothing that can be said in favour of Desdemona, either by herself or by Emilia, because he is convinced that she is a whore and as such one to whom lying is second nature.

It is not simply males who scorn Bianca because of her profession – Emilia is equally ready to upbraid her: 'Fie on thee strumpet.' Emilia is furious that Bianca has dared to speak to her as though she were her social and moral equal. We, however, have been convinced that Bianca's love for Cassio is sincere and this sincerity makes her forgetful of her own safety when she rushes in to comfort him when he is wounded. Clearly her pallor is due to her anxiety for the man she loves and not guilt, as Iago intimates.

Both Emilia and Desdemona die defending their own versions of a love that transcends self and selfish considerations. Bianca lives on, but her survival has its own hint of tragedy, since the object of her love will have no further use for what she has to offer him. Bianca is not even present at the play's conclusion.

MACBETH

(2007 and 2009 exams)

The story

The play is set in Scotland where, at the beginning of the play, Duncan is king. Scotland is at war with Norway. Macbeth is captain of the Scottish forces and possesses the title 'Thane of Glamis'. Lady Macbeth is his wife. Both characters are exceedingly ambitious. Macbeth is rewarded with the title 'Thane of Glamis' because of his valour and personal courage in the battle against Norway. Before he hears of this reward, on his return from the battlefield he meets three witches. They prophesy to him that he will be king hereafter. They tell Banquo, another general, that he will be father to kings. Macbeth is clearly influenced by these prophecies and it is obvious that he has secretly nourished ambitions for kingship.

Lady Macbeth persuades her husband to murder Duncan, who comes to spend the night in their castle at Inverness. After the murder, Duncan's two sons, Malcolm and Donalbain, escape to England and Ireland, respectively. Banquo begins to suspect that Macbeth is the murderer, but he himself is killed shortly before the banquet, which officially inaugurates Macbeth as king. At the banquet, Banquo's ghost appears to Macbeth to mock him. Lady Macbeth defends Macbeth loyally. Macbeth slaughters Macduff's wife and children because Macduff goes to England for help. In England the king is called Edward. He is a good and saintly man who offers to help them regain the throne of Scotland and get rid of Macbeth. In England an army of 10,000 men is mobilised and Siward, a general, together with Macduff and Malcolm, resolve to kill Macbeth and restore Malcolm as lawful king of Scotland.

Meanwhile, Lady Macbeth, who has committed herself fully to evil-doing, now begins to go mad and finally commits suicide. Macbeth pays one last visit to the witches, who show him three false visions. He is misled into thinking he will never be killed by any man born of a woman. However, Macduff kills him in the end, telling him that he was 'ripped untimely from his mother's womb'. In the end, Malcolm is invested with kingship and order is restored to Scotland.

Themes
- Evil and deception, false appearance and equivocation.
- Ambition.
- Kingship.
- Loyalty and betrayal.
- The supernatural.

Genre
The play is from the genre of tragedy and explores the world of supernatural evil.

The witches represent the metaphysical world of evil spirits. They can be seen as archetypal tempters recreating the original temptation that led to the fall of man.

Structure of the play
The play is divided into five main acts. The final destruction of evil and the triumph of good are shown in the concluding scene. The banquet scene is used ironically. It is supposed to confirm Macbeth's power as king, yet as the events proceed in this scene, Macbeth steadily loses control and the scene concludes in chaos. Furthermore, the conclusion of this scene demonstrates the beginnings of the rift between Lady Macbeth and her husband. She becomes haunted by guilt-ridden fantasies, while he develops into a ruthless, hardened murderer.

The plot revolves around the witches' wicked instigations to tempt Macbeth with thoughts of kingship and the evil consequences that ensue.

Style of the play

There is an abundance of blood-dominated imagery, which shows the power of evil and violence in the play.

Irony

Both Macbeth and his wife become victims of irony in this play because their hunger for kingship overrides all moral considerations and turns out to be a disastrous state of being for them. The many references to washing, cleansing and sleeping are all used in a deeply ironic way throughout the play. Both become obsessed with guilt and sleeplessness as a result of their crimes.

Soliloquies

Shakespeare's soliloquies serve many functions. The three characters that use soliloquies in this play are Macbeth, Lady Macbeth and Banquo. In general, the soliloquy furnishes us with a deeper insight into the mentality of that particular character and we can also gain information about the plot. The images used in a soliloquy usually highlight themes or main features of the character.

Cultural context

Under this heading are the following:
* kingship
* the witches
* the political situation.

The monarch at this time was a sacred figure with divine sanction. No earthly individual had a right to put an end to the rule of a king – this was God's right only. Therefore, regicide, or the killing of a king, was no ordinary crime.

The witches represent the supernatural world of evil that was prevalent in Scotland in the early seventeenth century.

The political situation is unstable. The values of order, harmony and stability are shown to be insecure. Under Duncan's rule Scotland has been subjected to rebellion from within (the betrayal of Cawdor) and invasion from without (the war with Norway).

General vision or viewpoint

Malcolm's victory restores order and harmony to Scotland. The leafy branches disguising the advance of the troops are symbolic of new life and hope for Scotland. Malcolm is the 'medicine of the sickly weal', who must 'purge' Scotland of the evil which Macbeth has reduced it to.

Both Macbeth and Lady Macbeth have betrayed themselves by falling for what is equivocal and illusory and now find that their actions and lives are meaningless. Time, life and death have lost all meaning for both. Macbeth's surrender of himself to evil has brought about nothing but a deep sense of emptiness and the futility of life:

Tomorrow, and tomorrow, and tomorrow,
Creeps in this petty pace from day to day,
To the last syllable of recorded time;
And all our yesterdays have lighted fools
The way to dusty death.

(Act V, Scene v)

Evil is shown to be self-destructive in all of Shakespeare's tragedies. Through the logic of events, Shakespeare shows that there is a universal moral law that one transgresses at one's peril.

Summary of the soliloquies
Macbeth's soliloquies

1. Act I, Scene iii. Macbeth's latent ambition is evident. He shows his vacillating moral outlook: 'cannot be ill, cannot be good'. His references to imaginary fears are ironic in light of the banquet scene and Lady Macbeth's breakdown.
2. Act I, Scene iv. Duncan's action in nominating his son Malcolm as successor to the throne is ironic and leads to this soliloquy. Macbeth uses the images of 'black' and 'deep' to show the evil nature of his desires.
3. Act I, Scene vii. This reveals the depths of Macbeth's conscience. It deals with the theme of justice and is a splendid assessment of Duncan's virtuous nature. There is an acknowledgment by Macbeth of his fatal flaw: 'I have no spur …'.
4. Act II, Scene i (the dagger soliloquy). This reveals the fact that Macbeth's moral sense has become corrupted. *Images of evil*: 'pale Hecate', 'bloody business', 'on the blade and dudgeon gouts of blood'.
5. Act III, Scene i. Macbeth's assessment of Banquo's qualities shows the threat to Macbeth while Banquo lives. The images show Macbeth's acknowledgment of the immorality of his deed: 'filed my mind', 'mine eternal jewel given to the common enemy of man'.
6. Act IV, Scene i. Macbeth announces his intention of destroying the Macduff family. He seeks to erase his bitter sense of how meaningless his life has become through this act of gratuitous violence: 'The very firstlings of my heart shall be | The firstlings of my hand'.
7. Act V, Scene iii. Macbeth gives us a glimpse of how hollow his life has become. He enumerates all the values he has lost because of his reign as a tyrant.

Lady Macbeth's soliloquies

1. Act I, Scene v. This is Lady Macbeth's assessment of her husband's character. She commits herself to evil to remove the obstacles that stand between him and the kingship. Images used here include 'the golden round', referring to kingship.
2. Act I, Scene v. She calls on evil to denature her (unsex her) in order to be filled with the necessary amount of murderous cruelty. In these soliloquies she suppresses not only her femininity but also her humanity.
3. Act III, Scene ii. This reflects dissatisfaction with kingship. Images here show us the quality of her life, a state of 'doubtful joy'.

Banquo's soliloquy

Act III, Scene i. Banquo's only soliloquy occurs when Macbeth has taken over kingship. It reveals that the virtuous Banquo may have been seduced by temptation and become morally tainted. Images that reflect a latent ambition that the witches' prophecies may come true include 'their speeches shine', 'May they not be my oracles as well, | And set me up in hope'.

Sample question and answer on Macbeth

'Would you agree with the statement that the witches in the play *Macbeth* are evil, malevolent creatures who originate deeds of blood and have power over the soul?' Discuss this statement with quotations from or reference to the play.

The witches are indeed creatures of evil who have access to secret knowledge; from the beginning of the play they know Macbeth's name: 'Hail to thee, Thane of Glamis'. However, the witches' power is limited. They can incite, tempt and induce characters to do evil, but they can never cause a character to commit sin or carry out evil deeds except indirectly. We see the limited quality of their powers early on in their own reference to the sailor:

> Though his bark cannot be lost,
> Yet it shall be tempest-tost.
> > (Act I, Scene iii)

The witches are agents of evil who seek to reverse the normal order of things and thereby obscure reality. From the outset they make their role clear – to create chaos from what is stable. The essence of their intention can be summed up in the lines

Fair is foul, and foul is fair
Hover through the fog and filthy air.
> (Act I, Scene i)

The witches are clearly intended to represent the metaphysical world of evil spirits roaming around Scotland. Their meetings take place in conditions suggestive of cosmic disorder. Their function on a symbolic level is to mirror the spirit of evil roaming around Scotland. They belong to the equivocal world of seeming. Their every action is a perversion of the natural order. They hover in 'the fog and filthy air'. They appear amid thunder and lightning. They are neither wholly male nor female; they look like women yet have beards:

> > you should be women,
> And yet your beards forbid me to interpret
> That you are so.
> > (Act I, Scene iii)

It is Banquo who recognises this satanic quality inherent in their natures when he asks the question:

What! Can the devil speak true?
>   (Act I, Scene iii)

Banquo also recognises their manner of working:

> And oftentimes, to win us to our harm,
> The instruments of darkness tell us truths,
> Win us with honest trifles, to betray's
> In deepest consequence.
>   (Act I, Scene iii)

Evil works through deception in the play. Shakespeare works the theme of appearance versus reality into the texture of his drama in order to clarify the whole theme of evil. The witches as instruments of evil operate in terms of false appearance. Their verse style is an indication of their function; their incantatory utterances communicate only ambiguous and uncertain meanings. In other words, the witches are 'imperfect speakers'.

Macbeth is in some way unconsciously bound up with the evil world of the witches from the very beginning of the play. His first words, 'so foul and fair a day I have not seen', are an unconscious echo of the witches' words in Act I, Scene i. From his first encounter with them, Macbeth falls victim to their fatal temptations. After this first meeting with them (Act I, Scene iii), Macbeth begins to move in a world of darkness, which is the domain of evil. It is no surprise, therefore, to hear him say shortly afterwards, 'Stars, hide your fires!' Macbeth is simultaneously attracted and repelled by the prophecies. He is 'rapt' in a world apart from his fellows. His soliloquy

> Two truths are told,
> As happy prologues to the swelling act
> Of the imperial theme.
>   (Act I, Scene iii)

shows us how he is beginning to become involved in the dark world of half-truths. This interior battle within Macbeth between good and evil is dramatised as a see-saw rhythm in his musings and in particular his soliloquies:

> This supernatural soliciting
> Cannot be ill, cannot be good;
>   (Act I, Scene iii)

It is obvious that Macbeth has begun to vacillate within himself in this juggling with the sense of good and evil. The witches tempt Macbeth with the possibility of kingship. However, he himself is his own destroyer. He is the one who falls victim to their fatal temptations and carries out murder after murder in his quest for 'sovereign sway and masterdom' (Act I, Scene v). So the witches indeed give rise to deeds of blood and violence through their subtle temptations, but they do not have power over the soul. Macbeth and his wife, Lady Macbeth, each end up as their own destroyer. They both go to their own damnation freely.

After carrying out the murder of Duncan, Macbeth is dominated by a sense of guilt and an agony of restlessness. His mind is full of scorpions, he cannot sleep and he stays alone, moody and savage. Everything within him condemns itself for being there. There is a fever in his blood, which urges him on to ceaseless action in his search for oblivion. Ambition, love of power and an instinct for self-preservation are too potent in him to permit him to give up. Motivated by a new will to live and a renewed desire for the crown, he challenges 'Fate' to come 'into the list'. He is 'bent to know, by the worst means the worst'. A frightful result ensues. He speaks no longer of conscience, remorse or pity, but instead becomes active and purposeful in his dedication to evil. By the time he has reached the witches in Act IV, Scene i, his relationship with them has changed. He is determined that

> Things bad begun make strong themselves by ill:
> (Act III, Scene ii)

His decision at this stage is free, fully conscious and deliberately calculated. He wishes to know the future even though there is universal chaos. After this last encounter with the witches, the whole flood of evil in his nature is unleashed. The final stage of their operation against him is shown in Hecate's words:

> raise such artificial sprites
> As by the strength of their illusion
> Shall draw him on to his confusion:
> (Act III, Scene v)

The apparitions that the witches show to Macbeth are mocking illusions. They offer a false confirmation of his own desires while at the same time symbolising through tragedy and violence the final birth of a new order. In this way they turn out to be dramatically ironic. It is Macbeth's tragedy, however, that he accepts the version of the world offered to him by the witches. Yet at no stage do they compel acceptance of what they offer to him. The crime to which they incite him is committed by himself and the responsibility for succumbing to the temptation is Macbeth's alone. He is his own betrayer. Macbeth's security depends on assumptions such as Birnham Wood moving to Dunsinane and the fact that no man born of a woman will harm him. His life depends on appearances like these. His realisation about the falsity of this world of appearance and half-truths comes too late; only at the end of the tragedy does he realise that the witches have been

> juggling fiends…
> That palter with us in a double sense;
> (Act V, Scene vii)

The witches tempt and entice. As evil agents they are catalysts with limited powers, but bring to the surface the latent evil that lies buried in the subconscious mind. Macbeth is his own destroyer and at every stage in the play freely chooses his own course of action and freely commits himself to the world of evil and violence.

COMMENT

This is a question about the witches and whether or not they are creatures of absolute evil who control the soul of a character. The answer shows how the evil inherent in the witches is not absolute, but simply sparks evil in others.

The first section of this answer explains the nature of the witches in the play and shows how they operate in deceiving characters.

The answer then develops by showing us the particular manner of the witches' evil operation in the play – their misleading language and statements.

The peculiar relationship between Macbeth and the witches is then outlined and Macbeth's free reactions are clearly drawn.

The answer concludes by demonstrating how the evil that governs the play begins in the witches' initial incitements, but is freely adopted by Macbeth himself and carried to a dreadful extreme.

THE TEMPEST

(2009 exam, comparative study only)

The play opens with a storm at sea. Alonso, who is King of Naples, is shipwrecked with his son, Ferdinand, Sebastian, his brother, and Antonio, who is now Duke of Milan, having usurped the throne from Prospero, his brother. Gonzalo, an honest counsellor to Alonso, is also part of the group. They are returning from the wedding of Alonso's daughter to the King of Tunis in Africa.

Miranda speaks to Prospero, who is her father, and tells him to abate the storm as a ship is in danger. She asks her father to tell her what happened to her before she came to the island, as she fails to recall anything. She learns that twelve years ago her father was the Duke of Milan and 'a prince of power'. Prospero tells Miranda about his brother, Antonio, who became ambitious for kingship once he was given a chance to help Prospero with affairs of state. Antonio dispossess Prospero of everything and makes himself the Duke of Milan. He allies himself to the King of Naples, becoming his subject. With help from the King of Naples, Antonio overthrows his own brother and drives him out of his lawful kingdom. Prospero and his daughter were put out to sea on a ship with no gear or tackle. They arrived at an island 'by Providence divine', having been given some food and water and some books by Gonzalo.

Prospero has the gift of magic charms and he has raised the storm at sea. Ariel is the spirit who raised the storm for Prospero and made the King's son, Ferdinand, afraid. Ariel asks Prospero for his liberty. Prospero reminds him of the foul witch Sycorax who was his former master. We learn that Caliban was her son, 'a freckled whelp hag-born'. Prospero reminds Ariel about how he rescued him from the clutches of this hag. Caliban is now Prospero's slave, who makes the fire and fetches the wood. Caliban curses Prospero because of the way he treats him. He states that he was first King of the island and that now Prospero keeps half of the island from him and treats him badly. Caliban tells Prospero that he taught him how to speak and the only profit he has gained from this is that he knows how to curse.

Ferdinand, the son of Alonso, the King of Naples, is now alone and separated from the rest of the group. When Miranda first meets him she thinks he is a thing divine, a noble man. He, on the other hand, sees her as a goddess. They both fall in love immediately. Prospero wants to test their love, so he accuses Ferdinand of being a spy. She stands up for Ferdinand but her father silences her.

Meanwhile, in Act II, Alonso and his crew of men are stranded on another part of the island. Gonzalo tries to mobilise their spirits, telling them how it is great to be alive. Alonso is grieving for the loss of his son and daughter. He feels that now that she is married in Tunis, he won't be able to see much of her. Gonzalo begins to speculate about the possibility of being King of the island and how he would behave in such a situation. He tells them that there would be no riches or poverty, no servants, no boundaries, no division of lands and no occupation carried out by the people if he were King. It would be a type of Utopia where Nature would bring about abundance to feed the people. There would be no crime committed and no felony.

Meanwhile, Ariel enters and overhears a conversation between Sebastian and Antonio, who plot to kill Alonso and take the Kingship of Naples. Ariel whispers in Gonzalo's ear to wake up and protect the King.

Stephano, a drunken butler, and Trinculo, the clown, meet Caliban. At first they think he is a fish and a monster because of his unnatural shape. Caliban begins to curse the 'tyrant' Prospero and swears allegiance to Stephano if he will act as his master.

In Act III, Prospero has compelled Ferdinand to act as slave and has engaged him in menial labor. Ferdinand meets with Miranda again and they both pledge their love for one another. They promise to be faithful to one another and to marry. Prospero overhears this conversation between them.

There is a comic interlude between Stephano, Trinculo the clown and Caliban. Caliban tells them to exact revenge on Prospero, to murder him and steal his books. At the same time, Ariel appears as an invisible spirit who keeps whispering 'you lie, you lie.'

Meanwhile, Prospero appears with several spirits and organises a banquet for Alonso and Antonio and the group who are stranded on another part of the island. The banquet no sooner appears before them than it disappears, and Ariel begins to tell them that they are 'men of sin'. Ariel accuses them of having expelled good Prospero from his throne and warns Alonso that he will be plagued by a life of suffering unless he repents and is sorry for what he has done. Alonso is stricken with grief and blames himself for the loss of his own son.

Act IV opens with Prospero giving permission to Ferdinand to marry Miranda. The spirits of Juno and Ceres begin to sing about marriage, fidelity and chastity. As the nymphs and reapers dance in joy at the happiness of Ferdinand and Miranda, Prospero realises that Caliban is plotting to kill him. Prospero expresses a long speech about the transience of life and mortality. Shortly after this, Stephano, Trinculo and Caliban enter and discover some robes. Stephano begins to parade in them, imagining how he would look as King. Caliban is intent on carrying out the murder of Prospero as soon as possible. Some spirits appear in the shape of dogs and hounds and chase the three away. Prospero promises Ariel his freedom shortly and also declares that his enemies will be punished.

In the final scene in Act V, Prospero and Ariel appear dressed in magic robes. Prospero has imprisoned Alonso and his men. Ariel tells Prospero that the men are deeply repentant and so Prospero declares that 'the rarer action is in virtue than in vengeance' (that virtue is more powerful than revenge) and so he decides to release them. Prospero realises that his magic has done its job, so he decides to renounce it. Prospero, meanwhile, has dressed up in his robes as Duke of Milan and he welcomes them. Alonso wakes up as if he had been in a dream of madness. He repents, resigns his dukedom and asks pardon from Prospero. Prospero accepts his pardon and accuses Sebastian and Antonio of treason and plotting. Then Alonso is reconciled with his son and learns that he is in love with the beautiful Miranda.

Prospero gives Ariel his freedom. He describes Caliban as a 'demi-devil', a 'thing of darkness'. Prospero asks Alonso to go with him to Milan to see the wedding of Ferdinand with his own daughter and that after that he, Prospero, will retire.

The play concludes with an epilogue spoken by Prospero to the audience declaring how his magic is gone, and the only strength left is his own, but that is weak. He states that he has got his dukedom and forgiven the deceiver. He wishes that art will enchant, and asks for prayers to free his faults.

Themes/issues
Kingship/power
Prospero was overthrown by his own brother, Antonio, as Duke of Milan and exiled to a remote island. When Prospero takes control of the island he tries to re-establish justice by assuming power over Ariel, the spirit with magic powers, and Caliban, who is a black slave with monster-like proportions. Prospero exerts his power over Caliban by getting him to work as a slave and he teaches him his own language. Caliban despises Prospero and is filled with animosity and thoughts of revenge against his master.

This relationship between Prospero and his slave, Caliban, could be read as that between an educated culture and an unlettered one, or as that between the coloniser and the colonised. Caliban despises the learning he got from his master and warns Stephano to burn his books before he kills him. However, Prospero turns out to be a good character in his actions. He promises freedom to Ariel, which he grants him at the end. He forgives his enemies and is reconciled with those people who wronged him earlier on in the play. Alonso, the King of Naples, is also a good character who repents for what he has done wrong.

Love
As in all of Shakespeare's plays, love has a dominant part to play. Miranda and Ferdinand fall in love as soon as they meet. Much of the play shows Prospero's attempts to test this love and to prove its quality. Even though Prospero treats Ferdinand as a

slave at certain stages, Ferdinand remains faithful to his beloved Miranda. The play concludes with the imminent marriage of Ferdinand and Miranda.

Genre

This play is described as 'tragicomic'. This play is allied with other plays that Shakespeare wrote in this era, among them *Pericles*, *Cymbeline* and *The Winter's Tale*. They are linked by magic, miracles and exotic locations, and also known as Shakespeare's 'romances'.

The Tempest is written in five acts and concludes with an epilogue. In this case, the epilogue is spoken by Prospero, the main character, to the audience and it sums up his wishes for the future.

Cultural context

This play was written between late 1610 and late 1611. This was a time when England was engaged in major expansion overseas, both the colonisation of Ireland and the colonisation of Virginia. England was coming up against the indigenous inhabitants of the New World. *The Tempest* island is set in the Mediterranean. The play has an African and a Mediterranean context. It deals with the nobility and their relationships. It also shows the function of slaves in that era in the figure of Caliban.

Prospero's island has similarities with a fantasyland rooted in the Old World. Prospero's attempts to use magic and magic spells can be equated with the work of the artist and perhaps with Shakespeare's own artistic creations.

Gonzalo's vivid description of an ideal society or a Utopia could come from current writings at the time of the play's publication about the New World.

General vision or viewpoint

This play was performed for King James I in 1611. The play takes a lighter and gentler tone than the tragedies. *The Tempest* seems to be one of the last plays written by Shakespeare. It is a very rich play, which can be read on many different levels, e.g. as a theatrical work showing the triumph of art over nature or as a critique of colonialism. In the latter respect, Caliban can be seen as a resident of the New World who is exploited by the European newcomers in the figures of Prospero and Miranda.

The general vision seems to be the power of forgiveness and love. In all Shakespeare's plays there is constant conflict between good and evil in man and in society. This is represented in the figure of Antonio, who betrayed Prospero and usurped his throne. This play dramatises the beauty of magic and good spirits and the final triumph of goodness through love and forgiveness.

TWELFTH NIGHT OR WHAT YOU WILL
(2007 exam)

The story

The title of the play comes from the twelfth night that comes at the end of the Christmas holidays, when work is forgotten and life is one of make-believe and joy. The story is set in Illyria on the shores of the Adriatic Sea. The story opens in the palace of Orsino, the Duke of Illyria, who is in love with a rich Countess by the name of Olivia. Olivia is not in love with the Duke.

There has been a violent storm on the seacoast of Illyria and Viola, a young girl who is shipwrecked, is mourning the death of her brother, whom she believes has drowned at sea. Viola disguises herself as a page, calls herself Cesario and offers herself to serve the Duke as his page.

Olivia has an uncle called Sir Toby Belch who drinks a lot. His friend, Sir Andrew Aguecheek, is in love with Olivia. Sir Toby is hoping that Olivia will marry Sir Andrew. They both sit up all night drinking and they get drunk.

The Duke of Illyria sends his new page, Viola, to woo Olivia for him. Ironically, Olivia falls in love with the page Viola. Olivia rejects a ring given to her by the Duke and instead sends Malvolio after Viola to return the ring. Viola is upset because now she is in a dilemma. She realises that Olivia is in love with her while she herself has fallen in love with the Duke. Meanwhile, Sebastian, Viola's twin brother, appears near a seacoast. He is speaking to a sea captain called Antonia who has saved him from drowning. Sebastian is bound for Count Orsino's court.

Sir Toby Belch and Sir Andrew have been drinking and are singing aloud even though it is midnight. Malvolio enters in anger and tries to quiet them. Malvolio is very self-righteous and even Maria, who is Olivia's servant, is tired of him. Maria becomes annoyed at Malvolio's pompous vanity and self-righteousness, so she decides to play a trick on him. She plans to write a love letter to Malvolio and make him think it comes from Olivia. She realises that Malvolio will fall for this as he 'is so crammed with excellences, that it is his ground of faith that all that look on him love him.'

Maria writes the letter and seals it with Olivia's seal. Sir Toby and Sir Andrew hide behind a tree along with Fabian, another servant. Malvolio finds the letter and believes all the false sentiments about Olivia's supposed love for him. The letter concludes with advice on how to please her best: 'in my presence still smile dear my sweet.' The letter also tells him to wear yellow stockings with the garters crossed, something which Olivia detests.

Viola returns to Olivia on behalf of the Duke to plead his suit. It is clear to everyone, including Sir Toby and Sir Andrew, that Olivia is in love with the handsome page. Sir Andrew, whose hopes of having Olivia's hand in marriage seem to be dashed, is now left with the alternative of challenging the page to a duel.

Sebastian, Viola's brother, is in town. Antonio lends him some money. He does not want to be seen as he has the reputation in Illyria of being a pirate. They agree to meet later in the suburbs.

Olivia becomes very melancholy because the page does not return her love. Furthermore, Malvolio has begun to annoy her deeply because he is behaving in a stupid manner with his yellow garters and his annoying smile. Sir Andrew is intent on fighting a duel with the page. Needless to say, Viola is not able to manage a sword and fears a conflict with Sir Andrew.

Antonio enters and thinks that the page is Sebastian. Antonio tries to rescue the page, or Sebastian, as he thinks, but he is apprehended by the Duke's officers as a pirate. He begs Viola to return the money he gave her on loan. She knows nothing about money, but begins to wonder whether or not her brother is alive in the light of what he has just said to her.

Shortly after this, Sir Andrew meets Sebastian and mistakes him for the page. Sebastian beats him. Olivia meets Sebastian and declares her love for him. She tells him she has organised the priest so that they can marry. Sebastian is totally confused but at the same time he is delighted with the offer and so he agrees.

Meanwhile, Malvolio has been locked into a dark chamber in Olivia's house to keep him quiet. The Clown appears and pretends he is Sir Topas and is chasing the devils away from him. Eventually Malvolio persuades the Clown to give him a pen and some paper so that he can write a letter to Olivia.

Outside on the street, Viola becomes confronted with a series of dilemmas. Antonio appears with officers and tells the Duke that he is not a pirate and accuses Viola of having betrayed his loyalty and friendship for denying that she knows him. With the appearance of Olivia, the situation becomes even more complicated. She tells the Duke that she has just married Viola, who totally denies the fact. Viola declares her love for the Duke. The entrance of the priest confirms Olivia's story and adds to the confusion. Furthermore, when Sir Andrew enters with his head sore from the beating he received, the situation reaches a peak of high comedy. He accuses Viola of having attacked him. She denies it vehemently. The situation is resolved with the arrival of Sebastian, who is delighted when he is reconciled with his twin sister, Viola.

Malvolio is released and finds out the truth about the letter. He is furious and declares that he will revenge himself on all of them. The Duke sends a messenger after him to declare peace. The play concludes on a cheerful note of joy and song.

Themes

Love

Love dominates the play. From the beginning, when she adopts a disguise as a handsome page, Viola becomes a messenger of love in the play on behalf of the Duke. She falls in love with him, however, and this makes the situation quite complicated. Much of the comedy in the play arises from the fact that many of the characters fall in love with the wrong person. Olivia falls in love with the page, Viola, who in turn happens to be in love with the Duke. At the same time, Malvolio, who is opinionated and dominated by a great deal of vanity, thinks that Olivia is in love with him. Both the Duke and Sir Andrew are in love with Olivia, even though she continually rebuffs them. At the conclusion of the play, the main characters find true love.

Mistaken identities

The theme of mistaken identity is developed from the beginning of the play. Viola, the twin sister of Sebastian, disguises herself as a page. For much of the play, everyone thinks she is a beautiful boy. This situation gives rise to a great deal of the comedy in the play. When Viola goes to Olivia on behalf of the Duke, Olivia falls in love with her, mistaking her for a handsome man. The situation reaches a climax at the conclusion with the return of Sebastian, Viola's twin brother. The characters' identities are revealed, and the play concludes happily with the union of the Duke and Viola and that between Olivia and Sebastian.

Genre

This is a romantic comedy written in five acts. There are many scenes made up of song and dance.

Cultural context

The cultural background is centered around the life of the nobility. The setting is Illyria, a place situated on the shores of the Adriatic Sea. Olivia's uncle, Sir Toby Belch, is obviously very wealthy and idle. He spends a good deal of time drinking with his friend, Sir Andrew Aguecheek. There are many servants and these have a lot of freedom in their lives. The play is set near a coast and we gain an insight into the life of a sailor through the characters of Antonio in particular and Sebastian.

General vision or viewpoint

The general vision or viewpoint in this play is very positive and light hearted. From the outset, relationships between people are shown to be genuine and important. Nearly all the characters in the play are in search of love in their lives. This search is shown to be quite eventful and funny as the story unfolds. The overall vision shows how difficulties can be overcome and how people can attain happiness when they find the right person.

12
Notes on Films

CHARACTERISTICS OF FILMS

This chapter contains some guidelines that can be used in answering questions in the comparative study section. There are also notes on all the films on the prescribed syllabus for Higher Level.

Il Postino	2007 exam
A Room with a View	2007 exam
Henry V	2007 exam
Witness	2007 exam
My Left Foot	2007, 2008 exams
Twelve Angry Men	2007, 2008 exams
Much Ado about Nothing	2008 exam
Strictly Ballroom	2008, 2009 exams
Cinema Paradiso	2008, 2009 exams
The Truman Show	2008, 2009 exams
Richard III	2009 exam
Inside I'm Dancing	2009 exam
The Third Man	2009 exam

A film is about people, places and situations. The way they are shown and the reason they are shown in a particular way varies greatly. A film is a narrative – it tells a story. Being able to say what a film is about, or the meaning of the story, is another way of identifying the themes or issues treated.

It is important to understand what particular values or views of life are represented in a film. A film can promote or criticise certain issues, depending on the stance taken by the director on the themes or issues being presented.

Examine what values or understanding of life the film emphasises or criticises. Ask yourself the following questions:
* Is there a coherent message or moral in the film? If not, why not?
* How does the film leave you at the end? Depressed? Sad? Happy? Why?

Film genres

A film-maker structures the story or narrative in a particular way. In other words, the viewpoint adopted by the film-maker in relation to the subject is what constitutes the film's genre. Film genres include detective story or thriller, western, romance, biography and social realism.

Features of the film genre

Films are made up of images that are photographed within a particular frame – the rectangle that contains the image. The camera frame controls what the audience sees and how they see it. According to what the film-maker is trying to say, this frame can control certain actions and eliminate others or it can direct attention in a particular direction, either towards an object or person or away from them.

Understanding the genre of a film means being able to ask and answer certain questions:

* Is there a pattern of striking camera movements, long shots or abrupt transitions?
* Why does the film end on this image?
* Why does the film start in the way it does?
* When was the film made?
* What does the title mean in relation to the story?
* Why are the credits presented in this particular way? Why are they presented against a particular background?

Every film uses patterns of repetition that are contrasted with certain important moments. One of the first steps in analysing the meaning of a film is recognising these patterns and understanding why they are important.

IL POSTINO

Directed by Michael Radford

(2007 exam)

The story

Mario is a young man who lives on an island off the coast of Italy. His father tells him to find a job so he applies for a job as a postman. He discovers that he has to bring the mail every day to a Chilean poet called Pablo Neruda, who has been exiled to Italy because he is a communist. Giorgio is Mario's boss and he has great veneration and respect for Pablo. Pablo writes love poems and as a result he receives a lot of mail from women. Pablo lives with his wife in a beautiful part of the island called Cala di Sotto. Mario gets one of Pablo's books and asks him to sign it for him but is upset that Pablo has not signed his full name, Mario Ruoppolo. Mario begins to read the book and becomes fascinated with it. Friendship blossoms between Mario and Pablo. Mario begins to speak to Pablo about poetry and metaphors and becomes a communist as well. Mr Di Cosmino is a local politician who spends his time looking for votes from the locals on the island.

After a while Mario falls in love with a beautiful girl called Beatrice. Mario asks Pablo to write him a poem for Beatrice. Beatrice lives with an aunt who opposes her relationship with Mario. Some time later the couple marry and Mario asks Pablo to be his best man. At the wedding Pablo receives a letter allowing him the freedom to return to Chile. Beatrice becomes pregnant and Mario decides to call the child Pablito. Mario follows all Pablo's movements by reading the newspapers and hears that he has been to Russia to receive an award. Mario receives a letter one day from Pablo's secretary asking him to send on some of the objects he left behind in the house. Mario returns to the house and begins to reminisce about all the good times he enjoyed while Pablo was there. Mario decides to tape the different sounds of the sea and the wind on the cliffs for Pablo. However, he never sends him the tape.

Shortly after this, Pablo returns to the island with his wife for a visit. Pablo meets Pablito, Mario's child, and Beatrice tells him that Mario is dead. He died as he was reading a poem he had written, dedicated to Pablo. The crowd at a communist meeting crushed him. The story concludes with the image of Pablo walking along the beach and listening to Mario's words on the tape.

Themes
- Friendship.
- Politics.
- Relationships.
- Love.
- Loyalty.

Friendship
One of the main themes in the film is the strong relationship between Pablo, the Chilean poet, and Mario, the Italian postman. Their relationship begins through Mario's fascination with Pablo's lifestyle and his poems. This friendship grows throughout the film and Mario becomes a communist, following in Pablo's footsteps.

Love
Pablo Neruda, the Chilean poet in the film, is known as the poet of love. This theme is shown in a very tender and sympathetic way. The love between Mario and his wife Beatrice is deep and strong. This love is not destined to last long, however, as Mario dies when his son is very young.

Genre
The genre of this film is social realism with a touch of romance. It is set in Italy and gives us a vivid picture of a small but united community.

Camera angles
There are many contrasting scenes used in this film to highlight the beauty of the Italian landscape and also many shots of the distinct type of buildings in this small village.

Cultural context
The particular cultural context is based on the values of a simple Italian village that survives mainly on fishing. There are realistic insights into certain types of characters, such as the man who runs the post office and who employs Mario. We also see glimpses of the political life in this community through the figure of Di Cosmino. Certain values of honesty and simplicity are set against those of self-interest and corruption. The women who are represented in the film work hard and seem to suffer a great deal in their lives, mainly from the poverty that surrounds them.

General vision or viewpoint
The treatment of human life and relationships in this film is tender and poignant. The general vision in this film is based on the inevitable suffering and joy inherent in life. Relationships are central in life and can contribute to changing the quality of a person's life and outlook. This is evident from the fact that Mario was greatly influenced by Pablo, the Chilean poet, and became a communist as a result. Pablo too was changed in his relationship with Mario and learned to appreciate certain values, such as loyalty and goodness. The overall general vision is positive.

A ROOM WITH A VIEW
Based on the book by E. M. Forster; directed by James Ivory

(2007 exam)

Historical and literary background
The film is based on the novel by E. M. Forster, first published in 1908, a time when England was still a colonial power.

The story
Lucy Honeychurch, a young Englishwoman, is on a visit to Florence, chaperoned by her cousin, Charlotte Bartlett. They have been led to believe that they will have a wonderful view at the Pensione Bertolini, but they are disappointed when they arrive. An English father and son overhear them when they express their dissatisfaction and promptly offer to exchange rooms. Charlotte, for her young cousin's sake, is offended at this presumption, especially since the young man is dangerously attractive. However, the rector of Lucy's parish in England, Mr Beebe, happens to be staying there as well; he offers to act as an intermediary and the rooms are exchanged without further ado.

The next morning Charlotte tours the city with Eleanor Lavish, a novelist she met at dinner the night before. Lucy goes for a walk alone and witnesses a violent street fight, in which a young man is seriously injured. She becomes weak and faints from the shock of what she has seen. Luckily, George Emerson, the young man she had met in the *pensione* (guesthouse), is there to help her back to her lodgings.

The following day all the English visitors arrange to go sightseeing as a group and the Emersons belong to the party. George and Lucy become separated from the others, and in a cornfield he kisses her. Charlotte witnesses what happens and after they return to the city she arranges for them to leave their rooms the next day. The women agree not to tell anyone what has happened to Lucy.

Back in England, Lucy accepts a proposal of marriage from Cecil Vyse, a pompous and arrogant snob. By chance, the Emersons take a house in the village of Summer Street, close to the Honeychurch residence. Mr Beebe and Lucy's brother, Freddy, invite George to go swimming in a nearby pond on his first day in the village. The men are high-spirited and naked and they chase each other around the pond. Unfortunately, this occurs at the same time that the ladies are taking their afternoon walk in the woods and they come upon the men in all their naked glory.

Freddy befriends George and he is regularly invited to the Honeychurch home to play tennis. Lucy is perturbed by George's renewed proximity; the contrast between George and the stuffy Cecil is obvious, which unsettles Lucy.

When Charlotte comes to stay with the family she is concerned for Lucy, fearing that George's presence will do harm to her engagement to Cecil. One day Cecil is reading aloud and criticising what he considers to be a dreadful novel and both Lucy and George are listening. The book happens to be by Eleanor Lavish, the woman who stayed in the same *pensione*, and is set in Florence. Cecil reads a paragraph exactly describing the scene where George kissed Lucy. On the way back into the house, out of sight of the others, George repeats the performance.

Lucy is upset by this and hurt that Charlotte told Eleanor Lavish after they had agreed not to tell anyone about what had happened in Italy. In Charlotte's presence she asks George to leave. George gives a passionate account of his love for her and tries to make her see that Cecil cares for her only as he would a prize possession. Lucy denies the fact that she may love George, but all the same she breaks off her engagement with Cecil soon afterwards.

When George sees that Lucy will not have him he decides to leave Summer Street, as he cannot bear to be near her. Lucy is shocked to see the furniture being removed from the house. Mr Emerson talks to her and makes a heartfelt plea to her to stop denying the truth. Realisation dawns on her that she does love George after all and the film ends with the two lovers on their honeymoon in the same *pensione* in Florence, where they kiss at the window of the 'room with a view'.

Themes
Love

A Room with a View is essentially a love story with a happy ending. Within the first ten minutes Lucy exchanges glances with George Emerson across the dinner table and we know that something is going to happen. Even Charlotte Bartlett can see this. She senses danger immediately and is extremely protective of Lucy.

The relationship develops the next day when George catches Lucy as she faints with horror at the sight of blood after a street fight. Lucy is naturally wary of him and gives the distinct impression that she does not trust her own feelings where he is concerned. On the way back to the *pensione* they pause for a while looking down on the river and George simply says, 'Something tremendous has happened.'

Unlike Lucy, who is unsure of her feelings, George knows that he is attracted to her and he acts on his instincts. He takes the opportunity to kiss her a second time after Cecil has read the paragraph based on their first encounter in Italy. He is more spontaneous when he acts like this, though he is reserved in company.

It is clear to the viewer that Lucy is attracted to George, but class barriers prevent her from admitting her love for him. It is only when her refusal to accept his love drives him away that she is jolted into the realisation that she does love him after all and cannot bear the thought of losing him.

The story draws a contrast between the idea of love and real love as it is evinced in everyday life. Cecil Vyse proposes to Lucy because he desires a wife who is suitable to his needs. Lucy comes from a fitting family, is attractive and she plays the piano very well. Cecil is emotionally shallow, but Lucy refuses to acknowledge that their relationship will be hollow and insincere. It is only when George arrives and passionately declares his love for her that Lucy realises what true love is.

Self-deception and self-realisation

It is obvious from the start that Lucy deceives herself about her feelings for George. On the day they meet, George's father is intrusive, pushy and generous almost to the point of rudeness, which emphasises the fact that they are from different classes. Charlotte is horrified at his manner and Lucy unconsciously knows that a relationship between herself and George would be unacceptable to her family.

On her return to England she is courted by Cecil Vyse, a man from the highest social class. This fact underlines the gap between herself and George. Lucy accepts Cecil's proposal of marriage because it seems the right thing to do. Cecil is neither physically nor emotionally attractive to her and as the story unfolds she finds him more unbearable, particularly when compared with George.

The plot is based on the fact that Lucy is lying not only to everyone else but to herself as well. Finally, realising that she cannot suppress her feelings any longer, she transcends the social barriers that separate her from her lover. Much of the viewer's enjoyment of this film comes from observing Lucy's struggle to admit her true feelings to herself and watching her succumb to them in the end.

Class

To the English upper and middle classes at the turn of the century, social position was crucial. In *A Room with a View*, snobbery, pretentiousness and the accompanying hypocrisy are glaringly exposed. Charlotte's attitude towards Mr Emerson in the *pensione* is a striking example of this. The Miss Alans, an elderly couple, also illustrate this when they sympathise with Charlotte and Lucy for having to endure Mr Emerson's insistence on exchanging rooms.

Cecil Vyse is an insufferable snob who sneers at everything that does not meet his standards. In fact, he shows how social standing and gentility do not necessarily go together: he is quite rude about Lucy's brother, Freddy, because he is not an academic and he makes Lucy's mother feel that she is not good enough for him.

It is Cecil who unwittingly organises the letting of the cottage in Summer Street to the Emersons. This is not done out of goodwill but to get the better of the owner and to punish him for being (in Cecil's opinion) a snob. It doesn't occur to him that George Emerson will be invited to socialise with people as genteel as the Honeychurch family.

It is because of her position in society that Lucy accepts Cecil's proposal and refuses to consider George's advances. There is too much at stake for her to contemplate disgracing herself and her family; the fact that Cecil continuously reminds her of the difference between his position and George's reinforces the point. It is Cecil who precipitates his own downfall through this approach, as Lucy begins to see that he is more in love with the idea of who he is than with selflessly giving himself to her in a loving relationship.

In the end, Lucy has the courage to overcome the social barriers that divide her and George and to follow her instincts. Much of the film concentrates on Lucy's emancipation from the restrictions imposed on her by her family and the society that surrounds her.

Genre
Romance.

Structure and style
Visual images and photography
The Florentine scene, with the view as the main focus, is a striking feature of the film. Art is an important topic, as the architecture of Florence illustrates. The stone carvings on the streets and the inside of a church are examined, paintings in the art gallery in London also feature and Cecil compares Lucy to a Leonardo da Vinci painting. The lovers kiss in a beautiful cornfield and later on in green countryside. The colour green is evident everywhere – England's lush landscape is seen in the swimming episode and in the tennis parties.

There are no significant changes in the lighting at any point in the film. Italy and England in the summer are both awash with light. England indoors is often in shadow, which sometimes varies according to the scene. When Lucy is refusing George the room is particularly dark. Most of this shadowy lighting reflects their relationship.

Language
The actors' accents are clearly drawn. Cecil Vyse in particular has what he considers to be a superior accent. His speeches are in a haughty tone and this is more exaggerated when he is criticising or demeaning someone. His language makes him sound and look ridiculous. Mr Emerson speaks with a plain and unadorned accent. He comes across as a more honest character who speaks as he feels and he stands out in contrast to Cecil, and in particular to the company he meets in Florence and England.

Symbols

The piano is a symbol in the film. Lucy plays it regularly, expressing her strongest emotions through her playing. It is Mr Beebe who is struck by the fact that her personality does not match the way she plays. He makes the point that if Lucy lived as she played, 'it will be very exciting for us, and for her.' He suspects that she will break out some day and that 'one day music and life will mingle.'

Cultural context

Two contrasting cultural backgrounds are depicted in this film: upper-class England and Florence. Bourgeois England is restrained and rigid, with great importance attached to certain codes of behaviour. Women are not allowed to travel alone but have to be chaperoned. The style of life is stiff and formal, which is shown in dress, speech, movement and social behaviour.

The culture of Florence, on the other hand, is rich and flamboyant. The atmosphere is open and bright; the streets are exciting and fascinating. We see open, airy streets and squares, impressive monuments and striking architecture. The Italians are a colourful and varied people; they have no problem chatting to foreigners or even engaging in a violent street fight. Thus, the social codes are radically different.

General vision or viewpoint

The general vision or viewpoint seems to be ambivalent about the England the film portrays. In one way it could be seen as a lightly critical satire of Edwardian society, while on another level it could be an affectionately observed comedy of manners.

HENRY V

By William Shakespeare; directed by Kenneth Branagh

(2007 exam)

The story

Henry V is King of England. As the film opens, we witness Henry planning to wage war on France over some disputed titles. He meets with some members of his advisory committee.

The French ambassador arrives with a packet of tennis balls from the French Dauphin. This gesture is a deliberate insult to Henry, who was formerly characterised as a reckless young man going by the name of Prince Hal.

Henry is determined to wage war on France as a result of this incident. Charles VI is King of France. Charles and his council are convinced of the superiority of the French army over the English. The English army numbers 12,000 men in comparison with the French, who number 60,000. The French troops prepare for battle with the English at Agincourt. Henry is unsure of the loyalty of his army and disguises himself on the eve of battle. In a series of conversations with various English soldiers, Henry becomes convinced of their support and loyalty and realises that their patriotism and determination are true and strong. Henry mobilises his troops continuously, urging them to fight for God and for England. He believes he is doing the right thing by engaging in battle. Just before the battle itself, he again urges his men to fight bravely for England, especially on this feast day of Crispin. The English are victorious and in spite of their relatively small numbers manage to massacre 10,000 French soldiers while sustaining few casualties themselves, as some noblemen are slain (only twenty-five men). Henry maintains that it was God who fought for them on this special feast day.

England is triumphant and Henry secures the hand in marriage of Katharine, the French princess. The film concludes with an image of the French king consenting to all reasonable terms and he signs the document in front of the English king. He gives Katharine to Henry in marriage. They pray for neighbourliness and Christian accord between their two countries. He prays to God to bind their two kingdoms together and that no jealousy will prevail. The French and English will receive each other in peace and harmony.

Themes
- War.
- Violence.
- Loyalty.
- Goodness.
- Friendship/love.

War

War in this film is seen as a glorious and brave event. Henry engages in many speeches to his troops, praising their courage and valour and declaring that this war has God's blessing. We see an image of the ideal hero in the figure of Henry V. He is brave in battle and loyal to his troops.

Goodness

There are many examples of this theme in the film. In the figure of Henry V we are shown a man who is kind and generous towards his subjects. We also see much good in Charles VI, King of France, a quiet and dignified man who believes in justice and mercy. The fact that Henry frequently invokes the name of God to help him on the battlefield also indicates that he believes in the justice of his cause.

Genre

The genre of this film is social realism and is based on the historical play written by William Shakespeare.

Camera angles

The film makes use of a variety of camera angles to highlight the bloody scenes of battle.

Cultural context

There are two contrasting world culturally. The film is shot in England and France. In both worlds there are some excruciating violent scenes. The time period is England and France in the fifteenth century. The particular cultural background is that of a Catholic king on the throne of England. Many of Henry's speeches are filled with references to God and his goodness and justice.

General vision or viewpoint

The general vision or viewpoint throughout this play is positive. Henry is a king who possesses a profound faith in God and his way of working. In the film the overall impression is that good will triumph and justice will prevail. The British troops fight a bloody battle against the French army, but they are constantly animated by Henry, who possesses a sure faith in divine providence. This faith stands to him at the conclusion. With England's victory over France and the securing of Katherine, the daughter of the French king, in marriage, justice and peace will prevail under Henry as king.

WITNESS

Directed by Peter Weir

(2007 exam)

The story

The story begins in 1984 in a community of Amish people in Pennsylvania. The opening sequence shows the funeral of Jacob, the husband of a young Amish woman called Rachel. She has a son called Samuel. Everyone in the community is dressed in black.

Rachel decides to pay a visit to her sister in Baltimore, taking Samuel with her. They arrive at the central train station and have to wait three hours there. The child wanders into the men's toilet and witnesses a man being killed with a knife by two other men. Samuel manages to escape. A police officer called John Book takes on the case. The man who was killed was a policeman. Rachel and Samuel are forced to stay and identify the man who carried out the crime. While Samuel is in the police station he sees a photograph of a coloured policeman and recognises him as the man who carried out the murder. The policeman is a narcotics officer, called McFee. Book goes to Paul Schaeffer, who is head of the police. Book realises that after a narcotics raid four years before, McFee has become involved in illegal dealings in narcotics worth over $22 million.

Paul tells Book that the FBI will take care of things. Book is shot at by McFee shortly after this in a car park. He then realises that the police are involved in the murder. Book decides to flee back to the Amish community with Rachel and Samuel. He rings his friend Carter in the police force and tells him to destroy all documentation on the affair.

Book sustains gunshot wounds and is forced to take refuge in the Amish community. His wounds are severe, but eventually he is restored to health. He begins to learn all the Amish customs and imbibes their culture, which is free from violence and governed by peace. He falls in love with Rachel.

Schaeffer and McFee carry out investigations to find Book. Carter is interrogated by Schaeffer and eventually killed. At one stage, some of the community go into town with Book and are antagonised by some local boys. The Amish do not fight, but Book is angered and fights the boys. The local police inform Schaeffer and his gang and they come to the Amish village to kill him. Book is in the barn and one of the men comes in with a gun. Book manages to kill him by making him fall into a huge container of grain. He picks up the man's gun and shoots McFee. Schaeffer comes into the barn with a gun held to Rachel's head. He warns Book that he will shoot her if he does not surrender. Book throws down his gun. In the meantime Samuel has rung the bell and all the Amish community come running from the fields to help. Schaeffer holds a gun to Book and leads him out of the barn. Book then stands with the community and attacks Schaeffer verbally. Schaeffer surrenders and is led away by the police. Book leaves Rachel and the community and returns to his job in Philadelphia at the end of the film.

Themes
- Violence and corruption.
- Loyalty and friendship.
- Trust.
- Peace and goodwill.
- Justice.

Loyalty and friendship
These virtues are strongly evident within the Amish community, in striking contrast to the grim, corrupt reality of deception and lies in the urban police force. Book is concerned not to expose Samuel to further danger and for that reason he discontinues the investigation into the crime. Book's friend Carter is also a police officer, who loses his life because of his loyalty to Book.

Peace and the power it brings
It is within the Amish community that, for the first time in his life, Book experiences the consolations of peace and hard work. In the Amish community violence is seen as destructive and for that reason none of the people carry a weapon of any type. When Book is living there he is forced to hand over his gun and we see him adapting readily to their simple but peaceful lifestyle.

Genre
The genre of this film is social realism. It makes use of a variety of camera angles to show the contrast between the two different communities.

Cultural context

The cultural context which is represented in this film is based on two totally contrasting worlds – the police force and the Amish community in Pennsylvania. Both worlds are dramatically opposed. The police force is riddled with corruption and violence and forms the catalyst of the plot. In contrast, there is a distinctly opposing vision given in the Amish community. Here, values of peace and respect for the sanctity of human life are foremost. Clothes, style of dress and behaviour, speech and food form a distinct contrast in both cultural worlds. Human life is sacrosanct in the world of the Amish, while life seems to be expendable and held in little value in urban society.

General vision or viewpoint

The general vision or viewpoint in this film is based on the fact that justice finally wins out in the end. Schaeffer, the corrupt head of the police, is eventually overthrown because of the unity among the Amish people. The loyalty and peace-loving values inherent in this Amish community triumph over the evil forces of corruption and violence at the end and the evil characters receive justice. Good triumphs, but at a price, as two police officers are murdered.

MY LEFT FOOT

Based on the book by Christy Brown; directed by Jim Sheridan

(2007 and 2008 exams)

Historical and literary background

The background of this film is working-class Dublin in the 1930s, a time of poverty and hardship.

The story

My Left Foot is based on the autobiography of Christy Brown, a writer and painter who was born with cerebral palsy into an impoverished family. The film begins with the mature Christy arriving at the house of Lord Castlewellan to participate in a presentation for charity. It then develops by means of flashback as it recalls Christy's attempts to overcome the limitations imposed by his condition. He is a strong and determined character who comes from a tough social background in which a person is expected to make out for himself.

Poverty is a central feature in the lives of the characters. Christy's father's moods fluctuate, as he finds it hard to accept Christy's limited ability. His mother, on the other hand, is a stalwart figure who quietly perseveres and patiently encourages Christy through all his vicissitudes. All his family unites to encourage him in his attempts at painting. It is significant that the first word he writes is 'Mother'.

His mother is an indispensable agent in his growth, continually sacrificing herself so that he will get all the help and encouragement he needs.

Later, Christy's father dies as he tries to build a room where Christy can carry out his work undisturbed. Christy falls in love with his therapist, who helps him to develop his talents. At the conclusion he marries the nurse, Mary, who is seen with him during the reception in the house of Lord Castlewellan.

Themes

Courage

The principal theme of this film is courage in the face of adversity, seen in the life of Christy Brown and his family. The superhuman struggle to overcome the personal limitations imposed by cerebral palsy and the corresponding courage that is shown by the characters triumph at the conclusion of the film.

Family

The power of the family is another theme of *My Left Foot*. We see how the support of his family generates a positive attitude in Christy, with the mother as a central figure of power and unity.

Love

The theme of love and the need for emotional security features strongly. It is seen as a powerful emotional force that transcends personal limitations and builds up the person.

Class

We get an insight into the class structure of society in this film. Christy belongs to the working class, while Lord Castlewellan's background is the Anglo-Irish ascendancy class; this is shown through such symbols as the big car, the butler and the long avenue lined with trees.

Genre
Biography

Structure and style
Visual images and photography
Close-ups are used to focus our attention on Christy's attempts to communicate, to show his frustrations or simply give expression to his feelings. Close-ups of the mother portray her anguish and suffering, while those of the father show his perplexity and confusion with the whole situation.

The streets are long and dark, suggesting the poverty of working-class Dublin. When Christy becomes famous the lighting significantly becomes brighter and there are more open spaces, as money has enlarged his possibilities.

Sound
The music is intense and dramatic, underlining the frustrations and tensions of the story.

Language
The language used is the Dublin working-class dialect of English.

Cultural context
The cultural background of this film is working-class Dublin in the early twentieth century, a time of relative poverty. Families are large but united and traditional hospitality and neighbourliness still exist. We see this in the frequent offers of neighbourly help, the street games organised by local teenagers and the family meals. The Catholic faith is a strong feature of life in this society, evident in the many religious images. The local pub is an important focal point in the life of the community. Significantly, when Christy writes his first words on the slate, his father carries him down to the pub for his first pint of stout. Christy is being initiated into manhood.

General vision or viewpoint
The general vision of this film is positive. The impression we are left with at the conclusion is the importance of struggle and optimism in the face of difficulties. The power of the mother is a central facet in consolidating unity and strength within Christy in spite of all the odds; she is a continuous source of hope and optimism.

Christy's own tenacity is also evident, not only in the way he develops his talents to an outstanding degree but in the strength with which he deals with people. This is evident at the conclusion when he nags the nurse to such a degree that she agrees to meet him that night. Later on he marries her.

TWELVE ANGRY MEN
Directed by Sidney Lumet

(2007 and 2008 exams)

The story

The story takes place in one room with twelve men who form part of a jury for a murder trial. The twelve men are assembled together to decide on the guilt of a young boy who has been accused of murdering his father. None of the men are given names. One member of the jury (we learn at the conclusion that he is called Davis) declares that the young boy is not guilty while the other eleven members firmly maintain that he is. The film is made up of dialogue to establish the truth about the circumstances. Each man attempts to offer a rational explanation on what he thinks has happened. They attempt to bring the matter to a quick conclusion while the member of the jury who supports the boy remains firm. The men are anxious to finish quickly and bring the whole matter to a reasonable conclusion, as all of them are strongly convinced of the boy's guilt.

As the film proceeds and the dialogue develops between the men, it becomes clear that many of the men who maintain the fact of this boy's guilt are governed by deep-seated prejudices. Some of these men maintain that the young boy's background of poverty and drugs makes his guilt inevitable. Another member of the jury is clearly prejudiced emotionally. He has a photograph of his own son, who has not spoken to him for over two years. It becomes clear that as a father he has failed to establish good communication with his son and for that reason he is antagonistic towards the young man on trial. Each scene shows us how the different men change their minds on the verdict. The men are restless and impatient and we see much hostility between them. They decide to take a secret vote and one new man from the jury votes that he is not guilty. They continue to argue among themselves, declaring that they cannot send a boy to his death in the electric chair on evidence that is not foolproof.

One by one the members of the jury begin to change their minds, having established that they now do not agree with the witnesses, doubting the truth of their testimony. They bring in the knife and while one is declaring that this is a unique knife, Davis produces a similar knife, which he bought in a local shop. One of the members is a foreigner, who reminds them to forget their personal prejudices and that they are deciding on the life of another human being. They also establish that the woman who testified to seeing the young boy killing his father wore glasses, but did not want to do so in court for reasons of vanity. Through building up a good deal of small details they begin to realise that they could be wrong and that the boy could be innocent. Gradually, as the evidence which had been brought against this boy begins to crumble, each man starts to change his mind and declare the boy not guilty. The film concludes with one man eventually breaking down and crying because his prejudice against the boy was rooted in a bad relationship with his own son. Every one of the twelve men votes not guilty at the conclusion.

Themes
- Prejudice.
- Truth.
- Integrity.
- Justice.

Genre
This is a classic black and white movie. All of the action takes place in one room. There are a few dramatic camera angles, ranging from close-ups to some well-composed medium shots. The music is plaintive and consists of a solo flute by Kenyon Hopkins.

Cultural context
The film is set in middle-class America. The opening sequence focuses on tall, imposing pillars of justice outside Manhattan's general sessions offices. It is set on a stifling hot summer's day, which mirrors the various passions and prejudices of the different men. The jury is made up of an all-male white group, mainly of middle-class status. The cultural background of the young boy accused of murdering his father is Puerto Rican. Much of the dialogue in the film reveals the different and contrasting cultural prejudices of the characters.

General vision or viewpoint
At one stage, one member of the jury reminds another man in the room that what they

are speaking about is 'not an exact science'. The whole film dramatises how uncertain human judgment can be and how it can be subject to error in small details. The importance of human life and its sacred quality is reaffirmed throughout this film. From the beginning, Davis, who refuses to condemn the young boy, is unsure of the facts of the case, but his main contention is that a young boy's life is at stake. Each member of the jury is forced to face their own personal prejudices and emotional states and try to squarely acknowledge the truth about the situation given the limitations of the facts presented. The need for deliberation and exact testimony in the judicial system becomes evident from the very beginning of this film.

MUCH ADO ABOUT NOTHING
By William Shakespeare; directed by Kenneth Branagh

(2008 exam)

Historical and literary background
Mediaeval Italy as seen through the eyes of William Shakespeare (sixteenth-century England) forms the historical background of this film.

The story
The story concerns two sets of lovers: Claudio and Hero and Beatrice and Benedick. Don Pedro, Prince of Aragón, returns victorious from battle with his 'illegitimate' brother Don John. Claudio is a follower of Don Pedro and he falls in love with Hero. Don John is jealous of his half-brother and he sullies Hero's reputation by implying that she is a wanton and unfaithful woman. Claudio believes him and breaks off their

proposed marriage. Meanwhile, Beatrice and Benedick spend their time sparring and insulting one another. Eventually they fall in love and decide to get married. Hero's reputation is salvaged and the film concludes with the two couples marrying. Don John is punished for his lies.

The plot develops by means of parties, picnics, courtships, witty scenes, parodies and many comic interludes.

Themes
- Relationships.
- Love.
- Deception/misunderstanding.
- Marriage.
- Happiness.

Love and courtship
The various entanglements that the different couples engage in throughout this humorous and light-hearted film dominate much of the content.

Deception and intrigue
This issue forms the framework for much of Shakespeare's work. Here Don John's jealousy of his brother gives rise to his efforts to defame Hero's reputation. Happily, things turn out well at the conclusion.

Structure and style
Visual images and photography
There are many images of large, bright gardens, with typical Sicilian architecture. There is a lot of sunshine and open spaces.

Music
The music is rich and joyous.

Genre
Romantic comedy.

Cultural context
The film is set in Messina, in Sicily, in the mid-seventeenth century. At the beginning we are given a picture of men returning from battle. They are seen as heroic and chivalric figures who have sacrificed their lives for other people. The women in the film are beautiful, gentle creatures who live in luxury, read poetry, eat rich food and drink wine. The lifestyle is rich and luxurious, filled with dance, song, wine and joy. They recite poetry, sing songs and talk about heroic deeds of romance and courage. Marriage is important in this society and virtues such as chastity and purity are held in high regard. The conclusion shows us an image of perfect happiness in the marriage of the two couples.

General vision or viewpoint

The overall general vision or viewpoint of this film is one of reconciliation and peace in the wake of misunderstanding and deception. In the unity of both couples in marriage we are given an image of perfect happiness and concord. The villain is destroyed and good triumphs at the conclusion.

STRICTLY BALLROOM
Directed by Baz Luhrmann

(2008 and 2009 exams)

Historical and literary background
This film is set in Australia during the 1970s.

The story

The story centres on the main character, Scott Hastings, and his attempts to win the Australian Pan-Pacific Dancing Competition. The film opens with Scott taking part in the Waratah Dance Championships. Barry Fife controls these competitions and will not allow dancers to change their style or steps. However, Scott wants to dance his own steps and this brings him into conflict with Barry Fife and his own mother, Shirley, who is determined that he shall win. Initially, Liz is Scott's dancing partner, but she refuses to dance with him because of his efforts to be innovative in his dancing style.

Scott's mother spends a great deal of time convincing him to conform to the rules of the Dancing Federation. Scott refuses and meets Fran, whose family is Spanish in origin. Fran lives with her grandmother and father at the back of a small bar. Fran and Scott spend a lot of time practising how to dance and secretly improve their steps, unknown to anyone.

Meanwhile, we learn more about Scott's father, Doug. We see him surreptitiously putting on records and dancing on his own a lot. It is clear that his wife outwardly despises him, as he is not a very assertive character. As the story develops, we also learn how Doug had the potential to be a prestigious dancer, but had tried to dance his own steps and was banned by the Federation.

Finally, Scott and Fran enter the Pan-Pacific Competition even though they are opposed by all the members of Scott's family and receive threats from Fife. The final sequence plays the song 'Love is in the Air', and everyone in the hall moves onto the dance floor in spite of Barry Fife's protestations and dances their own individual style. Fife's corrupt manoeuverings are defeated at the conclusion.

Themes
* Power and corruption.
* Deception.
* Self-expression and individuality.
* Love and romance.

Genre

This film belongs to the genre of romance with touches of absurd humour throughout. The director makes use of caricature to mock, as is seen in Barry Fife's capacity to bully people.

There are also comic touches in the documentary-style interventions from Shirley, who is intent on trying to explain to the viewer how her son must become a champion.

Camera angles

A variety of camera angles are used, mainly of different styles of dancing and of the various events.

Flashback

The film opens with a flashback to the Waratah Championships, which establishes the competitive atmosphere of the film. It also introduces the leading characters who will govern the story's plot.

Cultural context

There are different social classes represented in the film. The culture is that of Australia, but it is restricted to dancing events and competitors.

We gain an insight into a contrasting cultural world through Fran's story. Her background represents a more traditional way of life than the flashy ballroom scenes. The Spanish culture is represented through the figure of her father and his friends and the flamboyant style of dancing which we see in their house.

General vision or viewpoint

The defeat of Barry Fife's wicked manoeuvrings and the success attained by Scott and Fran in dancing in an individual style represent a change in the traditional system, which has obviously operated in this federation for years. The fact that Doug, Scott's father, was considered a failure when in reality he was trying to perfect his art made him appear weak in his own family. With the introduction of a new style of dancing, expressed by Scott and Fran, not only is Fife's corrupt system exposed and destroyed, but Doug's status as a dancer is restored and he is vindicated before his family.

The values of love and selflessness are made apparent in the sincere union of Scott and Fran.

CINEMA PARADISO
Written and directed by Giuseppe Tornatore.

(2008 and 2009 exams)

Historical and literary background
Cinema Paradiso begins in a small Sicilian town in the 1940s, shortly after the Second World War. This was a time when the cinema was just developing. It made a huge impact on the people of Sicily, who in many ways were isolated from the cultural developments of mainland Italy.

The story
The story deals with Salvatore de Gito, a successful film director, who hears about the death of Alfredo. A flashback recalls Salvatore's youth and adolescence in a small Sicilian town and shows his relationship with Alfredo, the local film projectionist, who becomes a father figure for him, as Salvatore's father has disappeared. Salvatore is fascinated by the local cinema and spends most of his youth there, helping Alfredo. He falls in love with the daughter of a banker, but they separate, and she leaves the town.

Eventually Alfredo persuades Salvatore to leave and get a better job, as he will never do anything worthwhile otherwise. The cinema is bought by a new owner, and the style changes. Formerly the priest could censor many things; now images are more permissive. The cinema is burned down, and a car park is put there instead. Salvatore returns after thirty years for Alfredo's funeral. It is clear that he has not found real love in his life.

Themes or issues
Love and relationships
One of the most powerful and endearing issues treated in this film is that of relationships. The relationship between the child Salvatore and Alfredo is perhaps the most tender and poignant. Alfredo is child-like in his nature and treats Salvatore almost as his own child. This relationship is strengthened when Salvatore saves Alfredo's life when the cinema catches fire. This relationship remains strongly embedded in the memory of the mature Salvatore years after he leaves the town.

The fascination of the cinema
The town community are characterised by their utter simplicity of nature. For them, the cinema is another world, which is filled with entertainment and excitement. Through the eyes of the child Salvatore we bear witness to the immense wonder filling these simple people as the screen reveals yet more images from another world. We also see the power of the local priest in the community to maintain moral standards, as he ruthlessly cuts any scenes that are morally offensive.

Change comes, however, and when a new owner takes over the cinema, the style of things becomes different. Censorship is less strict, but the cinema is closed to make way for a car park.

Genre
Social realism.

Structure and style
Visual images and photography
A variety of camera angles is used in the film. At the end of the film the technique of superimposing one picture over another is used, and this is done brilliantly, giving the effect of a reflection in a car window as Salvatore looks out on the countryside.

There is a clever variation at the funeral, when the shot is taken from inside the hearse, looking out at the mourners. The picture resembles a television screen, surrounded by the rear window of the hearse. The camera techniques are more varied here at the end, showing the viewers that things have really changed since Salvatore left thirty or more years ago, and now everything is presented differently.

Language
The film is in the Sicilian dialect of Italian; it is also issued with English subtitles. Much of the richness of the language and the meaning will be lost on the non-Italian viewer. However, the facial expressions of Toto as a child and the tender expressions of Salvatore are all the more meaningful.

Cultural context
The cultural context of this film is Sicily during a period from just after the war to about thirty years later. There is a strong emphasis on the changes that take place in

the Sicilian style of life during this period. At first the people are simple, ignorant of urban life, and they worship the world of cinema with awe. The projectionist, Alfredo, is a representative of this type of community – a simple man, who cannot read or write. The power of the priest in the community is evident in the way he censors unsuitable material in the films.

As the lifestyle changes, however, the people become more sophisticated and less satisfied with the films shown. The ownership of the cinema changes hands, and the priest no longer exercises control over the films shown. The old and rather tame romances are gone and more vibrant genres take their place: people are now watching westerns, thrillers and passionate love stories. Economic change brings about the eventual closure of the cinema to make way for a car park.

General vision or viewpoint
The general vision of this film is an overview of the rapid changes in Sicily and, by inference, throughout much of Europe over a forty-year period after the Second World War. The narrator does not seem to like these changes, yet there is a sense of inevitability about it all. At the end, as Toto gazes at the old square he knew as a boy, now filled with cars and noise, there is a definite sadness. The message is to be one of disappointment that life has changed in such a way.

The most shocking part is when the cinema is knocked down to make room for a car park. That says it all. The cinema, which stood for the old cultural values, is gone.

THE TRUMAN SHOW
Peter Weir

(2008 and 2009 exams)

The story
The film starts with an image of a man facing the camera and saying, 'We have become bored with phony actors giving us phony emotions while the world we inhabit is in some respects counterfeit. There is nothing fake about Truman himself.' The next scene shows us Truman facing into a camera. He is a middle-class American man married to Meryl, a respectable woman, and living in the suburbs. We are given several images of him travelling to work and greeting the neighbors with a big smile and the words 'Good morning, good evening and good night.' As he meets people he recognises, we begin to realise that he is pictured against the backdrop of various advertisements for different things, such as beer or food.

Truman arrives at work in his office and we see him trying to cut a picture of a girl from a magazine. Later on, there is a flashback where we see that he has a phobia of water because of the fact that his father drowned when Truman was a young boy while they were fishing. It is obvious that Truman blames himself for this experience.

Truman dreams about going to Fiji to experience a different life there. When Truman explains this longing to Meryl, she reminds him about his financial obligations and how she hopes they will have a baby. When Truman is going to bed that night with Meryl, the camera focuses on two men looking at a television, saying, 'You never see anything.' One day, Truman suddenly sees a man who he thinks is his dad, but then two men grab this man and Truman nearly kills himself pursuing them. He goes to his mother and tells her what he saw. It becomes obvious that Truman is being set up for something and everyone else is in on it. He begins to reminisce in the basement looking at old photos of himself and his dad. Meryl comes down to him with a big smile and tells him to 'throw out the mower and get one of the new rotaries'. Then the camera switches to an image of two waitresses looking at Truman on the screen.

Truman meets a beautiful girl called Lauren Garland at a dance and later on in the library. They escape to a beach and she tells him that they have very little time together and how 'everyone knows everything you do'. A man arrives in a car and announces he is her father and that she is mentally unstable. Lauren keeps repeating that it's a fake, a set-up, but she is taken away. She tells him her real name is Sylvia. The two waitresses watching the screen then comment on the fact that he should have taken her to Fiji and how he 'married the other one on the rebound'.

Shortly after this, Truman is driving to work and his radio begins to crackle and he hears a voice saying how he is heading down Lancaster Square. Truman begins to realise that they are talking about him. He becomes suspicious and begins to wonder if he is being followed. He sees a lift in the hotel with food and no backing on the wall. Truman goes to his friend, Marlon, for advice, but Marlon only laughs at him and says it is all nonsense.

Truman decides to do something unpredictable, so he arrives at the hospital in his pyjamas one morning and announces that he is going to Fiji. This is a humorous incident, as Meryl is in the operating theatre. It is obvious that Meryl is in on the whole thing. When he tries to book a flight to Fiji, he is told there is nothing for at least a month.

Truman takes Meryl in the car and begins to act madly. He insists on driving to Fiji and she becomes hysterical. When he drives near the water he cannot go over it, as his fear is too great. Back home, he challenges Meryl to tell him what is happening. She hands him cocoa with nuts and he becomes frantic. She shouts out 'do something' and then he knows that something bigger is happening. Marlon arrives with beer. Truman has a long conversation with Marlon about the fact that everyone is 'in on it'. Marlon insists that he is a loyal friend who is not in on it, and would never lie to him, as Truman is the 'closest thing [he] ever had to a brother'.

We learn that the story about Truman is a TV show in its thirtieth year and is a huge success. We are given an interview with the show's creator, Christof, and we learn how they manufactured ways to keep Truman on the island by creating a fear of water and the ocean. Christof explains how he has 5,000 cameras now but started with just one on Truman before he was born. We are shown a picture of Truman with a camera in the cot. We learn that the show is on 24 hours a day. Everything on the show is also a way of advertising. Sylvia rings and tells Christof that he is a liar and a manipulator. He answers that he has given Truman a chance to live a normal life.

Truman moves down to his basement and the cameramen are unable to keep contact with him. They begin to panic at the studios and realise he is sleeping in the basement. Marlon goes to the basement, where he discovers that Truman has disappeared. Transmission of the show is cut while everyone goes to search for Truman. Sirens sound all over the city and a whole group of people are marching in troops, looking for him with torches. Truman's mother, father and Marlon are at the front of the crowd. They find him on the sea, sailing away, and they resume transmission.

Truman comes onto the camera with a sailor's cap and he is looking at the photo of the girl. He is on a boat called the *Santa Maria*. Christof organises a storm over the boat to frighten him and Truman nearly dies. The storm increases in intensity and the boat is smashed. Truman survives, however, and suddenly he hears what seems to be a gunshot. He has reached a wall, which he cannot break through. Truman is broken-hearted. He walks around the edge of this horizon and up some steps, which is marked 'exit'. He opens a door and speaks to Christof, who tells him how his show gives hope and joy to millions, and how he has been watching him all his life. Truman then turns to the camera and says, 'In case I don't see you, good afternoon, good evening and good night.' He then goes up the steps and opens the door at the top. We see Sylvia running joyously down some stairs while Christof takes off his glasses in disgust.

Themes
Reality and illusion
From the outset it is clear that Truman is being used as a pawn in a game. It only becomes clear as the story develops that he is being deceived about the reality of his own life. All his family and friends, with the exception of Sylvia, hide the truth from him that he is the central actor of his own show. His life is a show that he creates for a worldwide audience. Everyone believes they are doing a great thing by offering joy to millions of people worldwide. Truman, however, walks away from this world at the conclusion.

Loyalty and betrayal
His friends and family betray Truman by not telling him that he is the chief actor in what is universally known as *The Truman Show*. His whole family deceives him about the truth of his life and all contribute to the show's continuous existence. Furthermore, the show is designed to advertise goods and many of his family and friends are shown against the backdrop of billboards advertising different types of merchandise.

Genre
This is a film of social realism which seems to point to the power of reality TV. Weir, the director, makes interesting use of the soliloquy (a speech addressed directly at the camera). The film opens with the film's creator, Christof, facing the camera directly. There are many instances of this technique. Christof is the creator of *The Truman Show*, so in essence he is explaining to the audience the mode in which it operates.

There is one use of flashback when Truman is sitting on a beach and he remembers the time when he was a young boy at sea with his father, who subsequently drowned. It becomes evident from this flashback that Truman blames himself.

Cultural context
The cultural context of this film is American middle-class suburbia. The film is set in the twentieth century and is a subtle presentation of the reality of media and the manner of its operation. It deals with consumerism and materialism in the twentieth century.

The characters' lifestyles are fairly affluent. It is a society where people live in pleasant, organised suburbia and have children. Truman works in an office and travels by car every day. The buildings represented in this small town of Seahaven are modern, and for the most part bright and new.

The power of television to generate huge income through reality shows lies at the essence of the film's content. Money is a huge factor motivating Christof, the show's creator, to sustain his deception over Truman, and also seems to govern Truman's family and sly friend. The film exposes the surreptitious and more sinister aspects of media control and underlines how people can become unconscious pawns in the media game.

General vision or viewpoint

Weir, the director of this film, seems to be highlighting the dangers of being manipulated and controlled by the media through Truman himself. The underlying idea seems to be that certain forces exist in society, such as advertising, consumerism and media influence, which, when combined, can rob a person of their identity and of the reality of who they really are. Truman's world is fake. All his family and seemingly loyal friends conspire together to delude him about the full reality of his life. He even believes he has contributed to the death of his own father. But the film shows that these are all lies and deception, and that Truman is the only honest man in this artificial world created by Christof. While the general vision or viewpoint certainly poses underlying questions about media control and our need to question this, Weir shows his audience how an individual always has freedom. Truman challenges the fake concept created by those around him and finally walks away freely.

RICHARD III

Directed by Robert Loncraine

(2009 exam)

Historical and literary background

The film *Richard III* is based on the historic War of the Roses, which took place between the House of Lancaster and the House of York. The film begins with the coronation of Edward, who is of the House of York, settled on the throne of England; King Henry, his predecessor, was murdered by Edward's brother Richard.

The story

In the opening sequence of this film we are told that civil war reigns in England, because the king is under attack from the rebel York family, who are fighting to put their eldest son on the throne. His youngest brother, Richard of Gloucester, leads Edward's army. Richard's tanks break down the walls of Tewkesbury and Henry and his father are shot.

Edward becomes King of England. He is married to Elizabeth and they have two sons, and a daughter also called Elizabeth. At the coronation ceremony of Edward, Richard gives the welcoming speech. Rivers, Queen Elizabeth's brother, who is an enemy of Richard's, arrives for Edward's coronation. Buckingham is an ally of Richard. He is a leading statesman who conspires with Richard at all stages.

Shortly after this Richard seduces Lady Anne, widow of Tewkesbury, whom he has murdered earlier. Richard announces to the audience that since he cannot prove himself as a lover because of his deformed shape, he is determined to prove himself as a villain. He frames Clarence, his brother, and has him committed to the Tower of London. Richard then suggests that Elizabeth has done this.

Richard then hires a man called Tyrell to murder Clarence, which he does while he is taking a bath, and drowns him in his own blood. Richard proceeds to inform Edward of this death as Edward is in the process of making peace between the various statesmen. On hearing the news Edward has a stroke and dies shortly afterwards. Richard murders Rivers.

Elizabeth's son is brought to London to be crowned king. Both he and his young brother are kept in the tower until the coronation ceremony. Hastings is Prime Minister. There is a meeting with the archbishop, Hastings, Buckingham and Richard, who is now the Lord Protector. Richard accuses Hastings of treachery and Tyrell executes him.

Both Richard and Buckingham then justify this execution to the Lord Mayor by claiming that Hastings plotted to kill Richard and Buckingham. Richard also insinuates that the two princes in the tower are bastard children who have no legitimate right to the throne.

The Lord Mayor wishes to crown Richard as king. Richard adopts a false show of piety and reluctance to take on responsibilities of kingship. Eventually he succumbs and is crowned king in a ceremony closely resembling a Nazi meeting.

After this ceremony Richmond is advised by the archbishop to flee to England for safety. There he mobilises an army to fight Richard.

Richard asks Buckingham to murder the two princes in the tower. Buckingham hesitates and reminds him of his earlier pledge to give him the earldom of Hereford. Richards replies that he is not in the giving mood. Buckingham, knowing his life is in danger, flees to France to join Richmond. Tyrell murders the two princes in the tower. Richard now plans to get rid of Anne and marry Elizabeth, the sister of the two young princes. Elizabeth's mother flees to England and young Elizabeth is married to Richmond shortly before the battle. Buckingham is captured by Richard's army, tortured and brutally murdered by Tyrell.

Richard's own mother has cursed him and prophesies that his end will be bloody and says that she will pray for Richmond's success in battle. Richard is tormented by nightmares on the night before the battle.

The battle takes places in daytime with tanks and modern military weapons. Richmond drives an army tank through the battlefield, intent on killing Richard. At the conclusion, Richmond and Richard are standing on the top of a dilapidated building.

Richard challenges Richmond to come to hell with him, and offers him his hand. Before Richmond shoots him, Richard falls backwards into a sea of fire.

Themes or issues
*   Kingship.
*   Violence, murder and corruption.
*   Betrayal.

Genre
The genre of this film is tragedy. It gives a vivid account of Richard's murderous movements both before and after he becomes king.

Soliloquy
This film makes frequent use of the traditional soliloquy. Richard, the villain of the film, engages in soliloquy frequently in the film. He announces his plot and justifies his behaviour through the use of soliloquy.

Music
Jazz music and the music of the 1920s forms the main background of this film. In particular, violence and violent actions are accompanied by strong jazz undertones.

Flashback
There is only one flashback in the film. This occurs when Tyrell informs Richard that the two princes are dead. We then see how they were smothered with a piece of red material.

Cultural context
The cultural setting of this film is England in the 1930s. It is a distinct modern setting for a film that is based on a king who ruled in England in the fifteenth century.

The coronation of Richard is almost Nazi-style. The red flag that is unfolded behind the grandstand and the red flags waved by the people who are gathered all resemble the swastika.

Close associations are drawn between the figure of Richard and that of Hitler. The dress is predominantly military-style uniforms that also resemble Nazi style.

The culture is rich and ornate: luxurious chandeliers, expensive carpets and paintings, large lobbies, elegant photographs and clothes are a hallmark of the atmosphere in this film.

General vision or viewpoint
The battle at the conclusion takes place during the day. The place is filled with army tanks and soldiers marching to their deaths. On the night before the battle Richard has nightmares and is haunted by his mother's last words, which condemned his actions. It is clear that he feels guilty, but suppresses his conscience and continues to justify his actions. In the morning of the battle, he mobilises his troops by preaching about the fact that conscience is a word cowards use.

Richmond is clearly intent on murdering Richard himself. He resolutely sets out in a military tank to kill him. Richard is finally trapped at the top of a dilapidated building and has lost the battle. Everyone around him is dead. He has murdered all his family and has no friends left. He fails to repent and instead recklessly challenges Richmond by offering him his hand with the words 'hand in hand to hell'. His drop into the sea of fire is symbolic of the fact that he has damned himself by his actions and refuses to repent. The accompanying music, 'I'm sitting on top of the world', is an ironic way of highlighting how Richmond has defeated the evil in Britain. Richmond is victorious. Heir to the house of Lancaster and married to Elizabeth, heir to the house of York, Richmond is the first of the Tudor line to rule England as Henry VII.

INSIDE I'M DANCING
Damien O'Donnell
(2009 exam)

The story
The opening sequence shows two young men in wheelchairs against the backdrop of dance music. The next scene moves inside an institution called Carraigmore Residential Home, where many handicapped people are sitting down in wheelchairs

looking at a cartoon on the television screen. The camera focuses on the face of one young man called Michael who has cerebral palsy. A cleaning lady begins to hoover the room and the flex scatters wildly against the wheelchairs. The young man gets upset because he sees the danger of this lead. He is unable to communicate, however, and when the supervisor enters asking everyone if they want mass, he becomes wild. Immediately after this, one of the attendants in the home falls over the hoover. We realise that this is what Michael was trying to tell her.

Then another young man with spiked hair and a pierced nose arrives at the home. Hs name is Rory O'Shea. He is suffering from Duchane muscular dystrophy. Rory is only able to move two of his fingers and his head very slightly. It is clear he is very rebellious, as he asks for the key to the door as soon as he arrives at the home. Rory is at odds with the atmosphere of the home from the outset. He plays very loud music as soon as he arrives and uses a lot of bad language. Rory understands Michael immediately and begins to develop a friendship with him. Rory's dad pays him regular visits. Rory is determined to get permission to live independently. He discovers that Michael's father is a very rich man who has dumped him in a home after the death of his wife and refuses to recognise him as his son because of the fact that he has cerebral palsy.

At one stage the residents of the home are collecting money on the street for their cause. Rory and Michael are involved in the collection. They collect some money and then go into a pub and meet two girls. They buy them drink with the money, and the girls get drunk. Then the two boys try to get into a club. Initially they are refused entry because they are in wheelchairs but Rory threatens them with the fact that they are discriminating against people who have a disability and warns them that they will have to pay a €2,000 fine. He pretends that Michael is a barrister. Once inside they use their wheelchairs to join in the fun of dancing. They also notice a young girl whom they learn later is called Siobhan dancing with other young people.

After this incident in the club, they return to the home, soaked and with no money. Eileen, the woman who is in charge of the home, is furious and blames Rory. Rory dresses up the next day in a suit and he and Mark go to meet with the Ability Ireland Board to request independent living for Rory. The Board, however, has heard how Rory mishandled the collection money and so they suggest that he return in six months' time. Rory is very angry after this encounter. It is clear that attaining independent living means a lot to him.

Shortly after this, Michael goes before the Board to look for independent living for himself. Rory accompanies him. The members of the Board are unable to understand Michael's efforts to speak, and so Rory is called upon to translate for him. Michael is granted permission to have what is called independent living and Rory goes with him as his friend and helper. They are now faced with the prospect of getting enough money together for a suitable flat.

Rory comes up with the idea of appealing to Michael's father for money. Rory behaves in an outrageous manner when he arrives at the father's office, and when he is refused access to the father, he shouts out how he is reporting 'a case of criminal neglect'. The father is shamed into giving them money. This is a very emotional scene, as Michael is clearly moved by coming face to face with his own father after so many years.

The two boys get a ground-floor flat with wheelchair access and with no rules or interference from anyone. They advertise for a personal assistant and they interview several candidates. None are suitable. Eventually they manage to convince the beautiful young girl Siobhan, who is working in a supermarket, to take the job. They have a wonderful time expressing their freedom and Siobhan manages the job as personal assistant very well.

Michael begins to fall in love with Siobhan. This is quite tragic, as it is clear that Siobhan sees her relationship with the two boys as nothing other than a job of taking care of two handicapped people who are both confined to wheelchairs. Rory watches this relationship between Michael and Siobhan developing, and becomes deeply cynical at the fact that handicapped people can never be loved by a girl and at the futility of Michael's love.

At one stage, in a fit of jollity and rebellion, Rory takes a car and crashes it. Siobhan begins to lose her patience with Rory, who becomes more aggressive and frustrated as he watches Michael falling helplessly in love. She has several verbal arguments. At one stage she walks out as he shouts out, 'I don't want your help, I don't want anyone's help.'

Rory's dad arrives with a birthday card for his twenty-first birthday. Siobhan meets an old friend and he invites them all to a fancy dress. Michael is deeply involved emotionally with Siobhan at this stage. She meets a boy friend at the dance and Michael wants to dance with her. At this stage she tells him that it's just a job. She resigns and brings another man along to replace her.

Michael is deeply upset and cries when she leaves. He goes out in his wheelchair one night and sits brooding on a bridge. Rory joins him and tells him that he is not the only one with a broken heart: 'you have the future, that's what I call a gift. Don't give it up. You can't give it up.' This is a very sad and tender scene. Both boys are crying and the scene is played against the backdrop of some very tender and poignant music. Rory makes a joke about suicide and they return home.

Shortly after this, Rory becomes sick and is taken away at night in an ambulance. He has pneumonia and is in intensive care. This is a very sad scene, with the two boys crying together in the hospital. Rory grabs Michael's fingers and tells him to 'be his own man'. Michael goes back to the Board to plead on Rory's behalf for independent living. He gets permission for him to live independently. He returns to the hospital to meet with Rory's father. Rory is dead. The film concludes with Rory's funeral, attended by his dad, Michael and Siobhan and several people from Carraigmore Home.

The last scene shows us an image of Michael returning to Rory's room and looking reflectively at Rory's wheelchair. He hears Rory's voice saying 'c'mon, are we going out?' The film concludes on a joyful note with an image of Michael in his wheelchair going into a large street on a busy day all on his own.

Themes

Friendship

One of the main themes in this film is the friendship between Rory and Michael. Both are handicapped and physically limited because of their illness. Their physical disability bonds them together from the outset of the film and contributes to enriching their relationship as the film develops. Adversity and suffering only serves the function of consolidating the friendship between the boys even more.

Communication

The film deals with two young boys who are handicapped because of different illnesses. Michael is suffering from cerebral palsy and Rory is suffering from muscular dystrophy. Both boys are able to communicate perfectly with one another. It is interesting that from the beginning of the film, we see how Michael is frustrated as no one is able to understand or communicate with him until Rory arrives. As soon as Rory arrives on the scene, Michael's face brightens up and his whole body becomes animated. There is a strong bond of understanding between them. Rory is the only character in the film that fully understands Michael. He fosters self-confidence within him, and this is evident at the conclusion, when Rory dies. Michael remains living independently and manages to travel into the city alone in his wheelchair.

Love and understanding

The film deals with the fact that even though people may suffer from physical disability, they still retain the capacity to love and be loved. This is particularly evident in the case of Siobhan, the beautiful young girl who spends some time working as a personal assistant for the boys. Michael falls passionately in love with her. Even though he may be suffering from cerebral palsy and is unable to communicate clearly, he still possesses the ability to love and wants to have that love reciprocated. Rory is very clever and quite cynical about this capacity in people who suffer from disability. Rory shows disgust in this part of this film, as he believes that no one can love a person with a disability. For this reason, he has a lot of arguments with Siobhan and eventually she leaves. However, Rory realises that the capacity for life is irreplaceable, and he warns Michael not to take life and the future for granted.

Genre

This is a modern film of social realism. It is a humorous film made up of many comic scenes.

Cultural context

The film is set in modern twentieth-century Dublin. The language used by the characters is rich with the Dublin dialect. All of the scenes are played in an urban area. We are given an insight into a typical Dublin pub in Ireland in the late twentieth century and also the modern disco when the boys insist on gaining admittance. We gain an insight into institutional life at the beginning of the film in Carraigmore

Residential Home. This is a typical style of urban institution, with its clean white walls and lack of character or atmosphere.

There is one scene when the two boys go to meet Fergus Connolly, who is a senior counsellor in the courts, and they look for money from him. Here we gain an insight into typical middle-class Dublin.

General vision or viewpoint

The overall vision in this film is very positive. The whole film deals exclusively with the situation of two handicapped boys, both young and both full of life and vigour. The director of the film seems to be intent on showing how the human spirit can triumph against adversity, especially when both are united. The two boys struggle together against all odds – lack of understanding from those around them, lack of financial means, frustration at doing ordinary things and inability to find expression for the strong love that dominates their hearts.

Yet in spite of all the difficulties and contradictions, the film has many positive elements. We witness the power of the human spirit and the great power inherent in friendship and its ability to transcend misunderstandings and difficulties.

THE THIRD MAN

Written by Graham Greene; directed by Carol Reed

(2009 exam)

Historical and literary background

The background of this film is Vienna just after the Second World War. Post-war Vienna was divided by the Allies into four occupation zones: the American, Soviet, English and French zones. The film is set against the background of general devastation and demoralisation in the wake of war. It was a time of corruption and illegal dealings on the black market. The background is typical of wartime: moral and spiritual destitution, poverty and corruption, desolation and anxiety, distrust and confusion of values.

The story

Holly Martins, a writer of pulp fiction, comes to Vienna to meet an old friend, Harry Lime, who has promised him a job. When he arrives he learns of the death of Lime in a car accident. He attends the funeral, where he meets Major Calloway, who is suspicious about Lime's activities. Martins undertakes to investigate the circumstances of Lime's death. He meets Anna, Lime's former girlfriend, who is working illegally in Vienna. Martins learns from Calloway that Lime was involved with dealings on the black market involving penicillin, causing a great number of deaths as a result.

Meanwhile he has discovered that Lime is not dead and he tries to meet him. He finally tricks him into a meeting, which gives rise to a chase through the sewers of Vienna, a chase that culminates in Martins shooting and killing Lime.

The story is told by means of a voice-over narration, which is the voice of Holly Martins. The plot revolves around the activities of Harry Lime in Vienna and his supposed death in a traffic accident. It develops through the medium of Holly Martins and his attempts to uncover the truth surrounding Lime's death. Various events occur to contribute to the tension, such as the appearance of Lime hidden in an archway outside Anna's flat one night, and the information given by Major Calloway about Lime's sleazy manoeuvrings. The falsification of Anna's passport consolidates Lime's guilt. The plot culminates in a magnificent scene in the sewers underneath the streets of Vienna, with Martins and Lime at the centre.

Themes or issues

War

War is a central issue in *The Third Man*, and the brutal effect of war on civilisation is shown throughout the film. It is shown on the surface level of society through the images of burned-out buildings, crumbling structures and general devastation. On another level the tragic effect of war is shown in the lives of the citizens. There are images of distrust and fear, a sense of helplessness and hopelessness in the aftermath of a catastrophe. These images percolate through the film and generate an atmosphere of distrust and suspicion. People are shown to be insecure and wary; camera angles suggest the fear and the suspicion in this society.

Finally, this corruption seeps through to the inner person. The black market mirrors the degeneration of humankind because of the corrupting effects of the war. The profound effects of Lime's actions are shown in the sick children at the hospital and are pitifully registered in the reaction of Martins, who up to now has compromised with Lime's evil doings. Lime allows himself to become completely cynical about life and people as he speaks to Martins in the carnival scene. War and all its evil effects are a strong element in this film.

Loyalty

This theme is a strong element in *The Third Man*. The character of Holly Martins, who alone tries to find out the truth about his friend, embodies this theme. He refuses to accept the fact that Lime is a dealer in black-market medicine, and he even gets himself embroiled in a fight in defending Lime's innocence.

Anna, Lime's girlfriend, also steadfastly adheres to her memory of him and will not accept the reality of his criminal nature. Right to the end Anna remains determined to uphold Lime's reputation. The long concluding sequence demonstrates in a vivid manner how strong her loyalty is. She is pictured walking down a long avenue filled with falling leaves while Martins remains standing on the roadside watching her. This image suggests that in spite of all that has happened, Lime still means everything to her.

Moral corruption

This theme is generally a corollary of war. The disastrous effects of war usually reveal in some way the particular taintings of moral corruption. Early on in the film there are images of dealings in stolen watches, of a dead body in the Vienna sewers, of racketeering and crime. According to Lime, corruption and double-dealing are the only way to survive and to deal successfully with life. As he preaches to his friend Martins in the fairground, 'in Italy for thirty years under the Borgias they had warfare, terror, murder and bloodshed, yet they produced Michaelangelo, Leonardo da Vinci and the Renaissance; yet in Switzerland, with brotherly love, five hundred years ago of democracy and peace, all they produced was the cuckoo clock.' According to this cynical view, corruption is an essential part of the way we survive in this world. However, this corruption backfires on Lime and his associates as Martins's conscience becomes more enlightened about the nature and consequences of Lime's evil doings. Lime is exposed at the conclusion and finally destroyed.

Genre

The Third Man is in the category of *film noir*, with features of the thriller. Film noir (literally 'dark film') is characterised by high-contrast black-and-white photography with low-key lighting, which creates a moody effect and gives a suspenseful quality to the story. The world portrayed by *film noir* has a dark look about it and generally shows the dark side of life.

The stock character in this type of film is the private detective, working in a world that conspires against him. In *The Third Man* Holly Martins is the detective who undertakes the investigation of the death of his friend Harry Lime. There is also a sense of entrapment or imprisonment by the individual; this is achieved by images of people pictured behind bars.

Another feature of this genre is the presence of a *'femme fatale'*. In *The Third Man* we have Anna, the woman torn between her love for Lime, her corrupt lover, and her duty to do what is right.

Structure and style
Visual images and photography
The film depicts imposing architecture, which creates an image of a rich, ornate background. It makes distinct use of many oblique shots. These tilted angles suggest a world caught off balance, a world that has lost its direction. The camera also focuses on different aspects of the characters in the film. A series of close-ups registers some ambiguous movements of people and facial expressions that are deliberately enigmatic. We notice, for example, the picture of the Austrian at the funeral in the beginning of the film with sly, furtive eyes registering the activities of Martins in the graveyard.

Much of the lighting is dark and shadowy, in keeping with this genre and that of the thriller. Movements are eerie and ominous; many images show figures in doorways looking out stealthily, or pictures of people behind bars, as if in prison. There are many cul-de-sacs, mainly shown at night. Much of the effect of the lighting and direction comes from the use of black-and-white photography.

Language
The various accents give a distinct tone to this film. When Martins arrives in Vienna he meets a porter who communicates the news of Lime's accident in broken English and a smattering of German. Much of the dialogue is sharp and tense, particularly that of Lime, whom we meet for the first time in the carnival scene. Here his language is short and clipped, suggesting that he is trying to deal with an awkward situation. Calloway's accent is upper-class English and long drawn out, in contrast with Martins, who speaks laconically, like the character he writes about in his pulp fiction.

Sound
The main sound in the film is the background music, played on a zither, a traditional stringed instrument, which gives an eerie atmosphere to the film. For the most part the music creates tension: there is no joy in it. After the funeral of Lime the music is long drawn out and creates a distinctly ominous atmosphere.

Symbols
There are many references to animals, to cats and budgies, all of which could suggest the theme of exploitation and abuse. The architecture of the house is of a heavy baroque type, which is rich in symbolic resonance. At the beginning, when Martins arrives in Vienna, we see him walking under a ladder outside a grand building decorated with an elaborate façade. Then the image is sharply undercut by the use of dramatic shadow, which gives the whole atmosphere of the film a distinctive symbolic resonance. The scene is set for a story involving crime and the underworld.

Cultural context
The Third Man is set in post-war Vienna. The opening sequence contains newsreel film that speaks about the black market and the moral decadence that often follows in the wake of war. War in the film is seen as something to be capitalised on; this gives the film a realistic edge. The culture depicted in Vienna is a civilised and educated one. The

military officer is seen as a moral compass in this world: he is a force that represents law and order, is shrewd and worldly-wise, with no illusions. Vienna is suffering from the effects of war: tea is scarce, clothes are shabby, buildings are derelict and people in general are depressed.

General vision or viewpoint

The film concludes cleverly on two different scenes that are skilfully juxtaposed. The first takes place in the sewer, with Lime at the centre of the police chase. The second takes place after Lime's funeral, as Anna walks in the long-drawn-out shot away from the grave and down the avenue of trees, with Martins standing beside the road. For this reason there are different statements or visions in the conclusion of the film. The general vision is that evil is punished. The wickedness and evil manoeuvrings of Lime catch up on him in the sewer: he is caught like a rat in his own trap. This image is significant. Lime has caused a great deal of suffering to innocent children and to people in general through his greed and selfishness. Martins experiences a moral trauma and confusion throughout the film. His dilemma springs on the one hand from his loyalty to his unscrupulous friend and on the other hand from his duty to what he knows is right and just. It is only at the hospital, when he becomes fully exposed to the brutal suffering caused by Lime's illegal trafficking in penicillin, that he is convinced of Lime's guilt. Shortly after this, he shoots Lime in the sewer.

As Anna continues to walk slowly out of the graveyard after the real burial of Lime, we bear witness to the astonishing loyalty of her love in spite of everything. The power of love is strong, and it can even blind one to evil. This seems to be implicit in the long shot at the conclusion as Anna, overwhelmed by grief, ignores Martins and walks on. Truth triumphs at the conclusion, but at a price.

Unseen Poetry

13

APPROACHING THE UNSEEN POEM

The first thing you must do when tackling an unseen poem is try to understand its meaning. The tone and the choice of words will help to convey the poem's meaning. You will find that the more times you read the poem, the more the meaning will become clear to you.

Some modern poetry has no clear and unequivocal meaning, and in fact is not meant to have a definite meaning. In many instances the meaning can be quite obscure, so don't worry about understanding the meaning immediately.

Remember, a poem can have many different interpretations. It is important to take risks when reading and to try to understand a poem's meaning.

A poem is based on communicating some emotion(s) to the reader through a particular choice of words and structure. To understand more deeply what the content or meaning of a particular poem is, we need to examine the following:

- ideas: the content or subject matter
- persona
- language.

Ideas

1. State the idea or attitude expressed in each component part or in each verse.
2. Are there key words or word repetitions strategically placed in order to express the main ideas? (Remember, poetry is emotion and may communicate through syntax, repetition or image association rather than logic.)
3. See why the verses are structured in the particular way they are.
4. Try to understand the relationship between the different parts of a poem – this will help to reveal its structure.
5. The theme(s) can be elicited or drawn out from grasping how the particular ideas or responses are developed in the poem.

Persona

1. Who is speaking in the poem? Is it the poet or is the poet pretending to be someone else?
2. To whom is the poet speaking – to a particular person or to a general audience?
3. What do we learn about the poet from the poem?

Language

When you analyse the style of a poem – that is, the language, tone, point of view and techniques used – it will help towards gaining a deeper understanding and interpretation of the poem.

The particular way in which language is used in a poem helps to give a shape and structure to the poem's thought and meaning.

The language of poetry is made up of:

- imagery
- words
- rhyme and rhythm
- alliteration
- assonance
- onomatopoeia
- ambiguity
- sound
- grammar
- metre.

Imagery

Imagery is any form of descriptive writing. Imagery focuses the meaning of the poem as a whole; it can also function to create atmosphere and establish a certain pattern within a poem. A poet can make use of language in many different ways to create imagery or word pictures. Don't just identify imagery – be able to say what its function in poetry is.

Imagery creates atmosphere and establishes a pattern within a poem. Imagery is effective when it is central to the poem's meaning.

When studying imagery in a poem, know how to identify the following:

- metaphor
- simile
- symbol.

Both metaphor and simile compare one thing with another. In a metaphor this similarity is implied, while a simile shows the comparison through the use of the words 'like' or 'as'. Similes are closer to ordinary speech; metaphors are more condensed and economical.

Simile: The fog descended like a blanket.
Metaphor: The blanket of fog descended.

A symbol is a word that stands for or points to a reality beyond itself. For example, flowers can symbolise the shortness of life. Some other examples include:
- sunrise: a new beginning
- water: purity
- a river: life
- the sea: eternity
- a garden: order
- spring: new life and energy
- autumn: maturity, fulfilment
- winter: old age and death

When you are examining symbols, an act of imagination is required before the meaning becomes fully clear. Aim at capturing the way in which a symbol glows or echoes with meaning. The statement or ideas that are being made do not make sense on the surface level – the sense or meaning of symbols must be inferred from some association, comparison, contrast or inversion of images and ideas used in the poem.

For example, take the following lines from T. S. Eliot's poem 'The Waste Land':

> Unreal City,
> Under the brown fog of a winter dawn,
> A crowd flowed over London Bridge, so many,
> I had not thought death had undone so many.

The fog and the winter dawn have many different meanings; they could refer to the spiritual apathy and stagnation that were a feature of the time when Eliot was writing the poem.

With regard to imagery in poetry, ask yourself the following questions:
- What does it say?
- Why is it used?
- Does it have connotations or sound effects?
- Does it fit into the context?
- How well does it acccomplish its task?

Words
Examine the way words work within a poem.

Appropriateness
Are the words that are used poetic, colloquial or abstract? If so, why?

Associations
Do the words have connotations or associations? Kavanagh here is suggesting religious renewal:

> … the green waters of the canal
> Pouring redemption for me …

This line from Eliot suggests fear and violence:

> Fleeing from the foreign faces and the foreign swords.

Allusions

An allusion is a reference to another book, event, person or place. The allusion may be implied or hinted. Sometimes the effect of an allusion may be to make something that is being said more significant, more ambiguous or more amusing.

Collocation

This occurs through an explosive, unexpected or sometimes contradictory combination of words, such as 'dense din', 'tremendous silence'. Consider these lines from Dylan Thomas:

> And as I was green and carefree, famous among the barns
> About the happy yard and singing as the farm was home.

Repetition

Repetition of a key word or phrase at different points can give emphasis to the power of the poem:

> And indeed there will be time ... there will be time, there will be time ... Time for you
> and time for me ...Time to turn back and descend the stair.

> I am tired with my own life and the lives of those after me,
> I am dying in my own death and the deaths of those after me.

Rhyme and rhythm

Rhythm can be used in poetry to add to the mood or atmosphere and therefore it can contribute to conveying the meaning more clearly. Effective rhythm is one where the stress falls on the crucial or important word. In the best poetry the rhythm and meaning of the words appear as one and not two things. Ask yourself whether it is significant that these thoughts and feelings have been expressed in this particular rhythm.

Internal rhyme occurs when a word in one line rhymes with another word in the same line:

> He found the forest track, he brought back
> This beak ...

The internal rhyme serves to emphasise a sense of movement:

> The grains beyond age, the dark veins of her mother.

The internal rhyme between 'grains' and 'veins' underlines the finality of death. Internal rhyme can serve the function of surprising the reader and quickening the pace of a line.

A line can be *end-stopped* with an *end rhyme* or it can run on into another line in a flow of thought. End rhyme occurs when two consecutive lines rhyme or alternate lines rhyme. Look at the following lines, which are an example of end rhyme:

If I were a dead leaf thou mightest bear, [a]
If I were swift cloud to fly with thee; [b]
A wave to pant beneath thy power, and share [a]

The impulse of thy strength, only less free [b]
Than thou, O uncontrollable! If even [c]
I were as in my boyhood, and could be [b]

The comrade of thy wanderings over Heaven, [c]
As then, when to outstrip thy skiey speed [d]
Scarce seemed a vision; I would ne'er have striven [c]

As thus with thee in prayer in my sore need. [d]

> (Percy Bysshe Shelley, 'Ode to the West Wind')

Rhythm sometimes exists to link words and ideas. It can also be used to suggest speed, calm, anger or monotony. Definite rhythm can make a particular point, for example:

Only thin smoke without flame
  From the heaps of couch-grass;
Yet this will go onward the same
  Though Dynasties pass.

The absence of rhythm can suggest fear, worry or aimlessness. Uneven rhythm is also used for a particular purpose, for example:

How the old Mountains drip with Sunset
How the Hemlocks burn –
How the Dun Brake is draped in Cinder
By the Wizard Sun –

How the old Steeples hand the Scarlet
Till the Ball is full –
Have I the lip of the Flamingo
That I dare to tell?

These lines are taken from a poem by Emily Dickinson. The uneven rhythm serves the purpose of building up an atmosphere in nature before the poet herself intrudes into the poem.

Alliteration

This is the repetition of the initial consonant. When you are dealing with an unseen poem, discuss the effect of alliteration – don't just give examples. Ask yourself whether or not it produces a distinctive tone and whether or not it is regularly spaced:

> I caught this morning morning's minion king-
> dom of daylight's dauphin, dapple-dawn-drawn Falcon, in ...

The alliteration of the *m* and *d* sounds here serves the function of conjuring up a sense of richness, majesty and power.

> I should hear him fly with the high fields
> and wake up to the farm forever fled from the childless land.

The idea of time passing is expressed here in the alliteration of the *f* sound.

> O wild west wind, thou breadth of Autumn's being ...

The *w* alliteration here enacts the poet's awe in the presence of such a mighty force.

Assonance

This is the repetition of identical vowel sounds. For example, look at the effect of assonance in the following lines from Tennyson:

> Lo! in the middle of the wood,
> the folded leaf is woo'd from out the bud
> Sun steep'd at noon, and in the moon
> Nightly dew-fed; and turning yellow
> Falls, and floats adown the air.

The combined effect of the assonance of the *a* sound creates an impression of rich abundance in nature.

Onomatopoeia

This is where the word conjures up the sound: 'wheeze', 'buzz', 'splash'.

> watch the crisping ripples on the beach
> Liplapping of Galilee.

Ambiguity

Ambiguity in poetry means the use of words to mean two or more different things. Many times a poet can enrich the meaning of a poem by using words that are ambiguous. Ambiguity can emphasise the many nuances or levels of meaning that can be found in poetic language.

Look at the following line:

> ... dapple-dawn-drawn Falcon ...

Does it mean that the falcon is etched against the landscape of the sky? Or does it mean that the falcon has been drawn out by the dawn into the sky?

> My heart in hiding
> Stirred for a bird ...

Does this mean that his heart is in hiding because he is a priest and therefore detached from the world? Or does it mean that he is literally hiding as he watches the bird in the sky?

> Fathering and all humbling darkness
> Tells with silence the last light breaking …

What exactly is meant by the term 'humbling darkness'? Does it mean that death will humble humankind, including the poet? Does it mean that darkness is death? If so, why 'humbling'?

All these examples illustrate the power of ambiguity in poetry.

Effects of sound

Don't just give examples – show the effect. For example, harshness can be conveyed by the use of the consonants *b, t, k*:

> Blight and famine, plague and earthquake, roaring deeps and fiery sands,
> Clanging fights, and flaming towns, and sinking ships, and praying hands.

A sense of smoothness can be conveyed by the use of certain vowels and also by the *s* sound:

> There is sweet music here that softer falls.

Grammar

Consider some of the grammatical devices used in poetry.
- The omission of 'and', verbs or commas. Ask yourself why.
- Adding 'and', commas, verbs or capital letters when not usual. Ask why.
- Short sentences. What is their purpose?
- Long sentences. Anger? Boredom? Movement?
- Unusual syntax. Look at the purpose.
- Word compounds – 'world sorrow', 'blue-bleak', 'leafy-with-love'. What are they saying? Why are they used?
- Word compression – using the smallest number of words to achieve maximum intensity. This can be used to convey a dense or intense meaning or it can be deliberately ambiguous.
- The unusual use of words – 'Pitched past pitch of grief,' 'More pangs will, schooled at forepangs, wilder wring'.
- Nouns made into verbs. Why?
- Coining of words. Why?

Metre

- A very short line can express emotion: joy, anger, hatred.
- A very long line – what effect does it have?
- Run-on lines can express movement, speed, growth or development.

METHOD OF ANSWERING QUESTIONS ON AN UNSEEN POEM

Remember that a poem is made up of content or subject matter. This content is shaped in a particular way and adds up to what is known as the structure or form.

1. Aim first of all to give a general summary of what the poem is about and the different stages in the poem.
2. Read the poem several times to grasp some idea of the meaning.
3. Examine the title of the poem and see what relation it may have to the content.
4. Assess what type of poem it is. Is it narrative, an argument, a philosophical insight into life, an ode, a lyric, a sonnet?
5. If the poem is a narrative, understand the main events. When you understand why the events follow one another in a particular way you will understand how the poem is designed. There are three elements common to poems that tell stories: expectation, surprise and reversal.
6. If the poem is a meditation on life, get the general meaning of what is being said.
7. If the poem is an argument, follow the main stages. Ask yourself why the argument moves from that stage to this. Look at the conclusion of the argument. Is it logical? Is it effective? Has it achieved what it set out to do? Am I convinced? Identify the main points and the different stages of the argument.
8. Look at the words and see whether they carry symbolic or emotive meaning. Ask yourself why this is so. Look for a particular *tone* – this is the voice, mood or outlook of the poet.
9. Show how figures of speech contribute to the poem. Remember, figures of speech can be metaphors, symbols, personification, similes, etc. Many times poems convey their meaning by implication, suggestion, word connotations or associations and not through explicit statement.
10. Be aware of your reaction to the poem. What thoughts or feelings do the words stir up in you? Remember that a poem does not have to make complete sense. Many times the power of poetry comes from its ability to establish or suggest many different levels of meaning and many possibilities.

QUESTIONS AND SAMPLE ANSWERS

Attempt your own answers first, then compare them with the sample answers given.

Epitaph on a Tyrant
W. H. Auden

Perfection, of a kind, was what he was after,
And the poetry he invented was easy to understand;
He knew human folly like the back of his hand,
And was greatly interested in armies and fleets;
When he laughed, respectable senators burst with laughter,
And when he cried the little children died in the street.

1. Write a short note on the structure of this poem.
2. What is the tone of the poem?
3. Comment on the poet's use of language.

Sample answers

1. The structure of this poem consists of one stanza. The poem is called 'Epitaph on a Tyrant' and for that reason the poet neatly and compactly expresses his tribute to this tyrant in six short sentences. There are no run-on lines; instead the poet uses end rhyme, in the words 'fleet' and 'street', 'after' and 'laughter', 'understand' and 'hand'. The function of this rhyming scheme is to convey an ironic vision of a man whose life yielded destruction.

> Perfection, of a kind, was what he was after, [a]
> And the poetry he invented was easy to understand; [b]
> He knew human folly like the back of his hand, [b]
> And was greatly interested in armies and fleets; [c]
> When he laughed, respectable senators burst with laughter, [a]
> And when he cried the little children died in the street. [c]

2. The tone of the poem is satirical: the poet is mocking or satirising the tyrant. In the second line he suggests that this tyrant's poetry was easy to understand. In other words, his deeds and life were motivated by selfish interests, such as trying to dominate people and murdering them. For example, 'when he cried the little children died in the street'. The effect of the whole poem is sobering.

3. The language used is restrained and terse. The poet seems to be wary of expressing himself in too much language. This poem is a portrait of a man who wielded power through bullying and brute force. The poet wishes to paint a graphic picture of this tyrant and for that reason he uses images that are arresting and dramatic. The poem is made up of one stanza, which says it all. The poet does not repeat himself and therefore the effect is much more dramatic and intense.

The Hippopotamus
T. S. Eliot

The broad-backed hippopotamus
Rests on his belly in the mud;
Although he seems so firm to us
He is merely flesh and blood.

Flesh and blood is weak and frail
Susceptible to nervous shock;
While the True Church can never fail
For it is based upon a rock.

The hippo's feeble steps may err
In compassing material ends,
While the True Church need never stir
To gather in its dividends.
The 'potamus can never reach
The mango on the mango-tree;
But fruits of pomegranate and peach
Refresh the Church from over sea.

At mating time the hippo's voice
Betrays inflections hoarse and odd,
But every week we hear rejoice
The Church, at being one with God.

The hippopotamus's day
Is passed in sleep; at night he hunts;
God works in a mysterious way –
The Church can sleep and feed at once.

I saw the 'potamus take wing
Ascending from the damp savannas,
And quiring angels round him sing
The praise of God, in loud hosannas.

Blood of the Lamb shall wash him clean
And him shall heavenly arms enfold,
Among the saints he shall be seen
Performing on a harp of gold.

He shall be washed as white as snow,
By all the martyr'd virgins kist,
While the True Church remains below
Wrapt in the old miasmal mist.

1. Discuss the use of contrast in this poem.
2. Comment on how the form of the poem develops the theme.
3. Examine the images in the poem and show how they contribute to the particular vision presented in the poem.

Sample answers

1. The poet develops his thoughts by drawing a contrast between the image of the hippopotamus and the Church. There is a striking contrast between the two images – the broad-backed hippopotamus resting in the mud on his belly and the image

presented to us of the Church that can never fail, based, as it is, 'upon a rock'. The poet seems to be illustrating the difference between the impermanence of material things, as shown through his symbol of the hippopotamus, and the permanence and power of the spiritual, as evinced in the images of the Church. Each stanza develops this contrast. As the poem develops we bear witness to the growing power of the Church, while simultaneously witnessing the weakness of material things. Images such as 'the 'potamus can never reach | The mango on the mango-tree' show the failure of material things to achieve permanence.

On the other hand, the poet may be illustrating the continuity and permanence of the Church in such lines as: 'But fruits of pomegranate and peach | Refresh the Church from over sea.'

At the conclusion of the poem, the poet skilfully fuses this contrast. The hippopotamus is surrounded by singing angels; he is seen among the saints and washed clean by the blood of the Lamb. Perhaps the poet is painting an image of the fate of those who are faithful to the Church.

2. The poem is structured in a series of nine stanzas, all of the same length. Each of the stanzas is structured in the same manner – four lines of verse – which makes subtle use of end rhyme. For example, look at the effect of the rhyme between the following words in the last three stanzas:

> I saw the 'potamus take wing [a]
> Ascending from the damp savannas, [b]
> And quiring angels round him sing [a]
> The praise of God, in loud hosannas. [b]
>
> Blood of the Lamb shall wash him clean [a]
> And him shall heavenly arms enfold, [b]
> Among the saints he shall be seen [a]
> Performing on a harp of gold. [b]
>
> He shall be washed as white as snow, [a]
> By all the martyr'd virgins kist, [b]
> While the True Church remains below [a]
> Wrapt in the old miasmal mist. [b]

The poet's use of rhyme between words such as 'wing' and 'sing', 'savannas' and 'hosannas' illustrates the striking contrast between the material and the spiritual worlds. He also makes effective use of repetition, for example, 'enfold' and 'gold' paint an image of triumph and glory at the conclusion.

3. The poet makes use of the unusual image of a hippopotamus to put forward his theme of the power of the Church. The images that describe the hippopotamus are earthy and real – resting in the mud on his belly, the vivid image of his broad back, his voice betraying 'inflections hoarse and odd' at mating time. These are images that are related to the earth, to earthly things. On the other hand, the images that describe the

Church's activity are more positive and unified, such as 'While the True Church need never stir | To gather in its dividends' and 'The Church can sleep and feed at once' and suggest an internal harmony and sense of oneness. The poet's use throughout the poem of emphatic repetition in phrases such as 'the True Church' intensifies this dramatic power of the Church.

Exposure
Wilfred Owen

I

Our brains ache, in the merciless iced east winds that knive us …
Wearied we keep awake because the night is silent …
Low, drooping flares confuse our memory of the salient …
Worried by silence, sentries whisper, curious, nervous,
     But nothing happens.

Watching we hear the mad gusts tugging on the wire,
Like twitching agonies of men among its brambles.
Northward, incessantly, the flickering gunnery rumbles,
Far off, like a dull rumour of some other war.
     What are we doing here?

The poignant misery of dawn begins to grow …
We only know war lasts, rain soaks, and clouds sag stormy,
Dawn massing in the east her melancholy army
Attacks once more in ranks on shivering ranks of grey,
     But nothing happens.

Sudden successive flights of bullets streak the silence.
Less deadly than the air that shudders black with snow,
With sidelong flowing flakes that flock, pause and renew,
We watch them wandering up and down the wind's nonchalance,
     But nothing happens.

II

Pale flakes with fingering stealth come feeling for our faces –
We cringe in holes, back on forgotten dreams, and stare, snow-dazed,
Deep into grassier ditches. So we drowse sun-dozed.
Littered with blossoms trickling where the blackbird fusses.
     Is it that we are dying?

Slowly our ghosts drag home: glimpsing the sunk fires, glozed
With crusted dark-red jewels; crickets jingle there;
For hours the innocent mice rejoice: the house is theirs;

Shutters and doors, all closed: on us the doors are closed –
  We turn back to our dying.

Since we believe not otherwise can kind fires burn;
Nor ever suns smile true on child, or field or fruit.
For God's invincible spring, our love is made afraid;
Therefore, not loath, we lie out here; therefore were born,
    For love of God seems dying.

Tonight, His frosty will fasten on this mud and us,
Shrivelling many hands, puckering foreheads crisp.
The burying-party, picks and shovels in their shaking grasp,
Pause over half-known faces. All their eyes are ice,
    But nothing happens.

1. This poem is a powerful comment on the effects of war. Identify the main feelings
    expressed in the poem. Show how these feelings are conveyed through the
    language and imagery.
2. Show how the poet has structured his thought in the poem and what the effect of
    such a structure is.
3. Identify the particular tone and attitude towards life in the speaker.

Sample answers
1. The poem opens with an image of men worn out and fearful as they struggle to keep
awake on a bitterly cold night. There is a feeling of tension in the last line of the first
stanza, which is underlined by the poet's use of sibilance: 'Worried by silence, sentries
whisper, curious, nervous'. The whole feeling is one of fearful apprehension about what
is going to happen. These feelings are given added momentum and intensity by the
reiterated use of the short, terse line 'But nothing happens.' The poet paints some
powerful images of fear and dread and builds the reader up to an expectation of
something momentous and dreadful. Then the line 'But nothing happens' serves the
function of emphasising this anxiety even more.

    There is a strong feeling throughout the poem of the futility and waste of war. This
is achieved by the use of the rhetorical question in the concluding line of the second
stanza: 'What are we doing here?' In a sense the poet answers this question in the next
stanza, in the grim line 'We only know war lasts, rain soaks, and clouds sag stormy'.
The brutal impact of war is registered vividly in these images.

    As the poem develops, the feelings within the poet change. In the fifth stanza the
poet asks, 'Is it that we are dying?' This leads him on to some nostalgic reminiscences
about his past life, the reality of life at home and his loved ones. But these images are
brutal and grim. The only reality of his former family life is mirrored in images such as
'sunk fires ... Shutters and doors, all closed: on us the doors are closed'. The only
reality is death.

Towards the end of the poem the poet's feelings become almost hopeless as he continues to depict the devastation caused by war. The sixth stanza is gloomy and shows how the poet's dreams have been killed by war to such an extent that even his love is gone:

> . . . our love is made afraid;
> Therefore, not loath, we lie out here; therefore were born,
> For love of God seems dying.

There are undertones of hopelessness and near-despair in these lines. The conclusion of the poem is filled with some chilling images:

> The burying-party, picks and shovels in their shaking grasp,
> Pause over half-known faces. All their eyes are ice ...

With these images of frost and snow, the poet seems to be saying how war robs people of feeling. The men's faces are only 'half-known': war has generated indifference and unfeeling attitudes.

2. The poem is structured in eight stanzas of equal length. Each stanza concludes on a short emphatic statement or question, which underlines the futility of war. In each stanza the poet has drawn a parallel between the world of nature and the plight of these men who are hiding in the trenches. The images from nature are wild and savage: 'the merciless iced east winds that knive us ... the mad gusts tugging on the wire, | Like twitching agonies of men among its brambles ... The poignant misery of dawn'. The function of such imagery is to emphasise the brutality experienced by these men because of the war.

The structure is coherent and compact. The particular effect of such a structure is to illustrate the real impact caused by war on the lives of people and how it wreaks devastation.

3. The tone of this poem is deeply dispiriting and negative. The speaker seems to lose faith in life as the poem develops and progresses. In the opening stanza he is caught in a situation of extreme suffering, surrounded by icy winds and a fearful apprehension and confusion about what is happening: 'drooping flares confuse our memory of the salient ... | Worried by silence ...'. This sense of bewilderment and confusion on the part of the speaker is given an added intensity by the concluding line of each stanza, such as, 'But nothing happens', 'What are we doing here?'

The tone of the poem reaches a climax of suffering as the men cringe in holes. The poet tries to escape from this anguish in the trenches by recalling images of home and loved ones. But these efforts only conjure up more images of death and loss and so the tone intensifies in its dark, pessimistic strain. This gives way to some sobering reflections on life, war and love. The poet concludes that he finds it hard to accept that 'kind fires burn; | Nor ever suns smile true on child, or field or fruit.' The alliteration here underlines the dark, negative aspect of the speaker's vision of things. The pointlessness of war and the loss of everything, including one's identity, are given striking expression in the concluding stanza, as the dead bodies are only half-known to the people who come to bury them.

You're
Sylvia Plath

Clownlike, happiest on your hands,
Feet to the stars, and moon-skulled,
Gilled like a fish. A common-sense
Thumbs-down on the dodo's mode.
Wrapped up in yourself like a spool,
Trawling your dark as owls do.
Mute as a turnip from the Fourth
Of July to All Fools' Day,
O high-riser, my little loaf.

Vague as fog and looked for like mail.
Farther off than Australia.
Bent-backed Atlas, our travelled prawn.
Snug as a bug and at home
Like a sprat in a pickle jug.
A creel of eels, all ripples.
Jumpy as a Mexican bean.
Right, like a well-done sum.
A clean slate, with your own face on.

1. What particular vision of things is given in this poem? Take into account the poet's unusual use of words.
2. Comment on the language used in this poem and how it communicates the ideas.
3. Write a short comment on the tone of the poem.

Sample answers

1. The title of the poem is 'You're'. The poem gives us an image of a certain type of character, who is happy as they act like a clown with their feet to the stars. As the poem develops, we get an insight into the type of character represented in the poem's title, 'wrapped in yourself like a spool'. There are implications of an isolated and deep character, 'trawling your dark as owls do'. The poet makes sustained use of simile to paint some interesting images for us of this unusual character: 'gilled like a fish', 'mute as a turnip', 'like a sprat', 'snug as a bug'. The general effect of the lines is of an impenetrable and inaccessible character, 'vague as fog and looked for like mail. | Farther off than Australia.'

 This portrait is varied. The character represented is as 'Jumpy as a Mexican bean', yet 'Right, like a well-done sum.' The poet uses a wide variety of imagery to paint this highly original portrait of a most interesting character.

2. The writer uses language in a highly original way. Much of the effect of this poem comes from the writer's striking use of simile. Almost every image is structured on some

clever similes: 'Gilled like a fish', 'Wrapped up in yourself like a spool', 'Right, like a well-done sum.' The use of the image 'feet to the stars' in the opening lines is cleverly juxtaposed with the metaphor 'high-riser' in the concluding line of the first stanza. The poet uses alliteration of the *r* sound to conjure up a sense of comfort and ease – 'like a sprat in a pickle jug, | A creel of eels, all ripples.' The effect is intensified by the use of assonance in 'creel of eels, all ripples.'

3. The tone of this poem is detached and factual. The poet is painting a strong picture of different features of a character and she does this through recording a series of clear, factual images in an objective tone: 'Clownlike, happiest on your hands, | Feet to the stars, and moon-skulled.'

14
Prescribed Poetry

In this chapter there are some sample questions on the prescribed poetry. A method of organising and assembling material for an answer on prescribed poetry is given. Study this method carefully and apply it to the questions on the prescribed poetry at the end of this chapter.

APPROACHING THE QUESTION

1. Rephrase or rewrite the question.
2. Take a stance on the question – decide to agree, disagree or partly agree.
3. Begin a draft of your answer, writing down seven or eight points that will form the framework of your answer. These points must be on different aspects of the question and must contain quotations or references. In addition, these points will form the basis of each of the paragraphs of your answer. The diagram illustrates these points more clearly.

Remember, a good Higher Level answer must be structured in paragraphs and all must develop the question asked. The concluding paragraph must tie up all your ideas and refer back to the question. In addition, a good conclusion makes a definitive statement on the question.

QUESTIONS AND SAMPLE ANSWERS

Study the following questions and draft answers on the poets Elizabeth Bishop, Eavan Boland and Keats. Follow the method given in answering questions like these. It can help to fully rewrite these questions as a first step. In your answers, always use quotations from or references to the poems.

There is a complete answer on Eavan Boland following the two draft answers.

ELIZABETH BISHOP

(2007 and 2009 exams)

Question 1

'Elizabeth Bishop's poems move from description towards moments of discovery, which can be joyful or devastating.' In your reading of Elizabeth Bishop's poetry, did you find this statement to be true? Support your answer by quotation from or reference to the poems on your course.

Stage 1: Rephrase the question
Would you agree with the statement that the poetry of Elizabeth Bishop moves from describing or drawing pictures to revealing moments of insight, which can be either happy or traumatic?

Sample opening paragraph
This statement is true. Bishop's poems move from describing and evoking certain moments of profound illumination and insight towards the revelation of a situation that can be either joyful or devastating. She is a highly subjective poet, as most of her topics spring from her own experience. The poems I propose to discuss are 'The Fish', 'At the Fishhouses' and 'In the Waiting Room'.

Paragraph 1
Discuss her descriptions in 'The Fish' and in particular her meticulous use of sharply observed detail. Pay attention to her use of colour and small details in lines such as:

> He was speckled with barnacles,
> fine rosettes of lime,
> and infested
> with tiny white sea-lice ...

Show how the fish almost becomes an objective symbol of the poet's own problems in the image of the rainbow (line 75): 'until everything was rainbow, rainbow, rainbow!' Discuss this central moment of illumination and show how this discovery is positive, a source of joy and added wisdom.

Paragraph 2

Discuss 'At the Fishhouses' and look at how Bishop uses a succession of vivid details in her description:

> an old man sits netting,
> his net, in the gloaming almost invisible,
> a dark purple-brown,
> and his shuttle worn and polished.

Describe and discuss how all these details conjure up a distinct atmosphere of seafaring people.

Comment on her use of small details in lines such as:

> The five fishhouses have steeply peaked roofs
> and narrow, cleated gangplanks slant up
> to storerooms in the gables
> for the wheelbarrows to be pushed up and down on.

Discuss how the change comes in this poem (line 45 onwards) and how the poet achieves this through her use of images that are now cold and deep. Discuss the reason for the repetition of certain images and how the colours change:

> The water seems suspended
> above the rounded grey and blue-grey stones.

The mode of discovery in the poem is gradual, deep, reflective and sobering. Discuss the fact that while this vision is neither joyful nor devastating, it certainly is a moving and emotional experience for the poet. Perhaps it is a wisdom that comes to her from her background – a neurotic mother and her own abandonment as a child.

Show how her vision at the conclusion is sobering, that this experience is unalterable:

> It is like what we imagine knowledge to be:
> dark, salt, clear, moving, utterly free,
> drawn from the cold hard mouth
> of the world, derived from the rocky breasts
> forever, flowing and drawn, and since
> our knowledge is historical, flowing and flown.

Paragraph 3

Show how 'In the Waiting Room' takes a simple situation and uses a descriptive and narrative approach to probe the meaning of her own sex on a deeper level.

Discuss the originality of approach – how on the basis of a simple descriptive narrative the poet merges the vision of herself with that of her aunt.

Show how she experiences a crisis of identity in the context of ordinary, banal images encountered in a waiting room:

> The waiting room
> was full of grown-up people,

artics and overcoats,
lamps and magazines.

Note her emphasis on the colour and movement of the volcano spilling over in rivulets of fire:

the inside of a volcano,
black, and full of ashes;
then it was spilling over
in rivulets of fire.

Note the description of the black women:

black, naked women with necks
wound round and round with wire
like the necks of light bulbs.

Comment on how she reacts to these images with fear and disgust.

Paragraph 4

Discuss 'Sestina' and how it is structured on some graphic domestic imagery. Comment on how it depicts a child seated at a kitchen table watching her grandmother preparing tea.

Discuss how the poet juxtaposes the image of the kettle boiling with the recurrent reference to 'drops of tears'. Show how these images change and develop in the poem to reveal a sorrowful moment of insight.

Develop the idea of how the whole notion of sorrow is firmly implanted in the child's mind by the conclusion of the poem.

Show how the reference to the child drawing 'another inscrutable house' underlines this unfathomable aspect of life and domestic bliss, which is a strong feature in Bishop's poetry.

Concluding paragraph

Discuss how all four poems operate on the level of simple, vivid and keen descriptive detail.

Show how this vision differs in each of her poems, revealing either joy or heartache. Conclude by showing how these various illuminations or insights display different aspects of the poet's life.

EAVAN BOLAND

(2008 exam)

Question 2

'Boland's poetry celebrates the domestic and the role of women in a world that is often violent and threatening.' Discuss this view, supporting your answer by quotation from or reference to the poems by Eavan Boland on your course.

Answer

Eavan Boland is a woman who writes against the background of Ireland and its history. She writes about a rich variety of different themes in her work. It is unquestionably true that Boland does celebrate women and their role in both the domestic situation and society in general. In addition, she communicates her vision of women against the backdrop of a world that is undoubtedly characterised by war and violence.

Many of her poems deal with the position of the woman. In all of them we are exposed to various facets of the woman, from her domestic role as caring mother in poems such as 'The Pomegranate', 'This Moment' and 'Child of Our Time' to the oppressed plight of a sterile woman in Famine times doomed to a life without children. Other poems, such as 'Outside History', discuss the role of the many women who were not recorded in the annals of Irish history in times of oppression for Ireland. 'Child of Our Time' vividly represents the situation of a mother confronting the death of a child because of needless acts of violence.

A simple poem entitled 'The War Horse' draws a dramatic parallel between a tinker's horse that is let loose from a camp on the Enniskerry Road and the influx of terrorist violence in the south of Ireland. Setting the scene in suburbia, Boland dramatically succeeds in fusing together the powerful image of a wild horse as it trots along the road of suburban Dublin one evening. This image becomes a sustained metaphor in the poem, through which she articulates her own insights and views on the reality of war and its impact on the south of Ireland.

In fifteen stanzas, all only two lines in length, Boland conveys the movement of this horse, the destruction left in its wake together with her own personal reactions to the whole situation, which are clear and sincere. She comments on how the horse has destroyed only a rose, which is expendable, a leaf of the laurel tree and a crocus. She uses these images to draw in the political theme and to articulate a strong and serious question about the reality of the commitment on the part of the south to terrorist violence: 'why should we care | If a rose, a hedge, a crocus are uprooted | Like corpses, remote, crushed, mutilated?'

She reiterates the fact that we are safe, however, that our fear of commitment has not been clearly or fully formulated and how, with the disappearance of the horse, this fear has vanished: 'But we, we are safe, our unformed fear | Of fierce commitment gone'. She moves on to show us how the neighbours use the shelter of the curtains to hide: 'Neighbours use the subterfuge | Of curtains.' Boland's reaction is one of gratitude when the horse passes her, 'Thankfully, passing us.' As she pauses she tells us that for a second only her blood is still with atavism. She is motivated by pride in her remote ancestors, but she returns to the present reality of the smashed rose, which reminds her of Ireland's violent history in the past.

In the poem 'The Famine Road' we are confronted with an image of a young woman who is unable to bear any children. She is dehumanised and humiliated, just like the victims of the Famine in the mid-nineteenth century. The world of British imperialism and colonisation are all set against the backdrop of this woman's plight. The poem is recounted from two different standpoints – a clinical, cold doctor and an inhumane, brutal English officer. The world is stark and threatening. The woman's problem is simply dismissed in cold, insensitive tones: 'take it well woman, grow | your garden, keep house, good-bye.'

The poem 'Child of Our Time' is written from the standpoint of a woman and mother in a world of terrorism and violence. The voice of the poem is a mother and woman who witness the needless death of a young child in terrorist violence in a city in the south of Ireland. The whole poem paints a vivid, grim picture of the utter futility of this type of warfare. The speaker addresses the world and pleads with them to learn some type of lesson from the death of this child.

It is certainly clear that Boland is a poet who represents Ireland and in particular the situation of the woman as woman and as mother. Through a rich range of various themes and poetic techniques, Boland succeeds in drawing some vibrant pictures of female sterility against a backdrop of oppression and famine. She uses some of her poems to articulate her public condemnation of violence and its consequences. She writes from the standpoint of a mother who witnesses the senseless waste of young life through the brutality of war. She is a valuable and realistic mouthpiece on behalf of a community suffering from the enormous impact of war and violence.

Sample answer on poetry

The following is a complete sample answer on a question about the poetry of Keats.

'The odes of Keats, taken together, can be seen as an investigation of the imagination's ability to cope with time and change.' In the case of any two odes on your course, test the truth of this statement. Support your answer by quotation from or reference to the poems.

Answer

In 'Ode to a Nightingale' and 'Ode on a Grecian Urn', Keats confronts the problem of reconciling the demands of a poetic imagination with life. He tries to escape from the miseries of life and seeks a form of compensation, either sensual or imaginative. In both odes Keats seeks to transcend the limitations imposed by time and change in life and instead to attain an ideal state of life, where beauty and happiness are the presiding values.

In 'Ode to a Nightingale' the poet is overwhelmed with the sorrow in this world: 'My heart aches, and a drowsy numbness pains my sense.' He seeks to escape from the harsh world of reality. He uses the symbol of wine as a vehicle of escape from 'the weariness, the fever and the fret' of this world. This impulse to leave the world inevitably leads to a recollection of actual life. Mortal existence has a distorted and ghastly resemblance to his own state of mind, as can be seen from the first stanza. As the poet hears the song of the nightingale, men sit and hear each other groan. In life, 'Beauty cannot keep her lustrous eyes,| Or new love pine at them beyond tomorrow.' The poet is lamenting the changes wrought by time to life and humankind.

To deal with this profound anguish brought about by the limited and imperfect nature of life, Keats desires to enter a visionary world of immortal and unmingled bliss: 'Away! Away! for I will fly to thee.' The vehicle of flight is no longer wine but poetry or fantasy. The poet now thinks of a verdant bower and describes it in rich, luxurious images: 'Through verdurous glooms and winding mossy ways.' This fourth stanza is a vivid assertion of the enormous power of the imagination to see more than the sensory eye.

Throughout this ode Keats steadily relinquishes his grip on actuality under the influence of the bird's song, and maintains that death is a climactic release. By the conclusion of the sixth stanza the bird has been transformed into a symbol: it is now an immortal bird living in a visionary realm. For the remainder of the poem the nightingale, even as a symbol, moves away from the human world – he is heard first by emperor, and clown, then by Ruth, the biblical figure, and finally 'in faery lands that are forlorn', because humans cannot live in them. For this reason the song of the nightingale is no longer happy: it is now a requiem or a 'plaintive anthem'.

As the poet awakens from his trance there is the suggestion that the visions stimulated by the song may have been illusory: 'the fancy cannot cheat so well, | As she is fam'd to do deceiving elf.' The departure of the bird is represented as the finding of a vision. The song does not merely fade, it is 'buried deep,' as if to imply the impossibility of ever hearing it. This could perhaps be an ironic reflection on the theme of death.

The poem ends with uncertainty and a question: 'Was it a vision or a waking dream?' Was the process that has taken place a momentary glimpse of truth (a vision) or a musing subjective one (half-dream)? Is the poet's inability to experience it now an awakening into reality or a lapse into sensibility? The conclusion of the poem is rich in possibilities.

On the other hand, the ability of the imagination to deal with change and time is developed in a thoroughly distinct manner in 'Ode on a Grecian Urn'. Both the vehicle of escape and the reality encountered are distinctly different in this poem.

This is a more objective poem than 'Ode to a Nightingale', structured on a series of clever paradoxes and ambiguity. The poet seeks to attain the immortalisation of beauty through the medium of a Grecian urn. The urn is ancient yet is of unblemished, youthful beauty, 'unravished'. The paradoxes continue as the poem develops: the urn is the bride of quietness, the foster-child of silence, yet also a historian. This rustic historian tells of a 'leaf-fringed legend' supplying neither names nor dates, nor exact facts, giving suggestive details only.

The poet reaches the central paradox of the poem in the image of 'Cold Pastoral'. The term 'pastoral' suggests something warm and idyllic, yet the urn tells its tale in cold marble, and not overtly but by teasing thought out of us. It seduces us away from an intellectual or rational mode of perception into an imaginative participation in its depicted life. The urn is beautiful, but, as the paradoxes of the poem have emphasised, this beauty stems from the imagination.

In this ode there is a stronger note of confidence and assurance in the ability of the artist to reconcile the reality of decay and life's limitations. The poet seems to draw a more positive conclusion here.

Towards the end of this ode Keats draws the conclusion that 'beauty is truth, truth beauty.' In a world of mystery and pain, beauty is the one great revelation of reality or truth. He reiterates what he has implied in his other odes: beauty can be embodied in a lasting form and therefore is truer than many aspects of life that we value. The poet, in practising his art, can give fixity to flux, as the unknown artist of the urn has done. This is precisely the 'message' that the Sylvan historian has conveyed to the poet. Immortality can be given to what is beautiful and passing, as long as the artist accepts that the life of the work of art must go hand in hand with the acceptance of life's limitations.

It can certainly be contended that in both odes Keats manifests the power of the imagination to deal with time and change. As can be seen from 'Ode to a Nightingale', the imagination cannot escape from oppressive reality. In fact, far from attaining a vision of ultimate truth, it achieves only a momentary illusion. On the other hand, 'Ode on a Grecian Urn' concludes on the idea that in a world of mystery and pain, the experience of beauty is the one great revelation of reality. If beauty is reality, then reality – the reality of suffering, the reality of experience intensely felt – can also yield beauty in itself and in art. Keats is struggling towards a vision that will comprehend all experience: joy, suffering, natural, ideal, transient and the eternal.

COMMENT

This question is based on the power of the imagination as it is manifested in the odes written by Keats. The answer clearly sets out the problems confronted by Keats with regard to the changes wrought by time. It begins by outlining the manner in which the poet uses the imagination in 'Ode to a Nightingale' to counteract the oppressiveness caused by time and mortality. The answer describes the techniques used by Keats in this ode to show the power of the imagination to transcend decay and the limitations of mortality.

The second part of this answer is based on 'Ode to a Grecian Urn'. The answer draws out the contrast between the different ways in which Keats uses the imagination to deal with these problems: time and change in life. The use of paradox is clearly outlined here.

The answer concludes by referring back to the question. It draws together the conclusions of both odes and demonstrates how 'Ode on a Grecian Urn' has been more successful in delineating the enormous power of the imagination to overcome the problems posed by time and change.

Answers to question 1 *(page 22–23)*

(a) When you look at the house from the outside it seems to have about twenty rooms.

(b) The writer makes use of short, terse sentences with both humour and sarcasm in order to maintain the reader's interest in the passage.

(c) Boyle, who is filled with self-delusion, sees himself as the man of the house.

(d) Many teenagers of this type come from homes where the parents are unable to control them properly or where the mother is at work and hasn't enough time for her children.

(e) I would be delighted if you would reply and let me know whether or not you are available, and the possible times.

(f) By this statement the writer means that people usually make a place what it is by their presence there.

Answers to question 2 *(page 23)*

(a) When he states his arguments he gives a balanced account of both sides.

(b) This can be found in a magazine bought by rich people. It would not be likely to feature in a newspaper, as there are too many photographs.

(c) The house is not the usual type, as it is old, enormous, and appears to have been restored.

(d) The environment surrounding a person can usually tell you a lot about them. If, for instance, you were in an untidy house you would presume that the owner was an easy-going type of character.

(e) The impression I get of Oprah from her programme gives me some indication of the type of person she is and of her lifestyle. I think her home would also tell me a lot about her.

(f) The picture of the mirror and the woman with the pearls suggests that this family has a luxurious lifestyle.

Answers to question 3 *(page 23)*

(a) The play is filled with examples of both jealousy and betrayal. For example, this is evident in the figure of Iago.

(b) University students consistently analyse their actions, for they may upset a friend or a teacher.

(c) I wish to inform you of the type of photographs and images that I would like included in my gallery.

(d) The difference between the cost price and the selling price rose.

(e) Trade fairs are a common commercial activity nowadays, many of them held in export markets.

(f) I believe the writer expresses himself and his observations of human motivations very well.

Answers to question 4 (page 23–24)

(a) I find myself struggling to retain my popularity.

(b) A time-and-motion study in this section would improve output.

(c) I am stuck in this claustrophobic condition, with no one knowing either the despair or the loneliness I am experiencing.

(d) We regret to inform you that the Boxhead golf clubs you ordered on 15 July are not in stock.

(e) The 15:20 train that runs on weekdays in summer will not run on Sundays in either winter or summer.

(f) These people soldier on, living on very little as they struggle for success.

Past Examination Papers

State Examinations Commission

LEAVING CERTIFICATE EXAMINATION, 2006

English – Higher Level – Paper I

Total Marks: 200

Wednesday, 7 June – Morning, 9.30 – 12.20

- This paper is divided into two sections,
  Section I COMPREHENDING and Section II COMPOSING.
- The paper contains **three** texts on the general theme of FEAR OF THE UNKNOWN.
- Candidates should familiarise themselves with each of the texts before beginning their answers.

- Both sections of this paper (COMPREHENDING and COMPOSING) must be attempted.
- Each section carries 100 marks.

SECTION I – COMPREHENDING
- Two questions, A and B, follow each text.
- Candidates must answer a Question A on one text and a Question B on a different text. Candidates must answer only one Question A and only one Question B.
- **N.B.** Candidates may NOT answer a Question A and a Question B on the same text.

SECTION II – COMPOSING
- Candidates must write on **one** of the compositions 1–7.

SECTION I
COMPREHENDING (100 Marks)

TEXT I
'WHAT SEEMS TO BE THE PROBLEM, LADY SARAH?'

In this extract (adapted from A Border Station, *by Shane Connaughton) a father and son are cutting down a tree. The father, a garda sergeant, has been given permission by Lady Sarah, a member of the landed gentry, to cut down a small tree on her lands. However, he decides to ignore her wishes and cut down a magnificent beech tree on the avenue leading to the Great House. We join the story as the tree falls...*

'She's going,' said his father. Branches quaking, the huge tree tilted, twisted and, fighting to stay upright, grabbed at a neighbouring tree but, bowing to its fate, keeled over and with a creaking goodbye-sigh rushed to the earth with a thunderous hurricane crash. The boy felt the shock waves in his feet and saw the light flood in to the space where the tree had stood. It was mad, he thought. Ridiculous. Lady Sarah was bound to find out. His father grinned.

'It'll see us in firewood for the winter, thank God.'

Tired out he sat on the tree-stump beside his father and had alternate swigs at the bottle of cold tea.

Hearing a noise he turned his head and instantly his body and blood went cold. Approaching along at the wheel of her antiquated Rolls Royce was Lady Sarah. Time stopped dead. His father gave a strangled groan and his face iced over in hatred. They were caught like rats in a trap.

The car crunched to a halt. He was terrified in case his father did something desperate and was all the more amazed when he saw him smiling and in high good nature waving to Lady Sarah as she, horror-stricken, stepped onto the drive. Wearing a peculiar 1920s hat and a flapping plastic mack she dismissed his father's greeting and staggered towards the tree.

'What have you done, Sergeant, what have you done!' she wailed. 'You have killed one of my beauties!'

Grabbing and clutching the stricken branches she buried herself in the copper coloured leaves.

'Oh Beatrice, Beatrice, my beauty, how has this occurred?'

His father winked.

'What's wrong, what seems to be the problem, Lady Sarah?'

'The problem,' she replied, stepping from the tree, 'is that you have murdered the wrong tree.' Behind the thick lenses of her spectacles her eyes were tiny red dots of dismay.

'Oh no, we haven't, have we?' howled his father, his face a dancing mask of pantomime surprise. 'Good Lord, I can't believe it. Are you sure Lady Sarah?'

'Oh yes I'm sure alright. I gave you a weakling ash, not this!'

Suddenly he turned on the boy and made as if to strike him.

'Didn't I tell you it wasn't this one? I told you all along.'

The boy hung his head in shame and didn't dare look at Lady Sarah because he knew she knew his father lied.

'I'll do anything I can by way of reparation, anything. I remember you saying the tree's name is Andy. I think that's what confused me. That and the boy. Beech wood is no good to me anyway. It's a poor burner. A weakling ash is just what I wanted, Lady Sarah.'

Once more he blamed the boy and made a run at him as if to hit him. Darting out of his way he went close to Lady Sarah and looked into her eyes.

She knew.

Turning away she faced the dead Beatrice and with her frail hand plucked a copper leaf. Resting on her fingers like a clot of blood, she held it to her mouth and nose and sighed as if kissing goodbye to a loved one. Tears welled in the boy's eyes. Lady Sarah looked very old, very sad, and a little frightened. She owned the great demesne, employed many people, but up against his father she knew the truth. He was the Garda Sergeant and she was just a lonely spinster, powerless to command. She needed him to protect her property. The law was hers but it was on his word that it was carried out.

Getting into her car, she spoke softly, her pride hurt, her spirit shocked. 'You may as well finish what you so cruelly started.'

'Well that's the only damn thing we can do now, Lady Sarah.'

Hours later as they drove home, though his body ached, the boy's soul raged rampant at the conquering smirk on his father's face.

N.B. Candidates may NOT answer Question A and Question B on the same text. Questions A and B carry 50 marks each.

QUESTION A

(i) Do you consider the first paragraph to be an example of good descriptive writing? Explain your view. (15)

(ii) How do the boy's feelings towards Lady Sarah change as the narrative progresses? Support your answer by reference to the text. (15)

(iii) A reader of the passage has commented: 'Both Lady Sarah and the father are powerful, but in different ways.'

What, in your opinion, would have led the reader to this conclusion? (20)

QUESTION B

'Hours later…the boy's soul raged…'

Imagine that, in an attempt to control his feelings, the boy writes into his diary an account of the incident and his reactions to it. Write out his diary entry. (50)

TEXT 2
GHOST WRITING

Jan Stevens is a ghost writer, that is, someone who writes books that are published as the work of someone else.

On Ghost Writing

I am a ghost writer. I write books that other people take credit for – people more famous than me, or busier, or who simply can't be trusted with a pen.

I have written for well-known authors, celebrities, and even for other ghost writers who found themselves over-worked. I have written legal thrillers, historical non-fiction, mysteries, and even ghost stories. However, my name doesn't appear on the covers of any of these books, or on their copyright page. My anonymity is complete. Sometimes, even the publishers don't know I exist. My name, of course, does appear on my contracts. To prevent confusion, the language of these contracts calls me the *ghost writer* and the other party is referred to as the *author*. Under the terms of my contracts, I'm forbidden from revealing the identity of my authors. Ghost writers have to keep their secrets, or face lawsuits.

Ghost writing can be challenging. For one thing, ghost writers have to write very quickly. We are often given work that has a looming deadline. I once wrote a 120,000-word novel in twelve weeks. That's 2,000 words every day for five days a week. Maintaining this sprinter's pace at marathon length was painful, requiring much solitude and coffee. However, I made my 2,000-word count every single day without fail. One of the advantages of ghost writing is that the *almost* right word will serve as well as the *right* word.

Some ghost writers I know are haunted by the loss of recognition and go to great lengths to put secret codes into their ghost novels. They concoct sentence-length acronyms or give minor characters anagrams of their own names, so that future historians will decipher the work's true author. Others enjoy private jokes: inserting the names of cats, roommates, or favourite restaurants into their ghosted books as a kind of petty claim to ownership.

A common question asked of ghost writers is, 'So, what do the *authors* actually do?' The answer covers a considerable range. I once wrote a novel from a fifty-page outline that provided specific adjectives and images for each chapter. Other authors provide only a paragraph or two. Some offer little guidance, but attack the finished work in minute detail. This ghost writer cares little because, by then, I'm busy haunting somewhere else.

As a rule, the most 'prolific' authors are the most detached. I've written five books for one man whom I've never met or spoken to, or even e-mailed. His editors, however, assure me that he has actually *read* the books, and that he rather enjoyed them.

A good ghost writer is expected to pick up an author's style by reading the author's other books. I often wonder if these were, in fact, written by yet another ghost writer. Am I a copy of a copy?

So, what of the ethics of ghost writing? Is ghost writing a case of false advertising? Is it simply bad manners? It can be argued that a book is simply a product; you either enjoy it or you don't, and the author's name is no more a personal signature than the Nike logo or any other well-known trademark. Moreover, publishing is a business like any other. As in every business in a market economy, the aim is to make profit from someone else's labour. I don't object to this. Indeed, someday I hope to come up with a get-rich idea, a detective or adventure series that will be hugely successful with the reading public. I'll write the first few books in the series, and then let some other poor ghost writer follow *my* instructions for a while.

After all, I've got to know quite a few ghost writers in the last decade. Between us, I could author twenty books a year without too much effort. Indeed, when I mentioned I was going to write this essay, one of them volunteered to write it for me!

(And how do you know she didn't?)

N.B. Candidates may NOT answer Question A and Question B on the same text. Questions A and B carry 50 marks each.

QUESTION A

(i)   On the evidence of this passage, what is the attitude of Jan Stevens to ghost writing? (15)

(ii) In your view, what is lost **and** gained by the 'author' in a ghost writing arrangement? Support your answer by reference to the text. (15)

(iii) Jan Stevens sets out to inform the reader on the topic of ghost writing. What features make this an interesting piece of informative writing? (20)

QUESTION B

Write a letter to a famous writer **or** celebrity **or** sports personality of your choice offering your services as a ghost writer for a future book. In your letter you should outline the reasons why you believe you would make a successful *ghost writer* for your chosen *author*. (50)

TEXT 3
PRETENCE
The following text consists of a visual and a written element.

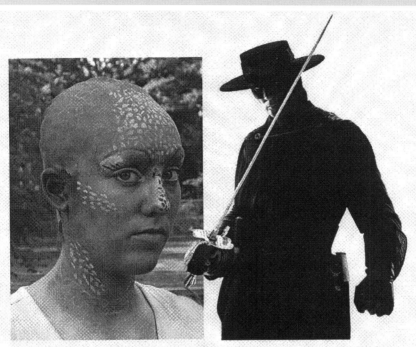

Masters of pretence

Make-believe

Diving?!

PRETENCE – Everybody's doing it!

Psychologists tell us that the habit of pretending is unique to the human species and begins in very early childhood. From about two years of age children engage in imaginary conversations with make-believe characters (talking to a doll, inventing an imaginary companion) or pretending to engage in a variety of adult activities (talking into a banana as if it were a telephone, pretending to cook and eat mud pies, pretending to be a teacher, a soldier, a Garda). The young of no other creature on earth behave like this.

It seems that this childhood role-playing is just training for later life where pretence is widespread. From the actor on stage shedding tears as he plays a tragic role for the hundredth time, to Ronaldo diving in the penalty area (again!), we are the masters of pretence.

Indeed, pretence often soothes the friction between people and promotes smoother relationships. Without it our world would be a crueler place. Can you imagine if everyone said, 'Let's stop all this pretence! Let's tell each other the unvarnished truth for a change!'

Imagine it's St Valentine's Day and the young, not so gallant lover comes to his tender lady's door. She twirls in her new dress and utters the invitation to praise. 'Well? How do I look?' And he replies truthfully, 'Well, let me see, dear. Hm... You know... I'd prefer you in something else!' In this case the absence of pretence might lead to a shorter than expected lifespan!

So why do we have this fascination with pretence?

Well, it is an expression of the two great gifts which make human beings unique: the gift of imagination and the ability to make one another happy.

N.B. Candidates may NOT answer Question A and Question B on the same text. Questions A and B carry 50 marks each.

QUESTION A

(i)   In your opinion, which of the visual images best expresses the theme of pretence? Explain your choice.   (15)
(ii) Taking the images as a group, do you think they go well with the written passage? Explain your answer.   (15)
(iii) Do you think the writer is justified in the conclusions drawn in the final paragraph? Explain your view.   (20)

QUESTION B

Advertising and young people – you report to the Advertising Standards Authority.

There is much discussion as to whether or not young people are being exploited by advertisers. Write a short report to the Advertising Standards Authority outlining your views on the matter.   (50)

SECTION II
COMPOSING (100 marks)

Write a composition on **any one** of the following.

Each composition carries 100 marks.

The composition assignments below are intended to reflect language study in the areas of information, argument, persuasion, narration and the aesthetic use of language.

1. 'Let's stop all this pretence! Let's tell each other the unvarnished truth for a change!' (TEXT 3)
    Write a personal essay in response to the above statement.

2. 'Maintaining this sprinter's pace at marathon length was painful...' (TEXT 2)
    Write an article for a magazine for young adult readers in which you give them advice about how to cope with the pressures of modern living.

3. 'It was mad...ridiculous.' (TEXT 1)
    Write a short story suggested by the above title.

4. '...Someday I hope to come up with a get-rich idea...' (TEXT 2)
    Write a magazine article (serious or light-hearted) in which you outline a get-rich idea of your own.

5. 'What seems to be the problem...?' (TEXT 1)
    Write the speech you would deliver to a group of world leaders in which you persuade them to deal with one or more of the world's problems.

6. 'Imagine it's St Valentine's Day...' (TEXT 3)
    Write an article for a popular magazine on the importance of romance in our lives.

7. **Write a short story prompted by one or more of the images in TEXT 3.**

State Examinations Commission
LEAVING CERTIFICATE EXAMINATION, 2006

English – Higher Level – Paper 2

Total Marks: 200

Wednesday, 7 June –Afternoon, 1.30–4.50

Candidates must attempt the following:

- **ONE** question from SECTION I – The Single Text
- **ONE** question from SECTION II – The Comparative Study
- **THE QUESTIONS** on the Unseen Poem from SECTION III – Poetry
- The questions on **ONE** of the Prescribed Poems from SECTION III – Poetry

N.B. Candidates must answer on Shakespearean Drama.
They may do so in SECTION I, The Single Text (*King Lear, As You Like It*) or in
SECTION II, The Comparative Study (*King Lear, As You Like It, Twelfth Night*)

SECTION I
THE SINGLE TEXT (60 marks)

Candidates must answer **one** question from this section (**A–E**).

A PRIDE AND PREJUDICE – Jane Austen
  (i) 'What fascinates the reader of *Pride and Prejudice* is the relationship between the central characters of Elizabeth and Mr Darcy.'
       Write a response to this statement, supporting your views by reference to the text.

OR

  (ii) 'In *Pride and Prejudice* Jane Austen laughs at the follies of her characters without being cruel to them.'
        To what extent would you agree with this view? Support your points by reference to the text.

B THE POISONWOOD BIBLE – Barbara Kingsolver
  (i) 'The main interest in *The Poisonwood Bible* lies in the Price family's experiences of a strange and different world.'
       To what extent would you agree with this view? Support your answer by reference to the text.

OR

  (ii) Write out the text of a talk you would give in answer to the question: 'Why read *The Poisonwood Bible*?' Support the points you make by reference to the novel.

C DEATH AND NIGHTINGALES – Eugene McCabe
  (i) 'Violence and deception govern the relationships in *Death and Nightingales*.'
       To what extent would you agree with this view? Support your answer by reference to the novel.

OR

  (ii) 'The mood or atmosphere of *Death and Nightingales* is a bleak one.'
        Write a response to this statement, supporting your views by reference to the text.

D AS YOU LIKE IT – William Shakespeare
  (i) What features of the drama *As You Like It* did you enjoy?
       Support your answer by reference to the text.

OR

  (ii) 'In the play *As You Like It*, Shakespeare upholds the value of romantic love.'
        Discuss this view of the play, supporting your points by reference to the text.

E   **KING LEAR** – William Shakespeare

   (i)   'In the play *King Lear*, the stories of Lear and Gloucester mirror one another in interesting ways.'
         Write a response to this view of the play, supporting your answer by reference to the text.

OR

   (ii) 'Reading or seeing *King Lear* is a horrifying as well as an uplifting experience.'
         Write a response to this view, supporting the points you make by reference to the text.

SECTION II
THE COMPARATIVE STUDY (70 marks)

Candidates must answer **one** question from **either A** – Theme or Issue **or B** – The Cultural Context.

In your answer you may not use the text you have answered on in **SECTION I** – The Single Text.

N.B. The questions use the word **text** to refer to all the different kinds of texts available for study on this course, i.e. novel, play, short story, autobiography, biography, travel writing and film. The questions use the word **author** to refer to novelists, playwrights, writers in all genres and film directors.

A   THEME OR ISSUE

1.   'In careful reading/viewing of key moments of texts we often find important themes or issues which are developed in the text as a whole.'

   (a)   Compare how key moments of two texts you have studied in your comparative course raised an important theme or issue.   (40)

   (b)   In the case of a third text, show how a key moment helped in your understanding of the same theme or issue discussed in part (a).   (30)

OR

2.   'The dramatic presentation of a theme or issue can add greatly to the impact of narrative texts.'
     Write an essay comparing how the presentation of a theme or issue common to the texts you have studied for your comparative course added to the impact of the texts.   (70)

B   THE CULTURAL CONTEXT

1.   'The cultural context of a narrative usually determines how the story will unfold.'

(a)   Compare the way in which the cultural context influenced the storyline in **two** of the texts you have studied in your comparative course.   (40)

(b)   Show how the cultural context influenced the storyline in a third text you have studied.   (30)

OR

2.   'Understanding the cultural context of a text adds to our enjoyment of a good narrative.'

In the light of the above statement, write an essay comparing the cultural contexts of the texts you have studied in your comparative course. Support the comparisons you make by reference to the texts.   (70)

SECTION III
POETRY (70 marks)

Candidates must answer **A** – Unseen Poem **and B** – Prescribed Poetry.

A   UNSEEN POEM (20 marks)

Answer **either** Question **1 or** Question **2**.

The Toy Horse

Somebody, when I was young, stole my toy horse,
The charm of my morning romps, my man's delight.
For two days I grieved, holding my sorrow like flowers
Between the bars of my sullen angry mind.

Next day I went out with evil in my heart,
Evil between my eyes and at the tips of my hands,
Looking for my enemy at the armed stations,
Until I found him, playing in his garden

With my toy horse, urgent in the battle
Against the enemies of his Unreason's land:
He was so happy, I gave him also
My vivid coloured crayons and my big glass marble.

Valentin Iremonger

1.   Do you think the poem gives a surprising insight into a childhood experience? In your answer you might consider:
– *the pattern of the child's thinking*
– *the words and images in the poem.*   (20)

OR

2. Write a response to the above poem, highlighting aspects of it that you liked and/or disliked. (20)

B   PRESCRIBED POETRY (50 marks)

Candidates must answer **one** of the following questions (**1–4**).

1. Write an introduction to the poetry of John Donne for new readers. Your introduction should cover the following:
   – *The ideas that were most important to him.*
   – *How you responded to his use of language and imagery.*
   Refer to the poems by John Donne that you have studied.

2. 'What Thomas Hardy's poetry means to me.'
   Write an essay in response to the above title. Your essay should include a discussion of his themes and the way he expresses them. Support the points you make by reference to the poetry on your course.

3. 'Reading the poetry of Elizabeth Bishop.'
   Write out the text of a talk that you would give to your class in response to the above title.
   Your talk should include the following:
   – *Your reactions to her themes or subject matter.*
   – *What you personally find interesting in her style of writing.*
   Refer to the poems by Elizabeth Bishop that you have studied.

4. 'Writing to Michael Longley.'
   Write a letter to Michael Longley telling him about your experience of studying his poetry. In your letter you should refer to his themes and the way he expresses them. Support the points you make by reference to the poetry on your course.

ACKNOWLEDGMENTS 2006 EXAMINATIONS

Penguin for an extract from *A Border Station* by Shane Connaughton; Colin Smythe Ltd for 'The Toy Horse' by Valentin Iremonger. The extract was adapted by the State Examinations Commission exclusively for the purposes of the Leaving Certificate English (Higher Level) examination paper (2006) and does not purport to be the author's original published text.

The publishers have made every effort to trace all copyright holders, but if they have inadvertently overlooked any they will be pleased to make the necessary arrangements at the first opportunity.

LEAVING CERTIFICATE EXAMINATION, 2005

English – Higher Level – Paper 1

Total Marks: 200
9.30 – 12.20

- This paper is divided into two sections,
  Section I COMPREHENDING and Section II COMPOSING.
- The paper contains **three** texts on the general theme of ORDINARY LIVES.
- Candidates should familiarise themselves with each of the texts before beginning their answers.

- Both sections of this paper (COMPREHENDING and COMPOSING) must be attempted.
- Each section carries 100 marks.

SECTION I – COMPREHENDING

- Two Questions, A and B, follow each text.
- Candidates must answer a Question A on one text and a Question B on a different text. Candidates must answer only one Question A and only one Question B.
- **N.B**. Candidates may NOT answer a Question A and a Question B on the same text.

SECTION II – COMPOSING

- Candidates must write on **one** of the compositions 1–7.

SECTION I
COMPREHENDING (100 marks)

TEXT 1
AN ORDINARY LIFE

Margaret Forster writes about her grandmother, Margaret Ann Hind, a domestic servant in Carlisle, a town in the north of England, in the 1890s. Her book is called Hidden Lives – A Family Memoir.

The life of Margaret Ann, my grandmother, was narrow. The physical hardship, the sheer energy and strength needed to get through each day, was commonplace. She *expected* to be down on her knees scrubbing, up to her elbows in boiling or freezing water, washing and rinsing dishes, rocking on her feet with weariness after hours of running up and down stairs. When she reminisced in later life, it was always without any trace of resentment. Her expectations were low. She was expected to carry on as she was until she dropped. Or married.

Marriage was always an option. Marriage was possibly, but not definitely, or even probably, an escape from servitude. If she married, she knew she'd still have to cook and clean and wash and mend, and without the help of the kind of servant she was to the Stephensons unless she married a rich man. The chances of this happening were nil. Who, in Carlisle, among the servant class, married rich men? Rich, eligible men were few and far between, and girls like Annie Stephenson from good families ever on the lookout for them. But there was rich and rich after all. Plenty of tradesmen around who did quite well for themselves, who could afford to rent or even to buy decent houses and to lead comfortable enough lives. The market was full of them. Plenty of money there, especially among the butchers, with Carlisle being such a big meat-eating place. On Saturday afternoons Margaret Ann would go to the market to buy the meat for Sunday. She went through the glass doors and down the little cobbled hill where the butchers' stalls now were. Some butchers had more than one stall. They had three or four together, positive empires. The meat hung from the ceiling on hooks, whole carcasses of pig and lamb and beef, and on the tiled counters below lay the cut-up portions; the bright red stewing steak, the dark slabs of liver, the great coils of pale, putty-coloured sausage, the crimson mounds of mince, the stiff rows of chops.

Thomas Hind was proprietor of stall number 4. This stall was clean. The carcasses didn't drip blood, the meat on the counter did not lie in puddles of it, the bin for fat wasn't nauseatingly visible. The floor always seemed freshly sawdusted, the aprons of the assistants were spotless. Even though his prices were not the cheapest, there was always a queue at Thomas Hind's. Margaret was a patient queuer. She never attempted to push herself forward but waited her turn calmly. She engaged in none of the banter that other customers seemed to like. She stated her requirement and that was that beyond a please and thank you. These were exactly the qualities which aroused Thomas Hind's interest. He noticed her precisely because of her curious quality of stillness. In 1893, when she first began buying meat from him, he was thirty-five years old and unmarried. His father had been a butcher and so had his grandfather, and as the only son he was always expected to take over the family business. His father had died when Thomas was a child and his mother, Jane, had become a butcher herself in order to keep the business going for Thomas to inherit. His debt to her was strong and he acknowledged it by now supporting not just her but two of his three sisters (the third had married). He was prosperous enough by then to marry. He was notoriously hard to satisfy and was teased about his high standards by his sisters who despaired of him ever approving of any girl. For four years he observed Margaret Ann quite contentedly, and then, when his mother died in 1897, decided the time had come for him to court her very seriously. Nothing impetuous about Tom.

So it was a slow affair, this courtship, three years of best boned and rolled sirloin, shoulder of lamb, leg of pork, three years of pounds of sausages, best back bacon, ham on the bone. A lot of meat, a lot of pleasantries, a lot of cap-doffing on Tom's part and head-inclining on Margaret Ann's. One Saturday, towards the end of the afternoon, when there were no assistants to hear and smirk, no customer other than Margaret Ann to hear and speculate, he asked her if she would care to go with him and his sisters out to Burgh marsh for a breath of sea air. He was very much afraid she would refuse, even be offended, but no, she smiled and said she knew his sisters from church and would be glad to accompany them if she could get time off.

N.B. Candidates may NOT answer Question A and Question B on the same text. Questions A and B carry 50 marks each.

QUESTION A

(i)   Write a paragraph in which you comment on the appropriateness of the title of this text, 'An Ordinary Life'.   (15)

(ii) What impressions of the characters of Thomas Hind and Margaret Ann do you get from this passage? Give reasons for your answer.   (15)

(iii) Did the description of the market bring it to life for you as a reader? Support your answer by reference to the text.   (20)

QUESTION B

'On Saturday afternoons Margaret Ann would go to the market to buy the meat for Sunday.'

Write **three diary entries** that Margaret Ann might have written over a series of Saturday evenings. Your writing should relate to her experience as described in the passage.   (50)

TEXT 2
ORDINARY LIVES IN WAR TIME

The following text consists of a written and visual element. The written text is adapted from an introduction by documentary photographer, Jenny Matthews, to her book of photographs entitled **Women and War.**

Mozambique 1986. Soldier with his baby son just before he returns to the front the next morning.

El Salvador 1986. An afternoon dance.

Bosnia 1994. Twenty-year-old Spanish soldier serving with UN waving Red Cross convoy over narrow bridge.

Eritrea 1988. Fighter back at base after battle.

INTRODUCTION by Jenny Matthews
From the beginning I was interested in covering foreign stories – starting with Central America in the early eighties, a bit off the map for the British media but an exciting place with revolutionary groups fighting guerrilla wars in the mountains.

One visit led to another and I learned about war. Although I have often worked where pictures in the news were of the frontline confrontation, I was more interested in what was going on behind the scenes, and that usually involved looking at how women were holding everything together. Some of the wars that I've tiptoed around have been major international conflicts – the Balkans, Middle East, Rwanda, Afghanistan – but others have been practically invisible.

I have not been everywhere and this is not a complete record of world conflict; it is my take on recent history, recognising the lives of remarkable women, ordinary people surviving as best they can. As I've travelled I've kept diaries, and the notes from these accompany the photos. All my work has been done in co-operation with a network of people, journalists, friends, fixers, drivers, translators, development workers. Without them it would be hard even to leave home. It has been a great privilege for me to be a photographer, to wander into other people's lives, often uninvited, but usually made embarrassingly welcome. I have lurked around some nasty corners of the world and come across the raw edges of life and death; an infinity of sorrow and fear, but more often than not, tempered with the hope that things will be better for the next generation.

N.B. Candidates may NOT answer Question A and Question B on the same text. Questions A and B carry 50 marks each.

QUESTION A

(i)   Which of the four images on page 308 makes the strongest impact on you? Give a reason for your answer. (15)

(ii) Do you think that the introduction to the collection of images is an interesting portrayal of Jenny's life as a news photographer? Give reasons for your answer. (15)

(iii) 'I learned about war . . . [but] I was more interested in what was going on behind the scenes.' From your reading of the introduction **and** the photographs, what impression do you have of how people's lives are touched by war? (20)

QUESTION B

Write a letter to a photographic magazine in which you propose **one** of the four images for the award **'Best War Photograph of the Year.'** (50)

TEXT 3
PUBLIC LIVES

Some people's lives seem far from ordinary. Modelled on articles from a number of celebrity magazines, the text below was written by a Leaving Certificate student. It offers a glimpse into the lifestyle of imaginary rock stock, Eva Maguire.

World exclusive! Irish Rock Diva speaks to readers from her Italian villa.

Hi, my name is Jerry Philips.

I interview sport stars, superstars, rock stars, divas, celebrities. My targets are the super wealthy, the faces of the moment, the famous; extraordinary lives that excite the curiosity and interest of ordinary people. I cover film premieres, music awards, Oscar ceremonies and star-studded parties: the significant global events of the world of entertainment.

This evening, I am in Florence, ensconced in a huge leather armchair in the waterfront palazzo home of Eva Maguire. In a rare, exclusive and candid interview, the 24-year-old rock superstar reveals where she sees her destiny and for the first time shares with *Celebrity* readers some of the secrets of her forthcoming wedding plans.

Our photo shoot shows her posing with one of her pet miniature greyhounds, wearing her favourite Jacqui Getty jewellery and

chic designer labels. As we discuss her plans for the future, personal and professional, candles light up her sun-baked, marble terrace with its glorious views over the Arno River, far from the terrace house of her childhood in a small Irish town. It has been a roller-coaster 18 months for this Irish-born music queen, originally from the midlands. Discovered on Christmas Eve, busking in Covent Garden, her rise to fame has been meteoric. She has achieved head-spinning global success, winning international music awards, packing concert venues and seeing her albums topping charts all over the world. Her first CD was the fastest-selling debut album to hit the UK charts and she is fast becoming a rock icon. Her life for the past year has been about L.A., London, New York and Monte Carlo. Some reviewers have criticised her ruthless quest for fame but she is certainly professional, hard-working and determined to succeed in a tough industry. She has been constantly under the media spotlight (and indeed, some would suggest that today's celebrity culture has gone too far), but says that her stable Irish family background has helped her to cope with the pressures of fame and with the world's press constantly on her doorstep.

'I'm a very reserved person,' she says, 'but this business is no place to be shrinking and insecure, it takes a certain attitude.' She stops and grins. 'The point is, I deal with projection all of the time. With a few smart changes, anyone can become a style goddess. Doors have opened for me and I am not afraid to take risks,' she says bluntly.

She is extraordinarily beautiful and astonishingly tough, steely and ambitious. Her golden hair frames features dominated by huge blue eyes. She wears a diamond and sapphire-studded ring on her left hand, reminding us that she is about to marry and share her future with Irish music promoter, Ross Kennedy. Three hundred Irish friends pack-jammed the luxurious K-Club last weekend in a pre-wedding bash.

International paparazzi are already gathering in the little Italian village where the ceremony will be held. It is expected that a galaxy of Hollywood celebrities, musicians and film producers will attend. It is even rumoured that some surprise politicians will be represented at the wedding. Limousines and helicopters have been arriving at the village for the past 48 hours. About 400 close friends of the couple are flying in from all over the world this weekend.

This spectacular event promises to knock off in style. Expect 600 doves to flock the Italian sky at the moment when the wedding vows are made and a church filled with tiny rosebuds, orchids and lily-of-the-valley. Pink, lilac and white are the colours chosen to predominate this glittering extravaganza. The couple intend to settle on the Italian Riviera. Welcome to their high-octane world of glitz, glamour, sleek yachts and private jets. The honeymoon will begin with a train journey on the Eastern and Oriental Express but the ultimate destination is a closely guarded secret. It is expected that the couple will party their way through the coming winter season in Italy.

N.B. Candidates may NOT answer Question A and Question B on the same text. Questions A and B carry 50 marks each.

QUESTION A

(i)   How in your view is Jerry Philip's attitude to the rock star, Eva Maguire, revealed in this article? Support your answer by reference to the text.   (15)

(ii) Does the kind of superstar lifestyle described in this passage appeal to you? Give reasons for your answer, supporting the points you make by reference to the text.
(15)

(iii) Do you find the style of writing in this magazine article appealing? Support your answer by detailed reference to the text.   (20)

QUESTION B

Imagine that as a reporter for a local newspaper you plan to interview a celebrity of your choice. Write a proposal/memo for the editor of your newspaper in which you explain why you want to interview this celebrity and giving an outline of the areas you hope to explore in the course of the interview.   (50)

SECTION II
COMPOSING (100 marks)

Write a composition on **any one** of the following.

Each composition carries 100 marks.

The composition assignments below are intended to reflect language study in the areas of information, argument, persuasion, narration and the aesthetic use of language.

1. '. . . my take on recent history . . .' (TEXT 2)
    Write a personal essay in which you discuss your views on a recent event or series of events in the world.

2. '. . . celebrity culture has gone too far . . .' (TEXT 3)
    Write a speech in which you attempt to persuade an audience that today's obsession with the lives of the rich and famous has gone too far.

3. '. . . ordinary people surviving as best they can.' (TEXT 2)
    You are responding to a radio competition to find an ordinary person whose life story will inspire others. Entries should include an account of the person's life and the reason(s) why it is inspirational. Write your competition entry.

4. '. . . the hope that things will be better for the next generation.' (TEXT 2)
    Write an article for a newspaper or magazine, outlining your vision of a better future.

5. 'She was expected to carry on as she was . . . he was always expected to take over the family business.' (TEXT 1)
    Write a personal essay on the part which other people's expectations play in our lives.

6. 'She engaged in none of the banter that other customers seemed to like.' (TEXT 1)
    You have been asked to give a talk to your class on the importance of not taking life too seriously. Write the talk you would give.

7. (a) **Write a short story suggested by one or more of the images in TEXT 2.**

    OR

    (b) **Write a short story suggested by the pair of images (the two houses) in TEXT 3.**

LEAVING CERTIFICATE EXAMINATION, 2005

English – Higher Level – Paper 2
Total Marks: 200
1.30 – 4.50

Candidates must attempt the following:
- **ONE** question from SECTION I – The Single Text
- **ONE** question from SECTION II – The Comparative Study
- **ONE** question on the Unseen Poem from SECTION III – Poetry
- **ONE** question on Prescribed Poetry from SECTION III – Poetry

N.B. Candidates must answer on Shakespearean Drama.
They may do so in SECTION I, The Single Text (*Hamlet, As You Like It*)
or in SECTION II, The Comparative Study (*Hamlet, As You Like It*)

SECTION I
THE SINGLE TEXT (60 marks)

Candidates must answer **one** question from this section (**A–E**).

A   WUTHERING HEIGHTS – Emily Brontë

(i)   'Heathcliff deserves the sympathy of the reader of *Wuthering Heights*.'

Write a response to this statement, supporting your views by reference to the text.

OR

(ii)   'The novel *Wuthering Heights* portrays a clash between two worlds represented by Wuthering Heights and Thrushcross Grange.'

Discuss this view of the novel, supporting your answer by reference to the text.

B   SILAS MARNER – George Eliot

(i)   'The story of *Silas Marner* has the magic of a fairy-tale, which leaves the reader feeling good about people.'

Write a response to this view of the novel, supporting your views by reference to the text.

OR

(ii)   'Godfrey Cass is not perfect, but, in the eyes of the reader, he is always a better man than his brother, Dunsey.'

Write your response to this statement, supporting it by reference to the text.

C   **AMONGST WOMEN** – John McGahern
(i)   'Michael Moran undoubtedly loves his sons, but his love contributes little to their happiness.'

Discuss this view of the relationship between Michael Moran and his sons. Support your answer by reference to the text.

OR

(ii)   'Unlike the men, the women in *Amongst Women* support each other very well.'

Discuss this statement, confining your attention to the female characters in the novel. Support your answer by reference to the text.

D   **HAMLET** – William Shakespeare

(i)   In your opinion, what is the appeal of the play *Hamlet* for a twenty-first-century audience?

Support the points you make by reference to the text.

OR

(ii)   'We admire Hamlet as much for his weaknesses as for his strengths.'

Write a response to this view of the character of Hamlet, supporting your points by reference to the text.

E   **AS YOU LIKE IT** – William Shakespeare

(i)   'Rosalind's attitudes and qualities make her a very attractive character.'

Do you agree with the above view? Support your answer by reference to the play.

OR

(ii)   'The play, *As You Like It*, presents many opportunities for dramatic performance.'

Write your response to the above statement, supporting your points by reference to the play.

SECTION II
THE COMPARATIVE STUDY (70 marks)

Candidates must answer **one** question from **either A** – The General Vision and Viewpoint **or B** – Literary Genre.

In your answer you may not use the text you have answered on in **SECTION I** – The Single Text.

N.B. The questions use the word **text** to refer to all the different kinds of texts available for study on this course, i.e. novel, play, short story, autobiography, biography, travel writing and film. The questions use the word **author** to refer to novelists, playwrights, writers in all genres and film-directors.

A   THE GENERAL VISION AND VIEWPOINT

1.   'Each text we read presents us with an outlook on life that may be bright or dark, or a combination of brightness and darkness.'

In the light of the above statement, compare the general vision and viewpoint in **at least two texts** you have studied in your comparative course.   (70)

OR

2.   (a)   With reference to **one** of the texts you have studied in your comparative course, write a note on the general vision and viewpoint in the text and on how it is communicated to the reader.   (30)

(b)   Compare the general vision and viewpoint in **two other texts** on your comparative course. Support the comparisons you make by reference to the texts.   (40)

B   LITERARY GENRE

1.   Write a talk to be given to Leaving Certificate students in which you explain the term *literary genre* and show them how to compare the telling of stories in **at least two texts** from the comparative course.   (70)

OR

2.   'Powerful images and incidents are features of all good story-telling.'

(a)   Show how this statement applies to **one** of the texts on your comparative course.   (30)

(b)   Compare the way in which powerful images and incidents are features of the story-telling in **two other texts** on your comparative course. Support the comparisons you make by reference to the texts.   (40)

SECTION III
POETRY (70 marks)

Candidates must answer **A** – Unseen Poem – **and B** – Prescribed Poetry.

A   UNSEEN POEM (20 marks)

Answer **either** Question **1** or Question **2**.

BACK YARD

Shine on, O moon of summer,
Shine to the leaves of grass, catalpa and oak,
All silver under your rain tonight.

An Italian boy is sending songs to you tonight from an accordion.
A Polish boy is out with his best girl; they marry next month;
                                    tonight they are throwing you kisses.

An old man next door is dreaming over a sheen
                            that sits in a cherry tree in his back yard.

The clocks say I must go—I stay here sitting on the back porch
                            drinking white thoughts you rain down.

                                            Shine on, O moon,
Shake out more and more silver changes.

                                            Carl Sandburg

---

1. (a)   Do you like the world that the poet describes in this poem? Give reasons for
          your answer, supporting them by reference to the text.   (10)
    (b)   Choose a line or two that you find particularly appealing and explain why.
                                                                              (10)

OR

2.   Write a personal response to the poem 'Back Yard'.   (20)

B   PRESCRIBED POETRY (50 marks)

Candidates must answer **one** of the following questions (**1–4**).

1.   'The appeal of Eavan Boland's poetry.'

     Using the above title, write an essay outlining what you consider to be the appeal
     of Boland's poetry. Support your points by reference to the poetry of Eavan Boland
     on your course.

2. What impact did the poetry of Emily Dickinson make on you as a reader? Your answer should deal with the following:
    –   *Your overall sense of the personality of the poet.*
    –   *The poet's use of language/imagery.*
    Refer to the poems by Emily Dickinson that you have studied.

3. Write about the feelings that T. S. Eliot's poetry creates in you and the aspects of his poetry (content and/or style) that help to create those feelings. Support your points by reference to the poetry of T. S. Eliot that you have read.

4. Write an article for a school magazine introducing the poetry of W. B. Yeats to Leaving Certificate students. Tell them what he wrote about and explain what you liked in his writing, suggesting some poems that you think they would enjoy reading. Support your points by reference to the poetry by W. B. Yeats that you have studied.

ACKNOWLEDGMENTS 2005 EXAMINATIONS

For permission to reproduce copyright material in these examination papers, the publishers gratefully acknowledge:

Penguin for the extract from *Hidden Lives: A Family Memoir* by Margaret Forster; University of Michigan Press for text and photos from *Women and War* by Jenny Matthews; and Harcourt Inc. for 'Back Yard' by Carl Sandburg. These extracts were adapted by the State Examinations Commission exclusively for the purposes of the Leaving Certificate English (Higher Level) examination paper (2005) and do not purport to be the authors' original published texts.

The publishers have made every effort to trace all copyright holders, but if they have inadvertently overlooked any they will be pleased to make the necessary arrangement at the first opportunity.

Sarah Bouguerra.

Sara Bouguerra.
J Sony
Saca Boug

Saca Bouguerra.
Sarah Bouguerra.
Racha Bouguerra.
Rayan Bouguerra.

Who done this?